# ADLERIAN COUNSELING

# ADLERIAN COUNSELING

# A Practitioner's Approach

# Fourth Edition

**Thomas J. Sweeney, Ph.D.**
*Ohio University*
*Athens, Ohio*

| USA | Publishing Office: | ACCELERATED DEVELOPMENT |
| | | *A member of the Taylor & Francis Group* |
| | | 325 Chestnut Street |
| | | Philadelphia, PA 19106 |
| | | Tel: (215) 625-8900 |
| | | Fax: (215) 625-2940 |
| | | |
| | Distribution Center: | ACCELERATED DEVELOPMENT |
| | | *A member of the Taylor & Francis Group* |
| | | 1900 Frost Road, Suite 101 |
| | | Bristol, PA 19007-1598 |
| | | Tel: (215) 785-5800 |
| | | Fax: (215) 785-5515 |
| | | |
| UK | | Taylor & Francis Ltd. |
| | | 1 Gunpowder Square |
| | | London EC4A 3DE |
| | | Tel: 171 583 0490 |
| | | Fax; 171 583 0581 |

**ADLERIAN COUNSELING: A Practitioner's Approach**

1 2 3 4 5 6 7 8 9 0

Printed by Hamilton Printing Company, Castelton, NY, 1998. This book was set in Times Roman by Blue Moon Editorial & Design. Copyediting by Christine L. Winter. Technical development by Cindy Long. Cover design by Nancy Abbott.

A CIP catalog record for this book is available from the British Library.
∞    The paper in this publication meets the requirements of the ANSI Standard Z39.48-1984 (Permanence of Paper)

**Library of Congress Cataloging-in-Publication Data**
Sweeney, Thomas John, 1936-
        Adlerian counseling : a practitioner's approach  / Thomas J.
Sweeney. —— 4th ed.
            p.    cm.
        Includes bibliographical references and index.
        ISBN 1-56032-510-0 (hardcover : alk. paper)
        1. Counseling. 2. Adler, Alfred, 1870-1937. 3. Adlerian
psychology. I. Title.

# ACKNOWLEDGMENTS

A variety of persons have contributed to this book directly or indirectly. Certainly, Dr. Rudolf Dreikurs is among those who come immediately to mind because of his charisma and genius in not only presenting but demonstrating Adlerian psychology. He truly lived what he taught. Also among those Adlerians who convinced me that this was more than another of the many approaches to helping were Bob Powers, a masterful teacher; Manford Sonstegard, the consummate counselor; and Harold Mosak, whose clinical skills with lifestyle assessment were excelled only by the love he and Birdie have shared with me both personally and professionally.

Another category of persons to whom I owe thanks are former students of mine who both enlightened and encouraged me as an Adlerian. I often tell the story of how Dr. Frank Walton of Columbia, SC convinced me to attend a summer session with Dr. Dreikurs and company at the Adler Institute in Chicago. It changed my life, personally and professionally. Likewise, Dr. Eugene Kelly of George Washington University has remained a friend and influence particularly in the realm of spirituality and its implications for wellness. Another of the graduates of the University of South Carolina, where my career as a counselor educator began, Dr. Gerry Gandy continues to write professionally and practices what we teach. More recently, Dr. Linda Maier, a graduate of the Ohio University program, I tease for living Adler even more than Adler.

Among professional associates who have been influential in broadening my appreciation for the many implications of Adlerian thought are Drs. Courtland Lee, Sam Gladding, and Don C. Locke. In addition to being outstanding educators and leaders for the profession, they model a way of life that is high in social interest and encourages optimum wellness in others. Certainly, the most influential colleague is also my dear friend, Dr. Mel Witmer. As chapter 2 reveals, he has a passion for life in all its dimensions. His patience, generous sharing of ideas, experiences, and optimism have been a continual source of encouragement.

When in need of good counsel, I also seek out the wisdom of Pat Witmer (Mel's wife), who embraced Adler and Dreikurs at a time in her life when it was needed most. Her clear understanding of the "ironclad logic of social living" qualifies her as a friend extraordinaire. Although not Adlerians per se, my dear friends and mentors, Dr. and Ms. Gilbert and Kathleen Wrenn are the embodiment of encouragement and exemplars of all that is caring in human nature. Likewise, Sisters Immaculata Paisant and Lois Wedl, Ph.D., give life to the message of Christ in a world where love is a verb as well as a noun. On more than one occasion, Drs. Charles Lewis and Joe Hollis also gave wise counsel and support when needed. Everyone should have friends such as these.

In earlier editions, I have noted that my parents, Thomas and Sarah Sweeney, provided me with the foundation for everything good that has been a part of my life. This is ever more true as I witness the courage and dignity with which my mother has lived with Alzheimer's disease. Now, as in my younger years, my mother's sister Ann and my Uncle Henry Grizer exemplify what I strive to be as a son, father, and partner. My children Elizabeth, Ann, Tom, Kate, and Mike and my nine grandchildren provide me the motivation to be my best. Likewise, Jill Myers has become an inspiration as one whose personal journey demonstrates the meaning of courage on a day-to-day nonheroic basis in service to self and others.

Most important, of course, is Dr. Jane E. Myers Sweeney. She challenges, encourages, and supports my every effort. She is a natural Adlerian but has yet to claim the title. She encourages me to live what I teach and be the best that I can be on all the dimensions of wellness. She helps make all that I teach come alive daily. In addition, she helped introduce me to Developmental Counseling and Therapy (DCT), from which my interest in its implications for Adlerians has come. In addition, I cannot thank her enough for critically reading and editing portions of this manuscript.

Finally, I wish to thank Ms. Kelley Rowland and Carole Dice for their help with the preparation of the manuscript. Thanks also to Nancy Conrad Ball for her assistance as a practitioner in critiquing parts of the manuscript.

# AUTHOR'S INTRODUCTION

This edition was written with the practitioner in mind, as were earlier editions of this book. Having had the privilege of both hearing and watching Dr. Rudolf Dreikurs teach and demonstrate the Individual Psychology of Alfred Adler, I am convinced that practitioners of all helping disciplines can benefit from the insights and methods of Adler and Dreikurs. Counselors and therapists of all types in all manner of work settings and with persons across the life span use this approach successfully. It is also applied successfully, however, by parents, teachers, paraprofessionals, and lay persons in homes, businesses, and educational settings.

Critical reviews of the earlier editions reported them to be useful, concise overviews of the theory and practice of what Adler called his Individual Psychology. For this fourth edition, every effort has been made to retain these characteristics while adding to, revising, and updating the material. Rather than deviating from Adler and Dreikurs, however, this work follows their line of thinking while incorporating research, methods, and techniques that expand upon Individual Psychology.

Adler's thinking was the forerunner of many of the approaches to psychology and counseling used widely today. Both his theory and methods are borrowed from liberally, often without note. Unfortunately, in the process of taking only parts of his thinking, some have missed essential components to the underlying philosophy and values upon which he based his practice. Without these, the methods and techniques are no more notable than many of those espoused by other approaches. Although they are indeed useful and beneficial in practice, their use begs the question, toward what changes are we assisting others?

Adler's answer was toward higher social interest, that is, something akin to a state of development characterized by one's personal confidence and competence to cope with life and a commitment to the common good of others. In the third edition, a basic model was presented based on research across disciplines that extended Adler's thoughts into a holistic conceptualization of both the life tasks and the qualities of persons successfully meeting them. Adler would have considered persons possessing these qualities high in social interest.

In this edition, the model has been refined, the research updated, and practical applications of the model introduced. My colleagues, Drs. Witmer and Myers, and I are genuinely excited by the reports of others who are using the developmental instrument related to this model in research and practice. In short, we are attempting to extend Adler's and Dreikurs' work in keeping with their thinking and practice.

Another dimension to this edition is the greater attention to the pluralistic nature of our society and, indeed, the world. While the efforts are relatively modest compared to the nature of the topics, the reader will find both cultural and gender topics addressed in this edition. As a forerunner of social democracy in this country, both Adler's and Dreikurs' works reflect the values and outlook consistent with today's need for greater respect and appreciation of differences.

Whereas Adler was primarily a practitioner and lecturer, Rudolf Dreikurs shared his experience through writing as well. He wrote practical, easily read papers and books concerning Individual Psychology and its uses. He also was recorded and filmed on different occasions conducting family and teacher consultation and counseling sessions. Even before his death in 1972, ample evidence was being exhibited that his students and colleagues would and could continue the work that he helped begin. His books, *The Challenge of Marriage* (1946) and *Social Equality: The Challenge of Today* (1971), were prophetic statements about the social changes within our society. More important, he addressed what is needed for changes to be in the best interests of all persons. This book is intended as a contribution to the continuation of his mission.

The first chapter is a short introduction to the man, the movement, and the psychology of Alfred Adler. For persons unfamiliar with his theory, it should serve as a basis for understanding the assumptions underlying the methods discussed in subsequent chapters. Not infrequently, persons new to this literature are surprised to learn how much is known to them through other counseling approaches. On the other hand, each chapter will reveal some unique applications of this approach. In addition, the section on validation of the theory and practice has been updated and new sections provide a basis for the multicultural and gender appropriateness of this approach.

Chapter 2 is entirely new as it is written. My long time friend and colleague, Dr. Mel Witmer, agreed to update the chapter and, in the process, completely rewrote the majority of it to accompany our revised and expanded model of wellness. This chapter represents only a portion of the extensive literature review and illustrations of the model's uses in practice, which he compiled during its development. The Wellness Evaluation of Lifestyle (WEL) instrument is briefly introduced as a measure of the components of the healthy person as presented in the model. It is already being used in research and practice. We have integrated the life tasks and forces influencing personality into a developmental, multidimensional model suitable for use in setting goals for counseling and education. As a consequence, we believe that it extends Adler's work beyond the broad concepts of social interest and makes it more useful to both practitioners and researchers alike.

Chapters 3 and 4 explain the dimensions and uses of natural and logical consequences. One often hears that "life is the best teacher." Indeed, natural consequences are the authors of much of what is learned about life. They are not alone, however, in teaching people how to live in harmony with one another. Adlerians pay particular attention to consequences as methods that follow the "ironclad logic of social living." We teach within this approach that "rules are for everyone." All beings experience negative consequences when they ignore the laws of nature. Social convention and society's laws have a force of their own as well. When understood and used wisely, social rules can be powerful, positive methods in helping people of all ages. Because these methods can be used effectively to correct "misbehavior," they are seized upon by some persons as the first and almost exclusive methods of choice. As will be revealed within the various sections, methods used in isolation of the total approach are bound to provide limited results at best and negative outcomes at worst. Encouragement should be the first method of choice.

Chapter 5 addresses the essential element of helping from an Adlerian perspective: encouragement. Nurturing courage is a key concept throughout Adlerian practice. It is a fundamental goal in all teaching and counseling. Definitions and methods of encouragement are supplemented with practice and self-assessment activities. The chapter also has been rewritten to include information on the concept of self-esteem and the stages of the change process. Drawing on the extensive work of Nathaniel Branden (1994), I present the "pillars of self-esteem." In addition, the need to assess readiness for change and to intervene appropriately at that stage is offered as a refinement to the intervention process. I also provide an illustration of how to use readiness-for-change assessment and an intervention for improving self-esteem.

Adlerians tend to be pragmatists. Much of what they use in teaching and counseling comes from the experience of others—parents, teachers, counselors, and, yes, children! Chapter 6 is about guiding all young people toward high levels of wellness. Building self-esteem and an internal sense of control are among the objectives. Cooperation as a preferred method of teaching and learning is presented. Case examples illustrate the goals of disruptive behavior, how to identify them, and corrective actions that complement the encouragement process. This is must reading for anyone who lives or works with young people. Rules of thumb, specific techniques, and useful methods are summarized within this chapter.

Lifestyle assessment is outlined and explained as an introduction to the uses of this technique. Although seen by some as mystical in the demonstrations of masterful clinicians, the serious student of Individual Psychology discovers that no magic is involved. Through study, practice, and experience one develops an intuitive competence that prepares the practitioner to hear, feel, and see that which the casual observer overlooks or mistakes for its meaning. Chapter 7 provides a guide for discovering the simplicity and interrelatedness, for example, of early recollections and present behavior. Applicable to persons of all ages, it can be an excellent tool for quickly establishing rapport and overcoming counselee resistance.

Chapter 8 explains the Adlerian counseling process. Each stage is explained and illustrated. In addition to examples taken from my work with young people, the use of early recollections as a tool for helping older persons is presented. Because "life review" has been observed as a common phenomenon among older persons, I advocate the use of Adlerian methods for more positive and long-lasting effects. This edition also has an innovation to the traditional Adlerian process. I have noted positive effects from incorporating some of Allen Ivey's (1990) Developmental Counseling and Therapy (DCT) methods into the counseling process. Thus, I have presented an overview of his assessment strategy and illustrate its use in a lifestyle case presentation and excerpts of a counseling session. It seems only fitting that Adlerians acknowledge and encourage the positive contributions of others to the practice of Individual Psychology. This case is presented at the end of chapter 8.

Adlerian career counseling as presented by my friend Mark Savickas is an innovation in its own right. I have used his methods in classes and workshops for several years. They are a wonderful illustration of how adaptive Individual Psychology is to the practical life tasks all people must address. I always have considered career counseling to be personal counseling, as opposed to some who think of it as data and information gathering for the purpose of making a single event decision. The elegance of these methods speak for themselves in practice. Career-style counseling, as Savickas illustrates in chapter 9, continues to be a significant addition to the Adlerian clinician's methods and practice.

Chapter 10 addresses one of the most challenging and, consequently, potentially most satisfying areas of counseling practice, couples counseling. Both the philosophical and psychological foundations of Adlerian practice are presented. In addition, the sociological perspective on the uncoupling process is explained in relation to its usefulness for assessment of success of the counseling process. A step-by-step case example is presented including specific techniques and methods potentially useful to facilitating the goals of counseling.

Family counseling and consultation are high priorities of most practitioners. This is one of the most widely recognized areas of expertise of Adlerians. Chapter 11 presents the Adlerian perspective while noting the similarities and complementary aspects of systems theory and practice to Adlerian counseling. A new section has been added to reflect what research tells us about strong families.

Consultation per se is frequently not differentiated from other helping methods by Adlerians. For purposes of chapter 11, a distinction between counseling and consultation is made. Underlying assumptions and strategies of the Adlerian consultant are outlined. In addition, stages in the process as they apply to parent and teacher conferences are illustrated. Because Adlerians make a practice of working with all the children in the family, an illustration of the children's conference is used. In additions, suggestions are made on how Adlerians can handle group demonstrations. Typical recommendations that most families find helpful illustrate how principles of Individual Psychology can be practically implemented for families. Because not all recommendations always result in the outcomes intended, I discuss a few common implementation errors. A full family consultation session is presented in the appendices along with a typical family meeting with young children.

The final chapter is about group procedures. Group methods are fundamental to Adlerian practice. Both Adler and Dreikurs are noted as being among the first to take counseling out of the dark little office into the auditorium, classroom, and community hall. Living together means living in groups. All practitioners need to have group skills in their repertoire. Discussion, consultation, and counseling groups, therefore, are logical methods of the Adlerian counselor. In chapter 12, each of these methods is discussed with reference to children and adults.

It is still true that one need not be an "Adlerian" to use and benefit from the ideas and methods described in this book. I do believe, however, that it is within the totality of this approach that the greatest good will be achieved. On the other hand, Adler indicated that he was not bound by his own creation. As noted by the additions and efforts toward innovation within this book, one can further his work best by creatively adapting and adding to it.

Thomas J. Sweeney
March 1998

# CONTENTS

## CHAPTER 9
## CAREER STYLE ASSESSMENT AND COUNSELING
*Mark L. Savickas*

# LIST OF FIGURES

# LIST OF FORMS

# LIST OF TABLES

## Chapter 1

# INDIVIDUAL PSYCHOLOGY: THE MAN, THE MOVEMENT, AND THE PSYCHOLOGY OF ALFRED ADLER

The Individual Psychology of Alfred Adler had its beginning in Vienna at the turn of the century. Adler began private practice as an ophthalmologist in 1898 but later turned to general practice, then to neurology, and later psychiatry. His first psychological paper, "The Physician as Educator," was published in 1904. Its major theme was clearly applicable to all educators. Adler emphasized the importance of the "child's confidence in his own strength," particularly in relation to guiding sick or pampered children (Ansbacher & Ansbacher, 1967). He believed that the child's greatest good fortune was the personal courage to cope with life. He instructed educators to help children develop discipline by allowing them to experience the natural consequences of their acts without fear of those who educate them. Throughout the remainder of his life, Adler was interested in child-rearing practices and the instruction of parents and teachers in what he considered to be important principles of guiding children.

Mosak and Dreikurs (1973) traced the similarities and differences between Adler and various philosophers and psychologists over the years. To some, Adler appears to be no more than a student of Freud who became a dissenter and pursued variations on psychoanalysis. Adler, however, revealed the outline of this theory in a publication that predated his contact with Freud. Although Adler's reason for joining Freud is not entirely clear, Freud invited him to join his Wednesday evening discussion group in 1902 after Adler had written two defenses of Freud's theories. It now appears more accurate to state that Adler was a colleague of Freud, because the evidence suggests that each influenced the other in some aspects of each other's theory.

From the perspective of visibility in history, Freud clearly has the greater renown. Prochaska and Norcross (1994) noted, however:

> Adler was clearly ahead of the learning curve in psychotherapy. His social recasting of Freudian theory predated the evolution of psychodynamic therapy; his task assignments foreshadowed the development of behavioral and other directive therapies; his specific techniques involving imagery and "as if" anticipated the cognitive therapies; and his community outreach and psychoeducational programs foreshadowed contemporary community mental health. Many of Adler's ideas have quietly permeated modern psychological thinking, often without notice. (p. 89)

In some respects, this anonymity has been a curiosity to followers of Adler. Differences between he and Freud were so significant that they eventually became antagonists. In his chapter comparing psychoanalytic and Adlerian theory, Gladding (1996) concluded with the following observations:

> Freudian and Adlerian theories differ in a number of ways even though they were developed at about the same time and in a similar environment. Psychoanalysis is biologically based and stresses causality, psychosexual development, the dynamics of the mind, and instincts. Adlerian theory, on the other hand, is socially based, interpersonal, and subjective. It emphasizes the future, holism, equalitarianism, and choice.

> The [Freudian] approach is not applicable for the client popu-
> lations that most counselors serve. The Adlerian approach,
> however, is widely practiced in school and institutional set-
> tings. Its popularity can be attributed to its hopefulness and
> its usefulness in multiple settings. (pp. 204–205)

Clearly, Adler viewed human beings as worthwhile, socially motivated, and capable of creative, independent action. The theory is so based upon the philosophy and values of social democracy that only in recent history has it begun to have an impact in education and psychology. Even today, however, comparatively few persons are aware of the Individual Psychology of Alfred Adler.

Ellenberger (1970) has stated the circumstances quite succinctly:

> Any attempt to assess the influences of Adler's work brings
> about a paradox. The impact of individual psychology stands
> beyond any doubt . . . [but] it would not be easy to find an-
> other author from which so much has been borrowed from
> all sides without acknowledgment than Alfred Adler. (p. 645)

This borrowing from Adlerian theory and methods tends to be true to such a degree that few persons who have ever studied child-rearing practices, education, or psychology could be considered unaware of Adler's ideas. On the other hand, few would remember his name were they asked to identify the author of these ideas. For example, although many people see at least a superficial parallel between Berne's (1964) theory of transactional analysis and Freud's concepts of id, ego, and superego, few individuals seem to know that this social interaction analysis is predicated on many of Adler's teachings concerning social living and psychological growth. Other major contributors to psychological theory and practice such as Viktor Frankl and Rollo May were students of Adler and on occasion credit him as a source of some of their ideas. Similarly, Eric Fromm, Karen Horney, and H. S. Sullivan integrate Adlerian psychology into their own systems—so much so that Ellenberger (1970, p. 860) observed that Horney's psychology "combines Adlerian teachings with Freudian terminology." Adler would be pleased with such broad-based incorporation of his ideas into the work of others. In fact, he anticipated it, as noted in recollections of him by family and friends. He is quoted as saying:

> "There might come a time," he said, "when one will not any more remember my name; one might even have forgotten that our school ever existed. But this does not matter because everybody working in our field will act as if he had studied with us!" (Manaster, Painter, Deutsch, & Overholt, 1977, p. 33)

## THE MAN

Adler has been described as an essentially simple man of great personal forcefulness and physical strength but at the same time gentle and humble in his manner. His personal orientation was toward the betterment of the human condition (Ansbacher, 1969). Adler was the second of six children. His brother Sigmund was 2 years his senior; Hermine, 1 year younger; Irma, 4 years younger; and Max and Richard, 7 and 14 years younger, respectively. There were two siblings, younger and older, who were deceased. Not surprising to Adlerians because of the concept of sibling rivalry, Adler perceived his older brother as his rival. His early school experiences were not entirely successful. He did so poorly in mathematics that his father was encouraged to place him in an apprenticeship in secondary school. Instead, Adler applied himself until he developed the needed skill in math.

Born on February 7, 1870, Adler's father was a middle-class Jewish merchant and his mother was a homemaker. His earlier years included poor health with rickets, pneumonia at the age of 5 years, and being run over by a vehicle. His health improving as he grew older, his interest in medicine was encouraged by his father and resulted in a degree from the University of Vienna in 1895. Adler described his interest in medicine as an effort to defeat death.

---

Individuals create their own evaluations and choices of how to respond to life events.

---

Adler's interest in why people respond differently to similar life events is reflected in his early attention to the *Study of Organ Inferiority and Its Physical Compensation: A Contribution to Clinical Medicine* (1907). His later lectures, books, and articles illustrated even more clearly the realization that individuals create their own evaluations and choices of how to respond to life events. According to a book of remembrances of those who knew the man, he obviously chose to enjoy life. Not one to miss a good time, he enjoyed telling stories and participating in singing sessions around a piano (Manaster, Painter, Deutsch, & Overholt, 1977).

After serving as a medical officer in World War I, he established a number of child-guidance clinics in the Vienna schools. Through these clinics, teachers, social workers, physicians, and others learned to understand children's behavior and how to help them. Through the clinics, which spread throughout Europe at that time, and his unique style of public lecture and demonstration, Adler developed a relatively small but significant following.

In 1935, when the Nazis began their oppression of Europe, Adler had to flee to the United States with his then radical, politically unacceptable ideas about a society of social equals. Although he had taught and lectured extensively in the United States, his death in 1937 while on tour in Scotland, left a significant void. His followers in the United States found great resistance by those who had adopted Freud's psychoanalysis. In addition, history shows that at the time the United States was far from truly accepting and practicing the equalitarian principles upon which Individual Psychology is based.

## THE MOVEMENT

With this background, one can only admire all the more the persistence and resiliency of Adler and those who followed him. Probably his most noted student and colleague, Dr. Rudolf Dreikurs, commands special mention. A prolific writer and founder of the Alfred Adler Institute of Chicago, through personal energy and talent he brought Adler's ideas into practical usefulness for thousands of parents, couples, and practitioners. His sense of urgency in teaching others how to live together was evident in his level of writing, lecturing, and counseling even until his death in 1972. Having recollections of him myself through lectures, counseling demonstrations, and informal talks, I can vouch for the fact that he lived what he taught. In their book on the life and works of Rudolf Dreikurs, *The Courage to Be Imperfect,* Terner and Pew (1978) helped readers to know him better through many anecdotes recalled by friends and students. One of their quotes from Dreikurs may help the reader to understand the man better:

> . . . I don't mind the patient criticizing me. I don't mind admitting that I have made a mistake—I very often make mistakes.
>
> We should not be afraid of making mistakes. . . . It is more important that we are human. It is unfortunate that one has to emphasize that today, because it is not the customary practice in psychotherapy to be human. Some psychiatrists wouldn't go to the elevator with the last patient of the day for fear of coming too close to him. They have to wait until the patient has gone down. "Don't come too close because that interferes with the therapeutic relationship." This is just the opposite of what I am saying. I want to function and to be recognized as a fellow human being. (p. 243)

Following Adler's conviction that our society was two generations removed from truly achieving equality, Dreikurs' (1946) book on marriage forecast the social revolution experienced in the United States since World War II. Ridiculed and rejected by many of his peers in medicine and psychiatry, Dreikurs lived long enough to see his books such as *Children the Challenge* (Dreikurs & Soltz, 1964) become best sellers among lay persons and professionals alike. Equally important, his work continues through his students and colleagues in the United States and abroad.

In addition to the center in Chicago, which offers accredited graduate degrees, Adlerian institutes offer certificates in child guidance, counseling, and psychotherapy in New York, Minneapolis,

Berkeley, and Toronto. The North American Society of Adlerian Psychology, headquartered in Chicago, regularly publishes newsletters and periodicals and sponsors workshops and conventions as sources of new developments, techniques, and research for interested persons. Adler's Individual Psychology is having an impact in its own right, particularly in the areas of child rearing and classroom behavior, and increasingly in other areas including marriage and family counseling, industrial relations, correctional counseling, and human relations groups.

## BASIC CONCEPTS

At the risk of oversimplifying Adler's theory, the following sections are offered as a foundation for subsequent chapters in which will be discussed the application of the Adlerian theory. Each chapter will elaborate further upon certain concepts as they apply to specific techniques or methods. The major thrust of this chapter, therefore, is to help the reader understand the significance of certain concepts without pursuing them in great detail or showing their application to specific methods or techniques.

### Socio-Teleo-Analytic

A number of assumptions, propositions, and beliefs can be listed under Adler's theory of personality. The essence of his system can be captured in part, however, by defining it as socio-teleo-analytic. Adler perceived humans as *social beings* with a natural inclination toward other people. Developmentally, human beings are one of the most dependent of all creatures at birth. Someone must nurture and care for them if they are to survive.

From early dependent experience and throughout life, human beings can be understood best as they interact with others. As children begin discovering themselves, others, and the world, their first impressions of the world are predicated upon contact with and through other people. As shall be seen later, these early impressions develop into rules about life that are used to help them understand, predict, and manage their world.

**Socio.** Adler believed that human beings had a basic inclination toward being a part of the larger social whole, a striving to feel belongingness, a willingness to serve the greater good for the betterment of humankind. He called this *Gemeinschaftsgefuhl*. The closest interpretation of this word in English is *social interest*. An expression of this inclination is observed in each person's striving to make a place for himself or herself and to feel belongingness.

Parents, significant other adults, and siblings offer opportunities for individuals to fashion their own notions about how to make their places in a group. Because cognitive processes and life experiences are quite limited for children, many of these notions or rules have limited value or can be quite unsatisfactory when viewed externally by someone observing their behaviors. These rules are perceived, nevertheless, and are helpful to individuals as they make choices, even though these processes and experiences remain largely unexamined in a critical manner.

The subjective or phenomenological view of individuals is necessary, therefore, if one is to understand their characteristic ways of moving through life. Adler referred to the basic notions that guide us through life as our style of life or, as more commonly referred to now, *lifestyle*. Adler characterized lifestyle as " . . . unity in each individual—in his thinking, feeling, acting; in his so-called conscious and unconscious, in every expression of his personality. This [self-consistent] unity we call the style of life of the individual" (Ansbacher & Ansbacher, 1967, p. 175).

Lifestyle is not determined by heredity or environment but both are important antecedents. Individuals decide how they think, value, and feel about being female, the oldest, or without the presence of a father. There is no ideal right or wrong lifestyle. Quite to the contrary, each lifestyle is unique.

Although Adler wished to emphasize the necessity of viewing human beings holistically (i.e., not in parts) when he coined the term *Individual Psychology*, he also wanted to underscore his belief in the uniqueness of each person. A superficial study of Individual Psychology might lead one to conclude that conformity was one of its objectives in practice. Not only would this conclusion be inaccurate, but also Adler would have stated that it is not even probable. In the same sense that finger and voice prints are unique, Adler observed that every individual fashions a unique way of moving through life.

Obviously, a psychology of personality that revealed no general or *nomothetic* rules of behavior upon which to base practice would be of little utility. As will be shown in subsequent chapters, Adlerian principles do indeed provide many useful guidelines. The significance of idiographic factors, however, is equally important. Adler stated:

> I believe that I am not bound by any strict rule or prejudice but prefer to subscribe to the principle: Everything can also be different. . . . General rules—even those laid down by Individual Psychology, of my own creation—should be regarded as nothing more than an aid to a preliminary illumination of the field of view in which the single individual can be found— or missed. (Ansbacher, 1969, pp. xx)

Adlerians are sometimes described as soft determinists; whereas freedom is not absolute, neither is determinism absolute. Predictions of human behavior must be stated in terms of probabilities of occurrence. Perfect correlation between what Adlerians refer to as antecedents and specific behaviors are elusive for many reasons. Not the least of these reasons is the belief that each individual has a creative capacity to transcend even standardized research conditions.

Therefore, Adler believed that individuals can be understood best within the social context of their transactions with others. He emphasized, however, the uniqueness of individuals. We create our unique ways of belonging, relating to others, being ourselves (i.e., our lifestyle). And it is by understanding the movement and process by which we make our place that we are understood as a person distinct from others.

**Teleo.**    *Teleo* denotes the goal-striving nature of human beings. Behavior is purposive even though this facet may be obscure to the observer. Individuals choose to act or not act because it serves some purpose and utility for them. Our anticipation of outcomes, events or consequences influences the present.

---

### Behavior is purposive.

---

Adler believed that human beings were not driven by instincts or molded by heredity, experience, or environment. Instead, he envisioned human beings as moving toward goals perceived as important to them.

> The science of Individual Psychology developed out of the effort to understand that mysterious creative power of life—that power which expresses itself in the desire to develop, to strive and to achieve—and even to compensate for defeats in one direction by striving for success in another. This power is teleological—it expresses itself in the striving after a goal. (Ansbacher, 1969, p. 1)

Much has been written about the significance of inferiority. Ansbacher (1969) notes that Adler did not give a clear answer as to which had primacy in the development of the human being, goal striving or inferiority feelings. Ansbacher believed that goal striving should have primacy although he could not be conclusive in supporting this position. However, Adler believed in the purposive nature of human striving. He observed that an individual's behavior could be understood best in relation to what he or she valued and moved toward achieving.

The teleological aspect of Adler's theory reveals the optimistic, encouraging nature of his position. Goals of behavior can be understood and anticipated. Individuals may choose to change the valuing of their goals and/or the behavior that they use in their striving. Individuals are not victims of circumstances beyond their control in an absolute way.

**Analytic.**   The *analytic* orientation to Individual Psychology is derived from the observation that most behavior is based upon that which is unconscious or nonunderstood (Mosak & Dreikurs, 1973). Individuals frequently report that they do not understand their behavior or motives. Closer inspection reveals that individuals often understand more than they willingly admit. In a helping relationship, they more readily accept direct confrontations on the purposes of their behavior including some purposes previously unknown to them.

Adler and his followers have developed techniques for helping individuals to discover basic notions about themselves, others, and life. He was influenced by Vaihinger's (1965) "philosophy of 'as if.'" He concurred with Vaihinger that individuals behave "as if" circumstances were absolutely true (e.g., life is dangerous, I am weak, or others cannot be trusted). Whereas some notions of individuals are stated clearly and believed beyond reproach, other notions are far more subtle and yet are a powerful influence on behavior. Adler referred to them as fictive notions.

So long as individuals function fairly well in their daily life, their notions remain unexamined. When their notions are challenged or proved ineffective in maintaining feelings of belonging, what is often termed as an "emotional" crisis develops. Such are the times when counseling or psychotherapy are sought most. Try as they may, individuals' behavioral responses are not synonymous. Behavior may change and show accommodation to varying circumstances including age, cultural milieu, and similar factors. Lifestyle is not believed to change except through psychotherapy, personally powerful life experiences, or causes such as brain injury, drugs, and so forth.

**Early Human Development**

As a means of studying Adler's psychology further, the development of personality as it unfolds from childbirth may be helpful. The child, thought totally dependent at birth, is by no means helpless in the strict sense of the term (Santrock, 1995). From the Adlerian point of view, even infants begin training adults far better than many parents train their children.

---

Love and parental interest are important ingredients to personality development.

---

On the assumption that infants typically receive attention and care from the moment of their birth, they are the cause of activity. They begin learning about life, themselves, and others in the most fundamental ways. Bodily functions contribute to much of this activity in the early hours and days of life. As feeding, elimination, and other comforts become routine, babies' attention may turn to the sounds, touch, and vague sights that intervene in their lives. Coping with these may involve crying, smiling, or any of a number of responses. Infants learn by their interpretation of the natural and social consequences that they experience with individuals around them. Adlerians often cite the example of perfectly healthy babies who do not cry, do not use their vocal capabilities. These cases have been babies born to deaf parents. These babies learn early that crying aloud serves no useful purpose; therefore, they simply wiggle, shed tears, and become red in the face.

In addition to heredity, the *family atmosphere* is a major component of one's development. The extent to which it is friendly, supportive, and encouraging as opposed to authoritarian, harsh, and suppressive is very important. On the other hand, many parents are overconcerned or overprotective and lose an unnecessary amount of sleep and energy attending to noises coming from the baby's room. As will be seen in later sections, Adler definitely believed that love and parental interest are important ingredients to personality development. Unfortunately, pampering and overprotecting can have negative consequences beyond what is reasonable. Children may perceive that they are not able, that others must take care of them, or that terrible things may happen when their parents are away. If corrective training is not instituted during their early years, such notions or variations on them may become a part of their lifestyle.

In most instances, children begin developing a sense of their strengths and weaknesses while attempting mastery over those aspects of development that seem within their reach. They also are beginning to make observations about their place in events around them. As their psychomotor capabilities develop, others' behavior toward them will change and they must decide how they will behave. If they are convinced of their belongingness and assess their capabilities as adequate, they will require less attention, service, and outward encouragement from those around them than previously. The *family and cultural values* can have a profound effect in this process. As children experience the emphasis placed on contributing, sharing, and enjoying as opposed to taking, withholding, or demanding, their sense of what is important develops. Likewise, the *adult models* that they observe will help them form ideas about what is appropriate male and female behavior, how one relates to the opposite gender, and how to make decisions or resolve differences.

Whether or not children make accurate assessments, they will behave according to their assessments. Adlerians believe that children usually are excellent observers, but they often are poor evaluators and interpreters of their experiences. As a consequence, feelings of inferiority are believed to be common because of their initial experiences as dependent, small, and socially inferior persons. Feelings of inferiority are not inherently good or bad. Individuals, for example, often move toward mastery and competence in compensations for these feelings. Through social interaction they further nurture their social interest and become persons others describe as fully functioning or self-actualizing. Children's responses to early experiences within the family unit, then, have implications for how they approach their life tasks.

## Family Constellation

Adler placed considerable importance on the *family constellation* or socio-psychological configuration of a family group. Essentially what Adler observed was the tendency of individuals holding similar positions in different families to assume similar characteristics, attitudes, and behaviors. As a consequence, the position of the oldest, second, and so forth became the common reference for one's family position. However, the differences not only in age but gender, number of siblings, cultural values attributed to gender roles, and related matters result in a need for understanding the psychological position of an individual in the family. Birth order or ordinal position (first, second, third) , per se, is not sufficient for the purposes of truly understanding one's perceived position. Nevertheless, references to family constellation most often include descriptions of the ordinal positions as though they were identical.

Children derive impressions of their place in the family, their world at the time, by comparing themselves with the siblings closest in age to them. In fact, we believe that *it is the sibling closest in age and most different from you that influenced your personality most*. Although much is said about birth order or ordinal position in relation to the family constellation, Adlerians are aware that it is the individual's *psychological* position that must be studied. A boy and girl in a family may be treated as two only children. Similarly, two children born 10 years apart may be reared like only children.

The perceptions and recollections of one's first 6 to 8 years of life will reveal his or her psychological position, for it is during these years, Adler observed, that the lifestyle is formed. As a consequence, *children more than plus or minus 6 years to the other children in the family are generally not in the same constellation.* Therefore, parents may have more than one constellation of children (e.g., first constellation [12-year-old—oldest, 11-year-old—middle, 10-year-old—youngest] and second constellation [2-year-old—only]).

With the qualification on family position noted, the ordinal descriptions of the positions deserve identification. Adlerians typically list five ordinal positions: oldest, second, middle, youngest, and only child. With each position is associated certain common characteristics, but these characteristics are nomothetic impressions that are to be quickly set aside when idiographic data about a given individual refutes validity of the common characteristics. They are, in fact, most useful in helping to uncover the uniqueness of individuals as references from which to discard ideas (e.g., how one is different from many other oldest children).

**Oldest.**   The oldest children can be typified as *ruler for a day*. They are the first and undisputed rulers of the family, the cause of glad tidings and happily the center of attention. One day a stranger appears in the house. Depending on the proximity in months or years, parental attitudes, gender difference, and other such variables, the oldest children evaluate the threat to their position in the family. On the average, they learn to take the newcomer in stride, especially if the parents are not too impressed with some likely acting-out behavior and provide encouragement for the oldest children to recognize their place as secure within the family.

Oldest children generally are able to relate well to adults, subscribe more readily to adult expectations and values, help at home particularly with the younger children, assume social responsibility, and develop socially acceptable ways of coping with life's tasks. The tendency of oldest children is to please adults and to strive for perfection as a guiding fictive goal, which can have serious consequences unless moderated over time.

**Second.**   The second children arrive to find someone already ahead of them. When within 6 years of the older child, and again depending on age and similar variables, second children typically will pursue their place in ways opposite to the older child. They may be less responsible, more independent, more demanding of service, and more interested in whatever the oldest does not pursue or master.

Second children often strive to be number one. The competition, referred to as *sibling rivalry*, can be quite intense in families that encourage comparisons between children. They can be portrayed by the illustration of persons in a foot race. Oldest children hear footsteps behind them and race to keep ahead. The second children see the person in front and feel that *if they just try harder*, maybe they can overtake them. Some individuals give up the race in discouragement. Others become admired as socially productive, although in some cases, they may gain only slight satisfaction from their efforts because they are motivated by the mistaken idea they must be productive to be valued as a person.

**Middle.**   Middle children acquire an added condition to their existence, a younger sibling. Often in families of three, the *middle children feel squeezed* in their position. They perceive themselves as singularly disadvantaged. They have few, if any, advantages of the oldest child and now their position as the baby has been supplanted. To help really convince them of their predicament, the oldest children often help take care of the youngest, thereby establishing for themselves an ally. The oldest may be seen as "bossy" toward the other children as well.

Middle children will likely still move in directions opposite to the older child. They may be more independent, rebellious, judgmental, and sensitive, and overtly seek assurances of their place with the parents. As is true with each position in the family, middle children can transcend these early perceptions through compensatory behavior that eventually works to their benefit. Each child often perceives his or her position as the most burdensome to bear. Middle children may express this disappointment more loudly.

However, middle children also have assets. Especially in larger families, they have the opportunity to learn from others' mistakes, to acquire negotiation and communication skills, and generally to cope with the politics of living. They also may be able to discover the unconventional solution to social situations through their tendency to see things differently than other members of the family.

**Youngest.**    Youngest children enjoy positions that they perceive as the center of attention. In addition to parents they have older siblings to entertain and provide them service. Although the youngest children might be troublesome at times, they have a protector to care for them. In fact, as youngest children get a little older, it is even fun to start something with the middle child and watch the older ally and the parents run to save the baby. They are often described as *cute, a charmer, and the family's baby,* no matter how old they become.

They may choose to use this charm and manipulative ways to just get by and enjoy life's many pleasures. On the other hand, with family values by both parents on achievement, they might be the hardest runners and greatest achievers of all if they perceive that as a way to make their place. They can be great entertainers and comfortable before an audience, whereas many people abhor, for example, public speaking.

**Only Child.** The only children may have the perceptions of the oldest child with one important exception. They are *never dethroned* and are less likely to feel the pressure of a close competitor. Only children may be perceived as quite mature for their age, comfortable with adults, responsible, cooperative, and developing mastery in cognitive skills. Their most likely perceived deficiency will be in relating to their peer group. Unlike the other youngsters, they may have little or no intimate give and take with other children. This can make early school experiences more difficult for these children as they begin coping with new life situations involving a peer group.

## The Five Major Life Tasks

Adler believed that everyone is confronted by at least three major life tasks: work, friendship, and love (Dreikurs, 1953). Research during the last several decades fortifies the position that these are indeed central life tasks to health and well-being. In addition, Mosak and Dreikurs (1967) identified a fourth and fifth task only alluded to by Adler. The fourth task is dealing with one's spiritual self in relation to the universe, God, or higher power. The fifth task concerns the individual's success in coping with self as subject, I, and as object, me.

**Work.** Equipped with their unique rules or guidelines about life, themselves, and others, individuals move from childhood to preadolescence, adolescence, and adulthood with a societal expectation that they will become more responsible, cooperative, and able to cope with life situations. Lack of success in the work task is fundamental to the most discouraged people in society. Although it does not require gainful employment, persons who find difficulty sustaining employment are in all probability individuals who lack confidence in their worth and ability.

In the school situation, failure and dropping out are tantamount to demotion and unemployment (i.e., loss of confidence and a sense of worth). Dreikurs (1968) believed that children who failed were not bad or lazy but, instead, discouraged. To face and fulfill one's life tasks requires the courage to be imperfect, to make mistakes, to fail occasionally but to try again. For too many children, school becomes a confirmation of their private assessment that they are not adequate. In later life, many of these individuals will be consistently unemployed, welfare recipients, or institutionalized. Although it appears difficult for persons to change in later life, Adlerians believe that one always has that capability.

**Friendship.** Dreikurs (1953) indicated that discouragement generally is not limited to one life task area. For example, most individuals can cope with the daily requirements of work whether by gainful employment or through service to others. Doubts, reservations, and fears may reveal themselves only at times. Friendship and intimate love relationships tend to be more demanding of cooperation, give and take, and respect. If an individual has persistent difficulties in either or both of these life tasks, discouragement is present that probably can be noted in the other areas as well. As will be noted in chapter 8, not all life task difficulties can be traced to psychosocial origin. Dreikurs (1946) has observed, however, that whenever individuals persistently complain, blame, make excuses, report fears, or discuss disabilities, they are revealing discouragement.

**Love.** Of the life tasks, love relationships require the greatest courage and faith in self and the other party. Basic values of respect, appreciation, and caring for the other party must be readily expressed or demonstrated in some manner to maintain and nurture the relationship. Decision making and conflict resolution competencies are essential. One's weaknesses, concerns, and peculiarities come under closer scrutiny than in most other life situations. Adlerians have observed, for example, that the very characteristics that attract individuals to one another also contribute to their friction in marriage.

Frequently, the European cultural value of *it's a man's world* orientation, which Adler discussed under the concept of masculine protest, encourages stereotyped notions such as "a real man brings home the family income" and "the woman cares for the children and serves the husband." Problems of partners generally do not surface openly until the relationship becomes quite disturbed, even though the problems could have been predicted on the basis of lifestyle analysis.

Not all such complementary, yet friction-producing, qualities can be stereotyped by societal circumstances. For example, in one case a husband always had the greatest regard for his wife's opinion, so much so that he depended on her to make most of the major family decisions because he doubted the reliability of his own decisions. On the other hand, she had admired his industriousness and goal-oriented attitudes toward life. After three children and several years of married life, the wife felt isolated from him. He never participated in family decisions; in fact, he was so busy with his work that she felt she meant hardly anything to him.

Initially, he felt threatened by her confrontations and somewhat confused by what seemed to be happening. She wanted him to work less and participate more in family decisions. Through counseling, they came to understand and anticipate their conflicts by establishing a new agreement for working together.

As Adler had noted, once the individuals understood their own movement through life, they could decide to change their attitudes and behavior with renewed respect for themselves and one another. They were able, in this case, to establish behavioral ways of short-circuiting old expectations, including the husband's low estimate of his decision-making ability.

**Spirituality.**  Spirituality only recently has become a major topic of consideration among the helping professions. There is a growing awareness that it is a part of the human condition to need and want to deal with personal existential issues. As noted in chapter 2, research is corroborating the position that *spirituality is a key component to both longevity and quality of life*. Until recently, it has been relegated principally to the responsibility of the clergy.

Questions regarding the purpose and meaning of life are universal. In fact, the increasingly multiculturalistic dimensions of our society appear to be contributing to a greater sensitivity and respect for spirituality as experienced and practiced, for example, by Native Americans, Asian Americans, and African Americans compared to the Western Judeo-Christian tradition and belief system (Gladding, 1996).

**Self.** The fifth task concerns the individual's success in coping with self. Popular literature abounds with self-help books, tapes, and seminars. Concepts such as self-esteem and self-efficacy are common themes. Many interesting studies of these and other self-focused concepts suggest that longevity and quality of life are related to one's basic attitudes and convictions about self-direction. Research, for example, fortifies the observation that the greater the extent to which individuals have an internal locus of control, then indices of positive health are also present to a greater extent. Chapter 5 includes further discussion on this topic.

Each of the major life tasks is presented in detail in chapter 2 as part of a new model of Adlerian conceptualization of holism and its implication for counseling practice. A research and clinical assessment instrument designed to measure the characteristics of the model of wellness based on major life tasks also is described.

## Function of Emotions and Feelings

Frequently, individuals tell counselors in a variety of ways that they cannot help themselves; they just feel so angry, sad, bored, or whatever that they *must* behave a certain way. Adler, of course, would not accept these evasions of responsibility. Although excuses take many forms, emotions often are identified as central to the problems that individuals bring to counselors.

---

One records impressions, including feelings,
for future reference.

---

Adler perceived emotions as tools necessary to the execution of behavior. Emotions are not considered entities unto themselves. Love, joy, anger, sadness, guilt, and fear do not come to us out of a vacuum. One must first perceive, value, feel, and then act.

Because much of one's valuing with regard to life, self, and others is a blueprint already stored in the unconscious thought processes, much of what is attributed to instant love, fear, or anger can be traced to one's lifestyle databank. As individuals grow and experience, they "record" impressions, including feelings, for future reference. Scientists now also believe that human beings "store" biochemical reactions in various parts of the body. Therefore, physiological responses seem to be a part of one's emotional memory of events.

Many counselees will wish to discredit this concept of emotions because it places responsibility on them for their present decisions and actions. As will be seen in subsequent chapters, Adlerians are very much interested in emotions but more as signposts to the individual's mistaken notions and their intentions. It is the messages individuals send themselves that build the energy they use to act.

Prior feelings help individuals process impressions of others to which they respond rather automatically, sometimes quite incorrectly. In the absence of knowledge or experience, individuals do not feel anything until they can fit it into their system of expectations. The expression, *as I think, I am,* is fundamental to understanding emotions as well as the behavior that follows.

Observers of the Adlerian counselor might conclude that he or she is very insensitive to the anger, complaining, blaming, tears, or affection expressed in a counseling session. If the emotions are tools used by the counselee to distract or otherwise manipulate the counselor from the goals for counseling, he or she indeed may seem unimpressed by their presence. Dreikurs stated that neurosis, a defense mechanism for denying responsibility for meeting one's life tasks, is a tribute to human ingenuity! He would say, do not be distracted by such creativity. It is the less visible feelings and attitudes that the Adlerian will pursue (e.g., isolation, alienation, lack of confidence, insecurity).

## Holistic View

The indivisibility of a person is a fundamental belief of this psychology. At a time when holistic approaches to medicine, mental health, and rehabilitation are coming to the forefront, the practitioner will find its usefulness apparent. When dealing with a wide range of people and circumstances, the probability of any one science or discipline being able to adequately explain, diagnose, or prescribe treatment for all the ills of people is nil. The author, therefore, continually seeks and incorporates new knowledge of human behavior into this approach.

In its most basic form, one recognizes the interaction between physical and psychological well-being. There are scientists who now observe that the distinction between mind and body is not only inaccurate but scientifically unsound. What traditionally has been associated with the chemistry of the brain and its function are now found to exist in other parts of the body. Biofeedback research and its application in stress management has helped to corroborate Adler's assumption that what one thinks can produce physiological symptoms similar to those of other origin. Infection, disease, and other injury to the body are potentially mood modifying (Sweeney & Witmer, 1991; Witmer & Sweeney, 1992). Fatigue, particularly due to distress, is symptomatic of the interaction of mind and body. Even personal experience suggests the validity of such a position.

Adler was not the first proponent of this point of view. As Witmer (1985) noted

> The concept of health and wellness as encompassing mind-body unity reaches back thousands of years to middle eastern religions, the ancient Greeks, and Far Eastern philosophies. Greek medical tradition like the Jewish healing tradition exemplified in Christ, treated the whole person. Mind and body were not separated but seen as interrelated and interdependent. (p. 43)

Adlerian practitioners also are aware that samples of an individuals behavior can help counselors to understand a more global life plan and direction of movement. Such behaviors, however, are only an approximation of the total and must be kept in proper perspective as such. One can anticipate, for example, that difficulty in sustaining friendships because of excessive demands for attention or unreliability would contribute to problems in marriage or love relationships. The greater intimacy, give and take, and equalitarian nature of love would be under even more stress than friendships. The fact that one chooses not to marry, however, would not necessarily indicate a lack of capacity for the personal commitment, empathy, and courage required in a loving relationship.

*Holism, then, is a point of view from which to understand human behavior as dynamic, self-directed, interrelated mind and body moving through life with a unique goal-oriented plan for having significance in relation to others.* Helping counselees change how they think and feel in their relationships with others, for example, can result in better physical health, greater satisfaction with their work, and increased joy and interest in other aspects of their life.

## Philosophy and Value System

Adlerians occasionally are charged with being manipulative in their practice. Dreikurs believed that this was true in the sense that when anyone influences another, he or she is manipulative. Dreikurs (1971), however, helped to open the Adlerian philosophy and value orientation to critical analysis. Adlerian presuppositions for practice rest upon a belief that individuals who are high in social interest will think of themselves and others as equals and behave accordingly. Dreikurs believed that if individuals valued themselves as equal to everyone else, the major problems of society would be virtually eliminated. He observed that in approximately 8,000 years of humankind's social existence, people have tried to function on the mistaken premises of authoritarian systems that continually fail to solve their problems.

As early as 1946, Dreikurs (1946) predicted that women, blacks, children, and other minorities would progressively demand equality, the unfulfilled American dream. Anyone reading his book on marriage would be inclined to believe it was written in the current decade rather than in the '40s. Adler, predating the world wars, similarly was far ahead of his time in this regard. Those who perceive themselves as being in power do not relinquish it readily. The upheaval of the last decades is evidence, however, that large groups of minorities, including children, no longer intend to tolerate disregard and inequality from the traditional "superiors." Authority from on high is questioned. Power among the few is suspect.

Dreikurs was concerned, however, that without education to a more satisfactory agreement among humankind, the underdogs would simply strive to overcome the top dogs and repeat the cycle at some further time. As a consequence, Dreikurs, following Adler's example, vigorously worked for change through social institutions that affected the quality of life of all persons but most particularly the underprivileged and disadvantaged. If he were alive today, he still would be an outspoken advocate for equality in an increasingly multicultural society.

In the same sense that many individuals strive toward goals of superiority, power, wealth, or position, groups similarly seek to be in control of others. The great emphasis in our society on competition and the external signs of superiority is further testimony to the preoccupation with control and influence. In such circumstances, cooperation too often becomes compromise of a temporary nature.

The democratic philosophy and values that Dreikurs (1971) proposed in lieu of those now found in society include

| Present | Proposed |
| --- | --- |
| Ambition | Enthusiasm |
| Righteousness | Friendliness |
| | Understanding |
| Obligation | Belongingness |
| | Participation |
| Conformity | Self-respect |
| | Self-improvement |
| Perfection | Courage |
| Rugged | Mutual help |
| Individualism | Cooperation |

Adlerians believe that one cannot make others do anything that they do not consider useful to them. Therefore, in spite of many efforts, some individuals will not change their behavior or attitudes even in the face of discomfort or inconvenience. This is predicated on the concept that all behavior is purposive (i.e., it serves a use for the individuals to pursue their goals). From their unique perceptions of life, the individuals may consider changing as dangerous or at least difficult.

On the other hand, Adler made a distinction between the behaviors that move individuals toward others (i.e., high social interest) and those that move them against or away from others (Ansbacher & Ansbacher, 1967). The latter behaviors were denoted as socially useless, self defeating behaviors. Whereas all behaviors are "useful" from the individual's point of view, the Adlerian value system would note that some attitudes detract from the individual's self-esteem and, consequently, social interest.

Attitudes and behaviors that result in an individual avoiding or failing to meet basic life tasks would be considered on the useless side of life by Adler. Because this is a *psychology of use and not inventory*, Adlerians do not typically label these behaviors in categories according to symptoms (although even Adlerians must use the statistical diagnostic categories of mental and emotional disorders in mental health practices based on third-party payment).

One way of conceptualizing the relative movement of an individual in the direction of social interest is depicted in Figure 1.1. Persons moving primarily on a vertical plane are most concerned about how they are doing in their endeavors. They constantly are evaluating and comparing their efforts to others or to a fictive notion of perfection that they strive to attain. Persons who actively move in this direction often are identified as productive, "successful" people in their field. A sad commentary on their striving is that they rarely gain much satisfaction from their efforts or the outcome because of a nagging concern that what was gained may be lost. The "can you top this" feeling may persist long after evidence substantiates the person's competence or adequacy.

**Low Social Interest:**

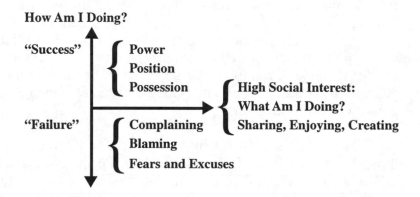

**Figure 1.1.** Social Interest Continua: Vertical (Low) vs.
    Horizontal (High).

The horizontal plane denotes movement toward enjoyment and
participation in life activities. Persons evaluate their activities on
the basis of the satisfaction they and/or others gain from them.
This portrayal of movement should not be construed to indicate
that high-social-interest individuals do not enjoy competition or
that low-social-interest persons gain no satisfaction from their work.
Actually most persons are somewhere in between the two directions of movement.

The difference might be observed, for example, in a competitive game or sport. High-social-interest persons may play very hard
to win but will have enjoyed the game, win or lose. Low-social-
interest individuals who lose, if they play at all, will in contrast
feel defeated, possibly even disgusted with themselves, until they
can reestablish themselves as winners. As will be illustrated in
chapter 6, Adlerians are conscious of this distinction particularly
with regard to the application of behavior modification techniques
in school situations. The indiscriminate use of rewards to reinforce achievement or social behavior also can reinforce the individual for moving vertically (extrinsic motivation) rather than hori-
zontally (intrinsic motivation).

# VALIDATION

Adlerian theory and practice are validated in part by its use and incorporation into several other systems or approaches to counseling. Virtually every major personality approach to counseling and psychotherapy, with the notable exception of traditional psychoanalysis, has incorporated Adlerian principles and techniques into its system. This is both an asset and one of its greatest liabilities. For although indeed Adler's work has influenced the work of others, its potential is still not fully realized.

## Theory

Social interest, ordinal position, early recollections, and other aspects of Adlerian theory have been investigated rather extensively. In fact, the number of studies has increased in the last 9 years over the previous 12-year period, 103 to 75, respectively (Watkins, 1992c). The number of studies in each area from 1982 to 1990 include birth order, 25 studies; early recollections, 23 studies; social interest, 21 studies; lifestyle, 7 studies; and other, 27 studies. The greatest increase has been in the area of early recollections. Unfortunately, many of these studies were limited in scope and lacking in sound methodology.

Watkins (1992a) noted the following regarding early memory research:

> In conclusion, Adlerian-oriented EM [early memory] research has increased substantially in the past ten years—seemingly more so comparatively than either Freudian, ego psychological, or cognitive-perceptual perspectives. This body of research as a whole provides some support for Adler's views about EM, but these studies are not without flaws (e.g., virtually no racial/cross cultural subjects have been included, no pilot studies have been conducted) . . . Currently, there is tentative support for Adler's views about EM's, but to draw any conclusions beyond that is inappropriate at this time. (p. 261)

Many studies have been conducted concerning birth order over the years. Watkins' (1992b) review of birth order research during the period 1981–1991 resulted in the following conclusions:

> Considering the limitations of these studies, the primary conclusions suggested by these data could be stated as:
>
> 1. firstborns often manifest characteristics consistent with the "firstborn profile" described in Adlerian literature (e.g., being more dominant, responsible);
>
> 2. achievement motivation patterns vary according to birth-order positions;
>
> 3. birth order when combined with the variable of sex (e.g., subjects' sex) relates to selected achievement variables and locus of control;
>
> 4. studies support the importance of "psychological position" in birth order research; and
>
> 5. some evidence suggests that birth-order effects vary as a result of ethnicity. (p. 365)

In the area of social interest, attempts at measuring this concept have had varying degrees of success. In another of his reviews of the period from 1981 to 1991, Watkins (1994) compared and contrasted the Social Interest Index (SII) (Greever, Tseng, & Friedland, 1973), the Social Interest Scale (SIS) (Crandall, 1975), and the Sulliman Scale of Social Interest (SSSI) (Sulliman, 1973). The SIS was the most used instrument ($n = 38$) during this period and the data were generally supportive of its validity and reliability. The SSSI also holds promise but there were limited data available at the time of the review.

Among the studies conducted during this period, two used both the SII and SIS in a linear composite of standardized scores (Leak & Williams, 1989). The authors predicted that social interest would be positively correlated with the hardiness components of commitment, challenge, and control and negatively correlate with the four facets of alienation (powerlessness, vegetativeness, nihilism, and adventurousness) in four contexts: family, work, others, and self. Hardiness is a concept found to be present in individuals who are able to overcome life adversities more readily than other individuals in similar circumstances.

Subjects in the two studies were undergraduates at a large state university ($n = 49$ males; $n = 38$ females) and others ($n = 103$ females) from a small, religiously affiliated university. The results of the two studies were similar but not identical. Social interest correlated significantly in the first study with two of three components of hardiness: commitment and control. The authors believe that the lack of correlation with the challenge scale was a function of the items having a strong rigidity-versus-impulsivity component unrelated to the concept of social interest. In the second study, neither challenge nor control correlated with social interest.

In the first study, all four predictions with respect to alienation and social interest were supported. The second study found three of four scales on alienation significantly correlated with social interest. Unfortunately, the authors did not control for differences by gender or ethnicity. The authors concluded:

> . . . the results of the two studies offer empirical support for Adlerian social interest theory. The relationship between social interest and diverse aspects of psychological hardiness and alienation support Adler's claim that social interest contributes strength and courage to a person. (Leak & Williams, 1989, p. 374)

Watkins (1992a, 1992b, 1992c, 1994) has provided a convenient summary and critique of the areas of research mentioned above. Anyone interested in conducting research in these areas should find Watkins' analyses and recommendation for future research helpful.

## Methods

Studies of Adlerian theory and methods with school-age children, their parents, and teachers have demonstrated effectiveness over the years. An interesting observation of some of these studies has been the greater usefulness of working with the adults who influence the children. Although working with the children is effective and desirable, efforts with their teachers and parents multiplies the long-term value of counselors' and psychologists' interventions.

A variety of studies (P. C. Burnett, 1988; Sweeney & Moses, 1979) have documented the usefulness of parent and teacher study-consultation groups. P. C. Burnett (1988) concluded

> The research studies . . . strongly support the effectiveness of Adlerian parenting programs. Changes in a positive direction were noted on measures of children's behavior, children's self-concept, parental behavior, and parental attitude. The studies were, on the whole, methodologically sound. (p. 74)

Shulman and Mosak (1988b) reported on studies of reliability, validity, and construct validity related to lifestyle assessment. For example, early recollections have been found to be more consistent than Thematic Apperception Test (TAT) protocols, which can be influenced by situational variables to a far greater extent. Other studies have demonstrated that changes in recollections reflect changes in the outlook and mental status of clinical populations. Shulman and Mosak noted

> Though far from exhaustive, the research is encouraging and almost universally supportive of Adlerian lifestyle conceptions. Continued research and empirical investigations will be required, however, to explore and clarify various issues and to delineate fine distinctions and differences. (p. 259)

Wheeler, Kern, and Curlette (1991) reported on more than 10 years of developmental work on the Life-Style Personality Inventory (LSPI). The LSPI was designed as an objective format measure of social interest and Adlerian lifestyle themes. The authors provided what they considered to be a strong case for the idea that lifestyle can be measured in a reliable and valid manner. Such a tool should be an asset in further research into this important area of investigation.

Subsequent chapters will cite other relevant research that pertain to specific topical areas. More and even better designed studies are needed, however, to add to the theory and practice of Adlerian psychology. Although Adlerian practitioners, including hundreds of lay group leaders and family education center volunteers, are satisfied with its utility and face validity, experimental data are needed to increase its credibility with publics of a different persuasion.

## Multicultural Considerations

Increasingly, questions are raised about the appropriateness of Adlerian theory and practice (as well as other approaches) from the perspective of various racial and ethnic groups. Such questions preceded the current attention to these groups because the works of Adler and Dreikurs have been translated into several other languages and have been found appropriate in other cultures. Nevertheless, such questions are all the more likely as the demographics of the United States continue to shift toward more Asian Americans/Pacific Islanders, African Americans, and Hispanics (Arciniega & Newlon, 1995). Equally notable is the fact that more than 50% of African Americans, Hispanics, and Native Americans are under the age of 25. As these populations continue to increase in number and age, the appropriateness of traditional counseling strategies will and should be challenged (Lee & Richardson, 1991).

Arciniega and Newlon (1995) provided a review of major theories using 11 racial and ethnic considerations. They rated the theories as follows: (+) positively; (–) negatively; (P) partially; or (0) not addressed. The 11 considerations and the ratings given for Adlerian theory were as follows:

1. Language (e.g., competent in the native language of the counselee), (0)

2. Family and social relations (e.g., respect for kinship ties, values, and minorities groups' strong sense of belonging and identity to the family groups), (+)

3. Time focus (e.g., events or situations are often viewed as more important than being on time), (P)

4. Nature—people relationships (e.g., acceptance [not subjugation] and harmony with nature coexisting without control), (P)

5. Holistic view (e.g., operate from the perspective of environment and themselves as a whole), (+)

6. Human activity and cooperation (e.g., includes cooperation, connectedness and loyalty to the group while feeling respect for who you are and not of having to become better), (+)

7. Identity (e.g., self-identity cannot be separated from cultural identity), (P)

8. Mental health (e.g., sensitivity to culturally different views of what is normal or abnormal), (+)

9. Spirituality and religion (e.g., treat spirituality and religion as an integral part of the group and its individuals, (+)

10. Responsibility (e.g., concept of collective responsibility is prioritized, family first, then group or community, and finally to self), (+)

11. Oppression and racism (e.g., whereas oppression exists for other groups, the physical characteristics of these minorities contribute to them being more easily identified for oppression and discrimination, and only Adlerians address this distinction), (+)

Adlerian theory, therefore, was rated positively on 7 of the 11 considerations, partially addressed three others, and "does not address" only one, language. Ivey's developmental theory was the next most culturally appropriate, with five positives and six ratings of partially responding to the considerations. The other theories evaluated were psychoanalytic, Jungian, existential, person-centered, Gestalt, transactional analysis, rational–emotive, cognitive–behavioral, reality therapy, and ecosystems. The authors noted the following about Adlerian theory:

> . . . of all the theories this one holds the great promise because of several characteristics. It focuses on the person in a familial and sociocultural context; it is involved in developing social interest and in contributing to others; and it emphasizes belonging, which supports the value system of these minorities groups. In addition, its emphasis on the role of the family and culture fits well with the values of these focus minority groups. Adlerian assumptions that people are equal, social and goal centered, and are holistic are congruent with the cultural values of these racial and ethnic groups. (p. 577)

From a cultural perspective, these authors reaffirm the Adlerian contention that the values that move persons toward social interest are also those that promote both the individual and the community. Contrary to a narrow interpretation of the Adlerian nurturing of social interest, it is out of respect for the individual's values and not to instill conformity that the counselor is motivated to intervene.

> The individual's unique subjective interpretation and perception are part of the Adlerian theory, and the client's values and views are honored and accepted. Adlerian goals are not aimed at deciding for clients what they should change about themselves. Rather, it works in collaboration with clients and their family networks. This theory offers a pragmatic approach that is flexible and uses a range of action-oriented cognitive techniques to explore personal problems within their sociocultural context. (Arciniega & Newlon, 1995, p. 578)

In an invited commentary on macrostrategies for delivery of mental health counseling services in the *Journal of Mental Health Counseling*, Corey (1991) offered the following:

> The basic assumptions of all these authors [Herr, Ivey, Rigazio-DiGilio, and Dinkmeyer] appear to rest on an Adlerian foundation that stresses prevention, policies that are

> growth producing, visions that inspire individuals to feel com-
> petent, the process of reaching out to others, and finding
> meaning and a sense of community in a social context. This
> context for understanding counseling practice makes far more
> sense to me than gearing practice toward a medical model
> that focuses largely on the internal dynamics of the individual
> and tends to ignore the impact of the individual's external
> environment. . . . From my vantage point, Adler's ideas are
> certainly compatible with many of the macrostrategies for
> future delivery of services to a culturally diverse population.
> (pp. 53–54)

The preceding assessments are especially notable because they
are offered by individuals who are not principally Adlerian in their
orientation. Although it is comforting to have such assessments,
the implementation of the theory into practice is still the responsibility of the counseling practitioner. By being congruent with the
philosophy, values, and practices of Adlerian theory, however, counseling practitioners increase the probability of being appropriate
in their interventions with culturally diverse groups.

## Gender Considerations

Adler was an outspoken advocate for women's rights. This
position no doubt contributed to his ideas receiving a less than
enthusiastic reception by those in power during much of this century. In one of his papers, he wrote of "The Alleged Inferiority of
Women" (1954):

> Boys actually do show greater talent for studies which are
> capable of preparing them for their masculine occupations
> but this is only a seemingly greater talent. If we investigate
> more closely we learn that the story of the lesser capability of
> women is a palpable fable. (p. 109)

Dreikurs (1953) described Adler's concept of the "masculine
protest" as a fictive goal men and women pursued to overcome
feelings of inferiority. Although it was more pronounced in Europe, he noted that equality of women was still far from a reality in
U.S. society. The masculine protest is predicated on the observa-

tion that men had more privileges, power, and overall advantages. In order to be equal, women protested for treatment equal to that of men. The "real man" image was further reinforced by heroes in the media.

As a consequence, a weak boy or man was disdained and only through protest could hope to gain equality. Girls and women had to protest to be treated like a man and, consequently, experience a sense of empowerment and respect. In the final analysis, Dreikurs believed that any system predicated on a lack of social equality was doomed to be unstable at the very least and, at its worst, to be unjust, oppressive, and disrespectful of individuals and groups.

Lee and Richardson (1991), in their work on culturally responsive counseling, identified sex role socialization as an important dynamic to consider across cultures. They noted

> Many racial or ethnic groups with non-European cultural origins have different perceptions of the role of men and women. These different gender perceptions can influence the expectations considered normal for development. Such differences, therefore, can account for fundamental differences in personality development for men and women. (p. 15)

Gender role differences, per se, do not necessarily constitute inequality. Inequities, however, can be inherent in the subculture of which an individual is a part. Such a reminder is needed when addressing the concerns of a specific counselee. Although an Adlerian will believe and behave in keeping with a value system fundamentally based on social equality, there is always a point in the process of counseling when a counselee is asked, "Do you want to change (that which seems to be a problem)?" The responsibility for change rests with the counselee. Indeed, without the cooperation of the counselee, no progress is possible.

On the other hand, Dreikurs was very direct in his assessments about the conflicts between genders. Role expectations, divisions of responsibility, and related matters were not to be the major focus of attention in counseling. Rather, finding solutions based on the fundamental valuing of each person as a social equal is essential. Who cooks, cares for the children, earns a paycheck, or takes the social initiative for the family is less a concern than the point that all such activities are valued as contributing to the good of all. Dreikurs would applaud couples or families who decided on task assignments based on competence rather than gender or other such arbitrary criteria. Chapters 10 and 11 address counseling with couples and families from the Adlerian perspective.

Also relevant to gender and discrimination is the partnerships and life choices of gays and lesbians. Such questions are raised in classes and workshops and there are occasionally references to early Adlerian works that include homosexuality as a form of neurosis. At least two points seem important to note. First, neurosis is indicative of those who choose to avoid meeting their life tasks through assumed disability. Therefore, individuals of whatever orientation grow (or do not) in social interest by meeting life head on (or not). One's orientation, then, does not in its nature constitute low social interest or neurosis. Second, like Adler, I believe that the individual is the only judge of what is useful for him or her regardless of what others may think. Of greater interest is whether the homosexual individual meets life's tasks responsibly, cooperatively, and happily.

One story about Adler is relevant at this point. This report came in the mid-1930s from a female family caseworker whose supervisor wanted her to consult with Dr. Adler regarding a 21-year-old man who was living "in sin" with an older man in Greenwich Village. She described the young man as very personable and highly intelligent. The following recounts her conversation with Dr. Adler:

> Suddenly the door to the inner sanctum opened, and a deep accented voice (which somehow matched his rotund, pudgy appearance) invited me to come in and be seated. Tobacco smoke and fumes hung in the small room like a tangible wall. He glanced for a moment at my report of "John," which lay on top of a vastly untidy desk, and he looked at me over his glasses. "You say this John—he is homosexual?"
>
> "Oh, yes," I replied.

"And is he happy, would you say?"

"Oh, yes," I replied.

"Well," leaning back in his swivel chair and putting his thumbs in his vest, "Why don't we leave him alone? Eh?" This was doubtless the most profound wisdom he could have shared with me. (Manaster et al., 1977, p. 82)

## ADLER AND BEYOND

Perhaps there is no greater challenge than being true to the principles of Adler and Dreikurs while not being bound by their time in the history of the helping professions. They were both proactive and ahead of their time in many respects. There is every reason to believe that they would be every bit as farsighted today if they were among us. Adler's daughter Alexandria made the following observation:

I would have loved my father to have seen the effect of drugs on psychosis. I am sure that he would have accepted it. He was always open to any progress. (Manaster et al., 1977, p. 57)

Prochaska and Norcross (1994) reported the results of a Delphi poll to ascertain, among other things, what 75 "experts" consider to be "hot and not hot" in the next millennium in terms of interventions and modalities.

. . . the consensus is that psychotherapy will become more directive, psychoeducational, present-centered, problem focused, and briefer in the next decade. . . . In terms of therapy formats, individuals, couples, family and group therapy are seen on the upward swing, but the huge transformation is expected in the length of therapy: short term is in, and long term is on its way out. (p. 486)

Also reported were questions about theoretical orientations and their predicted increase or decrease in importance. Although Adlerian theory was not specifically mentioned, as is often the case, "psychodynamic/neo-Freudian" was cited; this category often is used to include Adlerians. The respondents predicted these approaches among the groups to decrease at least slightly in the coming years. The irony in these predictions is in the relevance of Adlerian values, interventions, and modalities and the lack of identification with this approach to future change.

In a society where economics are a driving force of many policy decisions, attention to these matters will be all the more important in the future. Now more than ever, there is an opportunity to contribute to the needs of society. To do so will require an effort that extends Adler's and Dreikurs' contributions further into the affairs of institutions and groups that shape the quality of life within society (Sweeney, 1999). Their legacy is a challenge to those who believe that society will be better served by the philosophy, the values, and the psychology of Alfred Adler.

## SUMMARY

The Individual Psychology of Alfred Adler is the forerunner of many other approaches to education, counseling, and therapy today. Even as other approaches incorporate or independently discover principles and methods essentially Adlerian in nature, Adlerian institutes, study groups, and practitioners continue to provide answers for otherwise discouraged and often bankrupt systems of institutions. Central concepts to this approach include

1. Human beings are social beings who are essentially self-determining, purposive, and creative (idiographic) in their approaches to making a place for themselves in life.

2. Individuals are best understood holistically in their functioning from a phenomenological (subjective) point of view.

3. The lifestyle—one's unique set of convictions about the self, life, and others—is the map or outline individuals use to guide themselves in approaching basic life tasks:

work, friendship, love, self, and spirit. Established between 6 and 8 years of age, it remains basically unexamined and unchanged under normal circumstances.

4. Unsuccessful coping with basic life tasks is a sign of discouragement. Discouragement can be overcome early in life more easily; however, it can always be overcome if the individual chooses to do so.

5. Social interest is Adler's conceptualization of a quality in human beings that constitutes their proclivity for being responsible, cooperative, and creative members of humankind. Persons high in social interest enjoy and like themselves, others, and life. Social interest must be nurtured, however, or the individual's faulty perceptions of himself or herself can result in discouraged, self-defeating behaviors.

6. Adlerians tend to subscribe to a value system based on social democracy, with equality of people at the core. Their approach to helping other people is basically educative and preventative in nature, although remedial and crisis intervention work is also carried out.

7. In an increasingly pluralistic, multicultural society, Adlerian theory holds "great promise" as the most appropriate theory on which to base counseling interventions. Likewise, fundamentally based on social democracy and social equality, it has been and is the single greatest advocate for social equality as a reality between males and females, majority and minority populations, different generations, and persons of any persuasion who are oppressed.

Further elaboration on these and related concepts may be found in the succeeding chapters in the discussion of methods and techniques of Individual Psychology with individuals and groups.

## STUDY QUESTIONS

**Directions:** Respond to the following in the spaces provided.

1. (a) Explain the concept of goal-directed behavior (i.e., behavior is purposive).



   (b) Do you agree? _____ If not, why?



2. What is meant by "socio-teleo-analytic" as descriptions for this approach?



3. (a) What is the function of emotions?



   (b) Where do emotions originate?



   (c) In what ways can emotions be useful or disruptive socially?

4. (a) Which of the life tasks is most easily met?

   (b) Which of the life tasks is most difficult to meet?

   (c) Explain your responses to "a" and "b."

5. Why is this approach considered to have "great promise" for minorities?

## Chapter 2

# TOWARD WELLNESS: THE GOAL OF HELPING

*J. Melvin Witmer and Thomas J. Sweeney*

Health to you! The Greek people use this as a greeting and farewell expression. The Greek word *yiasoo*, which means "health to you," has its historical origins with Hygea, the goddess of health. She was an expert on teaching the ways of living in harmony with nature in order to prevent disease. The Hebrew word *shalom* has been used historically as a greeting and farewell to express a personal wish of peace and "completeness" or sense of wholeness to another person. In German, *Gesundheit* is used to wish health and wholesomeness. *Health* shares a root meaning in Old English with the words *hale*, *heal*, and *whole*. All of these terms express a wish for soundness of body, free from disease or infirmity, in which inner harmony, balance, and wholeness may exist. Many cultures have language expressions that convey a message of well-being for greeting another person.

In the third edition of *Adlerian Counseling* (Sweeney, 1989), research across disciplines was cited to substantiate the theoreti-

43

cal concepts of Adlerian theory with respect to its holistic orientation, the major life tasks, characteristics of healthy persons, and how these related to both longevity and quality of life. Subsequently, the authors (J. E. Myers, Witmer, & Sweeney, 1995; Sweeney & Witmer, 1991; Witmer, 1989; Witmer & Sweeney, 1992) expanded and refined their model of wellness over the life span to incorporate additional concepts considered to be important to human growth and development.

In keeping with a desire to help move Adlerian thinking to the forefront of education, counseling, and psychotherapy, this chapter is designed to expand, enhance, and refine what Adler and especially Dreikurs anticipated through their vision. There is compelling evidence that, as a nation, the United States must redirect its focus, priorities, and resources from sickness and remediation to wellness and prevention across the life span. In 1979, the U.S. Public Health Service reported that at least 53% of deaths are caused by self-destructive and negligent behavior that result in premature deaths. Recent sources attribute two thirds of all deaths to preventable conditions ("Six Convincing Reasons to Exercise," 1994). Yet it is estimated that only 1 to 3% of the annual health care bill in this country goes to preventive services (University of California at Berkeley, 1993). Mental health fares no better. In any one year, 22% of the population suffers from mental illness—28% if drug abuse is included ("When Mental Illness Strikes," 1993).

Today, holistic health has become an approach to the well-being of people that includes the prevention of illness. This is the first generation in human history to know what constitutes a "whole person." People now possess enough knowledge to craft their own lives intelligently, deliberately, and responsibly. Matters of fate are now more matters of choice. The term *holistic* does not denote a specific procedure or form of treatment, but is a philosophy, an attitude, a mindset. In a broad sense, it involves taking into account the person's physical, mental, and emotional states, social relationships, spiritual orientation, and life habits. Different methods, techniques, and knowledge bases are used to understand, treat, and enhance the well-being of the individual.

Certain leaders in the health field, however, argue that even the focus on holistic health is too much on disease or its prevention. The authors of this book agree. Consequently, we use the term *wellness* to describe what we believe is more health enhancing, proactive, and positive than the traditional models of human development. To be really healthy is to feel great, to enjoy life, not just postpone death or disease. Wellness as we define it is a way of life oriented toward optimal health and well-being in which mind, body, and spirit are integrated by the individual to live life more fully within the human and natural community. Ideally, it is the optimum state of health and well-being that each individual is capable of achieving.

High levels of wellness include a genuine zest for being alive. We occasionally incorporate the term *wholeness* into our descriptions and discussion. This is to emphasize the interdependence and relatedness of the components of wellness. The available research as well as clinical experience tend to fortify the position that all of the components that constitute well-being deserve and require development. As will be noted in the next sections, for example, cultivating a healthy sense of humor is no less important than effective critical thinking skills.

What follows is an introduction to wellness as a central, organizing, motivating purpose to human development, an explanation of the "wheel of wellness" over the life span (Figure 2.1) as dynamic and multidimensional in nature, an overview of the Wellness Evaluation of Lifestyle (WEL) assessment instrument (J. E. Myers et al., 1995), and some examples of how the model can be used in the context of the Adlerian philosophy and values espoused by Dreikurs (1971).

## WELLNESS OVER THE LIFE SPAN

What is the origin and nature of wholeness? Does a single motivating force move and influence the organism toward health and wellness? Adler (1927/1954), in his writings to acquaint the general public with the fundamentals of Individual Psychology, observed that, "The psychic life is a complex of aggressive and security-finding activities whose final purpose is to guarantee the continued existence on this earth of the human organism, and to enable him to securely accomplish his development" (p. 28).

Maslow (1970), in his pioneering work that led to the development of humanistic psychology, studied the characteristics of healthy persons. He noted that

> Human life will never be understood unless its highest aspirations are taken into account. Growth, self-actualization, the striving toward health, the quest for identity and autonomy, the yearning for excellence (and other ways of phrasing "upward") must by now be accepted beyond question as a widespread and perhaps universal human tendency. (pp. xii–xiii)

Witmer (1985), after reviewing the work of Adler, Maslow, and others as well as the research on human development, noted that two counteracting forces function to sustain life and fulfill the individual's potential for health and happiness.

> One force strives to protect and defend the self, both physical and psychological self. This protective force clings to safety and defensiveness tending to provide security, afraid to move away from that which is known. It is afraid of independence, freedom, separateness, and newness. The other force impels the individual toward wholeness and uniqueness of self, toward fuller functioning of pleasures and capacities. It moves forward and outward to create and enhance its existence. One force provides safety and satisfaction, the other growth and satisfaction. (p. 15)

Human behavior, then, is directed toward a goal. "The psychic life of man is determined by his goal" (Adler, 1927/1954, p. 29). This teleology, striving toward a goal, is ever present in the movement and activities of the individual. Therefore, to understand the goal of an individual, one must note the present activities and their meaning to the individual (i.e., what outcome[s] is anticipated). Instead of looking to the past for cause, human motivation is best understood by one's intentions and anticipation (i.e., what one expects to gain from such activities). Both conscious and subconsciously motivated actions are viewed as reflecting the intent or outcome desired by the person.

In order to develop and protect their growth and well-being, as noted in chapter 1, individuals formulate what Adler called a *style of life* or *lifestyle*. To realize their goal, individuals create a way of living that is motivated by their *fictional goal*. In early childhood, the person develops a fictional image of what he or she has to do to enhance and protect existence. This fictional image becomes a central goal of the person's lifestyle, guided by subjective notions of what one has to be like or do to be safe, to feel a sense of belonging, or to be superior. All of these notions are uniquely perceived by the individual as essential to well-being.

However, the fictional goal may be either self-defeating or self-enhancing because the person's private logic (i.e., unique convictions about life, self, and others) is influenced by genetic, cultural, and family factors. Discovering these fictional goals becomes an important process in counseling to eliminate self-defeating thoughts and behavior or to facilitate self-enhancing thoughts and behavior in reaching toward wellness.

The authors of this book believe that all human beings have the capacity to live life more fully; to learn new knowledge and skills throughout life, to enjoy new perspectives on themselves, life, and others; and to learn from experience how to appreciate what they have, who they are, and what is essential to experiencing satisfaction with their lives. Our purpose in counseling is to help individuals in this quest.

Considerable research has accumulated in the last three decades that describes the characteristics of the healthy person, especially the psychological dimensions of wellness. Maslow's work (1968, 1970), in which he identified the characteristics of self-actualizing people, is a part of what has become an ever-expanding knowledge base about healthy people. Anthropology (neoteny), quality of life and well-being research, longevity research, personality and behavior, behavioral medicine, stress research, psychoneuroimmunology, and health psychology have forged an impressive array of data.

The following section describes the wheel of wellness (Figure 2.1), which metaphorically represents the characteristics of healthy persons over the life span. The life tasks originally conceptualized by Adler and Dreikurs through which persons express their lifestyle are central to this model. In addition, it includes forces that act on the individual for good or for bad with respect to health and wellness (e.g., family, community, media, and environment).

## WHEEL OF WELLNESS

The "wheel of wellness" (Figure 2.1) has evolved over time to represent more accurately our conceptualization of both Individual Psychology and the research across disciplines that address factors influencing life satisfaction and longevity. We are aware that there are other models that contain similar components to those in this model. In light of the attention to these topics in the media as well as professional literature, this is not surprising. What we think is unique, however, is the incorporation of Adler's psychology, including its methods, and Dreikurs' attention to the philosophy and values of an equalitarian society, with the research across disciplines as they relate to health and wellness. In addition, we envision this as a multidimensional, dynamic process of human development rather than a static, descriptive picture of the components.

We draw the readers' attention to the center of the wheel. The life task of spirituality is at the center of wellness. Much like Maslow's highest level of development, although central to wellness, it is not easily accessed by the individual or others except as the other components develop as well. The spokes of the wheel are those related to the life task of self. We refer to these as the self-direction components. These inner components are what interact with others through the life tasks of work and leisure, friendship, and love as an expression of what is referred to as self.

The outer rings of the wheel represent the institutions and conditions that influence each individual's development. Each of these contributes or thwarts development toward wellness throughout the life span. In the following sections, each of the components of the wheel is discussed in more detail.

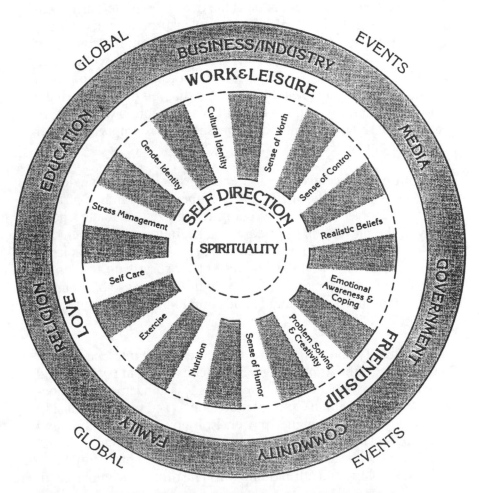

**Figure 2.1** Wheel of Wellness. Copyright 1996, J. Melvin Witmer, Thomas J. Sweeney, & Jane E. Myers. Reprinted with permission.

## Life Task One: Spirituality

> We are not human beings having a spiritual experience. We
> are spiritual beings having a human experience.

>                                    Teilhard de Chardin

Adler (1929/1964) believed that God is the greatest manifestation of the goal of perfection; he is the one "who is eternally complete, who directs the stars, who is master of fates, who elevates man from lowliness to Himself, who speaks from the cosmos to every single human soul" (p. 275). As lofty as this may seem, Levin and Vanderpool (1987), in a review of more than 250 empirical studies of religion and health, suggested that religion is the single most important factor in the individual's perception of quality of life and that religious affiliation is the single most important factor in maintaining a healthy lifestyle.

Until quite recently, religion and spirituality were neglected dimensions of quality-of-life and well-being research. Spiritual beliefs and practices are now being recognized as related positively to the prevention of disease, the healing process when disease occurs, and the global dimension of well-being. That spirituality is a factor in wellness should not be surprising because it embraces hope and optimism, purpose in life, a sense of security, influence through prayer, family and community relationships, and altruistic activities.

Spirituality and religion are sometimes used interchangeably but do have different meanings. Spirituality is more personal and private, yet universal and inclusive. It is less concerned with doctrine or theology about God and more concerned with relationship to or oneness with a higher power. Religion is more public and structured, usually accompanied by a prescribed dogma and a set of practices with sanctions for disobedience. Acceptance of a formalized theology and affiliation with an institution is emphasized.

Spirituality transcends religion and the culture in which one grew up. It is that common experience that reaches across cultures when one communes with the eternal spirit, whether one calls it

God, Allah, or some other divine name. In the traditional sense, it is the presence of a soul that is the seat of the moral or religious nature of the person.

Developing a spiritual nature might be considered as discovering and attaining those qualities of the spirit that enhance total well-being and help the individual and others achieve a greater potential. These qualities, when viewed across religions and time, embody certain fundamental characteristics that tend to be universal in nature. Six dimensions appears as common elements in the literature on spirituality and the world's religions. They constitute what may be referred to as spiritual pathways. These pathways are (a) recognition of a higher power or being—faith, (b) worship, prayer, and self-reflection—harmony, (c) knowledge of the divine—enlightenment, (d) meaning in life—purpose, (e) giving and receiving—love and compassion, and (f) living the faith—co-creation and service. These six pathways can be used as a basis for including the spiritual life task in a developmental approach to counseling. These are presented in more detail in a subsequent section of this chapter to illustrate some practical applications in the development of spirituality.

## Life Task Two: Self-Direction

If spirituality is the soul and character of the individual, the life task of self-direction is the personality and personal habits. Self-direction is the way in which an individual regulates, directs, and disciplines the self in the transactions of everyday activities as well in the pursuit of long-range goals. These attributes of the person provide a unique identity that is frequently characterized as the major component of one's personality. Personality is the sum of an individual's unique adjustment to life, including major traits, temperament, interests, drives, values, self-concept (i.e., "I–me" as subject), abilities, and emotional patterns.

This uniquely human capacity to be mindful and aware of their lives enables people to self-regulate and self-determine their present and future. Body processes are automatically regulated but can be consciously altered. Mindfulness gives individuals the potential to control their thoughts and emotions and voluntarily direct their efforts toward the enhancement of their lives.

The personality attributes of self-direction on the wheel of wellness help the individual to understand and manage the world in a meaningful way. The essential elements are drawn from health and wholeness research (Dreher, 1995; Goleman & Gurin, 1993; Witmer, 1989). The 12 spokes constitute areas of competence that contribute to the well-being of individuals (Hafen, Frandsen, Karren, & Hooker, 1992; D. G. Myers, 1992; Pelletier, 1994). They range from sense of worth to cultural identity. The personality traits that make up individuals' beliefs and behaviors enable them to think and act in healthy ways. Each one will be briefly described for their application to the striving for wellness.

**Sense of Worth.**   The concept of sense of worth is often explained in terms of self-acceptance, self-respect, and self-esteem. Its attributes are the sum of one's sense of regard and the value assigned to oneself. Whereas self-concept is descriptive of the self, both physical and psychological, self-worth or self-esteem is an evaluation of the self-positive or -negative, good or bad. This self-evaluation profoundly affects the quality of life experienced. Healthy self-evaluation (i.e., self-love) will include feeling good about and accepting one's capabilities, limitations, gender, race, and related aspects of self.

The foremost authority and research pioneer on the topic of self-esteem, Nathaniel Branden (1994), stated that self-esteem is "(1) confidence in our ability to think, confidence in our ability to cope with the basic challenges of life; and (2) confidence in our rights to be successful and happy, the feeling of being worthy, deserving, entitled to assert our needs and wants, achieve our values, and enjoy the fruits of our efforts" (p. 4). Individuals with a positive sense of worth tend to approach their basic life tasks with a confidence and expectation that they will be successful and happy in all that they do. As Branden noted, more than a feeling or judgment, positive self-assessment is a motivator. It inspires one to act when others hesitate.

Sense of worth is influenced by heredity, family, culture, gender, education, community, and society at large, as in the case of discrimination. Although these influences affect how individuals view life, themselves, and others, they are on the whole, antecedents, not causes of our thoughts, emotions, and behaviors. The family is the incubator of sense of worth, with the early years being most decisive in establishing one's sense of worth. Parents with high self-esteem can provide a healthy climate for the child. The environment of the school plays a major role in the development of self-esteem. Spiritual, work, and friendship experiences all influence how one evaluates self. To feel genuinely loved and affirmed by parents and other significant people in one's life is of incalculable value to building self-esteem.

Satisfaction with one's self was one of the strongest contributors to well-being and satisfaction with life in general in Campbell's (1981) long-term research. Later research by D. G. Myers (1992) confirmed the importance of self-esteem in contributing to happiness. People with high self-esteem are less vulnerable to physical illnesses, less likely to abuse drugs, more independent of pressures to conform, and more persistent at difficult tasks. Research reviewed by Hafen et al. (1992) illustrated how self-esteem is a preventive factor to illness, hurries recovery from illness, and in general enhances well-being. Belief in oneself is one of the most powerful forces available for protecting one's health and promoting a longer, more satisfying life.

**Sense of Control.**   Adler (1927/1954) seemed to equate the goal of superiority with power, presumably for the purpose of significance and overcoming feelings of inferiority. If power is comparable to control, then much scientific evidence is accumulating to support its potency for wellness. Beliefs about personal control have to do with feelings about mastery and confidence in what one can do. Frequently in the literature, it is described as competence, locus of control, or self-efficacy. Lack of control or a feeling of powerlessness is a condition in which the individual perceives self as having little or no power to influence events or regulate one's own emotions.

Control can be general beliefs one has about control of events and outcomes or a belief that a particular situation can be shaped or influenced. It also can be viewed as beliefs about internal control and external control. Those with internal control believe that events are contingent upon one's actions and, as such, yield more effort and persistence in achievement situations. An external locus of control refers to the belief that events are contingent upon luck, chance, fate, others, or powers beyond one's influence.

Having a sense of control enhances one's overall ability to cope with stress, reduces the likelihood of illness, and lessens negative emotions such as depression, anxiety, and anger (Ornstein & Sobel, 1989; Pelletier, 1994; Peterson & Bossio, 1991). Persons with a sense of inner control are more likely to collect information about disease and maintenance, take action to improve health habits, and engage in preventive care (Strickland, 1978). A person's decision to take more control over mind and body can be described as will, and is essential to the holistic approach to wellness. When one's will becomes active, then responsible participation in the healing process occurs.

Sense of control also seems essential to self-esteem. Sagan (1987), in his comprehensive work in examining the factors that influence health and wellness in various nations, wrote that those with a high level of self-esteem also have an inner locus of control. They are confident of their ability to make competent decisions. They believe that what they think and do will matter. Outcomes are not determined by gods, chance, or persons of influence. They have confidence in themselves and their ability to control their own lives.

**Realistic Beliefs.** Healthy people have a keen sense of reality, seeing reality more as it is, not as they might want or desire it to be. They recognize that which is rational and logical as well as that which is distorted or wishful thinking. This accuracy in the perception of reality leads to their enhanced ability to accept what is true, to come to conclusions, and to be logical and mentally efficient (Hafen et al., 1992; Maslow, 1968; Peterson & Bossio, 1991).

Private logic is the Adlerian concept of how personal beliefs guide people's feelings and behavior. It is a "biased apperception" about life, self, and others. Each person constructs a view of reality made up of beliefs or "personal truths" that guide the individual in explaining the way things are. The greater the discrepancy between private logic and reality, the greater the probability for inappropriate behavior in response to life events.

Unhealthy persons who have mood disturbances are not emotionally sick, but mentally wrong. That is, they are thinking irrational thoughts, practicing faulty reasoning, or living by maladaptive rules made up in the form of unrealistic or inappropriate "shoulds," "oughts," and "don'ts." Research and clinical evidence have documented that negative thoughts that cause emotional turmoil nearly always contain gross distortions or unrealistic expectations (A. T. Beck, 1984; J. S. Beck, 1995; Ellis, 1962; Freeman & DeWolf, 1992; Seligman, 1990).

Research by Witmer, Rich, Barcikowski, and Mague (1983) indicated that persons with a positive outlook and those who scored lowest on Ellis' (1962) irrational beliefs were less anxious and had fewer physical symptoms. The five irrational beliefs contributing to stress were as follows: (a) The past continues to influence me so much that it is hard for me to change or prevent bad things from happening; (b) I can't help getting down on myself when I fail at something or when something goes wrong; (c) It is very important to me to be liked and loved by almost everyone I meet; (d) I must be perfectly competent, adequate, and achieving in all that I do to consider myself worthwhile; and (e) I have little control over my moods, which are caused mostly by events outside of myself. Such thoughts as these are the source of negative emotions and inappropriate behavior. They are unrealistic beliefs.

**Emotional Awareness and Coping.** Adlerians note that emotions are the metaphorical "steam" that propels individuals to action or fortifies them against that which they fear or resist. Emotions can be used to manipulate others, for example, through tears or tyranny. The capacity to express a full range of emotions appropriately is indicative of high social interest. Human emotions can be summarized by nine primary or core themes: anger, anxiety, sadness, guilt, shame, disgust, interest/excitement, love/compassion, happiness/joy (Ekman, 1989; Izard, 1977; Lazarus, 1991).

"Self-actualizing" and psychologically healthy people were described by Maslow (1970) as relatively spontaneous in behavior and far more spontaneous than others in their inner life, thoughts, impulses, emotions, desires, and opinions. A childlike simplicity and authenticity are at the core of their responsiveness to events. Their relationships are essentially free of defensiveness and deceptiveness. They are sensitive to the predicaments of others. They appreciate their own positive circumstances and approach life with a continuing freshness and wonderment. They experience and willingly share their emotions with others in a spontaneous way.

Emotional intelligence is now getting some respect from researchers (Ekman & Davidson, 1994; Gardner, 1983; Goleman, 1995; Lazarus, 1991). Gardner (1983) identified emotional intelligence as one of seven multiple intelligences, calling it personal intelligence, which has two aspects. One is the capacity to access one's own feeling life—the capacity to instantly make discriminations among these feelings, label them, and to draw on them as a means of understanding and guiding one's behavior. The other personal intelligence turns outward, to other individuals. The capacity here is to notice and make distinctions among other individuals, their moods, temperaments, motivations, and intentions. Adlerians say that it is the capacity to empathize.

Behavioral medicine, psychosomatic medicine, and psychoneuroimmunology have established a relationship between thoughts, feelings, and illness (Dacher, 1991; Hafen et al., 1992; Locke & Colligan, 1986). When negative emotions become chronic or are suppressed, they can become destructive to well-being. Repressed emotions have been linked with a number of illnesses such as cardiovascular and immunity-related diseases.

Hostility seems to be a major contributor to high blood pressure, coronary artery disease, and death among those who have the competitive, hard-driving type A personality (Hafen et al., 1992;

Williams, 1989). Researchers have gathered a wealth of data suggesting that chronic anger is so damaging to the body that it ranks with cigarette smoking, obesity, and a high-fat diet as a powerful risk factor for early death (Williams, 1989).

Research findings also suggest that anxiety, loneliness, and depression are associated with suppressing the immune system, thus increasing the chance for illness to occur (Hafen et al., 1992; Locke, Kraus, Leserman, Hurst, Heisel, & Williams, 1984; Temoshok & Dreher, 1992). How individuals think and feel alters the strength of their immune system. In studying the mind–body factors of cancer patients, Temoshok and Dreher (1992) observed a behavior pattern they termed "Type C" behavior. Approximately three fourths of the patients displayed most or all of the following: (a) They were nonexpressors of anger, often unaware of any feelings of anger, past or present; (b) they tended not to experience or express other negative emotions, namely anxiety, fear, and sadness; (c) they were patient, unassertive, cooperative, and appeasing in work, social, and family relationships; and (d) they were overly concerned with meeting the needs of others and insufficiently engaged in meeting their own needs.

By contrast, the appropriate expression of negative emotions and the presence of positive emotions seem to strengthen immune function (Dillon, Minchoff, & Baker, 1985; Hafen et al., 1992; McClelland, Ross, & Patel, 1985). Indeed, ongoing responses to daily events influence bodily functions. Not only does a negative mood result in lower antibody response but a positive mood is associated with a higher antibody response (Stone, Cox, Valdimarsdottir, Jandorf, & Neale, 1987).

**Problem Solving and Creativity.** When reduced to its basic elements, thinking is primarily a problem-solving process (Montagu, 1981). According to Montagu, the need to think soundly is accompanied by a cluster of traits characteristic of the developing child. These traits include the need to know, the need to learn, the need to organize, curiosity, and a sense of wonder. Explorativeness, experimental-mindedness, flexibility, open-mindedness, imagination, and creativity are additional intellectual characteristics that enable a person to master the environment and pursue mental, artistic, and productive activities that challenge thinking and produce satisfaction.

The full breadth of this wellness characteristic can be better understood by Gardner's (1983) theory of multiple intelligences. He argued that everyone possesses at least seven intelligences, most of which have been widely overlooked in this IQ testing–oriented society. Gardner broke out of the narrow molds of intelligence and information processing to present a rich conception of human abilities. Although they have a biological basis, each is influenced by the environment and culture.

A brief description of each aspect of intelligence is provided to suggest the implications that they have for the wellness model:

*Linguistics or language.* The poet, scientist, leader, business person, and lay person all rely heavily on words to solve problems, communicate, and express opinions.

*Musical.* Whether performer, composer, or participant in the family sing-a-long, everyone develops an appreciation for music.

*Logical–mathematical.* Whether with material objects or abstract symbols, relationships are explored for ordering, re-ordering, and assigning quantity.

*Spatial.* With the capacity to create a mental image, a person can use imagery to solve problems, invent new objects, and perform in the visual–spatial arts such as sculpture and painting.

*Bodily–kinesthetic.* Using the body in highly differentiated and skillful ways enables one to express feelings and perform physical activities.

*Intrapersonal.* The core capacity here is access to one's own feeling life, to instantly discriminate among the various feelings, and draw on them as a means for understanding and guiding one's behavior.

*Interpersonal.* The core capacity is the ability to notice and make distinctions among other individuals and, in particular, among moods, temperaments, motivations, and intentions.

Each of these aspects of intelligence has implications for the problem-solving method, which is usually described as having five or six steps. Learning the skills related to these six problem-solving steps empowers individuals to solve intellectual, task, and interpersonal problems. The six steps are (a) identify the problem; (b) explore alternatives as possible solutions; (c) evaluate the alternatives including value/ethical judgments; (d) choose a solution; (e) apply the solution; and (f) evaluate the outcome.

Maslow found that creativity was a universal characteristic of self-actualizing people whom he studied. They demonstrated a special kind of creativeness, originality, and inventiveness. These characteristics have commonly been observed in children. Researchers and personnel working with older persons have noted how involving them in intellectually stimulating and creative tasks has the effects of regeneration and rejuvenation. Being mentally active and creative enriches the quality of life along with longevity (Bortz, 1991; Pelletier, 1981).

The "use it or lose it" maxim seems to be true for all ages, but especially for older persons. In some ways the mind is like a muscle; it has to be exercised to maintain health and increase capacity. Disengaging from life and mentally stimulating activities is a major contributor to the loss of well-being, perhaps more than disease and aging. Use of the brain along with physical exercise influence brain function in a positive way (Bortz, 1991).

**Sense of Humor.**   Adler (1927/1954) emphasized the therapeutic use of humor. He felt that therapists, in addition to specific training, should have "a jovial attitude . . . blessed with cheerfulness and good humor . . . " (p. 201). Indeed, as noted in chapter 1,

Adler practiced what he preached. The reference to "good humor" is notable. Sometimes referred to as "dark humor," sarcasm or similar derogatory use of cultural, racial, gender, or related stereotypical characteristics of individuals or groups can be unhealthy in its very nature. Therefore, we wish to differentiate and be clear that it is positive humor only to which we refer.

Humor seems to unfold naturally in children as young as 2 months. By the time they reach primary school age, children may average 300 laughs a day, compared to 15 for adults. As Montagu (1981) observed across cultures, "It is natural for children to laugh and to see humor in all sorts of things, whether they be real or imagined, or of their own creation" (p. 175). Playfulness, imagination, and creativity are closely allied with sense of humor.

Humor, particularly when it is accompanied by laughter, promotes physiological, psychological, and social change. The skeletal muscles become more relaxed, breathing changes, and the brain is believed to release certain chemicals that positively affect well-being, serving as an analgesic, a relaxant, or energizer, even boosting the immune system (Hafen et al., 1992).

Humor creates an open flexibility for problem solving, reduces defensiveness, and improves communication while neutralizing stress (Cousins, 1979; Loehr & McLaughlin, 1986; Moody, 1978). Psychologically, the right kind of humor overrides negative emotions associated with "unsound" thinking, dissipating such thoughts at least for a time, and opens the possibility to changes in perception (Mosak, 1987).

The social power of humor is well known. It is a potent force to reduce interpersonal conflict, tension, or unpleasant situations. It is also a mode of communication, often permitting the expression of ideas or feelings that would otherwise be difficult to express. Through positive humor one can think and say things that would seem risky if done seriously (Falk & Hill, 1992).

The use of humor as an effective method for adaptation to life was one of the mature defenses that Vaillant (1977) identified in the ongoing follow-up study of more than 200 Harvard graduates over a 30-year period. Health surveys were correlated with psychological tests each year. Those with the best adjustment used more humor than those with poorer adjustment. Humor is seen as an antidote for distress, but healthy because it allows both the idea and the affect to coexist in consciousness.

**Nutrition.**   Nutritional research has demonstrated that there is a relationship between what people eat, their health, their moods, and their performance (Rosenfeld, 1995; Wurtman, 1986). Five nutrients are necessary for good health: proteins, carbohydrates, fats, vitamins, and minerals. Water is the sixth substance essential for life sustenance. Eating habits and food preferences have ethnic, religious, and cultural origins. They are established early in life and consequently become difficult to change with increasing age.

The nation's eating and drinking habits have been implicated in 6 of the 10 leading causes of death: heart disease, cancer, stroke, diabetes, atherosclerosis, and chronic liver disease and cirrhosis. Several nonfatal but potentially disabling disorders such as osteoporosis and diverticulitis are implicated by diet ("Are You Eating Right?" 1992; Rosenfeld, 1995). Diet is implicated in one third of cancer deaths and a large proportion of heart attacks. Diet, however, is only one component in the development of disease; heredity, environment, and lifestyle all fit into the equation and interact with diet in complex and unknown ways.

Food is frequently used to reduce stress (Wurtman, 1986). People eat out of boredom, anxiety, or guilt, to distract themselves, and to take a "feeling break." Addiction to food is linked with the release of a brain substance called beta-endorphin, which serves as a natural opiate that may temporarily relieve pain and stress and give one a slight emotional high.

Obesity is a major problem, with about 1 of every 3 adults and 1 in 10 young children being more than 20% overweight—a commonly used definition of obesity ("Getting in Shape," 1996; Rosenfeld, 1995). The incidence of coronary heart disease, cancer, and diabetes increases significantly with being overweight, affecting the quality and longevity of life (Kozora, 1987).

Current knowledge indicates people in the United States are paying a high price for their high-fat, high-calorie, low-nutrient, low-fiber, processed-food diet. Whereas medical science has conquered most infectious diseases, the degenerative diseases are claiming more lives. Degenerative diseases linked to diet and lifestyle are heart disease, cancer, stroke, obesity, diabetes, and osteoporosis (Kozora, 1987). Medical research has established a relationship between diet, physical health, and emotional well-being. Just as a poor diet can be life debilitating, a proper diet can be life enhancing.

**Exercise.** Despite the recognized value of physical activity, relatively few Americans are regularly active. Only 22% of U.S. adults engage in leisure time physical activity at the level recommended for health benefits in *Healthy People 2000*, published by the U.S. Dept. of Health and Human Services in 1990 (U.S. Public Health Service, 1990). Fully 24% of adult Americans are completely sedentary. The remaining 54% are inadequately active and are greatly in need of more physical activity ("Summary Statement—Workshop on Physical Activity and Public Health," 1993). Participation in regular physical activity increased from the 1960s into the 1980s but has plateaued in the last decade.

Why are so few Americans physically active? The move from the Agricultural Age to the Industrial Age and now the Information Age has resulted in machine power replacing muscle power. Less than a century ago, 40 to 50% of the energy required to run factories and farms came from muscle power. Now less than 1% is required. Early in this decade, only 20% of the U.S. adult population could be described as "active" in any substantial way (Bortz, 1991). Percentages are even worse for older citizens. The importance of high-intensity exercise has been overemphasized in the media. To offset this, a group of experts from centers for disease prevention and control and sports medicine reviewed the scientific evidence and concluded that every American adult should accumulate 30 minutes or more of moderate-intensity physical activity over the course of most days of the week ("Summary Statement—Workshop on Physical Activity and Public Health," 1993). Examples of activities noted include walking up stairs (instead of taking the elevator), gardening, raking leaves, dancing, and walking part or all the way to or from work. The recommended 30 minutes may also come from planned exercise or recreation such as jogging, playing tennis, swimming, cycling, or walking 2 miles briskly.

The body was made for physical activity. Inactivity leads to stress and disease, a shorter life span, and in general a deterioration of the vital body functions. A person is physically fit if capable of cardiorespiratory endurance, flexibility in muscular movement, and strength and endurance in the use of muscles. The benefits of moderate exercise may be the most important finding for preventive medicine for the coming decades ("Exercise: A Prescription for Health," 1992). Several thousand studies of exercise now confirm the physical and psychological benefits that contribute to the quality of life and longevity (Bortz, 1991; "Does Exercise Boost Immunity?" 1995; "Exercise for the Ages," 1996; "Losing Weight," 1993; "Six Convincing Reasons to Exercise," 1994; "Strength Training for Everyone," 1991).

**Self-Care.**   A basic principle of the Adlerian philosophy presented in this book is the need to take responsibility for one's own health and well-being through personal habits that enhance wellness. Taking responsibility for one's wellness requires preventive behavior as well as remedial treatment. Learning to provide more self-care can boost esteem, improve health, and reduce health care costs, as was demonstrated in the education of arthritis sufferers (Lorig, 1992).

Three aspects of self-care constitute this dimension. First are the safety habits that are learned in order to protect oneself from injury or death. Wearing a seat belt reduces the risk of serious injury should one be involved in an automobile accident. Using sunscreen or wearing protective clothing when exposed to the sun can prevent skin cancer many years later. Being careful regarding safety in the home, neighborhood, workplace, transportation, and leisure activities can mean the difference between life and death or health and a serious disability.

Second, health care that includes periodic medical checkups may prevent a disease or enable one to get early treatment. Good medical and dental care requires preventive measures such as immunizations, regular examinations recommended according to gender and age, and proper treatment when illness, injury, or disease symptoms appear.

A third aspect of self-care is avoiding harmful substances, both those that might be ingested and toxic substances in the environment. Harmful uses of alcohol, tobacco, and drugs take an incalculable toll on individuals, families, and the community. Resulting health care costs and economic losses make such abuse one of the major social problems in the United States. The personal and interpersonal problems created by substance abuse add billions of dollars to physical and mental health care costs, not to mention the pain and misery of individuals.

Self-care is proactive in nature. It requires no one else to intervene and is a clear statement of positive self-esteem that affirms self-efficacy. It is one aspect of self-regulation through which anyone can gain almost immediate satisfaction by implementing even modest changes in habits. Gender differences in self-care account for a significant portion of the longevity difference of 7 years between males and females (Goldberg, 1993). Women, in general, are more attuned to taking care of themselves. Apparently, many men have much to learn from women about such things. On the other hand, many women can improve the quality of their lives through better attention to their own needs as opposed to the needs of others.

**Stress Management.**   To be optimally healthy, one must be able to cope with life's daily requirements and hassles while minimizing the detrimental effects of excess stress. Managing this stress includes any attempt to neutralize the stress arousal, return to a state of comfort, and cope with the situation with a sense of competence. Coping systems include spiritual, physical, emotional, mental, and behavioral responses. Coping can be healthy and growth enhancing or unhealthy when lacking the capacity to meet the demands of a particular situation. Such skills alter either the source of stress or the experience of stress.

Stress is an unavoidable fact of life. Some stress is part of everyone's life. Certain kinds of stress are actually helpful—the kind that arouses the mind–body systems, making one feel very much alive and motivating a person to meet the demands and challenges of the day. But too much stress or the wrong kind can have negative effects on the mind and body (Goldberger & Breznitz, 1993).

Stress has been found to be related to a whole host of symptoms, illnesses, and diseases. Prolonged stress can cause the mind–body systems to malfunction or break down. Daily strain on these systems can result in chronic fatigue, pain, or disease. Stress-related conditions or illnesses have been identified for each of the following systems: cardiovascular, digestive, muscular, respiratory, reproductive, hormonal, skin, immunity, mental, and emotional. At some point the body will even self-destruct in its attempt to meet the demands the mind makes on it.

The emotions are early indicators to alert the mind–body of possible harm, loss, challenge, or change. The presence of any one of five negative emotions may be a signal of stress: anger, anxiety, sadness, guilt, or shame. However, the emotion that is almost synonymous with stress in the lay person's mind is anxiety or tension. Stress, anxiety, and tension are often used interchangeably. Even in the professional literature, anxiety is reported as the key emotional indicator of stress (Michelson & Ascher, 1987). Stress-coping techniques are usually aimed at alleviating tension and anxiety. The absence of positive emotions is also a negative factor contributing to stress.

One person's stress is another person's challenge. One's perception of an event determines the mind–body response rather than the event itself. Stress occurs when the person appraises a situation as taxing or exceeding one's resources and ability to cope, endangering well-being (Lazarus & Folkman, 1984). This is clearly what Adler had in mind when he spoke of the private logic of individuals and how their "biased apperceptions" contributed to their social and personal problems.

**Gender Identity.** Dreikurs noted the significance of gender identity in the development of one's lifestyle. He raised consciousness to the importance both genders play in influencing the development of the child's convictions about self as male or female and the relationships between the genders. The biology of sex and the psychology of gender affect human emotions, motivations, thoughts, and behavior (Beall & Sternberg, 1993). Although gender-linked qualities are largely culturally determined, individuals must choose how to use these qualities for enhancing their own well-being. This becomes difficult when sex-role typing, either for males or females, is debilitating and constrictive to growth (Wainrib, 1992). A healthy gender identity seeks to be satisfied with the physical, psychological, and social qualities and roles one has carved out as a male or female. Positive affiliations with both genders add to total well-being.

Gender identity and gender role identity need to be understood as different aspects of gender development. Gender role includes "the social prescriptions or stereotypes associated with each sex, to which an individual may or may not conform" (Huyck, 1990, p. 24). Gender role identity refers to the degree to which a person identifies with or displays societally defined masculine or feminine behavior (Mintz & O'Neil, 1990). Gender identity is viewed as involving the introspective part of gender role, such as gender-linked qualities that one sees (or would like to see) as part of the self (Money, 1973).

Gender differences center around intellectual development, moral development, personality attributes, patterns of relationship formation, and health. They are embedded within a cultural context that interacts with personal traits. Although changes indeed are occurring, most children still are reared according to predominate gender-role stereotypes. Boys and men are socialized to be emotionally inhibited, assertive, powerful, independent, and sexual.

Girls and women are socialized to be emotional, nurturing, and possessing strong relational needs (Cowher, 1995). Girls appear to have or develop a capacity for empathy that is greater than that of boys.

For boys and young men, there appears to be a greater propensity to demonstrate competency in the world, either through play or mastery (Cosse, 1992). The evidence supports a developmental pathway for females based on interpersonal, empathic relatedness, but they have considerable latitude for crossing over to a male developmental pathway. Women tend to form relationships via a supportive, enabling, and facilitative manner (Maccoby, 1990). They place a great deal of significance on relationships as they develop a sense of self. Males follow a pathway leading to autonomy and mastery of the environment, with no pressure to pass over to the female pathway of development. In fact, those who do so risk rejection from other males. Assertiveness, competition, and winning are valued, with intimacy needs and connectedness being less important than for females.

A masculinity model is used in U.S. society to define success as well as to explain psychological well-being (Burnett, Anderson, & Hepner, 1995; Cook, 1987). Achievement, competition, and independence are encouraged more by the environmental press than sensitivity, emotional expressiveness, and satisfaction in relationships. Individuals who possess a larger number of masculine characteristics report greater self-esteem than do those with less of those traits. Those low in individual masculinity, especially women, are at a particular risk for decreased self-esteem. When there is lack of congruence between individual and cultural factors, greater risk for psychological difficulties exists. This certainly would seem to be true for individuals with a same-sex orientation as well. How much biological and hormonal factors contribute to the differences in gender development is in the early stages of inquiry (Kenrick, 1987).

Because what is considered gender appropriate varies across cultures, gender identity must be considered in the context of the person's culture and the extent to which the individual is satisfied with his or her male–female characteristics. When there is distress due to intrapersonal conflict on gender identity or with the environment on gender role, psychological well-being is likely to be affected. When attempting to improve mental and emotional health, an emphasis should focus on the person–environment factors and the interactions related to one's masculinity–femininity rather than personality variables alone (Cook, 1985).

**Cultural Identity.** Everyone lives within a cultural context. In a multicultural society such as the United States, each person belongs either to a majority or minority culture. As the media, computers, and rapid transportation reduce the distance, physically as well as through communications, between people, a global, multicultural environment has evolved. Culture, therefore, must be considered when attempting to understand the factors that contribute to wellness. It is part of the environment and all behavior is shaped by culture; consequently, whatever one does is culturally influenced (Segall, Dasen, Berry, & Poortinga, 1990).

Culture, ethnicity, and race have distinct differences in their meanings. Race refers more to the biological and physical commonalities such as skin color and hair texture. Ethnicity includes the commonalities of a group such as a shared biological heritage, common language, beliefs, norms, values, and behaviors. Similarities of religion, history, and common ancestry make up a shared sociocultural heritage. Culture is the more inclusive term that goes beyond ethnic and national boundaries. A culture-general view broadly defined, and the one to be used here, includes "demographic variables (e.g., age, gender, place of residence), status variables (e.g., social, educational, economic), and affiliations (formal and informal), as well as ethnographic variables such as nationality, ethnicity, language, and religion" (Pederson, 1994, p. 16). Culture-specific refers to a more limited view of culture such as similarities of religion, history, and common ancestry or the characteristics of an ethnic group (Pederson, 1994; Sue & Sue, 1990).

In a pluralistic society, a positive cultural identity is made when persons, through an inner sense of security, can appreciate unique, beneficial aspects of their own culture and those in the mainstream culture (Sue & Sue, 1990). When cross-cultural respect exists between the dominant and minority cultures, the conflicts, discomforts, and destructive forces are minimized. The minority culture is not necessarily in conflict with dominant cultural ways. Conflicts and oppression are resolved while being free to accept or reject those aspects of a culture that are not seen as desirable. This integrative awareness stage of cultural identity encourages a strong sense of self-worth and confidence and a sense of pride in one's group without accepting group values unequivocally. There is a reaching out toward different minority groups in order to understand their cultural values, and selective appreciation for the values and activities of the dominant culture.

Identity is inseparable from the culture that shapes it. When oppression from a dominant culture limits power, status, and economic opportunities, deprivation and deficits occur. A healthy cultural identity is dependent on individuals taking active control of their personal identity and the majority culture taking responsibility for removing barriers. A mature, connected identity is fundamental to acceptance of self and others and to rejection of prejudice (Hoare, 1991). This means including and accepting others who have different cultural values and perspectives. Learning to accept others' differences is one of the fundamental challenges to both individuals and societies throughout the world. Encouraging strong racial or ethnic identity can result in healthier individuals more able to cope with a multicultural society.

Support for the psychological resilience of those strong in racial or ethnic identity has been provided by E. J. Smith (1991). Individuals who are embedded in their culture tend to be more "ethnically hardy" and resilient than those who are more marginal with respect to their culture. Being embedded in or living among one's own ethnic group appears to be healthy. Having their own social and institutional affiliations enhances the resiliency of ethnic minorities to ethnic identity conflicts such as exist in the United States between whites and blacks.

The happiness research of D. G. Myers (1992) provided an example of how a positive cultural identity contributes to well-being and self-esteem. He defined subjective well-being as feelings of happiness and sense of satisfaction with life. Being white and educated does give an advantage, but not as much as might be expected because self-esteem is a well-spring of well-being. African Americans do not suffer from lower self-esteem when compared to whites (D. G. Myers, 1992). How can this be?

People of various stigmatized groups maintain self-esteem in three ways: they value the things at which they excel; they attribute problems to prejudice; and they compare themselves to those in their own group (Crocker & Major, 1989). This explains, in part, how it is possible for persons in a minority culture to attain a comparable level of wellness to those in the majority culture. These attitudes are fundamentally Adlerian in nature. What individuals think about their circumstances is what is most important, not the value others attribute to them.

When there is oppression, discrimination, and educational and economic deprivation, however, many members of minorities will suffer in physical and psychological health. Individuals lower on the socioeconomic hierarchy also are more likely to be exposed to environmental hazards, including pathogens and carcinogens. The conditions accompanying the "culture of poverty" increase the risk of physical and psychological problems (E. J. Smith, 1985). The mind–body–spirit connection demands that for wellness to be a reality, all forms of prejudice expressed through discrimination of any kind toward culturally different groups must be eliminated. One way to move toward less prejudice between groups of persons is to help instill in individuals genuine cultural and ethnic pride in their heritage.

Benefits to be derived from acceptance of one's ethnic, racial, or cultural heritage include a longer and more satisfying life. Another benefit of a positive cultural identity is being able to appreciate the positive attributes of those who are culturally different from oneself. Therefore, by helping to build a positive cultural identity in others, one also can contribute to the eradication of discrimination and prejudice toward all persons.

## Life Task Three: Work and Leisure

Work as a life task was thought by Adler to be the most important for the maintenance of life. Inability to fulfill this task was regarded as being a symptom of a serious illness (Dreikurs, 1953). Most people somehow fulfill this task and only the most discouraged people evade it. Adler defined occupational work as any work that is useful to the community whether for monetary gain or not. Included are gainful employment, child rearing, homemaking, volunteer services, educational endeavors, and innumerable other activities that engage individuals in activities meaningful to themselves and others. The play of children and the many leisure-time activities of adults have been added as an extension of Adler's concept of work as a life task.

The play of children was considered by Adler (1927/1954) as their "work" in preparation for the future. Attitudes, relationships, and competencies are developed. Montagu (1981) noted that play is one of the clearest early childhood traits. Playing for the fun of it without any particular goal leads to broadening of perspectives, new discoveries, exploration, and mastery of the environment. The creative ability to play is one of the criteria of mental health.

The role of work and leisure fulfilling this life task may be one and the same for a few people but clearly separate activities for most. When work satisfies the psychic and social needs of the person, separate leisure activities become less essential. Leisure activities, however, tend to satisfy the psychic and social needs of the individual because they have been freely chosen for their potential to bring personal satisfaction. Technological changes and greater affluence during the 20th century have added time and energy for individuals to pursue more leisure-time activities. With the emergence of a value change in the 1970s, Yankelovich (1978) compared work and leisure for sources of satisfaction. Only 21% of respondents said that work meant more to them than leisure. This was true even though a majority (60%) said that although they enjoyed their work, it was not their major source of satisfaction.

The different purposes that work can serve have been summarized by Herr and Cramer (1988). Economic purposes include the obvious resources to purchase goods and services, evidence of success, and assets to purchase leisure or free time. Psychological purposes include self-esteem, self-efficacy (control), identity, a feeling of mastery and competence, and meaning in life. Social benefits include a place to meet people, a feeling of being valued or needed by others, social status, and potential friendships. A work group is a sort of mini-culture where social needs are met and its own set of values and norms are developed (Tart, 1986). The answer to why people work has no simple answer and varies from person to person. Motives for working are influenced by a variety of very personal values, beliefs, attitudes, and outlooks (McDaniels & Gysbers, 1992).

How should one characterize a healthy job? A summary of the research supports the following qualities that buffer the effects of stress and enhance the quality of life in the workplace (Karasek & Theorell, 1990; Knoop, 1994; Renwick & Lawler, 1978). Although the list is biased toward the psychosocial aspects of work, we must recognize that other work conditions and environmental factors influence physical health as well as mental and emotional well-being:

- Use of one's abilities and knowledge; opportunity to learn new skills and abilities

- Autonomy; some freedom to influence task performance and the outcome

- Control over demands, both psychological and physical

- Cooperation and esteem from others

- Democratic decision-making and conflict resolution procedures

- Meaningfulness of work

- Integration of family and community life with work

- Good safety and environmental conditions

Can leisure satisfaction replace job satisfaction? Both can be a major source of intrinsic satisfaction (McDaniels & Gysbers, 1992). A high level of job satisfaction compares to the satisfaction from personally chosen leisure activities. Employment, however, makes demands that are stress producing and tends to provide for extrinsic rewards for making a product or providing a service. For most people, leisure satisfaction complements whatever satisfaction is gained from work. Some people even on a full-time basis gain as much or more satisfaction from leisure. Economic security is a factor in determining whether full-time leisure can replace the life satisfaction gained from work. The coupling of work and leisure makes up one's career development over the life span, a concept useful to career counselors and lay persons (McDaniels & Gysbers, 1992).

Leisure can be defined as engaging in self-determined activities and experiences for mostly intrinsic satisfactions that are available due to having discretionary income and time. The activity may be physical, social, intellectual, volunteer, creative, or some combination of all five (McDaniels & Gysbers, 1992). Major objectives of Americans during leisure hours are to spend time with the family, seek companionship, relax, learn new things, think and reflect, and keep informed about current events. Recreation and volunteer activities are important for relaxation and social interests. U.S. workers now view leisure as a necessity, not a luxury.

What makes for satisfying work and leisure? What is the psychological explanation for the intrinsically satisfying experiences? Whether it is work or play, certain activities are pleasurable. They challenge or engage one's skills and interests, bringing pleasure to the mind and body. When these challenges engage one's skills, one often becomes so absorbed in the flow of the activity that one loses consciousness of self and time. This state of consciousness is called "flow," an optimal state in which the individual loses awareness of self and time while being highly engaged in the task at hand (Csikszentmihalyi, 1990).

For more than two decades, Csikszentmihalyi has been studying states of "optimal experience"—those times when people report feelings of concentration and deep enjoyment. Everyone experiences flow from time to time. When in this zone of consciousness, excitement and joy are enhanced while anxiety and boredom are minimal. Flow can occur in a wide range of settings and activities. Examples are meaningful work, hobbies, music, art, walking, athletics, games, gardening, dancing, intellectual pursuits, solitude, and being with others. Generally they require few material resources, but they demand relatively high investment of psychic energy. People typically feel intense gratification, strong, alert, in effortless control, free of self-consciousness, and highly engaged in the activity. When at its peak, time and emotional problems seem to disappear, and there is a feeling of transcendence. Young children appear to be in flow much of the time. Leisure especially gives people opportunity to direct their mental energy toward activities that engage the senses and challenge their abilities. The experience is best when the tasks are neither too difficult nor too simple for one's abilities. The accumulation of such experiences makes up the joy of living.

Both research and personal experience confirm the significance of both work and leisure in contributing to health and wellness. Conversely, the absence of either or both contribute to all matter of physical, psychological, spiritual, and emotional maladies within individuals.

## Life Task Four: Friendship

Fundamental to understanding human behavior is the meaning that social interest has for each individual in seeking life satisfaction and maintaining well-being. Adler (1927/1954) considered "social interest" or "social feeling" as innate to human nature; that is, we are born with the capacity and need to be connected with each other and in a cosmic relationship. Therefore, the broad meaning of social interest is a "sense of fellowship in the human community" (p. 38). This awareness of universal connectedness and interrelatedness of human beings combine to form a willingness to cooperate with others for the common good. Seeking to belong or making a place for oneself in relationship to others is a primary motivation for human behavior. Empathy, cooperation, and altruism are manifestations of social interest. Nurturing one's capacity for empathy leads to altruistic behavior. Individuals regularly helping others are as likely to reap health benefits as people who exercise, meditate, or confide on a regular basis (Luks, 1992).

Friendship is used to describe all those social relationships that involve connection with others, either individually or in community, but do not have a marital, sexual, or familial commitment. Relationships that are formed on the basis of a fairly long-term, mutual commitment to one another and involve intimacy with family or friends are discussed under the fifth life task of love. Differences between the two life tasks are defined according to the nature of the relationship, the level of emotional attachment, and the extent of self-disclosure. Work, neighborhood, community, recreational, leisure-time activities, and extended family are the primary sources for friendships in this life task.

The desire for interpersonal attachments is a fundamental human motivation, as concluded by Baumeister and Leary (1995) in their review of research. Two main aspects of this need to belong are frequent, positive interactions with the same persons and a framework of long-term, stable caring and concern. Support for the need to belong as being intrinsic comes from a number of areas: (a) people in all cultures readily form social relationships; (b) once relationships are established, resistance to ending them is strong; (c) thoughts and feelings are affected by relationships, both positive feelings (joy, contentment) and negative feelings (anxiety and depression) when rejected; and (d) the lack of supportive relationships has been linked to many negative consequences such as mental and physical illness, crime, and suicide. Satisfying the need to belong depends more on the quality than on the quantity of relationships.

Friendships are constantly evolving, changing, and growing. Different levels of friendship exist. General acquaintances make up occasional, casual contacts but no particular bonds. Special-interest friends involve at least one common bond and some ongoing contact through work, worship, recreation, education, or civic activity. Significant others include a close bond in which individuals become more sharing, trusting, and supportive. Intimate relationships are very special, limited to a few in number, and take time and work. They involve an openness, honesty, emotional closeness, and mutual commitment. Confidants are likely to come from significant others or intimate relationships.

Social support is the term used to describe the degree to which a person's basic social needs are met through interaction with other people (Cohen & Syme, 1985). It is the resources that other people provide, both tangible and intangible. Social support has three types of functions (Schafer, Coyne, & Lazarus, 1982). These consist of (a) emotional support—attachment, reassurance, being able to rely on and confide in a person; (b) tangible support—involving direct aid such as loans, gifts, and services, such as doing a chore or caring for someone who is ill; and (c) information support—providing information, advice, or feedback.

Social support appears to contribute to wellness in at least two different ways. It provides a buffering effect, protecting the person from the adverse effects of stress and life events by preventing illness or minimizing the ill effects of a disease. Social support may also have a direct effect by enhancing one's mental and physical health. Feeling liked, affirmed, and encouraged by friends and family promotes both health and happiness. Research on the physical and psychological effects of social supports or lack thereof indicates that people indeed need and benefit from their social relationships throughout the life span.

**Life Task Five: Love**

As noted in chapters 1 and 10, both Adler and Dreikurs addressed love relationships as one of the most challenging and rewarding of the life tasks. This life task is challenging because it requires both courage and commitment to fulfill. Its rewards, however, are multiple in physical, emotional, and psychological health as well as contributing to longevity.

The life task of love includes those relationships that are intimate, trusting, self-disclosing, cooperative, compassionate, and usually long term in commitment. Some sense of attachment or bonding maintains a connectedness with those who are loved. Passion or sexual relations are often a part of the love relationship between life partners. As to the levels of friendship identified under the friendship life task, significant others and intimate relationships constitute the social network of love. Family, extended family, couples, and close friends embody this level of social interest. Acceptance, affirmation, and affection are the ingredients of social support most likely to be found in close relationships.

The power and beauty of love have been acclaimed by poets, philosophers, religious teachers, writers, musicians, and artists. Only in the last two decades have social and behavioral scientists been able to confirm the health benefits of love relationships and social support. Such qualities as trust, intimacy, caring, companionship, and giving of oneself to others have been supported by research as promoting well-being and longevity. Pitirim Sorokin (1967), a sociologist at Harvard University and forerunner of the scientific study of love, described love as the single most powerful force for influencing and changing human behavior.

Love has many different meanings. At least five kinds of love exist in human relationships (Bradshaw, 1992; Fromm, 1956; May, 1969). First is parental love, an unconditional affirmation of the child's needs and its nurturing; self-love begins very early as the child seeks to satisfy its own needs and enhance its well-being, both of which are an affirmation of one's life and growth; sibling and friendship love become important in middle childhood; romantic and sexual love unfold in adolescence; and the most advanced and mature form of love is *agape*, a word the ancient Greeks used to describe a self-giving love that is selfless, nondemanding, and devoted to the well-being of others. The self-giving love is a spiritual type love that is unconditional, creative, and life giving. Intimacy, meaning, emotion, and even a sense of mystery encompass this type of love, which Moore (1994) described as soulful. Such relationships usually last for a lifetime. Although these different forms of love occur developmentally in everyone's life, they exist throughout the life span as a source of life-giving energy.

The sources of satisfaction from long-term relationships differ according to age, stage of life, and gender. Age and gender differences were found by Argyle and Furnham (1983). Women derive more satisfaction in the emotional support area from friends and family; men get more satisfaction from spouses and work superiors or associates. Older people derive more satisfaction from family and neighbors, younger people from friends and work associates.

In early adolescence, the sexual drive awakens, reaches its peak in early adulthood, and continues throughout adulthood, with a gradual decline occurring in older years. For most persons, the fulfillment of the life task of love includes the desire for sexual satisfaction, procreation, and the continuation of life through children. No one dies, however, from lack of sex because individual survival does not depend on it, although the survival of the species does. The extent to which sexual satisfaction contributes to longevity and health is unknown.

The depth and quality of personal relationships appear to be the key factors in the health benefits that have been observed. Some relationships are unhealthy and, in fact, may facilitate illness. Mental and physical illness increases when individuals are experiencing relationship difficulties. Work performance may suffer. Studies have shown that unhappy marriages, continued emotional conflict after a divorce, or the death of a spouse can lead to impaired immune function. Researchers have shown that mortality rates for all causes of death are consistently higher for divorced, single, and widowed individuals of both sexes and all races (Berkman & Syme, 1979; Lynch, 1977). The differences are greatest at younger ages and most apparent among men.

Satisfactory resolution of conflict appears essential for a stable, lasting relationship. Gottman (1995), after studying more than 200 couples over 20 years, concluded that a lasting marriage results from a couple's ability to resolve the conflicts that are inevitable in any relationship. Healthy marriages tend to settle into one of three styles of problem solving: compromise to calmly work out their problems to mutual satisfaction; passionate dispute until reaching some sort of accord; and conflict-avoiding or -minimizing in which the couple has agreed to disagree and make light of their differences. Regardless of the style, what separates the contented couples from those in marital misery, is a balance between positive and negative feelings and actions toward each other. By balance, Gottman meant at least a 5-to-1 ratio, with five times as much positive interaction between the couple as there is negative.

Gottman's research revealed the conditions essential for communicating or "fighting fairly," regardless of style for resolving conflicts. Criticism of character and personality, contempt by put-downs, defensiveness by blaming or denying responsibility, and stonewalling by refusing to respond are warning signs that a relationship is headed for trouble. On the basis of studies from a total of 20 years of research and 1,000 couples, Notarius and Markman (1993) concluded that the vital element is how couples handle conflict.

The closeness (or intimacy) of the relationship seems to be the especially important factor. In this context, intimacy does not necessarily mean physical or sexual contact, but rather a warm relationship in which an individual can share thoughts and feelings. Having the capacity to confide and disclosing one's thoughts and feelings are powerful aspects of maintaining wellness. In a series of studies over more than a decade, Pennebaker (1990) confirmed the mental and physical health benefits of opening up and disclosing thoughts and feelings around upsetting events. Emotional catharsis or just the facts of the event will not provide the therapeutic benefits. Both must be present in the mode one chooses to self-disclose whether it be to a spouse, to a close friend, in a diary or journal, to a counselor, or with clergy. Disclosing one's deepest thoughts and feelings around painful childhood memories and recent personal hassles and traumas can result in improved moods, more positive outlook, greater physical health, and improved immunity functioning. Other studies support the health benefits of having a confidant.

Looking at the effects of divorce is another way to understand how relationships affect total well-being. More than 50% of first marriages in the United States end in divorce. Second marriages have a 60% rate of success. The health hazards of divorce have been summarized by Hafen et al. (1992). Divorced adults have higher rates of heart disease, cancer, pneumonia, high blood pressure, depression, alcoholism, traffic accidents, homicide, suicide, and accidental deaths than do persons who are married. They also have poorer immune function, which lowers resistance to disease (Kiecolt-Glaser et al., 1993). These facts are generally true for both men and women. Men, however, seem to suffer the most from divorce, suffering from more disease and earlier death.

Unhappily married persons are worse off than those divorced, according to the research (Sarason, Sarason, & Pierce, 1990). Simply being married does not give one a better chance for being psychologically well adjusted or physically healthier, but being happily married does. Persons who report marital dissatisfaction are at a greater risk for all kinds of illness. Poorer mental health, especially depression, exists among persons who are unhappily married.

The research does not bode well for the stepfamily. Children in a stepfamily are not much better off than those living with a single parent. The nature and rate of problem behavior is similar to that of single-parent families (Blankenhorn, 1995). What seems to matter most in determining its emotional health is how the family functions together, whether intact, single parent, or stepfamily. Scarf's (1995) work indicated that a family's emotional health is determined by how it handles power, intimacy, and conflict.

Effects of divorce on children are often more profound and longer lasting than on adults, according to a summary by Hafen et al. (1992). In addition to health problems, most children involved in divorce suffer emotional and behavioral changes, financial disadvantages, and a wide range of social and academic difficulties. They visit health clinics and physicians more often, are more likely to develop psychosomatic disorders, and are prone to become depressed, be aggressive, and suffer regression in development. Boys, more than girls, suffer from poor self-concept, bed-wetting, a sense of sorrow, anger, withdrawal, and frequent fighting. Children of divorce are also likely to be lower achievers, truant, late, absent, and subject to disciplinary action at school. Children living in dysfunctional families, regardless of family structure, are vulnerable to the same ill effects as children from divorces families. For children especially, a stable identification with a place and home seems to represent an important predictor of health (Cohen & Syme, 1985).

In sum, healthy marriages and healthy families give similar benefits. For men, women, and children, the committed relationship provides protection against physical and mental illness, increased longevity, and a greater sense of well-being. The health benefits tend to be greater for men than women. Single women who have never married may fare almost as well in health and longevity because of the capacity to establish and sustain intimate relationships through friends and family. Love relationships, therefore, although challenging in their requirements for personal courage, resourcefulness, and caring for others, are a powerful source of positive well-being for both genders throughout the life span.

## Life Forces

Both Adler and Dreikurs devoted the majority of their efforts to educating others on the influence of the family, the school, and the community at large on the healthy development of social interest. Dreikurs, for example, participated in the 1970 White House Conference on Children as an advocate for more responsible involvement of government in the welfare of children. Although Individual Psychology acknowledges the creative capacity of individuals to form the attitudes and adopt the values that guide them throughout life, one also must be cognizant of the powerful influences of institutions and the environment on the perceptions and alternative choices of individuals.

Development and performance of the five life tasks are influenced by forces from within the individual and from outside in the way societal institutions function to achieve their purposes. The outer circle of the model as illustrated in Figure 2.1 represents the life forces as major societal institutions that impinge on the health and well-being of each individual.

**Family.** Healthy marriage, family, and other close relationships provide similar benefits. For children especially, the benefits of a healthy family are crucial to personal and social development and adjustment. However, marriage and other forms of a committed relationship are for better or worse. Social ties can have negative effects on couples, children, caregivers, and close friendships. In fact, the physical and psychological consequences of negative relationships can be a serious health hazard (Burg & Seeman, 1994). Trust, intimacy, and sharing oneself with other persons have by their very nature a degree of risk. The risk carries with it the potential for physical and psychological harm, rejection, and the loss of family, financial, and social security. One enters into committed love relationships, however, with the expectation that they will bring joy and some of life's greatest satisfactions.

**Religion.** The place of religion in the lives of Americans is without question (Gallup & Castelli, 1989; Kelly, 1995; Naisbitt & Aburdene, 1990; Warner, 1993). Opinion polls for decades have provided evidence that Americans are a religious people, with church membership and attendance now identical to what they were in the 1930s. People in the United States believe in God, Allah, the Buddha, the Great Spirit, and divine beings with other titles who are the essence of the energy or consciousness in the universe. Only 8% claim no religious affiliation. In public opinion polls, more than 90% have consistently said they believe in God, 70% believe in life after death, 80% believe that God still works miracles, and prayer is "an important part" of the daily lives of 76% of those polled. On any given week, about 40% of Americans can be found attending a worship service, although 69% claim membership in a congregation. More than two thirds of parents ensure that their children get a religious education.

**Education.** Education has unlimited potential for creating a community in which the characteristics of the healthy person can be nurtured. Growth is both incidental and intentional and, next to the family, education provides the greatest opportunity for all of the 16 dimensions of wellness to be developed. When implementing a holistic approach to education, the most effective method is modeling a lifestyle of wellness. When integrated into the curriculum and a school climate that is encouraging, learning and living a healthy lifestyle becomes a process likely to extend over the life span.

**Community.**   With social mobility, industrialization, urbanization, and the breakup of the extended family has come the fragmentation of a sense of community in American life. The interdependence built into the small town and rural social structure of earlier years seems unnecessary at an economic level but is essential today for fulfilling the needs at a social level. The ingredients of community building need to be identified, then built into the social and architectural fabric of cities, towns, and rural areas. Support groups, religious groups, and work groups should all nurture a feeling of connectedness and a belief that everyone's destiny is intertwined, yet as individuals, retaining a healthy degree of independence.

**Media.**   Shaped by the norms of society, the media also shape people's values and public policies. Because they have the power to mold people's attitudes, beliefs, and desires, the media must be considered for the potential they have for positive influence as well as negative. Given the fact that children watch on average 25 to 30 hours of commercial television a week with little or no supervision, one must consider its potential for harm as well as good. An overwhelming majority of the studies on the relationship between TV and violence in children conclude that children who watch television violence are more prone to use physical aggression than those who do not watch so much.

**Government.**   Three underlying values promulgated in the Declaration of Independence are life, liberty, and the pursuit of happiness. Government policies and practices do have an impact on human behavior and attitudes. With a vision of wellness and prevention and through far-sighted leadership, the government can promote policies that influence every U.S. citizen (e.g., by lowering the death rate of children and extending the longevity of adults). One recent example is the report on *Healthy People 2000* (U.S. Public Health Service, 1990), which set the nation's health-promotion and disease-prevention goals for the decade.

**Business/Industry.** Although the workplace exists primarily as an economic force for the production of goods and services, it can be designed in a way that elements of the wellness and prevention model will contribute to its financial health. Healthier people are more productive, creative, cooperative, competent, and committed; miss fewer workdays; and have fewer illnesses. The relationship between health and worker productivity is being recognized by the business community (Pelletier, 1994). Many of the larger industries have not only started employee assistance programs but have initiated wellness programs that include such components as smoking cessation, control of alcohol and substance abuse, coping with stress, good nutrition, exercise, effective communication, noise reduction, and control of toxic substances.

### Global Events and Cosmic Consciousness

Beyond the life forces are global events (Figure 2.1) that impact everyday living and the quality of life. Wars, hunger, disease, poverty, environmental pollution, overpopulation, violation of human rights, economic exploitation, unemployment, and competition for limited resources are heavy clouds across the international sky. All are part of the ecology of living in a "global village" on the planet Earth. In an increasingly smaller world due to rapid transportation, mass media, and instant communications, society cannot afford to ignore these events if it wishes to build a "neighborhood village" that is committed to a lifestyle of wellness and prevention.

## WELLNESS EVALUATION OF LIFESTYLE (WEL)

The preceding sections described the theoretical constructs associated with wellness. The Wellness Evaluation of Lifestyle (WEL) was constructed to measure the 16 key dimensions of healthy functioning depicted in the wheel of wellness illustrated in Figure 2.1 (J. E. Myers, et al., 1995). The original form of the WEL included 114 items written at the high school reading level (Witmer, Sweeney, & Myers, 1994). A subsequent version included 100 items written at the seventh grade reading level (J. E. Myers et al., 1995). A Likert-type format is used, and respondents report the extent to which the items, or statements about wellness, reflect their personal lifestyle choices.

The WEL provides scores for each of the 16 dimensions of wellness in the model plus composite scores for total self-direction (a summary of scores on the 12 self-direction scales) and total wellness (the sum of all scores on the inventory). A short scale titled "perceived wellness" is included to measure an individual's perception of his or her overall wellness.

Scores for the WEL scales are presented as a percentage of the total possible points for each subscale. Thus, each score represents a point on a continuum from low-level wellness to high-level wellness. Naturally, because the items are representative only of the types of attitudes and behaviors associated with high levels of wellness, it is possible to score at the 100th percentile on a subscale but, in exploring the full scope of the topical area (e.g., exercise) still find areas for improvement. Likewise, some individuals may misunderstand the use of norms for such an inventory. For this reason, we suggest that norms not be used in most counseling cases. Some individuals may believe that little more improvement can be made if they have a high percentile score in an area of the WEL compared to persons like themselves. Likewise, they may be unduly discouraged by consistently low scores compared to others in the norm groups.

The test–retest reliabilities for the subscales of the WEL range from .68 to .94, with a median of .80 for groups of undergraduates and counseling graduate students. Validity was examined by comparing scores on the Testwell, developed by the National Wellness Institute. These scores ranged from .44 to .77 for a group of 44 graduate students in counseling (J. E. Myers, Witmer, & Sweeney, 1996). Due to the developmental nature of the instrument, new data collection and analyses are ongoing. The results of these analyses can be obtained for research purposes through the authors.

Completion of the inventory requires 10 to 15 minutes, and it may be completed either by an individual or in a group setting.

Scoring services provide both individual scale scores and a profile that provides a graphic comparison of subscale scores. (*Note:* Copies of the WEL [114-item form] and scoring services are available from MINDGARDEN, P.O. Box 60669, Palo Alto, CA 94699.)

## WELLNESS: PRACTICAL
## INTERVENTION TECHNIQUES

Throughout Adlerian practice there is an underlying theme of encouragement. Without encouragement, corrective methods will be ineffective or, at their worst, hurtful in their impact. Each chapter within this book includes methods, techniques, and suggestions for encouragement toward the goal of optimizing wellness. In an effort to help add specificity and focus to the traditional Adlerian concepts and methods, the model of wellness was created as represented in the wheel of wellness (Figure 2.1).

What follows are brief overviews of a few of the concepts and illustrations of practical applications of the model whether using the WEL as a clinical tool or simply by observation of what counselees need help in improving. Those that have been chosen for illustration include some, such as spirituality, that have not been found in Adlerian or counseling literature until recently. In addition, a few of the concepts and techniques related to self-direction are illustrated (realistic beliefs, humor, and stress management). The life tasks of work and leisure, friendship, and love are developed in subsequent chapters as well.

For illustrations of all of the concepts and suggestions for each, the reader is referred to *The WEL Workbook* (J. E. Myers et al., 1996). In addition, the reader may wish to review these illustrations after reading the section on readiness for change in chapter 5. The success of any intervention is directly related to the counselees' readiness for specific activities at a given point in their development (Prochaska & DiClemente, 1984). Ascertaining the stage of readiness and using intervention techniques appropriate to that stage increase the probability of movement toward new goals and behavior.

## Pathways to Spirituality

Spirituality may be conceived of as a state of being that transcends the challenges of this life and enriches that which is ordinary in everyone's life. Like all treasures of life, spirituality cannot be attained by pursuing it as a trophy or goal. Rather, one surrenders to that experiencing of self that transcends words of explanation. Each person must choose when and how to begin. Pathways to spirituality include faith (recognition of a higher power); harmony (prayer, worship, and self-reflection); enlightenment (knowledge of the divine); purpose (meaning in life); love and compassion (giving and receiving); and co-creating and service (living the faith) (Witmer, 1996). The following descriptions and practical activities relate to three of these pathways (faith, harmony, and purpose).

One caveat concerns the counselor's personal beliefs. For the purposes of discussion of spirituality, as is true for any topic for which one lacks competence or comfort with a topic, referral to another counselor is appropriate when spiritual matters are beyond the scope of one's practice. In one case, a counselee expressed considerable distress with the prospect of an impending divorce because of very deeply held convictions about what the Lord expected of Christians as found in the Bible. The "helper" responded, "I haven't any idea what you are talking about . . . " and made no effort to provide assistance or referral. The rationale in defense of such action was "we are here for the psychological needs of clients, not their spiritual ones." Clearly, a holistic, wellness orientation to counseling as proposed here refutes such a shallow rationale and raises ethical questions about such treatment as well.

On the other hand, entering into spiritual exploration carries with it responsibility for maintaining ethically appropriate objectivity as a companion rather than guide for a counselee. This is especially so if one's practice is not notably specialized in matters of religious values. Having noted that ethical practice requires careful consideration of these matters, we hope that more counselors will develop competence in matters of spirituality and help more of their counselees in their process of self-discovery.

**Faith: Recognition of a Higher Power.**   The first pathway is acknowledging in one's consciousness that some power greater than oneself exists. This is usually not a rational, cerebral choice alone, if at all. To acknowledge a higher power is more intuitive, more creative, more personal than most life experiences. It is a matter of faith. One god, one power, one force or energy is a characteristic of the world's major religions. Through nature and the world of thought, the individual is in awe of the universe and desires to experience the universe as a single significant whole. A direct question about one's beliefs may be all that is required to open exploration of the topic when appropriate to the issues at hand.

Called the Tao by Lao Tsu (Bolen, 1979), the experience of a unifying principle in the universe to which everything relates underlies the major Eastern religions—Hinduism, Buddhism, Confucianism, Taoism, and Zen. Although each religion may call the experience by a separate name, each holds that all phenomena—people, animals, plants, and objects from atomic particles to galaxies—are aspects of the One. The Creator exists in and through everything.

A characteristic that distinguished Judaism in its early centuries from the other religions in the Mediterranean region was its adherence to one god called Jehovah. The existence of one power is personified as God and Jesus Christ in Christianity. Mohammed, the prophet who founded Islam, called this one god Allah.

Hope and optimism motivate people to become co-creators with the force of the universe in anticipation of future events. Optimism is a factor that nourishes spiritual wellness. As such, it is an expression of hope that with a certain degree of confidence, one can either expect the best possible outcome or dwell on the most hopeful aspects of the situation. Both dimensions of optimism are important—the expectation of a desirable outcome and focusing on the positive aspects of the situation.

Only in recent years has scientific attention been devoted to the possibility that optimism may have beneficial health effects.

Various studies have shown that optimism is an important factor in coping with stress and is linked to physical and psychological health (Peterson & Bossio, 1991; Scheier & Carver, 1987; Seligman, 1990; Witmer & Rich, 1995; Witmer et al., 1983).

**Practical Activity on Faith.** Invite counselees to keep a journal of expectations and circumstances surrounding them for a few days up to a week. Expectations about any events important to them may be recorded, for example, that they will complete a project, that a friend will follow through on a promise, that they will have enough money to keep up with their needs for the week. At the next session, the list may be reviewed with attention to the following: Were the expectations positive or negative? Were more positive expectations met than not? Is there a pattern to the expectations and outcomes? What emotions were a part of the outcome of these events? Follow-up discussion can focus on counselees' convictions or beliefs about a higher power, the importance or influence that this has in their life, and how these beliefs affect their day-to-day dealings with stressful circumstances, challenges, and opportunities.

**Harmony: Prayer, Worship, and Self-Reflection.** Traditionally religion and spirituality have sought peace, guidance, and contact with the universal force through meditation, prayer, worship, contemplation, or introspection. If one defines prayer as every kind of inward communion or communication with the power recognized as divine, it becomes in a broad sense the very essence of religion. Such prayers would include prayers of petition, thanksgiving, confession, and communion. Rituals give structure and substance to a prayerful attitude whether in public or private worship. When this prayerful attitude is extended to a moment-by-moment awareness of our spirituality, one has an ever-present reverence for life.

Solitude and a sense of detachment are essential conditions for pursuing this pathway. Letting go of that which encumbers them, frees people to become more like the divine spirit. Prayer, meditation, reading spiritual literature, and contemplation are practices that provide direction and inspiration.

Included as part of the inner experience is the mystical. The rational limits of consciousness are exceeded, boundaries are removed, and the mind goes beyond the usual senses in receiving sudden insights, illuminations, or revelations. The experience is often unanticipated, timeless, and mostly inexplicable. To experience the mysterious is to transcend the ordinary by rising above or going beyond the usual experience, thought, or belief.

This receptive mode of consciousness may be accompanied by a sense of awe or reverence, losing one's sense of time and space, an inner harmony, ecstasy, unconditional acceptance, security, contentment, or joyfulness. One's life is imbued with a certain sacredness.

**Practical Activity Toward Harmony.** Even for persons who attend some form of religious service regularly as well as those who do not, meditation tends to be absent in their lives. A variety of small books with inspirational readings may serve as a simple introduction to the practice of quiet meditation. The greatest commitment to such practice begins with a decision to make a time and place for doing it.

For some people, either the morning or evening are the best times. The place may be in their favorite room, whereas for others it is their place of worship, possibly during the day when others are busy elsewhere. The simplicity of the task, however, is deceptive. True meditation is an art developed over time with patience. The readings help to give one structure. Over time, the individual learns to quiet the mind in order to listen to the soul. It is important, therefore, to establish habits for the occasion without expectations for outcomes.

The outcomes will follow even initially with a greater sense of being centered, calmed, and relaxed. For the initiate, however, these are easily lost in the stress and rush of ordinary activities. Like relaxation techniques, establishing a pattern for practicing and reinforcing the habits is essential. Regularly taking time to center one's consciousness on spiritual matters can provide insight, inspiration, and serenity. Invite counselees to think of several rituals they could practice, then choose at least one they are willing to make part of their lives. Rituals can include a daily devotion time, a weekly walk in solitude with nature, lighting a candle for a particular observance, or an annual spiritual retreat.

**Purpose: Meaning in Life.** Purposiveness (teleology) in the psychic life is central to Adlerian psychology: *"The psychic life of man is determined by his goal.* No human being can think, feel, will, dream, without all these activities being determined, continued, modified and directed toward an ever-present objective"* (Adler, 1927/1954, p. 29). Human behavior is, therefore, understood as directed toward a goal.

Spiritually, the divine takes a human form to fulfill a purpose. A common belief is that each person has a unique talent and a way of expressing it. In point of fact, all persons have many talents from which to develop their uniqueness. The purpose in life focuses on what one is here to give back to life. To do this, first, one must seek the true or spiritual self inside—an image of what one can become. Second, one must develop the talents and gifts that are unique to one's capacities and interests. Last is the service to humanity in ways that make the world a better place to live.

Purposiveness is found through the different life tasks. Being involved as a participant in shaping one's destiny as well as one's daily experience sustains the will to live. For some people, it may be centered on family relationships, for others their career, and a yet for others it may be a community service.

**Practical Activity on Life Purpose.** Using lifestyle assessment and techniques similar to those in chapters 7, 8, and 9, the counselor can guide counselees through an exploration of life themes and interests that move them toward a knowledge of self in relation to life and others. Early recollections, for example, often reveal interest in other people and a compassion for their predicaments as well as talents, characteristics, and attributes. Heroes and heroines likewise disclose service to other themes or qualities of resourcefulness, courage, and purpose. The search for meaning in life is inherent in the entire lifestyle assessment and interactive process. The counselor sensitive to this potential has much more to offer in the way of advancing spiritual exploration than has been used in the past. Using this potential as a part of the counseling process can provide a new and meaningful dimension to Adlerian counseling.

One activity to help counselees is to draw a spiritual lifeline. Using a sheet of paper to draw a time and events line, the counselees illustrate their spiritual development thus far in life. Starting with their earliest memories, they are invited to recall those religious and spiritual experiences that have impacted them, positively or negatively. They may place negative experiences below the line and the positive ones above. Include the expected and unexpected experiences and events, those within an organized religion and those outside. They may think of persons, places, and events that have molded their faith and spiritual values. A guided reflection on the meaning of these experiences to their current outlook on life follows. Finally, they should draw a new projection of the future on this same line to include desired spiritual experiences followed by an exploration of how this will impact positively on their lives.

## Facilitating Self-Direction

Within the wheel of wellness (Figure 2.1), self-direction as a life task has 12 components. The titles given to these components are intended to convey movement, purposiveness, and personal power. They are individually and collectively dynamic in nature. All are important to the whole and each influences the others.

Occasionally, we will be asked by individuals while discussing their WEL scores, How many of these components must be "high" for me to be "well"? I am reminded of a sign in the dentist's office that reads, "You don't have to floss all of your teeth, only the one's you wish to keep!" We have selected a few of the self-direction dimensions for illustration among those commonly addressed in counseling and workshops. They include realistic beliefs, sense of humor, and stress management. All dimensions of the wellness model deserve attention, however, and each will be important to different counselees at different points in their lives.

**Fostering Realistic Beliefs.** How does the thought–mood connection work? The human mind has a continuous flow of thoughts and images, perhaps as many as 50 per minute. These thoughts and images occur in the form of self-talk and images that create individual scenarios within one's mind. The body believes everything the mind says and consequently acts on those thoughts (Levine, 1991). What makes it difficult is that these thoughts and images usually occur automatically and one responds emotionally, physiologically, and behaviorally as though they truthfully represented reality (Dacher, 1991). Without some kind of monitoring and evaluation of these thoughts and images, one continues to feel bad, make poor decisions, and fail in achieving goals. Although some automatic thoughts are true, many are either untrue or have just a grain of truth.

Four steps are essential for coping more effectively with situations that create distress or dissatisfaction:

1. Identify the situation and feelings that are associated with the thoughts and images. Note the self-talk (script) that is used to explain the situation (past, present, or future).

2. Evaluate the self-talk to test its validity. Is it positive or negative; rational or irrational; true of untrue? Discuss, debate, and discount that which doesn't make sense. Challenge false assumptions, overgeneralizations, irrational or unrealistic expectations, and thinking that magnifies the negative and minimizes the positive.

3. Choose an alternative thought, belief, or explanation for the situation. Note how it will change what you say to yourself and the subsequent feelings that result from a different script.

4. Practice the alternative thought and explanation for the situation by using it on a regular basis. Do you feel differently and does the new self-talk stand the reality test? Note the evidence that supports your new self-talk.

**Practical Activities on Realistic Beliefs.** The following are recommendations for use with counselees who wish to improve their check on realistic beliefs:

1. Do a mind scan at various times during the day, particularly when you have negative feelings. Listen to your thoughts or watch the pictures that are on the screen of your mind. Decide what you want to do about these thoughts and images. Tell yourself, "I have the power to choose what I will think about." Write a note on the specifics of what it is you desire thinking and feeling.

2. Make a list of the "shoulds" and "oughts" that you have come to believe (e.g., "I should always do what other people expect of me."). Note the self-talk and the related feelings.

3. Note the frequency of your negative and positive thoughts. What is the ratio? One negative thought cancels out many positive ones. Are you optimistic or pessimistic about life?

4. When you evaluate yourself, others, or a situation, do you unreasonably magnify the negative and/or minimize the positive?

5. Do you overgeneralize by making a sweeping negative conclusion that goes far beyond what is justified by the situation?

Positive thoughts perform at least four functions: (a) they help you solve problems; (b) they are based on verifiable events or information shared by others; (c) they result in you feeling the way you like to feel most of the time; and (d) they contribute to positive relationships with others. After each of the above activities, determine which are your best thoughts and which new ones can help you do better than you have in the past.

**Nurturing a Sense of Humor.** Many persons who come for counseling reveal a "life is serious business" outlook that is trait more than state in origin. It is fundamental to their lifestyle. Across sessions, the counselor can be alert to the presence and emergence of a sense of humor in the counselee. Such behavior is one indicator of progress. However, humor can be used defensively to avoid painful content and feelings. As such, the counselee and counselor must break through the protective facade to deal with genuine feelings and beliefs. When the counselor uses humor, it should never be in the form of a put-down of the individual or a group. If overused, used inappropriately, or poorly timed, humor can seriously detract from movement toward the goals of counseling (Gladding, 1995).

If humor has an effective role in counseling and psychotherapy and is good medicine for treating illnesses, how much more important might it be for enhancing wellness? Adler and Dreikurs, as noted in chapter 1, were masterful in their use of humor throughout their counseling and teaching.

**Practical Activities for Nurturing a Sense of Humor.** The following may be offered as assignments for counselees:

- Make it a point to read daily your favorite cartoons, comic strips, and jokes. Share them with others during the day.

- For an evening of relaxation, rent a video of your favorite comedian or a comedy film. Plan for at least an hour of humorous relaxation.

- Send humorous notes or cartoons to friends or coworkers. Put a humorous note in the pockets or shoes of someone living in your house.

- Be intentional about telling a funny story or using spontaneous humor in response to everyday happenings or encounters.

- Adopt an attitude of playfulness. Be open to silly, irreverent (or irrelevant) thoughts and doing the unexpected thing.

**Stress Management.** A holistic approach to preventing and managing stress would include all of the other 15 wellness dimensions. However, methods and techniques have been developed with specific application to managing stress arousal (Girdano, Everly, & Dusek, 1993; Kabat-Zinn, 1990; Kleinke, 1991; Lehrer & Woolfolk, 1993). They are summarized according to their emphasis on physical, mental, or behavioral/environmental methods and techniques:

> *Physiological—Relaxation* (Benson & Stuart, 1992; Kabat-Zinn, 1990, 1994; Schwartz & Associates, 1995). Controlled breathing; body scan for tension; meditation—yoga, transcendental meditation, or mindfulness; relaxation response (Benson & Stuart, 1992); progressive relaxation; autogenic training; biofeedback; hypnosuggestion.

> *Physiological—Physical Fitness* (Ornish, 1990; Weil, 1995). Exercise; nutrition and eating habits.

> *Cognitive* (J. S. Beck, 1995; Borysenko & Borysenko, 1994; Miller, 1991; Shealy & Myss, 1993). Controlling thoughts (thought stopping); changing mistaken ideas: faulty beliefs, reasoning, and rules; optimism and positive thinking; values affirmation (organizing and managing priorities); visual imagery; reframing (giving different interpretation to the event); problem solving.

> *Behavioral/Environmental* (Archer, 1991; J. C. Smith, 1993). Assertiveness; relationship and communication skill building; time management; allowing for leisure activities; avoiding the stressor; medical, spiritual, psychological consultation; change job situation.

The practical ideas that follow illustrate briefly one method from each of the four strategies.

**Practical Activities on Stress Management.**  Although many people have read about the negative effects of stress, too few actually attempt to practice stress management techniques. The following are known to be effective if practiced by counselees as suggested:

- Breathing and relaxation: During stressful moments, experiment with how an awareness of your breathing for as little as 15 seconds can have an immediate calming effect. Make it a ritual to take time out during the day to spend 10 to 15 minutes in silence just being aware (mindful) of your breathing, allowing the full cycle of inhaling and exhaling, occasionally taking a deeper and longer breath.

- Become intentional about accumulating at least 30 minutes a day in physical movement. Start with stretching in the morning. During the day include time walking to work from your home or your car, walking up stairs, housework, yard work, and gardening.

- Use visualization to practice your performance in an upcoming event, one that has aroused a little anxiety. Close your eyes and imagine the situation as you expect it to be. Breathe slowly and deeply. See yourself approaching the situation with confidence and as you wish it to be. Rehearse how you want to act and what you might say. Feel a sense of inner control as you do this. See the ending in the way you would really like it to be. End the visualization feeling confident about your performance and positive about yourself.

- If you suffer from "hurry sickness," try time management. How you use time is related to goals and priorities. Goals and priorities come from values, so you will need to do a values assessment. List the 5 to 10 most important values (short term and long term). Connect these values to your use of time. Eliminate or reduce the time spent doing the activities of lesser value. Use a daily and weekly scheduling calendar to plan, monitor, and revise where you allocate your time.

## WELLNESS IN ACTION

The preceding section is only an introduction to the concepts and many activities that can be addressed through a wellness orientation to helping. Although the concept of social interest is useful in understanding Adler's thoughts on the motivation of healthy persons, a review of Adlerian literature suggests that both researchers and practitioners find the construct difficult to define, to measure, and to cultivate in practice or research. Our efforts to further define what Adler intended resulted in the development of the wheel of wellness (Figure 2.1). Like Adler, however, we are not bound by or to this model. As new research and practice advance our knowledge, we expect the model to change or to be replaced by better representations of what it is we attempt to achieve with our efforts as Adlerian counselors and researchers. In the meantime, we believe that it can be a useful addition to those who study and practice Adlerian interventions.

## SUMMARY

Among mental health theorists, there has been a movement to identify with a position that speaks to efficacy and outcomes and a need to match techniques to diagnosable client symptoms (Prochaska & Norcross, 1994). In the heyday of behaviorism, Rudolf Dreikurs took every opportunity to expose its flaws. If Dreikurs were here today, he would no doubt speak as passionately to the pitfalls of technology and the seduction to only that which appears quantifiable. Perhaps not as articulate but nevertheless every bit as convinced, we note that in the absence of a philosophical context, a statement of values, and an appreciation for the uniqueness as well as interdependence of each human being, our techniques, no matter how effective, are only tools.

In this chapter, we have put forth a position for wellness as the ultimate goal of counseling, not the remediation or elimination of dysfunction. We hope that over time this position will be embraced by all Adlerians as an extension of what Adler and Dreikurs had in mind when they first laid the foundation for Individual Psychology and the concept of social interest.

As is noted in other chapters, there is growing evidence of the validity of Adler's and Dreikurs' thoughts and teaching as related to the vast majority of individuals who benefit from developmental as well as remedial counseling and psychotherapy. It is particularly for those individuals, couples, families, and groups that this approach is appropriate. With the dimensions of wellness over the life span added to the Adlerian concepts of life tasks, social interest, and holism, we believe that those theorists and practitioners holding to other approaches would do well to reexamine Adlerian theory for that which is absent in their own approaches.

## Chapter 3

# NATURAL CONSEQUENCES: LIFE'S RULES ARE FOR EVERYONE

Have you ever

locked your car keys in the car?

found in the checkout line that you had left your cash and checkbook at home?

stubbed your toe while walking without shoes?

lost or broken something of value because of carelessness?

All of these events can be powerful influences on behavior. All have certain characteristics in common. Each results in an undesirable, sometimes painful, consequence. Each is the result of short-sightedness with respect to possible outcomes. In each case, no one else is involved (i.e., the natural consequence follows without the intervention of anyone else).

Such experiences prompt comments such as "experience is our best teacher" or "learning through the school of hard knocks." Much can be said about the value of personal experience as a guide to learning how to cope with life. Such learning has its disadvantages, however. For example, real bodily harm or even death can be a result of a serious oversight. In other cases, an individual may overreact to possible consequences and develop fears that impede other areas of personal development. Also some consequences take an indefinite period of time to have an effect (e.g., not brushing one's teeth eventually causes cavities or unhealthy gums). In short, natural consequences affect how one learns to cope with life, but intelligent use of them is important for such consequences to have a positive influence.

## ACTION DIMENSIONS

The action dimensions—natural consequences, logical consequences, and encouragement—of the Adlerian approach are the foundation of the educative process.

### Natural Consequences

This consequence is the result of an ill-advised behavior and will follow without the intervention of another person. For example, if you neglect to take your clothes to the laundry, they do not get cleaned; if the children do not place their dirty clothes in the laundry hamper, they do not get cleaned.

### Logical Consequences

This consequence is the result of an ill-advised behavior and can follow logically even though it requires the purposeful intervention of another person. For example, if others must pick up your belongings, they also may decide where to place them. A logical consequence would follow that you would have to do without the use of your belongings during this period of time.

### Encouragement

This dimension denotes the process by which one develops the faith and self-confidence needed to cope successfully with any predicament, defeat, or task; whatever the circumstance, individuals know that they have a place, that they belong, and that they will survive.

## EXPERIENCING NATURAL CONSEQUENCES

Natural consequences are the negative outcomes of an ill-advised behavior that follow without the intervention of another person. These are among the great social levelers in nature. Regardless of your social stature, if you violate "commonsense" rules about life, nature has its own recourse! You can be sure that heads of government sometimes stub their toes while fumbling around their bedrooms in the dark. Likewise, the most expensive automobile will not run unless the driver remembers to keep fuel in its gas tank. You can see how each person's equality is reinforced by recognition that nature's laws apply to all persons regardless of sex, age, race, and so forth. Such rules are for everyone!

From a historical perspective, the use of natural consequences as an aid to child rearing is by no means new. Spencer (1885) supported Rousseau's concepts of 100 years earlier and condemned the harsh treatment accorded many children by parents and other adults. Spencer believed that punishment debased children rather than prepared them for the demands of adult life. As a more proper alternative, he discussed what Adlerians identify as a natural consequence:

> When a child falls or runs his head against a table, the remembrance of which tends to make it more careful; and by repetition of such experience, it is eventually disciplined into proper guidance of its movements. . . . So deep an impression is produced by one or two events of this kind, that no persuasion will afterwards induce it thus to disregard the laws of its constitution . . . they are simply the unavoidable consequences of the deeds which they follow: are nothing more than the inevitable reactions entailed by the child's actions. (Spencer, 1885, pp. 161–163)

Everyone has learned important lessons about the natural order from such experiences. Thus, individuals have a very useful tool in helping others to accept responsibility for their actions.

Without explaining, nagging, or pleading, one can "let nature take its course" and allow natural consequences to enforce the order that impinges on everyone.

## PRACTICAL IMPLICATIONS

So many illustrations of natural consequences are operating that only a few should help you begin a list of your own. Carelessness in watching where you are going can result in bumps and bruises. Most children have ignored admonitions to "not run so fast" and fallen hard enough to hurt themselves. Touching hot plates or kettles contributes to continued caution even when you are mature enough to discriminate between those items that may be dangerous and those that are not. Some adults pay little attention to their automobile fuel gauges or "idiot" light for oil. Inconveniences and costly repair bills are a result of such carelessness. Likewise, oversleeping, overeating, working to the point of exhaustion, forgetting tools needed to do a job, or allowing work to accumulate beyond a reasonable point all constitute situations that contribute to natural consequences.

### Self-Study Situations

Now try to select one or more consequences to each action by asking the following question: What happens if no one intervenes in a positive or negative way?

1. You never pick up your clothes
   - _____ a. they remain dirty
   - _____ b. they get more soiled
   - _____ c. you run out of clothes
   - _____ d. someone else must pick them up

2. You go to a store late
   - _____ a. store is closed
   - _____ b. someone must open it for you
   - _____ c. you may be inconvenienced
   - _____ d. you become angry

3. You do not complete          _____ a. someone else does it for
   your work                                you
                                 _____ b. you may have to do it at
                                         another potentially less
                                         convenient time
                                 _____ c. you have more to do the
                                         next time
                                 _____ d. you may lack the knowl-
                                         edge, skill, or experience
                                         needed for a future task

4. You ignore the natural       _____ a. you may get bruised or
   laws                                    injured
                                 _____ b. someone must protect you
                                 _____ c. you run into or over that
                                         which is around you
                                 _____ d. your insurance rates go up

To help fully understand some of the subtleties of discriminating among the alternatives, find someone with whom to compare responses if possible. Then check the appropriate answers at the bottom of this page.

Frequently someone will indicate that a natural consequence is anger or a similar emotional reaction. Emotions, however, are not an unavoidable consequences or inevitable reaction to an experience. People differ in their emotional reactions to identical events. Therefore, emotional reactions are not natural consequences. Likewise, to have an automobile accident while "ignoring the natural laws of motion" may result in higher insurance rates, but this requires the intervention of someone else. Because of a number of circumstances, the insurance company may choose not to change your rates.

Occasionally the question of dangerous circumstances will arise. When we speak of this situation as a common sense approach, the need for judgment is implied. In fact, mastery of the subject

---

**Key:** 1. a, b, c; 2. a, c; 3. b, c, d; 4. a, c

can be determined in part by one's ability to discriminate in the use of general rules. Knowing when it is most appropriate to make an exception to a general rule connotes one evidence of mastery. Sometimes you may choose not to intervene and protect a young person from a fall or bump because he or she has insisted on discovering the consequence for himself or herself. Likewise, you may choose to stop providing a colleague, friend, or spouse with a way out for "forgetting" tools, supplies, appointments, and so forth, when it becomes apparent that you (and others) only serve to reinforce self-defeating and/or irresponsible behavior. On the other hand, no one could stand aside while a 2- or 3-year-old ran into a busy thoroughfare or someone proceeded to light a cigarette in an area of gas fumes.

The imagined prospect of youngsters maiming or killing themselves has been the enslavement of many adults. In discussions with many youngsters and on the basis of years of observation, a general truth seems apparent. On the average, no one chooses to seriously injure himself or herself purposely. Some may flirt with danger but generally with an expectation that they will not be injured. Some few young people and adults seem compelled to test themselves as daredevils. These people are the exceptions. More often, as one cartoonist noted in a discussion between two youngsters, they "have to plan their emergencies very carefully in advance!" in order to impress the adults in their lives.

---

Children plan their emergencies to
impress adults.

---

In one parent study group, a parent was convinced her son was "bound and determined to do himself in." Based on other information, the group questioned this assumption but the parent felt compelled to protect him from all manner of dangers. Two sessions later, the parent returned a believer in the group's admonitions. That week while the parent was in the process of preparing supper, the boy was seen to be walking on the peak of the garage roof. Suddenly he lost his footing and fell. Convinced that he had finally done it this time, the parent ran into the backyard. There behind the garage, sitting on top of a large carefully piled layer of leaves, was the son, grinning from ear to ear. No one needed to explain his motivation and a more motivated parent study group participant could not be found!

Children are not the only ones whose behavior causes problems. When a family member, roommate, or coworker persistently abuses common courtesy, allowing natural consequences to occur may be the solution. For example, many homemakers complain that their spouses tend to come home later than expected but looking for a fresh, still hot meal. The obvious consequence is a cold meal. In fact, when family members don't make it home and/or don't call to say that they will be delayed, some families agree that the late arrivers get leftovers. In such instances, no comments taunt the late arriver nor angry feelings because a good meal was not had by all. Silence is golden and friendliness an asset.

This last point is particularly important to understand. Because many people are accustomed to the use of punishment as a method of discipline, they want the offender to suffer! They believe that it isn't enough to no longer be in conflict; they want revenge or retribution! When in such a mental state, some natural consequences may seem mild indeed. Revenge and desire for retribution tend to escalate a conflict whereas natural consequences do not. Because no one need intervene, the force of reality is the teacher. You can remain friendly and unperturbed by what formerly had been an annoying situation. Statements of "I told you so" or "Now you'll know better than to do that" are unnecessary, if not also unkind. They also increase the probability of further conflict. Be patient and recognize that more responsible behavior will follow as the consequences prove their own value as a source of learning.

On a more serious note, the literature on alcohol and other substance abusers supports the position that often family and friends enable loved ones to continue in their self- and other-destructive behavior by excusing them from the consequences of their behavior. Whether it is being expected to clean up after vomiting (natural consequence) or not being allowed the use of the car (logical consequence), the enforcement of reasonable but firm rules is essential to any intervention program. Better that such intervention begin sooner rather than later for the benefit of all parties involved. Such "tough love" can save lives and relationships. Obviously, in such situations, other therapeutic interventions also will be necessary.

## SUMMARY

This chapter was designed to heighten awareness of life's methods of teaching responsible behavior and attitudes. By studying how each person has learned through experiencing natural consequences, one is better able to implement them as methods for allowing others to accept responsibility for their behavior. Subsequent chapters help illustrate the uses and usefulness of natural consequences. The next chapter is particularly valuable as a further extension of consequences into the social domain.

## STUDY QUESTIONS

**Directions:** Respond to the following in the spaces provided.

1. Why does the title to this chapter include "Rules Are for Everyone"?

2. Cite two or three illustrations from your experience that were important lessons based on natural consequences.

3. Give one example of how you might allow someone you know to experience a natural consequence that could contribute to more responsible behavior on his or her part.

4. Under what circumstances might you choose to allow natural consequences to take place?

5. Under what circumstances might you choose to intervene to prevent someone else from experiencing a natural consequence?

## ACTIVITIES

A natural consequence is the result of an ill-advised behavior and will follow without the intervention of another person.

I.  A.  Check those of the following that could be examples of natural consequences:

| Action | Natural Consequence |
|---|---|
| 1. You forget to water your plants | ____ a. they die<br>____ b. they lose leaves or blooms<br>____ c. they may need to be replaced<br>____ d. someone else must do it |
| 2. You lock your keys in the car | ____ a. you may miss an appointment<br>____ b. someone must open it for you<br>____ c. you may be inconvenienced<br>____ d. you become depressed |

| **Action** | **Natural Consequence** |
|---|---|
| 3. You don't tie your shoelaces | ____ a. someone else does it for you<br>____ b. you trip on your laces<br>____ c. your shoes fit badly and may hurt<br>____ d. in an emergency, you can't move quickly enough to reach safety |
| 4. You go on vacation without money | ____ a. you must borrow and pay interest<br>____ b. someone must give you money<br>____ c. you cannot do some of the things you planned to do<br>____ d. you lose fun time trying to get money for things you need |

B. Now reach a consensus with your partner and/or group members about appropriate natural consequences.

C. Check your responses with those of the key.

` II. A. List one or more natural consequence to each of the following if another person does not intervene.

| **Action** | **Natural Consequence** |
|---|---|
| 1. You misplace needed materials: | |

---

**Key:** 1. a, b, c; 2. a, c; 3. b, c, d; 4. c, d

| **Action** | **Natural Consequence** |
|---|---|

2. You forget a dental appointment:

3. You are careless with tools:

4. You do not bathe:

5. You do not get enough sleep:

6. You miss one or more meals:

7. You abuse belongings:

8. You forget to bring necessary clothes,
   equipment, or materials:

B. Share your list of natural consequences with the group
   and participate in discussion.

III. A. Identify three or more natural consequences you have
experienced, even vicariously, that remain as important
influences on your behavior.

**When you did this**          **This (unfortunate)**
**(ill advised) ...**          **consequence followed . . .**

1.

2.

3.

B. Share your responses with your partner or group members. Do others agree that the consequences you listed
are logical consequences? Why or why not? Discuss
other participants' responses.

## Chapter 4

# LOGICAL CONSEQUENCES: SOCIETY'S LESSONS

As noted in the previous chapter, natural consequences are powerful influences on our behavior. They do, however, have limitations. For this reason, social conventions in the form of understandings, mores, rules, and laws have an impact of their own. A lack of understanding or ignorance of these contributes to difficulties among people of different ethnic or national origin. Western businessmen, for example, are only beginning to appreciate the subtleties to conducting business with Arabs, Chinese, or Japanese businessmen. Likewise, agreements within and between families will differ so much that arrangements for a wedding can be tantamount to war!

For those who ascribe to the rules and mores of a given group, to violate them is to invite the social consequences as a result. Such consequences generally will be accepted as a logical outcome of the ill-advised behavior of one of its members. The influence of peer opinion and consensus contributes to the power of the rules over individuals. Although individuals probably will not like the consequences, they tend to accept them because they apply to all members and the rules are intended to contribute to the better-

ment of individuals as well as the group. Unlike natural consequences, logical (social) consequences are not unavoidable consequences of the deeds that they follow. Their definition and application, therefore, are more complex and require a context in which
they operate.

## COMPARISONS OF CONSEQUENCES
## AND PUNISHMENT

Logical consequences are the negative outcome of an ill-advised behavior and can logically follow even though the consequence requires the purposeful intervention of one or more other
persons. For example, if you leave your belongings in places that
cause inconvenience to others, others may move them to places
inconvenient to you. A logical consequence would follow in that
you may have to do without the use of the belongings during this
period of time. Some persons new to the concepts of natural and
logical consequences will equate them with punishment. This conclusion is an error that is well illustrated by Dreikurs and Grey
(1968). The comparison in Table 4.1 can help distinguish between
consequences and punishment.

## ASPECTS OF LOGICAL CONSEQUENCES

Certain aspects contribute to the successful implementing of
consequences. Three of these aspects are attitudes, choices, and
actions.

### Attitudes

The importance of maintaining a friendly attitude and helping
to establish choices cannot be overemphasized. Angry feelings can
be evoked in conflict for a variety of reasons. At such times, personal power gets translated into an ultimatum—"you do it my way
or else!" Conflicts are escalated into major wars and cooperation
goes out the window.

Friendly attitudes can be maintained when (a) you can perceive other alternatives to your behavior besides arguing and (b)

## TABLE 4.1
## Comparison of Consequences and Punishment

| Consequences | Punishment |
| --- | --- |
| Expresses the reality of the social order of the situation not of the person | Expresses the power of a personal authority—*Authoritarian* |
| Logically related to the disruptive behavior | Not logical, only an arbitrary connection between disruptive behavior and consequences |
| Involves no element of moral judgment | Inevitably involves some moral judgment |
| Concerned only with what will happen now | Concerned with the past |
| Relationship and atmosphere are friendly; resentment is minimized | Often anger is present, either overtly or covertly; resentment is frequent |
| Develops intrinsic motivation and self-discipline | Depends on extrinsic motivation |
| No submission or humiliation | Often requires submission or humiliation |
| Freedom of choices within limits | No alternatives or choice |
| Consequences are acceptable | Punishment is at best only tolerable |
| Thoughtful and deliberate | Often impulsive |
| Person feels important | Person feels belittled |
| Choice given once only | Often involves endless nagging |
| Uses action | Uses talking and coercion |

you are not preoccupied with winning or losing. Angry feelings can be facilitative when they are expressed without disrespect to oneself or the other person. They even may be encouraging, as illustrated in chapter 5. On the whole, however, Adlerians recommend that you extricate yourself from power struggles.

Because at least two people are required to have a fight, Dreikurs recommended that *you take the sail out of their wind.* When angry feelings have subsided, a discussion of what transpired and why (i.e., what purpose was served) may be helpful in reestablishing a friendly relationship. This discussion does not mean giving in. Rather, you side step the power struggle until calmer circumstances prevail. One simple technique is to go to the bathroom (i.e., the bathroom technique). As comical as it may sound, parents, children, and spouses report that it does indeed bring greater harmony to the family! Persons in work settings report equally good results with coworkers and bosses!

---

Extricate yourself from struggles.

---

Logical consequences inflicted in anger increase the probability that the recipients will perceive them as revenge or punishment. If the recipient is prone to conflicts with power or revenge as a goal, logical consequences as a method may be ineffective in any case. As a method, however, it gives you a recourse if no natural consequences are available or reasonable (waiting for the proverbial roof to fall in may take too long or inflict damage of too permanent a nature).

## Choices

Choices are another aspect of successfully implementing logical consequences. The magic in giving choices sometimes astounds persons unfamiliar with these methods. No one appreciates an ultimatum, particularly when there is personal tension between the parties involved. Sometimes, however, simply perceiving that one has some degree of influence and choice is sufficient to allay defensiveness and resistance. Studies under laboratory conditions have indicated, for example, that persons who *perceive* themselves as having control over an otherwise annoying environmental situation will be less distressed than persons who are told that they have no control, even though neither group had control of the experimental factors. One practical illustration of this phenomenon was shared by a parent study group member who applied this principle in her work as receptionist for an ophthalmologist.

Occasionally patients would balk at having medication put into their eyes. During one such episode, she asked the physician if he would like a suggestion for dealing with this. He followed her advice and asked the patient if he would like both drops at the same time or prefer to have them one at a time. The patient made his choice and the physician was forever grateful because it proved effective with other patients as well. Persons preoccupied with control are particularly open to being more cooperative when given choices.

---

The magic in giving choices
astounds persons.

---

Teachers and parents have reported similar results with youngsters. One such illustration comes from a teacher who was bothered by a pupil who persistently rocked back on his chair. In spite of warnings about school rules, the pupil would tip the chair back on the two legs. Eventually the teacher asked if he would like to sit on all four legs like the other pupils or sit on just the two legs. He indicated that he would prefer to use just two. She placed two books under the front legs so that the chair tilted back at a safe but uncomfortable angle. After a time, he removed the books and there was no further problem during the remainder of the year. In this case, the teacher wisely offered a choice and creatively established a logical consequence.

## Action, Not Words

Another important aspect to the successful implementation of natural and logical consequences is that action, not words, helps ensure that fewer misunderstandings will follow. In the last example, once the choice was made, the teacher said no more. Especially when the boy decided to remove the books and be seated properly, her attention to other matters made it clear that she was not concerned about having her way. Had she made any comments, she could have run the risk of being misunderstood even though she may have meant well. Adults, no less than children, appreciate being allowed to cooperate quietly without fanfare when they decide it is once again in their best interest.

## NEW RULES

As noted earlier, every group, organization, or family has rules that influence the behavior of its members. What is appropriate to that group of persons interacting with one another becomes learned through a variety of responses by its members. I wish to call attention to the value of new rules based on the philosophy and values of a socially equalitarian democracy. The old rules tend to be predicated upon an authoritarian philosophy and value system that deny or thwart the rights and respect for those under the influence of those in power. Contrary to what authoritarians argue, chaos is not the outcome of shared rights and responsibilities. I share Dreikurs' desire to have all leaders of social institutions learn the methods and techniques of social democracy. Such leaders include parents, teachers, business executives, and politicians.

The practical application of new rules in a family, classroom, or business can result in greater empowerment of individuals to work for not only their success but that of the group. Logical consequences, as will be illustrated in the activities at the end of this chapter, often require thoughtfulness and creativity. Both of these are qualities well within the capabilities of most parents as well as others who are in positions of leadership. New rules deliberately designed to empower, to show respect, and to expect responsible, common sense decisions will change the family, classroom, and work environment. Each will become a setting in which conflicts can be resolved, where diversity because of culture, gender, or similar factors will be assets, and where each person experiences higher self-esteem through personal contributions and collaboration.

## SUMMARY

Logical consequences, as noted in this chapter, are powerful influences upon the development of individuals and groups. Adlerians raise consciousness to their use in positive, empowering ways. Rather than techniques to merely shape and modify another's behavior, they are means for liberating discouraged persons from the bondage of self defeating attitudes, emotions, and behaviors. They empower and encourage through choices, responsibility, and respect.

## STUDY QUESTIONS

**Directions:** Respond to the following in the spaces provided.

1. List four or more distinctions between consequences and punishment.

2. Cite two or more illustrations from your experience that you can now distinguish as natural versus logical consequences.

3. Why should logical consequences apply to everyone in a common social group? What problems develop if they do not?

4. When are logical consequences likely to be least effective?

## ACTIVITIES

Logical consequences are the logical outcome of an ill-advised act and require the intervention of another person to ensure their impact. Normally, the individual has one or more alternative choices to a given situation. The logical relationship of the act to outcome helps the individual accept responsibility for the misjudgment and its subsequent correction.

**Examples:**

| Action | Logical Consequence |
|---|---|
| Child does not get dressed in the morning | No breakfast if adult must use time to help with dressing instead of making breakfast |

> Child leaves clothes lying in hallway      Others may put them where they please

I.  A.  List one or more logical consequences to each of the following. Ask yourself, What happens if someone intervenes? What happens if that becomes a rule for everyone (i.e., what if the logic of how to behave is mimicked)?

| **Action** | **Logical Consequence** |
|---|---|
| 1. Uses others' materials, equipment, or clothes without permission | |
| 2. Neglects to inform others where he or she is going, when he or she will return, and so forth | |
| 3. Persistently allows supplies to run low (e.g., car low on gas when it is returned) | |

4. Comes to regularly scheduled activities late (e.g., reading circle, class, or family meetings)

5. Does not listen to instructions the first time

6. Regularly solicits assistance after bedtime or at other times inconvenient to others

7. When called to come in, never comes the first time

8. Does not carry out trash, cut grass, and so forth, without being nagged or threatened

B.  Share your list of logical consequences with the group and participate in discussion.

II. A.  Identify three or more logical consequences that have been used successfully to help you or others experience the outcome of ill-advised behavior. Did others intervene? Was a "new rule" adopted?

| Ill-Advised Behavior | Logical Consequence Experienced |
|---|---|
| 1. | |
| 2. | |
| 3. | |

B. Share your responses with your partner or group members. Do others agree that the consequences you listed are logical consequences? Why or why not? Discuss other participants' responses.

## Chapter 5

# ENCOURAGEMENT: THE KEY TO CHANGE— THE ESSENTIAL ELEMENT OF HELPING

In John Kennedy's *Profiles in Courage* (1956), he described events surrounding acts of courage by legislators who found themselves at significant moments in history, unpopular with the constituents who had voted them into office. In each case, Kennedy illustrated how these individuals rose above partisan politics and the prevailing social practices of the day to act on principles fundamental to a better society. Not all of them had been true to the public trust throughout their careers, quite the contrary. On the other hand, several faced certain defeat and potential bodily harm if they acted counter to the popular opinion. When they did speak out, for example, against slavery, all of the negative consequences one would expect befell them. Kennedy believed that everyone has such opportunities in their lives when they must look into their own souls to determine how they shall act.

The cultivation of that quality which prompts one to act responsibly, deliberately, and with conviction is the subject of this chapter. Sometimes it is evident when one is faced with negative consequences and acts to serve a greater good than personal advantage. Equally important, it frees one to live fully as an active participant each moment of each day.

The essential element in the concept of encouragement is courage. Gandhi said,

> Courage is the one sure foundation of character. Without courage there can be no morality, no religion, no love. One cannot follow truth or love so long as one is subject to fear. (Nehru, 1958, p. i)

It is that quality of approaching life courageously that raises individuals' consciousness to the beauty all around them, to the intrinsic value in a new experience, or to the satisfaction in making a new discovery or mastering new skill. Optimally, everyone would greet each day as a new opportunity with an expectation that regardless of temporary negative circumstances, they would not only survive but thrive in the future. Not because of some good fortune but because they choose to perceive life in this manner, it would be true for them.

---

Individuals create their own expectations
of how life will treat them and how well
they will respond.

---

Increasingly, research and clinical experience tend to corroborate the observations of Adler. He noted that individuals create their expectations of how life will treat them and how well they will respond. Basically, people tend to place themselves in one of two broad categories. One group perceives themselves as captains of their ship or masters of their own destiny. By contrast, others deny that they can do much more than avoid a catastrophe from circumstances beyond their control. The latter group may take either passive or active attitudes and behavior (i.e., accepting their fate or challenging whatever force[s] they perceive as creating constraints). Persons in the passive group tend toward a disruptive behavior goal of inadequacy. Other such goals are discussed in chapter 6.

Even as adults, some people deny responsibility for meeting life's tasks. They ask innocently, How could I assume responsibility for events over which I have no control? The active group, by contrast, tests for the limits. Daredevils, gamblers, and criminals of various sorts all tend to have a desire to "beat the odds," to experience a personal triumph in the face of a compelling force. In their discouragement, they have mistaken the meaning of their acts as something noble or necessary in order to be somebody of worth in an otherwise oppressive environment.

Obviously, there are matters of degree in the two broad categories. Witness the number of persons who subscribe to horoscope services or carry good luck charms. Many of these same people ostensibly believe in "free will" as a gift of the Creator. One is not surprised, then, by the variety and degrees of behavior that reflect discouragement in one's attitude toward coping with new or difficult life situations.

Early childhood experiences increase the probability but *do not determine* the orientation that a person assumes toward life. For example, the socialization process includes teaching children what is inappropriate or harmful. Adlerians believe that in order for children to develop into self-confident, healthy adults, they also need to know that you have faith in their abilities and that you accept them for who they are, not only what they do.

Children tend to be constantly reminded of their limitations. Consider the 4-year-old who can't reach the faucet, see the top of the counter, needs help cutting his food, and cannot quite snap his pants after going to the bathroom. Adults expect children to need help and know that they will soon be able to take care of themselves. In the eyes of a child, however, never having experienced full self-reliance, these temporary limitations can be perceived as signs of inferiority.

Given consistent encouragement, one can increase the probability that children will accept these shortcomings for what they are and keep trying to do their best. They will decide that, although they sometimes fail at what they attempt, this does not mean that they are a failure. By contrast, children whose limitations are exaggerated through comparison to siblings, who experiences overprotection or other responses that impart a lack of respect and faith in them as an individual, may grow up feeling that they are inferior or otherwise unequal to the business of life.

## ON BELIEVING IN ONE'S SELF

Literature on biofeedback research and stress management clearly demonstrate the capacity of individuals to create the moods and emotions that they wish to experience (Witmer & Sweeney, 1992). They also lend empirical data to Adler's assumption that emotions are tools to help people achieve their goals. By purposely practicing body relaxation and positive mental images, individual's learn to overcome debilitating stress resulting from real or imagined circumstances. In fact, research has established that the body's responses to perceived images does not distinguish between those experiences that are vicarious and those that are real. The body responds in the same way, for example, to imagined or real stressors if the individual believes that a real threat is imminent. On the other hand, application of these same principles helps persons who experience chronic pain to overcome its negative impact on other aspects of their lives.

In my experience, discouraged persons have difficulty setting goals and having faith in themselves to do what the situation requires for them to be successful. There are what I consider situational or temporary conditions to which individuals respond with discouragement. The loss of a loved one, illness, prolonged fatigue, lack of proper nutrition, and such contribute to discouragement. The high-social-interest person tends to become less discouraged (i.e., less depressed), less prone to persist in withdrawal, and more likely to begin helping others as a means of overcoming their grief. They choose to redirect themselves, establish new goals and new expectations, and regain satisfaction in the relatively simple, readily available satisfactions in life.

The low-social-interest person tends to use the situational or temporary conditions as an excuse for not acting responsibly and, when called for, with courage. A societal consequence of this circumstance is millions of dollars each year spent on sustenance for persons who have psychologically dropped out of society as a contributing member. Not everyone on welfare is low in social interest any more than everyone who is gainfully employed is high in social interest. As an imperfect society, although still better than many, the United States has yet to secure social equality for all of its people and thereby contributes to the very discouragement that it wishes to ameliorate. A practical social consequence of this lack of equality is lost talent, lawlessness, and expenditure of resources for corrective purposes rather than prevention. Another way to address this lack of courage and the conviction of believing in one's capacities to cope is through the concept of self-esteem.

## SELF-ESTEEM

The concept of self-esteem is often explained in terms of self-acceptance and self-respect. In some popular literature, positive self-talk practiced throughout the day is portrayed as a technique for overcoming poor self-concept. Were change that easy or the explanations quite so simple, there would be little need for so many books, workshops, and speakers on the topic of self-esteem!

The foremost authority and pioneer in research on the topic of self-esteem, Nathaniel Branden (1994), stated that self-esteem is

> 1. confidence in our ability to think, confidence in our ability to cope with the basic challenges of life; and 2. confidence in our right to be successful and happy, the feeling of being worthy, deserving, entitled to assert our needs and wants, achieve our values, and enjoy the fruits of our efforts. (p. 4)

Positive self-worth is central to experiencing positive self-esteem, but it is an achievement earned by meeting life's tasks on a day-to-day basis, often without great fanfare or acknowledgment by others. Achievement is both a product and promoter of what is called self-efficacy. Self-efficacy is confidence in one's ability to reason, problem solve, think creatively and cope with the basic tasks of life. This is not done in a vacuum.

Choices must be made. One is, for example, correct or incorrect, honest or dishonest, courageous or cowardly in what one does. The effect of these choices and actions on one's sense of worth varies not only at the time but over time. One's sense of worth can increase or diminish depending on choices made. As a consequence, responsibility for one's sense of worth involves much more than "feel good" thoughts. Moral decision making, action, and honesty with oneself are keys to a genuine foundation for a positive sense of self worth.

In my experiences over many years of counseling and teaching, I have found that most individuals discount their competencies, accomplishments, and capabilities to cope—far more than claiming unwarranted success. In fact, the worst prejudice that counselees hold is the faulty self-evaluations of themselves. One of the counselor's most important contributions to a counselee is to help her or him discover and celebrate the genuinely positive attributes and accomplishments already present or achieved. On the other hand, helping counselees to learn and act on sound decision making provides them with the tools that they require to not only sustain but enhance their sense of worth.

## Consequences of Self-Esteem

Self-esteem is the result of a human process so fundamental that it is a part of what constitutes human nature. From the time of birth, one begins experiencing life as pleasurable, satisfying, safe, supportive, or not. Individuals are alert to signs that convey what they can expect from others, their own efforts, and life in general. Although this process of seeking cues continues throughout people's lives, their earliest experiences tend to establish the expectations that will guide them throughout the remainder of their lives.

As a consequence, people tend to filter new experiences according to their expectations. Equally important, they create new experiences that will reinforce their self-fulfilling prophesies about themselves, others, and life. Left unchallenged and unexamined, their early self-assessments tend to guide their thoughts, emotions, and actions much like an autopilot that has been preprogrammed to a distance destination. Therefore, early life experiences are the repository of anticipation of future success or lack thereof in meeting life tasks. Individuals with a positive sense of worth tend to approach their basic life tasks with a confidence and expectation that they will be successful and happy in all that they do. This fundamental difference between individuals with high and low sense of worth also explains the power of these convictions.

As Branden (1994) noted, more than a feeling or judgment, positive self-assessment is a motivator. It inspires one to act when others hesitate. Apart from generalities, however, individuals also tend to differentiate between those activities and tasks that they prefer, find easier to do, and receive encouragement for in their interactions with others. When functioning within those areas of talent, interest and experience, confidence and action are reinforced both intrinsically and extrinsically. Contrary to what some authors and speakers may propose, there are no gimmicks to developing and sustaining a positive sense of worth. It is vital to a happy life but it is earned one day at a time, one choice at a time.

In an extensive presentation of the attributes and processes associated with self-esteem, Branden (1994) identified what he calls the "pillars of self-esteem." He identified them as

1. *Living consciously:* to seek to be aware of everything that bears on my actions, purposes, values, and goals—to the best of my ability, whatever that ability may be—and to behave in accordance with that which I see and know.

2. *Practicing self-acceptance:* (a) to be on my own side—to be for myself; (b) to make real to myself, without denial

or evasion, that I think what I think, feel what I feel, desire what I desire, have done what I have done, and am what I am; a refusal to regard any part of myself—my body, my emotions, my thoughts, my actions, my dreams—as anything but a legitimate part of me; (c) to accept responsibility for my errors and wrongdoings but with compassionate interest in the motives that prompted them. Accepting, compassionate interest does not encourage undesired behavior but instead reduces the likelihood of it recurring.

3. *Practicing self-responsibility:* to take responsibility for my actions and the attainment of my goals. It is essential to experiencing self-control and competency and being worthy of happiness.

4. *Practicing self-assertiveness:* the willingness to stand up for myself, to be who I am openly, and to treat myself with respect in all human encounters.

5. *Practicing living purposefully:* to use my powers of attainment of goals I have selected in all spheres of my life— studying, working, parenting, love relationships, leisure activities—and in small as well as large matters of life.

6. *Practicing personal integrity:* to be able to answer affirmatively to such questions as: Am I honest, reliable, and trustworthy? Do I keep my promises? Do I do the things that I say I admire and not do the things that I say I deplore? Am I fair and just in my dealings with others?

7. Acting courageously and persistently on the first six pillars of self-esteem when to do so may not be easy.

The remainder of this chapter is devoted to methods and techniques of intervention designed to encourage others. A first step is to assess readiness for change in an effort to ascertain the appropriate intervention for the individual developmentally.

## ASSESSMENT AND INTERVENTION

### Readiness for Change

Assessment is never complete unless a readiness for change is also noted. In this instance, the operative word is readiness. Readiness may be determined through dialogue on issues related to the topics and items above, follow through on suggestions for "homework" tasks and activities, or, for example, evidence and reports of persistence with behavior change when to make excuses would have been understandable.

The following are readiness levels on which to base a decision to proceed with further work and for determining the types of activities to suggest:

*Level 1: Pre-awareness.* Individuals are not aware of their responsibility related to self-defeating attitudes or behaviors.

*Level 2: Awareness.* Individuals are aware that they have some responsibility for the nature of their life experiences, relationships, and challenges, but they are uncertain about what to do to change and have not made a commitment to change.

*Level 3: Anticipatory.* Attitudes and behaviors that illustrate that individuals are willing to commit to change for better self-directed health are candidates for proceeding with the development of a plan for change.

*Level 4: Action.* This is the level at which individuals demonstrate a readiness to develop healthier attitudes and behaviors through the implementation of a plan for change.

*Level 5: Maintenance.* Such individuals are fully aware of their responsibility and opportunity to direct their attitudes and behaviors in healthful and satisfying ways.

## Interventions by Readiness Stage

Each of the levels of readiness requires a different kind of intervention and follow through. The following discussion of intervention levels addresses general considerations according to readiness for change with respect to self-esteem. They are appropriate for consideration of any personal plan for change. They are based in part on the work of Prochaska and DiClemente (1984), who found that both self-change and counseling-induced change stages have similarities that represent attitudes, intentions, and behaviors related to an individual's status in the cycle of change. Ascertaining the stage of change of a counselee helps the counselor choose interventions more likely to be effective and realistic with regard to the counselee's readiness for change.

**Intervention Stage 1: Pre-Awareness.** At this stage, individuals do not recognize that they have a problem. Others often can recognize the need and, indeed, may insist on counseling as a remedy. If there is some degree of cooperation, individuals may be asked to discuss life experiences that have contributed to their self-evaluation of worth (e.g., parents, siblings, friends, teachers, acquaintances, and coworkers). An exploration of events over time (i.e., from childhood to the present) will reveal both overt and covert messages of self-esteem assimilated into the self-talk of the individual.

Identifying and focusing on such messages opens the entire realm of how one can live life "as if" someone else were in control and whose opinions are the only ones that are valid. The major purpose of these interventions is to raise consciousness to self-defeating attitudes and behaviors and their negative consequences to living life more fully. It is worth noting that some individuals will respond positively to this type of dialogue and express a desire to immediately embark on change. One caution is to move slowly at first and, after expressing a willingness to accompany them through the change process, even suggest that they may not be ready for change (i.e., old attitudes and habits are familiar, even useful, and have been supported by years of self-fulfilling expectations as well as those of others).

One homework assignment is to develop a list of challenges to change using categories and topics like those discussed in antecedents of sense of worth (e.g., personal, family, friends, society, and so forth), attitudes, and behaviors. Likewise, assets for change is another list that can be developed and supplemented over time. Discussion of these lists is valuable in raising awareness to the desirability of change (see benefits of positive self-esteem above) and the agents for and against change.

**Intervention Stage 2: Awareness.** Based on prior discussions and behaviors, the counselor may move into a more formal assessment. The WEL items found in Appendix A on sense of worth or the "pillars of self-esteem" above may be used to draw attention to an essential component of self-esteem. Discussions will help to fortify emotional as well as informational arousal associated with positive change. The outcome of this intervention will be a clear awareness of the antecedents and consequences of one's sense of worth, the self-talk and emotional states associated with the current sense of worth, and a growing conviction that change will be worth any effort required.

**Intervention Stage 3: Anticipatory.** As with each of the first stages of readiness and intervention, preparation for change is essential to successful outcomes. The development of a plan for change will address goals (clearly stated and attainable), include successive approximations to the goals including emotional and behavioral benefits, and provide a calendar for starting, evaluating progress, celebrating gains and effort, and refining and sustaining target outcomes. Help with anticipating the antecedents of old behaviors and accompanying emotions fortifies individuals for the likelihood of being inclined to rely on the more familiar unhealthy coping strategies. Thought stopping (i.e., catching one's self in the moment of irrational thoughts and feelings) is a useful technique and can be practiced during counseling sessions. Another technique is rehearsing situations that will arise and role-playing new behaviors until an emotional arousal of positive feelings is present.

Environment changes likely will be necessary as well. Old friends, places frequented, and so forth will need to be avoided and new associations identified for support of the new, healthy behaviors. In the likely event that family members are a part of the old environment in which poor self-evaluation occurred, a family intervention at some point can be very important if not essential in some cases. The conclusion of this intervention level should result in a feeling and conviction that success is possible with action and the benefits are well worth the effort.

In a realm somewhat unfamiliar to professional helpers except those with religious preparation as well, there are those instances when it is a forgiving spirit that must be addressed (Simon & Simon, 1990). To err is human, the saying goes, to forgive is divine. Adlerian counselors are inclined to note that "guilt feelings are for good intentions that we do not have." Stated another way, if one can truly say that one is sorry and will not do it again, then guilt feelings are not necessary. Regret, yes, restitution, maybe, but guilt feelings (and low self-esteem), no. Go forth and do good might well be the new focus. Helping others to thoughtfully and emotionally address these sources of low self-esteem may be critically important to change. Equally important, there may be a need to lower anxiety over possible (if not likely) relapses to old habits.

**Intervention Stage 4: Action.** Implementation of a plan of action is truly a commitment to stopping old familiar ways of thinking, feeling, and behaving and establishing new ways for solving old problems. For this to be possible, the plan must be put into action with known points for reassessment, refinement, and celebration. Encouragement throughout is possible by focusing on assets, effort, indications of progress, patience with inconsistency, forgiveness for errors, and rewards for small as well as large gains in change.

**Intervention Stage 5: Maintenance.** There are at least two kinds of situations that could merit intervention at this level. First, an individual has successfully implemented a plan of action, has experienced success, and is prepared to explore other dimensions of a healthy lifestyle. The second kind of situation could involve individuals who already experience positive thoughts and emotions in this area but desire suggestions for enhancing and affirming them in their healthy thoughts and habits.

As is true of all dimensions of wellness, one does not arrive at a state of optimum functioning as in earning an award. The process is ongoing, life long, and continually in need of nurturing. Therefore, recommendations for enhancing and sustaining a healthy sense of worth can prepare individuals for the days and transitions in their lives when they may be tested by life circumstances and others to the very depths of their personhood. Lists of books, multimedia tapes, workshops, and so forth that address topics on sense of worth, self-esteem, and related topics may be suggested for a diet of regular support. Journaling is another method used to help individuals remain reflective and introspective on a continuing basis.

## Self-Development Application

In the event that the reader is interested in this area for self-development or in helping to guide someone else, the following steps and suggestions are offered in preparation for developing and implementing a plan of action:

1. *Readiness and self-assessment.* Self-help has its benefits and its shortcomings. Objectivity is always an issue. However, it is the subjective that is truly most important to all of us. Whether I "like" myself or not is purely subjective. Others, whose opinions are also subjective, may refute or corroborate my opinion but it is my opinion that affects my emotions and my actions. Optimally, I will value myself positively and others will reinforce this conviction. At the outset, however, there is a good chance that if I have a low sense of worth, I have been too hard on myself and others have done little to improve this opinion.

   Using the following descriptions, determine at what level of readiness you consider yourself to be at this moment:

   *Level 1: Pre-Awareness.* If you are attempting this activity, you have passed this level. Congratulations!

   *Level 2: Awareness.* Although I do not have the sense of worth that I desire, I have few or no ideas of what to do about changing it. (If you have read and understood the material in this chapter, you have most likely passed this level. Congratulations again! If, however, you skimmed or overlooked the earlier material, this may be a good time to go back to the beginning of the chapter and study it more deliberately.)

*Level 3: Anticipatory.* If you have found reading material such as this chapter interesting and potentially useful, you may be at this level, especially if you are thinking about applying it to your own life.

*Level 4: Action.* If you have been planning some specific changes in your thoughts, feelings, and behaviors that should result in a more positive sense of worth, you are a candidate for change.

*Level 5: Maintenance.* If you have a basically positive sense of worth on most occasions and circumstances, you may be interested primarily in means to reaffirm and enhance those convictions.

2. *Developing a plan of action.* Individuals at levels 3, 4, and 5 are different in their entry level but each is prepared to develop a plan of action. People who use outlines, lists, and other such specificity have a higher probability of achieving their goals. Therefore, we encourage even the most laid back, live-and-let-live persons to prepare a written plan. For those who are truly at level 3 or higher, the following are elements of a plan for your use:

a. Assessment: Summarize in short descriptive statements or phrases the extent to which you feel or think you

   i. are confident in your ability to think, confident in your ability to cope with the basic challenges of life (i.e., work/school, friendship/social, love/family);

   ii. are confident in your right to be successful and happy;

   iii. feel worthy, deserving, and entitled to assert your needs and wants, achieve your values;

iv. enjoy the fruits of your efforts; and

v. are confident in your ability to reason, problem solve, think creatively, and cope with the basic tasks of life (Branden, 1994, p. 4).

### Example

I think that I usually think clearly about most issues in my life. There are times, however, when I feel uncertain about when my "wants" are selfish versus natural and deserved. At these times, I doubt my right to pleasure, enjoyment, or satisfaction.

I seem to be respected and liked at work. My close friends are few but that's really okay. My family life is not perfect (i.e., my mother and I disagree about the proper rearing of my children, but I am comfortable with my way of doing it). My spouse and I respect and love each other but since the children, we have become somewhat insulated from expressing our wants (particularly sexually) and needs (for companionship). At times, I wonder if it's me (not desirable) or just circumstances or both. I guess that part of my feelings are related to not speaking about it to my spouse in case I don't like what I hear (that I'm not particularly desirable, fun, interesting, etc.).

b. Develop focus areas: Using your assessment summary, identify key words and concepts to develop a list of specific thoughts, feelings, and behaviors that will

i. affirm your self-esteem,

ii. enhance your self-esteem, or

iii. challenge your self-esteem.

### Example

i. Affirmations

I think clearly, problem solve, and make appropriate decisions in most situations.

I am a competent, dependable worker.

I have friends who like me and I like them.

I think of myself as a competent parent.

My spouse and I respect and love one another.

ii. Enhancements

I can solve new problems or challenges in my life.

I have resources (self and others) that will help me.

I have a right to enjoy the fruits of my labor.

iii. Challenges

I have doubts about my expectations for my spouse.

I am reluctant to talk about my wants and needs.

I am afraid to find out my spouse may find me less desirable.

My hesitancy to address these issues with my spouse makes me feel bad about myself.

c. Focus on desired change: In simple but specific language, state what you want to happen to improve your self-esteem.

**Example**

I want to address my concerns about our mutual marital wants and needs in an open, honest, and loving way.

d. Plan: State what you are willing to do, when, and under what circumstances.

**Example**

What: I will initiate a conversation with my spouse regarding the "insulating" that I feel. I will use my best problem-solving abilities to introduce this as a discussion from which both of us can feel better and contribute to greater intimacy in our relationship.

When and under what circumstances: I will plan this for an evening this week (Wednesday) when we can have a baby sitter and dinner out together without the interruptions of the kids.

3. *Considerations during implementation.* Create a supportive environment, minimize negative contacts, celebrate progress, and emphasize assets that will further enhance the desired change and/or sustain desired thoughts, feelings, and behavior.

**Example**

We have married friends whose company we enjoy. All of us laugh a lot in good fun. I will help set a time for us to be together in the near future (preferably within the week).

4. *Considerations for maintenance.* Plan for the necessary resources, habits, and so forth that will be required to sustain your progress.

**Example**

Evenings used to be a time for us to share what had gone on during the day, to unwind, and to feel close to each other. I am going to suggest that we start doing this again on a regular basis. This will mean getting the kids to bed and agreeing to no interruptions except in unusual circumstances.

This plan is only representative of the kinds of thoughts, feelings, and behaviors that can be addressed. The statements and activities are designed to empower the individual. Self-efficacy is enhanced. Problem solving is paired with desired outcomes including positive emotions. They are deliberately set within achievable timelines and realistic behaviors. Achieving the desired thoughts, feelings, and behaviors in small increments helps to ensure success. Within the context of a more comprehensive educational or treatment plan, progress toward establishing and sustaining a positive sense of worth is increased.

## DEFINITION AND ASSUMPTIONS

Encouragement inspires or helps others toward a conviction that they can work on finding solutions and that they can cope with any predicament. Some basic assumptions about encouragement are extensions of the concepts presented in chapter 1 concerning high and low social interest.

The following principles apply to encouragement with regard to someone's actions. Each principle is followed by an example of an encouraging statement (E) and an example of a discouraging statement (D).

1. *What* one is doing is more important than how one is doing it.

    E:  That's a beautiful shine on your car. What did you do to get it that way?

    D:  I'll bet you take better care of your car than anyone else in town. (comparing)

2. The *present* is the focus more so than the past or future.

    E:  It's obvious that you're really enjoying this project by the time and energy that you're giving to it.

    D:  Now why don't you work this hard all the time?!

3. The *deed* is what is important rather than the doer.

> E:  I really appreciate your help. Thanks!

> D:  You're such a good boy. You always do the right thing!

*or* when correcting

> E:  I really feel angry when you ask for food and then don't eat it.

> D:  You're always wasting food—you're just plain irresponsible.

4. The *effort* is to be emphasized rather than the outcome.

> E:  By golly, I enjoyed that game. If I can just learn to be more patient and not rush the ball, next time I should be able to give you a better match! (emphasis on progress, what to do, and enjoying increased competence)

> D:  You were lucky this time, but I'll beat you for sure next time, no matter what it takes! (it's winning that counts!)

5. *Intrinsic* motivation (i.e., satisfaction, enjoyment, or challenge) rather than extrinsic motivation (i.e., reward or punishment) is expressed.

> E:  I spend hours taking pictures. Nothing gives me more pleasure than capturing a moment in time that reflects the beauty in life!

> D:  What do I get for doing it? What's in it for me?

6. What is *being learned* matters more than what is not being learned.

> E:  You've just about mastered addition and subtraction. That will be very helpful to you in learning division and multi-

plication. Now let's look at a couple of problems that give you difficulty and get you help mastering them.

D:  We're going to have to go on, and you'll need to get help at home or division's going to be hard for you.

7. What is *being done correctly* is stressed more than what is not being done correctly.

E:  You got 84 out of 100 correct on the addition and subtraction problems. With just a little more effort, I know that you'll be able to go on to division and multiplication.

D:  You missed 16 out of a 100.

The encouraging person practices these behaviors until they are genuine and spontaneous. Conversely, many people are prone to discourage others quite unconsciously. I am reminded of a television sports interview that captured the essential difference with respect to intrinsic versus extrinsic motivation as it relates to competition. In this instance, a downhill skier had just lost the championship by literally fractions of a second. Immediately after the results were announced, a commentator interviewed the skier and asked, "You lost the championship by only fractions of a second. Knowing that now, how would you run the race differently?" The skier replied, "I wouldn't. It was a good run. I gave it my best effort and everything went as planned." The commentator continued, "But you lost by only fractions of a second. Might you have pushed off a little harder at the start or attack the track a little differently?" The skier: "Not really. It was an exhilarating run. I did my best. The other fellow just went a little faster!"

The commentator tried again in disbelief to elicit regret or disappointment from the skier. The skier was comfortable, however, that it was a good run, that he had done his best, and to be second, third, or whatever was not his primary criteria. No doubt he would prefer to win. His goal does include winning, but factors exist over which he does not have control (e.g., the other skier going a little faster!). This brings us to another aspect of encouragement that I believe is a unique contribution to an understanding of helping others.

## ESSENCE OF ENCOURAGEMENT

Life circumstances are subject to many factors beyond the control of individuals. Attitudes, expectations, and self-beliefs, however, are within the control of the individual. Assisting individuals to minimize the impact of noncontrollable factors and to maximize their use of controllable factors in enriching their own life experiences is of the essence in helping them.

Uncontrollable factors include, for example, the family into which one is born, the school system, neighborhood, economic environment, talents, handicaps, and physical characteristics shaped by genetic contributions of parents. Many other factors might be considered accidents of nature.

Among the controllable factors, on the other hand, are attitudes toward environmental circumstances, knowledge about self and others, and behavior that supports one's attitudes, expectations, and self-beliefs. Concerning the basic life task of work, for example, career choices (chapter 9), like other personal choices, are in the realm of controllable factors. Maximizing one's control over career choices includes

- developing positive work habits;

- learning the value of purposeful attention to physical appearance;

- learning how to locate, assess, and use career information; and

- developing knowledge and skill with valuing, decision making, goal setting, planning, and follow through.

Minimizing the impact of noncontrollable factors includes

- acquiring information about economic trends and job requirements;

- raising consciousness about social attitudes and practices that can be unnecessary constraints, such as sex stereotyping; and

- seeking out examples of individuals with similar handicaps who overcame them to pursue their career choices.

---

All people start out life with a desire to discover, develop mastery, and enjoy life.

---

In short, a major thrust of encouragement is helping individuals establish goals, attitudes, and competencies they need to cope with life as they experience it. Some adults express concern that this fosters mediocrity in performance. Nothing could be further from the truth. All people start life with a desire to discover, develop mastery, and enjoy life. Through encouragement, one feeds these inclinations and brings them to consciousness to be enjoyed all the more. What parent hasn't experienced a young child saying "No, I want to do it myself"? Who can't recall the deep satisfaction at developing mastery of a new task or problem, whether tying one's shoe or solving a geometry problem?

I often am struck by adults' preoccupation with toilet training, eating habits, and bed times. All these activities involve intrinsic satisfiers (i.e., pleasure, relief, and self-assertiveness). With five children to help rear, I have had many occasions to carry a tired, grumpy young one to bed. On the way, with a head against my shoulder, I speak of how good it's going to feel between the cool, clean sheets—stretching out, curling up, thinking pleasant thoughts—oh, how good it will feel to be rested, and what fun you will have when you get up! All of our children enjoy a good rest!

Likewise, toilet habits are no particular problem. When a youngster is ready to assume responsibility, a little help is all that is needed. Being too impressed with when the baby book says it might happen prompts anxious parents—and kids who know how to elicit more attention and service from a parent who is anxious about such matters. On the other hand, asking children how they feel when they finish heightens awareness of the relief and pleasure involved. You also can talk about the good feelings associated with taking care of oneself.

When one is working on a new task or problem, help in ensuring success is always appreciated. How much help is needed varies with individuals but success does encourage further effort. Inch by inch anything is a cinch! Regardless of age, people enjoy discovery and mastery.

I remember well the experience of helping a 35-year-old Catholic nun learn to water ski. For a nun at that time, to even be seen in public in other than the traditional habit was quite novel. She had been excited, however, by the prospect of learning to water ski since she was a young girl. Not much athletically inclined and also now accustomed to a more sedate life, she struggled time after time to bring herself out of the water. Finally, after many tries, she succeeded in a relatively short but significant ride. The expression of exhilaration on her face could not be explained adequately. Even now, one of her happiest recollections is the day she mastered water skiing. Some may say, "but she never became an accomplished water skier," and that's quite right; however, that was not her goal. The same "true grit" with which she attacked water skiing could be found in other areas of her interests.

The definition of success that I use corresponds to this philosophy. In this case

> Success is the progressive realization of predetermined, worthwhile goals and a well-balanced life.

Success, therefore, is a process not an event. Students in school can consider themselves already successful as they progress through school; not only when they graduate. Parents can consider themselves successful even as they see their children struggling with life's challenges; not only when the "children" graduate from college, get a job, or whatever other event they might otherwise set as a goal. By this definition, planfulness is deliberate. Setting goals and milestones to their achievement is deliberate. Valuing is central to the process as goals are determined to be "worthwhile" by the individual. Finally, there is a balance to such a life; that is, physical health and mental health are maintained through loving family relationships, attention to good eating habits, hygiene, cooperative work relationships, and so forth. With this definition, anyone can be helped to see themselves as successful. Chapter 2 provides a model of wellness based in part on this definition.

If each of us enjoys life, enjoys learning, and strives to be the best we can be at whatever we choose, can anyone ask more? With proper encouragement, more young people will grow up like the skier in the earlier example, capable of being champions in their own minds because they enjoy doing their best at whatever they choose.

## COMMUNICATING ENCOURAGEMENT

Research and experience have revealed that most people are not particularly effective listeners or communicators when others need their help. Being able both to reflect others' feelings and to communicate your own effectively increases the probability that better interpersonal relationships will be established. Most neophyte helpers believe that advice, information, or questions for more specific details are the main tools for helping others. Although these techniques have a place, too, they are what can be called "action" dimensions of helping. When used early in response to others, these techniques actually have been found to be subtractive rather than helpful. They instead discourage the person further. Empathic (feeling) understanding in communicating appears to be a central, necessary condition in a helping relationship. The facilitative dimension of helping, then, is prerequisite to the action dimension.

A vocabulary of feeling terms is listed in Figure 5.1. A review of these terms can be helpful in developing more effective communication skills. Note, for example, which terms you use most

| | | | | |
|---|---|---|---|---|
| absurd | contempt | fervent | intimidated | satisfied |
| adequate | contented | fidgety | joy | scared |
| adventuresome | crushed | fine | jubilant | seductive |
| affectionate | daring | flabbergasted | mad | self-reliant |
| afraid | deflated | flustered | marvelous | sentimental |
| aggravated | dejected | forlorn | meek | skittish |
| agony | delight | fulfilled | melancholy | sorrow |
| agreeable | depressed | gallant | merry | splendid |
| amused | desirable | gay | miserable | stricken |
| angry | despair | ghastly | mortified | stunned |
| anguish | desperate | gladness | numb | sulky |
| animosity | disagreeable | gleeful | obsessed | suspicious |
| anxious | disappointed | good | odd | terror |
| apprehensive | discontented | grateful | offended | thankful |
| ardent | disgust | great | overcome | timid |
| arrogant | disheartened | grief | overjoyed | tormented |
| ashamed | dislike | grouchy | pang | tremendous |
| astounded | disquieted | guilty | peaceful | triumph |
| awful | distrustful | happy | phony | troubled |
| bewitching | disturbed | heartbroken | pleased | trustful |
| bitter | downcast | hopeful | pleasure | uneasy |
| blissful | eager | hopeless | plucky | unfortunate |
| bored | earnest | horrible | proud | unhappy |
| bothered | ecstasy | hostile | regret | unnerved |
| breathless | elated | humble | relaxed | voluptuous |
| buoyant | emotional | humiliated | relived | warm |
| captivated | encouraged | hurt | repelled | weary |
| charming | enraged | impatient | resentment | winsome |
| cheerful | enthusiastic | indifferent | resignation | wistful |
| close | excited | indignation | resolute | witty |
| comfortable | exhilarated | insecure | restless | wonderful |
| complacent | fantastic | insincere | revealing | worried |
| confident | fascinated | inspired | ridiculous | |
| confused | fearful | intimate | sad | |

**Figure 5.1.** Feeling Words.

comfortably and often. As you review the terms, consider how some are more specific and state feelings of greater intensity. For example, instead of "upset," you might say more accurately, "embarrassed," "disappointed," or "angry." Improving your vocabulary helps provide greater resources for you as a facilitative listener and communicator. In my experience, many people lack an adequate vocabulary for this purpose.

When communicating that you have listened to and understand what someone else is experiencing, accuracy, specificity, concreteness, and immediacy are important ingredients. A choice of terms is a major tool in this process. For example, "Even now you feel pleased that you made the proper choice" compared to "Well that's nice. It sounds like you're pretty happy about it."

Study the set of discrimination categories and responses listed in the following section. At the end of the chapter, rate the responses in the self-practice exercises. The purpose of these exercises is to provide basic competency practice in discrimination between responses that are subtractive, interchangeable, and additive. Role playing and guided practice in empathic communication can greatly enhance one's skill.

Also worth noting are the categories and intensity of feelings. For example, feelings can range in types from happy, sad, fearful, uncertain to anger. In addition, the intensity and power of the feelings vary significantly. I recall the following exchange with a 6-year-old:

Counselor:   And when you don't get your way it upsets you.

Child:       It makes me mad!!!

She wanted to make sure that I understood! One can feel excited, jubilant, or thrilled. These are strong feelings, too. On the other hand, one may feel good, cheerful, or optimistic. These are more moderate feelings. By contrast, to say someone is upset tells little without a context. For example, I can be embarrassed, disappointed, angry, or sad. All of these are forms of being upset, but what a difference a suitable response would be to each. Therefore, attention to the nuances in feelings adds intensity and vitality to the communications. This specificity and richness of affective responses facilitates rapport building in a relationship.

## Discrimination Categories and Response Examples for Communications

Stem: I really want to do well in school. I mean, I really try, but . . . I just can't seem to keep up. You know, it's just so hard . . . knowing how to study, doing well on tests, and now writing reports! It really worries me. . . .

### Subtractive.

- Definitely hurtful to sense of belonging, adequacy, or security

Response Example: "You're the kind of person who is always talking but never gets to work. Take your talk somewhere else. I'm busy."

- May simply change the subject, making further subject exploration by speaker difficult or impossible

Response Example: "Yeah, well, that's how it goes. Say, did you see the game last night?"

- Type and/or intensity of feeling ignored; content oriented although not necessarily accurate (e.g., asks for more information or makes specific suggestions without indicating awareness of what was stated)

Response Examples: "So you don't know how to study effectively."

"Have you talked to your teacher about it?"

## Interchangeable.

- Restates content and feeling or, in many cases, reflects feeling tone with only necessary content included; even without the speaker's comments, a third party could determine essentially what was conveyed

Response Examples:   "You're really worried because you can't keep up with your school work no matter how hard you try."

"Doing well is really important to you, but no matter how hard you try, you still can't seem to do well enough."

## Additive.

- Clarifies content and feelings expressed, often stated more succinctly, and increases probability of further exploration by individual; immediacy and specificity are often present

Response Example: "You want to do well, but it's really discouraging and kinda scary because it seems to be getting more difficult all the time."

- Adds new dimensions to exploration of feeling and content by speaker; enhances, for example, speaker's capacity to deal with thoughts and feelings of belonging, adequacy, or security; may be confrontation or action oriented but always within a context of nonpossessive regard and empathy

Response Example: "To do well seems so important, but now you're wondering, can I really do it? Do I have what it takes?"

## Discrimination Exercises for Communications

### Exercise 5.1.

**Directions:** Rate each of the following responses as S (subtractive), I (interchangeable), or A (additive) in their helpfulness to the individual speaking. Check your responses with the key that follows.

Excerpt 1: *My husband comes home tired, complains about how hard he's worked all day and then proceeds to criticize what I haven't gotten done! With three kids and my mother-in-law dropping in several times a week, I'm absolutely beside myself!*

_____ a. Is your mother-in-law aware of how her visits upset your work schedule?

_____ b. Sounds like you need to talk with someone.

_____ c. Your husband's attitude really is insensitive to your situation; just thinking about it makes you angry.

_____ d. I can remember feeling that way myself.

Excerpt 2: *I went in to see my supervisor about a problem I'm having with one of my coworkers. Before I knew what was happening, she was asking me what I'd done to bring this on! After working here for 14 years with no problems, I felt hurt and betrayed.*

_____ a. You really feel betrayed by your supervisor—she completely missed the point of your conference—now you don't think you can trust her.

_____ b. How long has she been with the company?

_____ c. In 14 years, you never had other problems?

_____ d. Your supervisor really hurt you. After all those years of good service, she questions you!

Excerpt 3:    *We had such a really good time at the beach that all my problems seem inconsequential now!*

_____ a:    That was some great trip to the beach! No problem seems too big or important that it can't be handled!

_____ b.    Which one did you go to?

_____ c.    How can you say that after all the money you must have spent!

_____ d.    Sounds like you're still enjoying it and all your problems seem less important!

Excerpt 4:    *After living with us almost as a member of the family for over a dozen years, our dog died this weekend and I still keep looking for him—expecting him to greet me when I come home. I feel so bad and yet I know he was just an animal.*

_____ a.    It seems hard to explain, but that dog was a member of the family. You miss him and really feel bad not having him there when you come home.

_____ b.    I know how you feel. I once had a parakeet I felt that way about.

_____ c.    Was he hit by a car or something?

_____ d.    There must be a lot of people who feel that way; haven't you heard about animal cemeteries?

| Key: | a. | b. | c. | d. |
|------|----|----|----|----|
| 1.   | S  | S  | A  | S  |
| 2.   | A  | S  | S  | I  |
| 3.   | I  | S  | S  | I  |
| 4.   | I  | S  | S  | S  |

### Exercise 5.2.

**Directions:** Rate each of the following responses as S (subtractive), I (interchangeable), or A (additive) in their helpfulness to the individual speaking. Check your responses with the key that follows. (The first two excerpts are from a child; the rest are from an adult.)

Excerpt 1:  *Boy, is she ever a great teacher! I mean she really makes coming to school fun. She even makes me feel that trying the problems is the best part!*

_____ a.  Wow, she sure is some kind of great teacher! I even feel like I'd like to be in her class, too!

_____ b.  How does she do that?

_____ c.  She's so great that even the toughest problems seem like fun. . . . It must be really exciting to be in her class!

_____ d.  Do you think the other kids like her class, too?

Excerpt 2:  *I don't ever get a chance to talk about the things I like. The other girls always pick their friends as discussion leaders. It isn't fair, and they just don't care, either.*

_____ a.  Why don't you tell them how you feel?

_____ b.  The other girls really make you feel bad when they purposely leave you out of the discussion.

_____ c.  It really doesn't seem fair for the other girls to exclude you from the discussion by always talking about their interests.

_____ d.  Aren't you being a little oversensitive? You have the same vote as the other girls and the same opportunity.

Excerpt 3: *The things we talked about at the last team meeting really worked! I can't get over it! Only one day later and already I can see an improvement. I really think we've hit a bonanza!*

_____ a.     Hey, that's wonderful! Sounds like you're right on top of this situation and really enjoying it.

_____ b.     Well, don't be too disappointed if things don't go as well tomorrow.

_____ c.     You'll have to tell us more about it at the next meeting.

_____ d.     What a great feeling! Only one day and things are already going better! Let's share it with everyone else!

Excerpt 4: *I really don't understand what's happened to Mary lately. She seems distant . . . unwilling to talk with me like we used to . . . with drugs and such so much in the news now, I don't know what to think.*

_____ a.     You feel worried about Mary's reluctance to confide in you as she used to . . . you're not at all sure what it could mean.

_____ b.     You really shouldn't worry; girls Mary's age all go through that stage.

_____ c.     Would you like me to get you a copy of a new government booklet on drugs? Maybe that would put your mind at ease.

_____ d.     It's upsetting to have Mary being distant with you . . . you feel somewhat powerless to help her at a time when she may benefit most from your guidance.

Excerpt 5:   *I'm sick and tired of always having to make do with second-rate materials. If they don't think enough of us as teachers, the least they could do is think of the kids. It's the same old story every year, "Well, you know we're on an austerity budget"!*

_____ a.   Yeah, it was that way at the last school where I taught, too.

_____ b.   I agree with you.

_____ c.   It's really frustrating to try doing a decent job of teaching with second-rate materials. . . . The least they could do is think of the kids.

_____ d.   It really is sad to think of how this affects the kids' school experience and no one in authority even seems to care . . .

## I Messages

Another aspect of verbal communication that deserves mention relates to minimizing the negative aspects of sharing angry or confrontative feelings. The basic principles involve "I messages" instead of "you messages." In lieu of nagging, complaining, or blaming, simply communicate the feelings that another's specific behavior tends to prompt in you. "I messages" (a) describe the behavior that is bothersome, (b) state your feeling about the consequence the behavior produces for you, and (c) include the consequence to you. Note the following example:

Behavior:   When you don't fill the car up with gas after using it

| Key: | a. | b. | c. | d. |
|------|----|----|----|----|
| 1. | A | S | I | S |
| 2. | S | I | I | S |
| 3. | I | S | S | A |
| 4. | I | S | S | A |
| 5. | S | S | I | I |

Feeling:      I feel angry.

Consequence:  Because I am delayed in getting to my office or appointment when I leave in the morning.

Compare the preceding statement to the following: "Well, you did it again! When are you going to start acting responsibly? I was late to work because the car had no gas in the tank!"

Not unlike logical consequences, using the "I message" formula while angry and visibly upset decreases its effectiveness. If your goal, however, is to maintain respect among all parties involved, you increase the probabilities that a successful solution can be found. As will be noted in the chapters on child guidance (chapter 6) and family consultation (chapter 11), being able to express one's genuine feelings, even angry feelings, can be facilitative when respect is inherent in the relationship. The fact that you are angry (or really happy) reflects your level of genuine interest and valuing. To show a continuing desire to work toward a satisfactory solution without warfare actually contributes to greater trust, intimacy, and respect.

I believe that the truly successful resolution of differences and conflict builds stronger, better relationships whether at work, among friends, or in marriage. In fact, differences can be seen as an opportunity instead of a threat to closer relationships. The practice of the methods and techniques of encouragement and conflict resolution increase the likelihood of healthier, more satisfying relationships.

**Further Application**

As noted at the beginning of this chapter, there are as many applications of these methods as there are social conflicts. With respect to adult relationships, the same steps are followed although techniques will vary. The most commonly violated aspect of conflict resolution concerns the first step, mutual respect. When one believes that someone else is mistaken or has done something wrong, one tends to begin the interaction by asking accusatory

questions, blaming, or pointing out the error, which tends to undermine the other person's sense of belonging, security, or adequacy. Action statements follow as to what should be done to correct the situation. Even though the suggestions may address what the situation requires to correct it, the violation of step one almost precludes successful resolution. Winning and losing become the outcome of such situations.

On the other hand, if mutual respect is established through active listening, good eye contact, and empathic communication, the other steps may not be executed optimally but the situation can still be resolved satisfactorily. When others perceive openness, flexibility, and respect as elements of efforts to solve differences, there is a much greater probability of success in achieving a satisfactory outcome.

Another way of expressing concern about another's behavior and/or attitudes can be characterized as facilitative confrontations. On occasion, sharing perceptions can be growth producing and helpful even though the perceptions speak to aspects of the person that one may find uncomfortable. I recall one such instance when an undergraduate in my human relations class had distinguished herself as the class clown. She was always good for a laugh. After getting to know her during the quarter, we had a conference concerning her relatively poor performance with the class assignments. I had noted that often she was the butt end of her pranks and jokes. I asked:

Counselor:    I wonder why you end up being the one everyone looks to for a laugh. Do you know?

Student:       No, I really don't.

Counselor:    I wonder, could it be that so long as you're good for a laugh, no one needs to take you seriously . . . that they keep you in your place as sorority or class clown because they feel more comfortable not considering your opinions, how you feel, what makes you happy . . . or sad . . .

Student:     (silent but pensive) . . . I've never quite put it that way before but I have wondered . . . do they really like me, no, do they respect me as a person. You think, "hey, does anybody care that I might not be here next quarter 'cause I'm flunking my courses?" . . . Yeah, that's it! (smiles) . . . so I'm the court jester, good for a laugh . . . I'll be darned!

Counselor:   Quite a discovery, but you know what . . . [no] . . . it isn't their fault either . . . [What do you mean?] . . . well, who said you had to be what they wanted? [oh, I see] . . . now the question is, what do you want to do about it? Would you like to change? [You bet!]

In this case, change was not so easy. As we pursued the situation further, I pointed out that because she lacked confidence in herself, she had developed many habits that earned her the reputation she now wanted changed. People expected her to perform, so to speak, as she always had. When one begins changing, others can become uncomfortable. All of a sudden you seem unpredictable! The combination of self-doubt and others' expectations is always a factor in such instances. She was able to accept my observations, even though they were psychologically distressing to her, because she experienced genuineness, nonpossessive caring, and empathic understanding in our relationship. Equally important, I helped her understand the purpose of her behavior. How it masked her fear of being a failure and gave her an excuse for not exploring her real capabilities and talents was revealed. This *hidden reason*, as Dreikurs called it, would no longer be as useful to her in avoiding her life tasks. More important, she was now free to have a good laugh and joke around or not, as she chose. She also began practicing behaviors that prompted others to perceive her as a more serious-minded, responsible student and friend. Effective verbal communication, then, involves several components. Most often the words one uses are the least important factors, although they, too, contribute to the overall effect. Key concepts include:

1. *reflective listening*, which reveals an awareness of the kind and intensity of feelings expressed;

2. *nonjudgmental attitudes*, which show respect for the individual even though you may not like what he or she has done;

3. *accepting responsibility* for your feelings and avoiding blaming, complaining, and nagging; and

4. *understanding the purpose of behavior* and how it may be self-defeating to the other person and/or yourself in finding solutions to life circumstances.

Studies of teacher–pupil interactions over the years tend to support the difficulty that both teachers and pupils experience in their interactions. In my experience as a lecturer in the United States and abroad, workshop participants, including teachers, generally agree that most interactions involve giving instructions, reminders, and reprimands. Parents are equally perplexed. Marriage and family interactions also tend to be less than encouraging in all but the strongest families (D. G. Myers, 1992; Stinnet & Defrain, 1985). What this suggests is that the most powerful learning methods available (i.e., modeling and example) are absent in the major environments where learning to cope with life is an expected outcome. In short, there is no more important mission than to model, teach, and perfect methods of encouragement if we are to cope successfully with the problems of our time.

## ON BEING ENCOURAGING

Attention to only verbal methods of encouragement leaves a significant gap in what is required. Adlerians stress the significance of action, not words, when coping with discipline problems. The same principle can be espoused for encouragement. Each person looks for evidence that what others say is revealed also in their behaviors. Nonverbal communication can be as simple as smiling or as involved as planning and conducting events specifically designed to reflect love, respect, and genuine caring for others.

Remembering and celebrating birthdays, anniversaries, and graduations constitute nonverbal messages of encouragement. At such times, the recipients may not remember exactly what was said or what was given to them, but they will remember the manner in which it was given.

Some illustrations of acts of encouragement include the following:

1. Helping someone do a job that might otherwise be done alone

2. Listening to someone describe a hobby, a vocation, or event that he or she wanted to share

3. Keeping busy and remaining patient while someone else completes a task he or she found difficult

4. Completing or doing another's task in order to let him or her have more leisure time

5. Sharing with a friend a book or item of value to you

6. Offering to do a favor without being asked

7. Sending letters of appreciation, thanks, or remembrance, especially when it might easily be overlooked

8. Intervening on another's behalf to help others appreciate his or her capabilities or contributions for a job to be done

Virtually any act that is given genuinely as an expression of appreciation, recognition, or acceptance of another person's qualities, talents, or behavior can be encouraging to that person. Sometimes individuals question why Adlerians tend to avoid reference to praise. There are several explanations for this tendency. First, most often, the goal of counseling is to help overcome evidence of discouragement in other persons. Referring to the explanation in chapter 1 of the vertical and horizontal planes on which people tend to move, praise by our definition tends to bring attention to how one is doing more than to what one is doing (e.g., "You're a good painter. You've done that well!"). Because discouraged persons tend to be preoccupied with how they are doing, we prefer to deemphasize it.

In the earlier case of the skier interviewed after losing a competition by only fractions of a second, to say he'd done a good job probably would have made little difference to him. In spite of the commentator's prompting, he already believed that he'd done his best! A good respected friend's praise for his run down the hill could be encouraging as an affirmation of what he already believed. **When in doubt about another's level of self-confidence, we believe that it is better not to praise.**

By dictionary definition, to praise is to express approval. In an authoritarian society or system, praise is a means of influence. Superiors "approve or disapprove" subordinates' work or behavior. Praise, then, is not an appropriate method for an equalitarian society. Praise also tends to bring attention to the person and not the act.

The personal tragedy of many persons can be traced to their early mistaken notions that in order to be somebody of importance they must perform to the satisfaction of others. On the one hand, some people decide what they will or will not do according to how it will please others, whereas some people will act only to displease others. In either case, the consequences are equally stifling. There are also many examples of businessmen, writers, actors, music stars, and others who excelled in the eyes of their publics only to die from substance abuse, personal abuses to their health, and various other behaviors of a discouraged person. In these instances, success with power, position, and possessions all proved shallow and depressing. Some people may argue that success ruined these individuals. The influence of fame and money corrupted them. The demands of their public life were too great. These arguments may seem compelling if you accept the premise that these individuals could exercise no influence over their time, their friends, and their associates.

By contrast, there are examples of other successful, high-visibility public figures, who in some cases, in spite of personal tragedy in their private lives, are excellent examples of high-social-interest persons. The comedian Bob Hope has used his quick sense of humor and personal charm to lift the spirits of servicemen and the less fortunate all over the world. He has been generous with his time, talent, and personal resources on behalf of many charities and causes. Never one to miss the humor in a situation, his humor is never purposely hurtful to anyone. As is noted in the chapters on consultation and counseling, helping others to laugh at the predicaments in life is therapeutic in itself. On the basis of that criteria, he could well be called Dr. Bob Hope!

---

Attention to appropriate touching can be an important process of encouragement.

---

One last observation about encouragement concerns touching. For a variety of reasons, touching others in U.S. society seems to have acquired a kind of taboo (Thayer, 1988). Among certain ethnic groups, hugging and kissing men and women alike is an accepted expression of love, friendship, and warmth. No greeting or celebration is complete without it. And yet, principally western European Victorian attitudes and practices seem to coexist in a society charged with pornography, moral indulgence, and preoccupation with sexual performance. This fact is particularly striking as new data accumulate that in the absence of fondling, cuddling, picking up, touching, and other signs of physical caring, even animals experience all manner of maladies, including, evidently, death in some situations. Case studies of human beings of all ages are likewise quite striking with respect to neglect in this area. For this reason, I believe that attention to appropriate touching can be an important factor in the process of encouragement.

In most instances, a simple but firm handshake, a touch on the arm or back, a kiss on the cheek, a hug, or a holding of hands is sufficient. Early in courting, couples hold hands, kiss, caress, and fondle as an expression of their affection. Babies tend to receive similar treatment early in their young lives. As children grow older, they tend to pull away from parental touching but generally about the same time that they discover opposite sex attractiveness. Cultivating appropriate social expressions of interest, caring, and support among same-gender and opposite-gender individuals without erotic overtones or connotations is desirable. Parents especially have many opportunities to model this with and for their children. Teachers working with young children likewise have many occasions when gentle touching to obtain attention or expressions of support would be helpful.

Nonverbal communication also can be attained by physical approximation (i.e., standing nearby or leaning over a table or desk to observe at close hand a piece of work or object). In each case, one's presence can be felt in a positive way by the other person. Learning what is appropriate or comfortable for another can often be determined simply by asking. For the purposes of this discussion, anyone in a helping role should be sensitive to behaviors that could be construed as sexual overtures or harassment. Likewise, as one gains appreciation for multicultural diversity, sensitivity to eye contact, physical approximation, gestures, and related nonverbal communications require deliberate exploration of the values, thoughts, and feelings of individuals whose cultural background is unknown to the helper (Lee & Richardson, 1991).

## SUMMARY

This chapter reviews various aspects of the most important element in promoting significant positive attitudes toward coping with life. Believing in oneself is influenced but not determined by others. In order to encourage others most effectively, you must believe in yourself. To have the courage to find solutions to life's predicaments is to have one of life's greatest assets.

Specific methods and techniques are available and, with practice, will make a difference in how you relate with others. Because encouragement is fundamental to Adlerian interventions, additional illustrations and explanations will be found in subsequent chapters. In addition, completing the study questions and the activities at the end of this chapter can be quite helpful. In conclusion, the person who encourages

1. *Respects* individuals as they are (even though you may not approve of specific behaviors)

2. *Shows faith*, which enables people to have faith in themselves

3. Has an *expectancy* that the person's ability will be sufficient to function satisfactorily

4. *Recognizes effort* as worthwhile

5. *Works through* and with *groups* (family, classmates, coworkers) to free and enhance the development of individuals

6. *Helps* each person experience a sense of *belonging* in the group

7. *Helps develop skills and attitudes* needed by others for coping through sequencing and pacing of experiences and knowledge to ensure success

8. *Uses individuals' interests* and assets to further their development

9. *Volunteers encouragement* to others without any effort or behavior necessary on their part

## STUDY QUESTIONS

**Directions:** Respond to the following in the spaces provided.

1. List qualities of an act of encouragement (e.g., more concerned with effort than with outcomes).

2. Why do you think Adlerians teach that you should cultivate the courage to be imperfect?

3. Give two or more illustrations that represent (a) someone
approaching life tasks on the vertical plane and (b) someone approaching life tasks on the horizontal plane

4. (a) Briefly describe "words that encourage" and give two
examples.

(b) Briefly describe "acts that encourage" and give two
examples.

## ACTIVITIES

To provide encouragement is to inspire or help others, particularly toward a conviction that they can work on finding solutions and that they can cope with any predicament

Actions that encourage have the following characteristics:

1. *What* one is doing is more important than how one is doing it.

2. The *present* is the focus more so than the past or future.

3. The *deed* is what is important rather than the doer.

4. The *effort* is to be emphasized rather than the outcome.

5. *Intrinsic* motivation (i.e., satisfaction, enjoyment, or challenge) rather than extrinsic motivation (i.e., reward or punishment) is expressed.

6   What is *being learned* matters more than what is not being learned.

7   What is *being done correctly* is stressed more than what is not being done correctly.

I.  A. For each circumstance below, select one or more actions that can be characterized generally as encouraging to others:

| **Circumstance** | **Response** |
|---|---|
| 1. Volunteers to help wash the dishes | _____ a. faint from surprise |
|  | _____ b. tell them how to do it |
|  | _____ c. remain cheerful and helpful no matter how it is done |

_____ d. tell the person you appreciated their help and company

2. Accidentally drops full dinner plate on the floor

_____ a. clean it up for them

_____ b. tell them to clean it up

_____ c. ask if they would like help cleaning it up

_____ d. say nothing unless it seems necessary

3. Brings home a treat for others

_____ a. express appreciation for the thoughtfulness

_____ b. ask where they got it

_____ c. openly enjoy it

_____ d. reciprocate by sharing at another time something that they would enjoy

4. Brings home report card

_____ a. explore with them what subjects they enjoy most

_____ b. sign it without reading it

_____ c. give money for good grades

_____ d. invite them to discuss what it means to them

---

**Key:** 1. c, d; 2. c, d; 3. a, c, d; 4. a, d

   B. Reach a consensus with your partner and/or group members about appropriate responses.

   C. Check your responses with those of the key.

   II. A. List one or more encouraging responses (verbal or nonverbal) to each of the following:

| **Circumstance** | **Response** |
|---|---|

**Someone else:**

1. is unable to complete an assignment in the time allotted

2. tends to be slow in motor skills

3. volunteers to help with bothersome assignments

4. washes the car

5. loses an item of special value to you

6. shares a common interest or hobby

7. has a special talent

8. takes a bath and goes to bed without being told (child)

   B. Share your list of encouraging responses with the group and participate in discussion.

III. A. Identify three or more situations in which others have been encouraging to you when you really appreciated their support.

**Situation**                     **Encouragement Response**

1.

2.

3.

B. Can you think of situations in which you felt more encouraged by what you did than by what others said or did (i.e., intrinsically motivated vs. extrinsically motivated)?

C. Under what circumstances do you find yourself feeling most discouraged? Can you identify the thoughts and feelings that influence your behavior at those times? Would you like to learn new ways of thinking and behaving in similar situations in the future?

D. Share the encouraging recollections you listed in Part A.

E. If you wish, you may share one of the circumstances in Part B.

F. If you wish, you may share one of the circumstances in Part C, asking the group and/or your partner in what new ways you might approach such a situation (i.e., thoughts and actions as a means of overcoming it).

IV. In the tables that follow, check the frequency applicable to your own behavior. Note that common activities can be used quite purposefully to encourage others.

## Verbal

*How often do you say something like*

| How often do you say something like | Daily | Weekly | Monthly | Yearly | Never or Not Applicable |
|---|---|---|---|---|---|
| 1. I really enjoyed your company. | | | | | |
| 2. I appreciated your help. | | | | | |
| 3. You seem to enjoy . . . . | | | | | |
| 4. I like your . . . . | | | | | |
| 5. I really like what I'm doing. | | | | | |
| 6. May I help? | | | | | |
| 7. Thanks. | | | | | |
| 8. That's unfortunate; is there anything I can do? | | | | | |
| 9. Can you tell me more about your hobby, trip, . . . ? | | | | | |
| 10. Would you teach me how to . . . . | | | | | |
| 11. I feel good about myself. | | | | | |
| 12. I'm really happy for you. | | | | | |

## Nonverbal

| How often do you do something such as: | Daily | Weekly | Monthly | Yearly | Never or Not Applicable |
|---|---|---|---|---|---|
| 1. Listen empathically to another share a concern or important event in his or her life. | | | | | |
| 2. Send letters, get well cards, and so forth, to let others know you care about them. | | | | | |
| 3. Remain patient when others are slow or less able. | | | | | |
| 4. Remember birthdays, anniversaries, or other important dates of loved ones and share them. | | | | | |
| 5. Realize that you really enjoy what you are doing or whom you are with. | | | | | |
| 6. Share with a friend something of value to you, such as a book or record. | | | | | |
| 7. Offer to do a favor for another without being asked. | | | | | |

## Chapter 6

# GUIDING CHILDREN TOWARD WELLNESS

The predicament of teachers and parents in guiding the young is much like the proverbial iceberg. Even the casual observer will note that young people are more openly rebellious and independent now than they were 20 or 25 years ago. Reports of violence against teachers have reached such proportions that some school boards have metal detectors, authorize searches of students coming in the buildings, and employ police to patrol the halls. This plan at best is bankruptcy in guiding young people. More common, however, are the hundreds of small to large hassles teachers and parents face every day in their contact with children and adolescents. Conscientious teachers and parents find themselves discouraged and defeated in their efforts to fulfill their most basic responsibilities. Under many of these circumstances, Adlerian methods and techniques have succeeded very well in correcting and preventing the conflict between adults and young people. The following review lays a foundation for supporting the general thrust of Adlerian child guidance.

## RELEVANT RESEARCH TO SCHOOLS AND HOME

### Building Self-Esteem, Achievement, and Internal Orientation

Coopersmith's often cited study (1967) is among those that reported mothers high in self-esteem were more likely to have children also high in self-esteem. The homes of these youngsters were characterized as being more active, contentious, and interactive than children with lower self-esteem. Also of note, the homes of high-self-esteem children have more and better defined rules by which to live than the children in the low-self-esteem groups. The opportunity for the high-self-esteem children, however, to discuss issues and differ with the opinion of the parents was also higher. Accommodation for the children's point of view is a hallmark within these families. In fact, these families tend to use more of what Adlerians call natural and logical consequences in lieu of coercive "punishment" and use encouragement as a more effective way of winning cooperation than extrinsic rewards.

The parents of high-self-esteem children apparently expect their children to strive for and comply with the standards they establish. These expectations represent a belief in their child's adequacy and a conviction that they have the ability to perform in whatever way is required to succeed. These convictions, when set at a reasonable level, represent a parental vote of confidence. To the child they provide a clear indication that what is desired is attainable. As a result, they give courage as well as direction.

Adlerian-like methods were the foundation used in building positive self-esteem in the children of the high-self-esteem mothers in Coopersmith's (1967) studies. In summarizing his conclusions, he stated that

> The most general statement about the antecedents of self-esteem can be given in terms of three conditions: total or near total acceptance of the children by the parents, clearly defined and enforced limits, and the respect and latitude for individual action that exists within the defined limits. (p. 236)

Likewise, teachers who believe that what they do makes a difference in student outcomes are more likely to convey this attitude to their students. Earlier studies in the 1970s and 1980s showed that students taught by highly internally motivated teachers tend to achieve more than students taught by externally motivated teachers. These teachers tend to encourage student goal setting, responsibility, and self-confidence, all of which are goals within Adlerian child guidance as well.

There is also some evidence that children can be guided to change their internal beliefs. Although these changes in attitude have not yet been studied in relation to student changes in achievement, there is evidence that "internally" oriented students are higher achievers than "externally" oriented students.

A large number of studies that relate to the concept of student locus of control have been conducted over the years. Like adults, internally oriented students believe that it is through their efforts and not "luck" that they achieve success. Conversely, externals tend to believe that ill fortune, circumstances over which they have no control, and related chance factors determine their destiny. Although the results are not consistently the same for boys and girls, research with elementary school age youngsters suggests that internally oriented students have higher achievement than externally oriented children.

Some studies have uncovered what researchers refer to as a "self-serving effect" (SSE) among these students. Essentially what they have found is an inclination of the able students to accept responsibility for their successes but to attribute failure to external circumstances at a higher rate than the less able student.

Studies also have shown that students with positive self-concepts are likely to have the SSE tendency. Stated another way, students who are high achievers and those with positive self-concepts tend to accept credit for their successes but deny accepting as much responsibility for their failures as compared to lower achievers and those students with lower self-concepts. The high-self-concept students would seem to insulate themselves when low achievement is encountered. Conversely, the low-self-concept students are more inclined to interpret the low achievement as a confirmation of what they already expected.

Unfortunately, there are still far too few studies that specifically identify Adlerian interventions for influencing self-concept. Hattie (1992) provided an in-depth analysis and conceptualization for self-concept theory and research that provides new directions for such works. Of interest to Adlerians will be those related to research considerations, including better defined, more cognitively oriented interventions with larger and more diverse populations, appropriate control of variables, and assessment tools specifically addressing the outcomes sought.

## Cooperation as a Desirable Process and Goal

There may be no more sacred "cow" in U.S. society than the preoccupation with competition and the goal of winning. Certainly, one would not wish to subscribe to a philosophy in which losing is better than winning or failing is better than succeeding. As noted in chapter 1, this is a win–win, no losers approach to human relations and life. As a consequence, we want to promote cooperative activities through which all youngsters can be "winners." For the doubtful, there are data to support such a position in the schools.

Johnson, Maruyama, Johnson, Nelson, and Skon (1981) reported a meta-analysis based on 122 studies dealing with the influence of cooperative, competitive, and individualistic goal structures on achievement. Their major findings deserve serious consideration by all educators.

> Cooperation promotes higher achievement than does interpersonal competition. These results hold true for all subject areas (language arts, reading, math, science, social studies, psychology, and physical education), for all age groups (although the results are stronger for pre-college students), and for tasks involving concept attainment, verbal problem solving, categorizing, spatial problem solving, retention and memory, motor performance, and guessing-judging-predicting. (pp. 56–57)

In addition, they noted that cooperation promotes higher achievement and productivity than individualistic efforts. Although less conclusive due to the number and types of studies conducted, there is some indication that cooperation without intergroup competition promotes higher achievement and productivity than cooperation used in conjunction with intergroup competition (e.g., as in team sports). In conclusion, the authors noted

> Given the general dissatisfaction with the level of competence achieved by students in the public school system, educators may wish to considerably increase the use of cooperative learning procedures to promote higher student achievement. (Johnson et al., 1981, p. 58)

Peer tutoring can be another effective way for schools to accomplish their purposes without greater funding or more professional staff. Studies have demonstrated peer tutoring produces both academic and social gains for the tutors as well as those being tutored. For example, teachers have used seventh and eighth grade low achievers to tutor second and third grade children of similar temperament, academic achievement, and type of problem. Each tutor spent 45 minutes a day, 4 days a week for 6 weeks tutoring the younger students at their school. The tutors developed quizzes and reported progress to the program supervisor.

The young-low achieving tutors were skeptical at first. Once they believed, however, that they were able to understand and help their charges, they participated very willingly. At the end of the experiment, both groups had shown improvement in their academic subjects and in their attitudes toward school. Of interest as well was the finding that the tutors moved significantly toward an internal belief system.

The age and sex of tutors may not matter so long as they are competent at the task to be learned. A same-age tutor may be more beneficial in those cases when the person being tutored lacks confidence in his or her ability to complete a task. Likewise, a same-sex tutor may be more effective when the models are good examples of their sex role.

Although there is still much research to be done, this brief review of findings should be sufficient to corroborate some of what Adler and many of his followers have believed over the years. Through grassroots practice in vivo, they have discovered that desirable outcomes in human relations could be realized with the attitudes, values, and practices described in this book. What follows are some of the principles and practices that relate specifically to child guidance. They are just as applicable, however, to older persons.

## PRINCIPLES OF CHILD GUIDANCE

Before one can presume to influence the behavior of another person, one must first establish premises on which actions are based. Teachers and parents, for example, often subscribe to cultural expectations that remain unexamined and yet central to their discouragement as they find themselves unable to fulfill these expectations. Adlerians especially try to expose the folly of the "good mother" or the "good teacher" who has perfect control of his or her children and who sees to their every need.

---

Each person, no matter how young, decides
how he or she will approach life tasks.

---

Central to the development of personality is the concept that each person, no matter how young, decides how he or she will approach life tasks. Genetic factors, family, friends, cultural values, and general environment definitely influence the individual's interpretations of what life means. What happens to the child or what he or she possesses genetically, however, is not as important to understand as how he or she values and consequently acts toward these circumstances. Respect for the child as a thinking, valuing human being is essential. As will be illustrated in later sections, all children are far more able than most adults credit them for being.

An important principle to understand is that one can influence another individual's behavior, but only under most extreme circumstances can one control another's attitudes and behavior. Dreikurs often said, you cannot make others do anything they choose not to do! This is important for two reasons. First, adults can be freed of the burden to do the impossible—control another human being. Second, it clarifies the first step in attempting to influence someone else's behavior—one often must change his or her own attitude and behavior first! This change is very hard for many teachers and parents to accept in practice. They ask, how can I teach or take care of my responsibilities if I cannot control the children? The answer is not so simple. It is by helping the children to learn self-discipline.

If adults realize that children make the best choices of which they are capable from the perceptions they have of the situations, the matter of the adult changing their own behavior can be more easily accepted. If what an adult does (e.g., telling or spanking) does not result in cooperation, continuing to do it in all probability will not help a problem situation. Changing one's own behavior, however, changes the alternatives open to the child and then he or she must decide anew how to respond.

Only the most discouraged person will move away from participation with others. Even the angry person needs someone with whom to fight. Adler believed that people naturally are inclined to move toward other people and to make a place for themselves. Consider a new person assessing where he or she fits in a group, if at all, and how to establish himself or herself as a member. Everyone experiences these feelings, each with his or her own expectations of what probably will happen. Teachers and parents can use this understanding to help children find their place in new ways and to establish new expectancies for how they can participate.

Cooperation, not conformity, is the goal of Adlerian work with children, parents, and teachers. Cooperation requires respect for self and others, shared responsibility, and a commitment to the tasks at hand. Occasionally, the author has heard an adult say, "He is lazy" or "She isn't motivated." Closer inspection reveals quite the opposite is true. Children expend considerable energy toward aggravating adults in very ingenious ways! Their goals are not toward cooperation with the adults, but they nonverbally agree to carry on a disagreement.

---

### Cooperation requires mutual respect and understanding.

---

Young children often say "no" even when they mean "yes." "No" is a statement of personal power to withhold cooperation. Too many adults become impressed with this expression and actually encourage children to use it more often by trying to correct it verbally. As children grow older, they learn "no" can be expressed in many subtle ways. For a child's social interest to be nurtured, he or she requires opportunities to develop mastery in those aspects of social living suited to his or her capabilities. From getting up in the morning to learning to help with family activities, a child requires opportunities to participate, share, and benefit from the labors of daily living. Too often, these opportunities are denied by the faulty notions of parents, on one hand, that they have an obligation to provide for the child's needs and, on the other, that they should assign to the growing youngster responsibilities that parents prefer not to do themselves. Such paradoxes are the foundation of many conflicts.

Cooperation, then, requires mutual respect and understanding. Talking together with genuine regard for the other's opinions, suggestions, and concerns is an important activity for all parties involved. This kind of communication requires practice and a new understanding of one's role as participant. Adlerians use group activities extensively as a means of educating and encouraging others in this type of communication.

A summary of Adlerian thoughts for adults who guide children follows:

1. Freeing myself of the mistaken notion that I should control the child's behavior

2. Accepting responsibility for changing my behavior first

3. Respecting the child or adolescent for making the best choices he or she can under the circumstances, as he or she perceives them

4. Realizing that children are attempting to make a place for themselves by whatever means seem available to them (i.e., socially useful or useless behavior)

5. Understanding that when children misbehave, it is an outward sign of their internal discouragement as participating members of our class or family

6. Committing myself to helping children learn self-discipline and cooperation by friendly participation in the daily tasks we all must fulfill

## GOALS OF DISRUPTIVE BEHAVIOR

The assumption that all behavior is purposive opens a very interesting area for exploration when one observes the myriad of behaviors in a classroom or family. The naive observer may conclude that children simply are active and playful. New student teachers may feel that pupils are bent on driving teachers out of the classroom—and sometimes pupils are. Adlerians have determined that children's disruptive behaviors can be categorized by their goals (i.e., what the children expect to achieve by these behaviors either consciously or unconsciously). Normally these goals are most easily recognized in the disturbing behaviors of children up to the age of 10. After this age, they can still be observed in the behavior of adolescents and adults but these behaviors become less inclusive and other goals also are sought by the older persons.

The four goals of disruptive behavior are attention seeking, power seeking, revenge seeking, and inadequacy or assumed disability. Explanation of each follows.

### Attention Seeking

To enjoy recognition is quite normal among children and adults. When attention seeking becomes an annoyance, however, it is a form of misbehavior and an early sign of discouragement. Dreikurs (1968) noted that attention-getting behaviors may be active-constructive (e.g., "perfect" child, bright sayings), passive-constructive (e.g., clinging vine, vanity), active-destructive (e.g., showing off, tyrant), or passive-destructive (e.g., speech impediments, fears). The two former types often are overlooked by adults because they are accompanied by "good" behaviors of the "model" child or "cute" behaviors of the charmer. Rarely are the persistent attention-seeking behaviors of the latter two overlooked. Tapping pencils, dropping books, forgetting instructions, coming in late, ad infinitum, distract adults every day and try their patience to the limit.

### Power Seeking

Children discover at a very early age, generally by the age of 2, the satisfaction of saying no. It is an assertion that "I can do what I want to do and you can't make me do anything I don't want to do!" This behavior also takes active- and passive-destructive forms. Some children will openly rebel, whereas others will simply be quietly stubborn. In either case, the adult generally knows that he or she has been challenged.

### Revenge Seeking

Adults often are most troubled by the active-destructive behaviors of revenge because of the moral judgments that accompany lying, stealing, or hurting others. Adults do not realize that when they use their power to punish a child, they model the kind of behavior that the child may decide will work for him or her, too, when attention and power fail.

### Inadequacy or Assumed Disability

The most passive children can be the most discouraged and the most difficult to help. Children who withdraw from daily life tasks may be overlooked by some adults. Their message is clear, however: "Don't expect anything from me because I don't have anything to give."

Not all behaviors will be easily classified into one goal area. For example, the more discouraged the youngster becomes, the more evidence of multiple goals will appear. The following case helps to illustrate this observation.

## Example: Charles

Charles was a bright, handsome, healthy looking 7-year-old in the first grade. He demonstrated early in the year a readiness for reading and math. His home situation was quite unsettled because of the recent divorce of his parents.

His disruptive behavior initially was excessive attention seeking in every imaginable way. The teachers tried to be understanding, reassuring, and generally sympathetic, but there were limits to their time and patience. Increasingly he resisted the teachers' instruction, spoke back to them (power), and began hurting children in the class (revenge). At this point, I was asked to visit the class. In one 10-minute period, Charles was out of his seat behaving in disruptive ways 14 times. Both teachers reported that on some days they were close to tears from trying to cope with him. He also was requesting to stay in during recess (inadequacy), was attempting none of his school work (inadequacy), and potentially was going to be denied the opportunity to ride the school bus because of his fighting.

As conscientious and well meaning as the teachers were, they were watching Charles become further removed from his classmates and convinced of his unworthiness. His insatiable attention-seeking behavior elicited a power response from the teachers; he responded to the challenge and ultimately was paddled by the principal. Threats of expulsion seemed only to strengthen his convictions. This process was reversed to an appreciable extent before the school year ended by encouragement and the use of logical and natural consequences. Lack of cooperation from his mother hampered a more satisfactory resolution of his problems. The kinds of corrective techniques that were used are discussed in a subsequent section.

## IDENTIFYING GOALS OF CHILDREN'S DISRUPTIVE BEHAVIOR

Knowing the goals of misbehavior can help adults to understand children better and to correct mistaken notions in pursuing these behaviors. To identify the goals and begin anticipating corrective action, four questions should be asked:

1. What did the youngster do?

2. What did you do?

3. How did the child respond to your action?

4. How did you feel?

---

Identify the goals of disruptive behavior and
begin anticipating corrective action.

---

An example will help to illustrate. The following excerpt is taken from a discussion between a teacher and a counselor.

Teacher: Jimmy is constantly getting out of his seat, talking to other children, raising his hand, or talking at the wrong time. He's really driving me up the wall!

Counselor: In your most recent encounter, what did he do and then what did you do?

Teacher: Well, just this morning I gave instructions for everyone to remain quiet while one of the children read from a book he had brought from home. Not 2 minutes later, Jimmy was singing to himself, looking out the window, and tapping his pencil! When I told him to listen, he stopped, but a short time later he was doing something else.

Counselor: In this case, would you say you were more annoyed than angry?

Teacher: Well, yes; most of the time he gets right back to
work, but I just wish he'd stop bugging me.

In this case, we see a child who is active-destructively seeking
attention. We know this goal by two pieces of information. First,
when the teacher "corrects" him, he stops what he was doing. Second, she feels more annoyed by his behavior than anything else.
This feeling is significant because children seeking power usually
will not stop their behavior until they have clearly challenged the
adult and provoked anger to some degree. Children seeking revenge will do what is necessary to elicit hurt, disappointment, or
similar feelings. Children wishing to affirm their inadequacy will
have succeeded when the adult finally says, "I give up, I can't do
anything with her!" or "He's just not smart enough." However said,
the feeling most often expressed by the adult is one of defeat. In
the previous case, attention appears to be the goal.

Making the assumption that a mistaken conviction or notion
about how they can make their place motivates their behavior,
Adlerians note that children usually are saying approximately the
following for each of the four goals:

Attention: I only really count when others notice and/or
serve me.

Power: I only really count when others know I can do
what I want to do.

Revenge: I can't be liked but I can hurt others and then
they'll know I count, too!

Inadequacy: I'm stupid, inadequate, really hopeless, so why
try—don't expect anything from me. Trying will
only prove it to everyone.

Children generally are not aware of the purposes of their actions. Many children stop their disruptive behavior when made

aware of its purpose by a counselor. Teachers and parents should refrain from confronting children with these observations unless they have training and supervised experience in the process. The possibility exits that the untrained adult will stereotype or label the youngster in a way that can only exacerbate the relationship.

Persons not acquainted with Adlerian psychology are some-times critical of the apparent oversimplification of these behaviors and question the validity of the assumptions behind the goals. In practice, counselors have ample opportunity to test these hypotheses as they talk with children. When confronted with "Could it be, Jimmy, that you want to keep your teacher busy with you to have her notice you," the counselor will see the recognition reflex, from a slight turning up of the lips to a broad smile or a knowing nod, that confirms that the counselor is on the right track. Whether or not the message is worded exactly right does not seem to be as important as presenting it in a friendly, caring manner.

Table 6.1 is not intended to be comprehensive, but it helps to illustrate the kinds of behavior that serve to achieve the child's goal. Occasionally someone will question how one determines that striving for excellence or pleasing is a mistaken goal. Referring to the concept of social interest and the questions one asks concerning reaction to a child's behavior, persons moving on the horizontal plane with a goal of excellence in some area of interest are intrinsically motivated. They do not require praise, an audience, or persistent reassurance. They enjoy the activity and will perform for others, but attention per se from others is merely nice, not necessary. Anyone who has lived or worked with a person who demands attention can discern the difference quite readily. People moving on the vertical plane constantly are assessing "how" they are doing, evaluating their performance, seeking assurances, brooding over mistakes or making excuses, and complaining or belittling others when circumstances don't suit them.

## Attention Deficit Disorder

Increasingly, there are reports of children being diagnosed with attention deficit disorder (ADD). Anyone who has worked with

these children realizes that business as usual is not possible. After appropriate clinical diagnosis and when administered properly, medications can be an important component for assisting these children. It is beyond the scope of this chapter to offer a discussion on diagnosis, and indeed there is a need to seek expert assistance

### TABLE 6.1
### Typical Behaviors Associated with the Four Goals of Disruptive Behavior

| Goal | Behaviors | |
|------|-----------|---|
| **ATTENTION** | Active-Constructive | Passive-Constructive |
| | cute remarks | excessive pleasantness |
| | performing stunts | excessive charm |
| | strive for excellence, | exaggerated conscien- |
| | industriousness to exclusion | tiousness |
| | of other activities | |
| | Active-Destructive | Passive-Destructive |
| | show off | bashfulness |
| | clown | fearfulness |
| | "infant terrible" | untidiness |
| | unpredictable | eating peculiarities |
| **POWER** | Active-Destructive | Passive-Destructive |
| | argues | laziness |
| | contradicts | stubbornness |
| | exhibits "bad" habits | disobedience |
| | exhibits temper tantrums | forgetful |
| | dawdles | |
| **REVENGE** | Active-Destructive | Passive-Destructive |
| | viciousness | obstructs |
| | stealing | undermines |
| | bed-wetting | irresponsible |
| | fighting | |
| **INADEQUACY** | | Passive-Destructive |
| | | indolence |
| | | ineptitude |
| | | stupidity |

and second opinions in such matters. However, it is even more important to emphasize that the same conditions that are necessary for children without ADD are critical for those so diagnosed.

Every adult needs to strive for consistency in their use of encouragement, choices, and consequences. In addition, cooperation from classmates is essential in any successful intervention plan. In my work as a consultant to teachers of such children, I have found that teachers of children with ADD require and deserve much support and encouragement as well. More co-leading of classroom meetings with the teachers, co-consultations with the principal and parents, assistance with other specialists who are providing special services, and direct counseling with the children individually is necessary.

Parent and/or teacher defensiveness can be a barrier to the kind of collaboration that is needed. Depending on prior experiences, parents and teachers may be justified in their complaints about the lack of cooperation by others in coping with the special needs of these children. Unfortunately, teachers and parents are often left to their own resources to cope with such children until they are exhausted in their efforts. The methods and steps of conflict resolution and problem solving outlined in chapter 11 will prove invaluable in these situations. What happens often in such situations is blaming and complaining, which heightens defensiveness and resistance to collaboration. Both parents and teachers are challenged by the child with ADD and want relief from the daily hassles.

Only after mutual respect has been established can solutions be discovered and acted upon. For this to be possible, a third person such as the school counselor is helpful to ensure that all parties' positions, thoughts, and feelings are heard and acknowledged. Differences of opinion can be accepted as valid from the perceptive of the speaker without agreement of those participating. After all points of view have been heard, the key question is, what can we do to be helpful? Due to the pervasiveness of this condition, a number of books and manuals are available outlining recommendations for home and school use. These should be available in developing a collaborative intervention plan. An individualized educational plan will no doubt be an outcome of such sessions. Planned, periodic follow-up will be necessary to ensure that progress is evaluated and new efforts considered.

## TYPICAL FAULTY GOALS OF ADOLESCENTS

Kelly and Sweeney (1979) identified 11 faulty goals of teenagers. Some of these goals are variations on the four mistaken goals of children. Basically, they reflect a lack of one or more of the elements of self-respect, respect for others, shared responsibility, or constructive cooperation. Unlike with the goals of children, however, the reactions of adults are all the more compounded by those of peers when responding to the disruptive behavior of adolescents. Perceived peer support, whether real or imagined, contributes to the faulty notions. In other instances, adult approval serves as a reinforcement to a mistaken notion of how to make one's place.

---

Typical faulty goals of adolescents reflect a lack of self-respect, respect for others, shared responsibility, or constructive cooperation.

---

All persons may exhibit evidence of one or more of these goals at various times in their lives. These goals are considered faulty only when the behaviors are used repeatedly despite being socially inappropriate or personally self-defeating. On the other hand, defiance, conformity, or withdrawal, for example, can be quite appropriate in certain situations.

Only when one is avoiding or denying responsibility for one or more life tasks (work, friendship, love) on a persistent basis is the faulty goal clearly identified. The experienced counselor can establish the validity of his or her observations by revealing what Dreikurs called the *hidden reason* to one's behavior in counseling. As is true of children, the teenager's recognition reflex such as a smile will help confirm the accuracy of your perceptions.

## Superiority, Conformity, and Popularity

The first three faulty goals involve some patterns of constructive behavior that often stimulate initial positive reactions from
others. The goals nevertheless are faulty because they seriously
constrain individual creativity and/or provoke competition at the
expense of cooperation.

**Superiority.** Adolescents with the goal of superiority strive
to be best at everything. They must get the highest grades, win
school elections, or gather top honors to themselves. They often
win high approval from adults. Their peers generally admire them,
but also consider them with a mix of envy, even annoyance, at
their competitiveness and success. If an adult tries to temper such
superachievers, they usually react with a justification of their efforts. The general strategy for correcting or rechanneling these
single-minded efforts involves avoiding blanket approval of
achievements that are feeding the excessive need to achieve. Attention to enjoyment, satisfaction, and sharing with others in their
activities and talents can refocus individuals' interest toward what
they are doing rather than how they are doing. It is especially important to foster the courage to be imperfect so that these superachievers are not crushed by failures or defeats.

**Conformity.** Living up completely to the standards of established society (school, church, etc.) is the goal. These teenagers
are literally young adults who have adopted the styles and manner
of establishment adults rather than their peers. They receive consistent approval from adults but frequently evoke annoyance in
many of their peers, except other adolescents with the same goal.
Because they conform to adults, corrective action from adults will
be received with courtesy and surface compliance, but with no
real change. As with the previous two goals, complete approval of
this behavior should be avoided. A program of corrective action
will encourage both increased social activities with peers and independent activities.

**Popularity.** Teenagers with this goal are accumulators of
friends and social contacts. They strive to be widely accepted and

recognized by everybody. They join and are active in many school organizations. Like the superachievers, they also often win the approval of adults and peers, although some of the latter will react with envy and annoyance. The initial reaction to corrective efforts is usually a friendly, even outwardly agreeable response. No real change in attitude or behavior results, however. To redirect these teenagers' behavior into more discriminating collaboration, corrective efforts should avoid blanket approval of popularity behavior and include strategies that encourage independent and personally self-assertive activities.

### Defiance, Promiscuity, and Inadequacy

The next three goals are more clearly disruptive or self-defeating and usually evoke negative reactions from adults.

**Defiance.**   Defiant teenagers want to be in complete control of or, at the very least, not controlled by adults. This goal is divided into three subcategories of defiant behavior, each with a characteristic pattern of behaviors and reactions. The first is the *independent struggle* in which there are innumerable arguments over dress, curfews, personal appearance, and a whole array of other matters. In fact, anything, no matter how trivial, is a point of contention. Adults react with annoyance and anger to being constantly disputed. However, because disagreements are primarily with adults and not peer standards, peers usually react with approval and sympathy. Any direct attempt to correct will only fuel further resistance. The general corrective strategy involves an avoidance of arguing at times of provocation and, during pleasant moments, indirect suggestions that respect the teenager's right to choose for oneself.

The *aggression goal* is more extreme than the independence struggle. In this case, teenagers strike out against others with fighting, vandalism, and delinquency. They evoke strong feelings of anger, hurt, and revenge in adults and are rejected by most of their peers. Corrective efforts that are built on angry efforts of punishment provoke more striking out. Although difficult, effective corrective efforts include control of the angry and hurt reaction and avoidance of angry striking back. What is needed is the patient building of a positive relationship, a mutual understanding of a positive relationship, a mutual understanding of reasonable limits, and a nonpunitive use of natural and logical consequences.

---

Effective corrective efforts include control
of your own anger and hurt reaction.

---

Defiance also can be expressed by *attempted suicide*. In adults, these teenagers evoke a mixture of fear and concern, usually with some anger. Such teens are usually out of touch with the predominant peer group and, although they may receive some sympathy, are often treated with indifference. Their reaction to correction is a passive nonimprovement. Effective correction blends avoidance of a hysterical reaction with a focused program of encouragement that uncovers and builds personal strengths.

**Sexual Promiscuity.** Teenagers with this goal are seeking a feeling of belonging and selfhood by proving themselves sexually. They are not only sexually active, but highly active in and defiant about their sexual behavior. Despite the greater openness about sex in our society, adults typically react with disgust and shock and most peers react with disapproval and rejection. Corrective advice is defiantly rejected. Effective correction includes an avoidance of the shock or disgust reaction and a program of interaction that encourages a desire for personal self-respect and the respect of others.

**Inadequacy.** Teenagers with this goal enjoy the victim role and seek much consolation for their shortcomings. They give up early in all their endeavors and proclaim their deficiencies and lack of abilities. They tend to evoke an initial feeling of pity from others, with adults tending to feel hopeless and peers tending to be indifferent. Corrective efforts may spur some meager efforts at improvement, but surrender quickly takes over again. Effective correction builds on the avoidance of a discouraged or pitying reaction and provides a program of opportunities for small successes with encouragement for improvement and achievement.

## Charm, Beauty, and Sexism

The next three goals have a superficial appearance of being personally and socially constructive. They are closely related to one another.

**Charm.** Charmers find their place not through genuine cooperation or productivity, but with smooth talk and pleasing manners. Initially, others are often charmed and flattered by them. With some adults the veneer of charm may eventually evoke annoyance. Among peers, a successful charmer will provoke a mixture of admiration and envy. When corrected, the charmer will turn on more charm, and if this does not work frequently will withdraw and sulk or pout. To redirect the charmer effectively, adults must not be taken in by the smooth behavior and must expect, with patience and without insult, productive behavior.

**Physical Beauty or Strength.** These teenagers rely completely on their good looks, physical strength, or abilities to define their place with others. They give excessive attention to these attributes and frequently evoke admiration, with some envy, in both adults and other teenagers. They ignore direct corrective efforts. For effective correction, the tendency to admire and praise physical attributes must be tempered, and a program of nonphysical activities (e.g. reading, volunteer charity work, art, etc.) should be developed and encouraged.

**Sexism.** This goal is a variation on the previous two goals and involves an overdevelopment of stereotypical masculine or feminine characteristics and behaviors. For teenage boys, it results in excessive macho behavior, and in girls it takes the form of clinging-vine behavior that combines an appearance of helplessness with underlying manipulation. Both adults and other teenagers generally are accepting of this behavior, although it eventually begins to grate or annoy after a while. Both males and females will reject direct corrective feedback. Alternative corrective strategies involve avoidance of blanket approval of the behavior and encouragement of positive attitudes and behaviors that are stereotypically associated with the opposite sex (e.g., child care and housework for males and competence in auto mechanics for females).

### Intellectuality and Religiosity

The final two goals have the appearance of positive directions for teenagers. However, they represent extremes that in reality inhibit full development.

**Intellectuality.**   These teenagers gain their feelings of value and belonging completely from "book" learning and from discussing ideas. They are the very bookish students who study, read, or discuss ideas most of the time. They have the approval of adults but most of their peers are indifferent toward them. Corrective action usually is met with an intellectual argument. Effective correction avoids simple approval of the overintellectual approach to life and encourages nonbookish social and leisure activities, greater awareness and acceptance of feelings, and openness to nonintellectual values generally.

**Religiosity.**   Teenagers with this goal seek belonging through an immersion in religious ideas and activities. They are regular and frequent church-goers, and religious themes pervade their conversations. Adults typically approve of their behavior; however, they also may experience some annoyance. Their peers are mostly indifferent, but other religious adolescents will give approval. If corrected, they will defend their position and even pity their corrector. In effective corrections, both simple approval and arguments are avoided, and independent and exploratory thinking and conversations are encouraged.

### Summary

In my experience, many people including teenagers do the right things for the wrong reasons. In the same manner that Ellis helped clients rid themselves of "shoulds" and "oughts," Adler recognized the counterproductive nature of an overbearing conscience, the relentless demands of superiority, or the destructiveness of self-denial. Although influenced by parents, peers, and others, thoughts and behaviors that serve these goals are, nevertheless, the self-made creation of the individual.

Your goal in counseling and guidance, therefore, does not require so much a change in behavior as a redirection of goals. For the individuals who strive to please others, the reason for pleasing may be changed to one of intrinsic satisfaction. They are freed of the mistaken idea that not to please would be catastrophic. In the chapter on counseling, this will be illustrated. The concept of motivation modification is underscored because through it, changes in one area of life tasks tend to be transferred into other personal domains as well.

## VIOLENCE AND SUBSTANCE ABUSE

Perhaps the fact that these topics are even mentioned is indicative of the loss of basic human decency and the spiritual bankruptcy of social institutions in society. These are symptoms of what Dreikurs feared for the American way of life. It is beyond the scope of this book to address the issues facing the youth of today, especially among minorities. We as a society are, however, either a part of the problem or a part of the solution for a better future.

After reading articles in the local newspapers which for months reported on violence, substance abuse, youth suicide, teen pregnancy, and related crimes such as vandalism in the schools, I developed and promoted a workshop on the prevention of violence in schools. I compiled a bibliography of research, methods, and techniques, developed handouts, and designed a workshop around Adlerian methods and related strategies. One publisher donated a variety of related books, manuals, and media for display. The fee for the workshop was intentionally made relatively modest compared to other such programs to encourage participation. In short, the turn out was modest as well. From a large metropolitan area, just over two dozen educators, local practitioners, and a minister from a distant community participated.

The local newspaper called to ask if I was an expert in violence! I noted that I had the statistics and examples of violence now present in schools but, indeed, I was promoting the prevention of violence in the schools. The reporter expressed little further interest in an interview.

Clearly, school personnel alone cannot ameliorate all the shortcomings of the home and community. Parents, especially those who must work to make a living for the family, cannot do it alone. Churches, social agencies, police departments, mental health agencies, the media, businesses, and local and state government must become a large, coordinated, cooperative unit. There are no magic wands and no magic approaches to solving the serious problems facing youth and those who attempt to guide them. If Dreikurs were alive today, he would likely say very simply, *this is our problem, what are we going to do about it?*

This strategy avoids moralizing. It is a practical, no nonsense, reality-based approach to the situation. If blaming, complaining, and making excuses can be avoided, an answer can be found within the philosophy, values, and methods Dreikurs (1971) advocated so eloquently. The successful efforts with which I am familiar to combat the discouragement, alienation, and concomitant symptoms of it among our youth have included methods and values consistent with Dreikurs' approach. Unfortunately, most of them are discrete programs or efforts by a single charismatic individual. Because so much political attention and resources have been devoted to the more punitive and reactionary methods, the successful, positive efforts tend to receive only limited media attention.

The following sections contain some of the time-tested methods and techniques that Adlerians have found effective across generations and many cultures. They can make a difference when implemented properly. To be implemented properly and address the serious youth problems facing communities all across this country will require an all out commitment as noted above. Otherwise, like other such efforts, they will succeed only for those who use them in situations over which they have a reasonable amount of control or influence. I believe that, fortunately, the majority of parents and educators are eager for collaboration, although the media would have you believe otherwise.

## CORRECTIVE ACTION

Because you are most often confronted with a problem before determining that preventative measures are required, you need to develop competence with corrective methods. As a consultant to adults working and living with young people, I have found it helpful to summarize what is required into four steps. These steps can be remembered easily by the acronym CARE.

1. *C*atch yourself—don't act impulsively.

2. *A*ssess goals: What goals are served by the behavior?

3. *R*espond with consequences and encouragement.

4. *E*xecute with consistency, friendliness, and respect.

Dreikurs frequently emphasized that before the adult can begin doing something correctly, he or she must stop doing that which is incorrect. Parents and teachers alike tend to behave toward their children the way their parents and teachers behaved toward them. Increasingly, the old methods do not work because they were based on an authority from on high that was never questioned. Adlerians have been teaching social democracy so well that young people now believe its precepts and behave accordingly—these are trying times for the old methods!

### Catch Yourself

Behavioral research on conditioning affirms the Adlerian notion that what most adults do impulsively when they respond to misbehavior is incorrect. Using the case of Jimmy who seeks attention, when asked what she did in response to his behavior, the teacher reported that she told him to stop his misbehavior. She gave him, then, the attention he sought. Not only did he receive the attention, he received reinforcement for misbehaving in a similar way again.

When adults are told that they must learn to catch themselves, they often believe that this will be difficult. In a manner of speaking it is difficult. On the other hand, there can be much satisfaction in observing the surprise our changed behavior elicited from the children. Initially, the adults are unclear about what else to do. They should be forewarned that when they stop doing what they used to do impulsively, the attention-seeking behaviors of some children will increase before they decrease. Convinced that they count only when they have attention and/or service, these children try desperately to reestablish the adult's part in their plan. This is one reason why preventative action is important, too.

Before proceeding to the other steps, a comment on talking deserves special note. In spite of research that suggests otherwise, most adults seem to behave as though words were the major means of communication. Whenever something does not suit them, they talk. They talk even though the children rarely listen. In fact, adults have nonverbal agreements with the children about when they should listen. Counseling and consultation with parents, teachers, and children reveal that such factors as the number of times instructions are repeated, pitch of voice, and voice inflection convey more to the children than what is said.

Adults tend to talk too much! Establish a new rule; give instructions once and after that they are repeated only under exceptional circumstances or when it is convenient. Make action, not words, the principal means of conveying intentions.

### Assess Goals

In its simplest form, disruptive behavior is evidence of feelings of discouragement. From this discouragement and lack of faith in themselves to meet life's daily tasks, people behave in ways that reinforce these notions. Adlerians refer to certain of these attitudes as self-fulfilling prophesies.

When one expects others not to like him or her and behaves as though they will not, other people generally do not like the person. To break this cycle of mistaken notions and expectations, adults must alter their behavior first. You may ask, "How can I behave differently when I am angry?"

Often adults become angry because they are judging and perceiving themselves as personally affronted. For example, a dad might think, "Look what Bill's doing now! I said he couldn't do that. Who does he think he is? Well, I'll just fix his wagon right now!" Then he talks, threatens, and otherwise carries on. The thoughts flash in milliseconds, the feelings swell up simultaneously; he may not even realize what actually transpired. He does, however, remember the feelings. The feelings linger even after the episode and can be resurrected easily later in a discussion. The question is, Can he develop new messages, new insights, and new alternatives to similar behaviors? The answer is "yes," with educational guidance, study, and practice.

---

Behavior is secondary to
understanding attitude.

---

A part of the new thought process will include an initial recognition that the behavior is secondary to the attitude of discouragement. When moralizing and judging are removed from the process, feelings of righteous indignation typically associated with disruptive behaviors dissipate. If you consider first the discouragement (i.e., the message the other person is saying and feeling within himself or herself) your feelings will change in most cases as well.

## Respond with Consequences and Encouragement

Having caught oneself and avoided doing the predictable, you will no doubt desire specific recommendations on how to proceed next. At this point, three major concepts in Adlerian methods presented in earlier chapters become the foundation of the responding action dimension of the guidance process. They arc natural consequences (chapter 3), logical consequences (chapter 4), and encouragement (chapter 5).

**Natural and Logical Consequences.**   The concept behind the effectiveness of natural and logical consequences is the logical order and pressure of reality. In the same sense that Adlerians believe there is a natural order of life, there is also a logical social order. Adults of all generations have tended to present these as rules and regulations to be accepted and followed without helping new generations to understand or discover the logic of social living. Some rules are illogical and arbitrary and children perceive this quickly. Such rules are fair game for conflicts in a power struggle. Patience in helping children and adolescents learn to experience the natural and logical order of daily living, however, is one of the keystones of effective guidance.

With social democracy as the basis for training methods, adults can extricate themselves from the arbitrary exercise of power. As will be seen in some of the examples taken from actual experiences of teachers and parents, the use of democratic methods including natural and logical consequences will result in many immediate corrections of previously persistent problems. Why they work effectively seems to be associated with rules of thumb such as the following:

1. Natural consequences are sought first, before considering a logical consequence.

2. "New rules" of the class or family generally are presented and/or discussed before implementation.

3. "New rules" apply to everyone, including the adults.

4. Alternatives are always open to the individual (e.g., "you can stop crying or go to your room and return when you are through crying").

5. Consistency in implementing the "rules" or consequences is followed with action, not words.

6. Logical consequences are avoided when power struggles are in process (i.e., angry feelings, evidence of power being exerted or challenged).

7. Friendliness prevails before, during, and after consequences are experienced from ill-advised acts of a family

or class member (e.g., "I told you so" comments do not precede or follow, verbally or nonverbally).

8. Encouragement for the many positive ways individuals share, participate, and cooperate are highlighted. Everyone is made to feel and know that they have a place and belong especially when they reveal discouraged behavior.

9. Time for having fun together is an important part of the planning that takes place.

Knowing about these methods will not eliminate errors or the occasional satisfaction of being angry and full of righteous indignation. Frequently, when adults report that certain behaviors are still being pursued by the children, omissions or errors in one or more of the rules of thumb are present. On occasion, adults should be aware that the consequences may not work and instead may backfire. A logical consequence inflicted in anger becomes a punishment.

Logical consequences do not work as effectively as natural consequences with power-oriented children because they tend to see the intervention by another as an exercise of power. If the adult is resentful or angry, the child is confirmed in his or her suspicion. Such lapses on the part of the adult can reaffirm the discouraged child's self-fulfilling prophesy.

---
Angry people are uncooperative.

---

Parents or teachers may rightfully wonder what to do when they are angry. They may ask, "Are angry feelings always bad?" To become angry is not unusual nor should it be "suppressed." How one expresses anger, however, is a different matter. When people become angry they also become uncooperative. This consequence involves power. Angry feelings can be expressed in ways that facilitate a relationship, but only when the respect of each party is preserved and caring is a genuine foundation of the relationship.

As a general rule, Adlerians recommend that adults extricate themselves from power struggles. Because at least two people are required to have a fight, Dreikurs (1968) recommended that you take "the sail out of their wind." When the angry feelings have subsided, a discussion of what transpired and why (i.e., what purpose was served) may be helpful in reestablishing a friendly relationship. Saving bad feelings for another day can be equated with saving "brown stamps" until you cash them in for a fight over some other unrelated topic on which you feel unjustly treated. Adlerians believe, for example, that regular opportunities for classes and families to meet and discuss common concerns is necessary to help avoid brown stamp collecting. Such meetings are discussed in chapter 11.

Coping with the goals of disruptive behavior, including examples of natural and logical consequences found in the next sections, can help eliminate the frustration and resultant anger some adults feel from not knowing what to do when action is required.

Table 6.2 summarizes the probable responses of children to reprimands according to the goal sought by the child and presents some recommended alternatives to correct these behaviors. Likewise, Table 6.3 summarizes faulty goals of adolescents, reactions of peers and adults, and alternatives to the expected responses.

The process of discovering natural and logical consequences is one that requires forethought and practice. Parent and teacher study groups, which are discussed in chapter 12, are particularly helpful in this regard. Remembering that the normal demands and logic of life are the source of these experiences, adults may ask three questions as a way of uncovering potential consequences that might be effective:

1. *What will likely happen if no one intervenes?* For example, if you don't remind them when to leave, they'll be late; if you don't pick up their clothes, they won't get washed.

2. *What can happen when "others" must intervene?* For example, if adult moves the belongings of the children; the

children cannot find their belongings when they want them; adult will prepare breakfast, but the children cannot have breakfast until they're dressed.

3. *What happens if "others" reciprocate or copy similar behavior?* For example, if the children will wash dishes only during TV commercials, the mother will cook supper only during TV commercials; if children are persistently late coming home, parents lock up the house and remain unavailable when children want to come in.

### TABLE 6.2
### Corrective Action to the Four Goals of Disruptive Behavior.

| Goal | Reprimand Results | Alternatives (Methods) |
|------|-------------------|------------------------|
| **ATTENTION** | Stops temporarily | Ignore small behavior; allow consequences to follow; do the unexpected (e.g., invite child to teach the class and give attention for positive behaviors) |
| **POWER** | Intensifies with challenge or withdraws to fight another time | Extricate self; offer alternatives; look for natural consequences |
| **REVENGE** | Seeks ways to get even and be more disliked | Sidestep power struggle; maintain order with minimum restraint; work with counselor and parents; affirm positive behaviors; expect the unexpected |
| **INADEQUACY** | If any behavior, withdraws | Be interested in him/her; encourage any effort; eliminate failure from his/her experience |

## TABLE 6.3
## Typical Faulty Goals of Adolescents

| Faulty Beliefs | Goals | Examples | Adult Reactions | Peer Group Corrective Feedback | Reaction to Corrective Methods | Alternative Corrective Methods |
|---|---|---|---|---|---|---|
| I AM WORTHWHILE AND BELONG ONLY: | | | | | | |
| When I am best | Superiority | Super striving for best grades, most honors, first in the class, etc. | Approval | Admiration | Justifies striving | Avoid blanket approval; encourage courage to be imperfect; encourage social cooperation |
| When I have widespread peer social acceptance | Popularity (social climbing) | Constantly attempting to obtain widespread peer social acceptance | Approval | Acceptance, subgroup envy, or annoyance | Superficial compliance; friendly disagreement | Avoid blanket approval; encourage independent activity |
| When I live up completely to all standards of established adult society | Conformity | Constantly trying to please, particularly adults rather than peers, with good behavior, grades, etc. | Approval | Annoyance (with some envy) | Superficial compliance | Avoid blanket approval; encourage peer social activities; encourage individuality |
| When I am in complete control or not being controlled | Defiance; independence; struggle | Arguments over hair, dress, etc. | Annoyance; irritation | Acceptance; approval | Continues to argue; defiant compliance | Avoid arguing; make suggestions at other times |
| | Aggression | Vandalism; fighting; delinquency | Anger; hurt; revenge | Rejection by most; subgroup acceptance | Strikes back | Avoid hurt and anger; don't strike back; reasonable use of limits and consequences |
| | Withdrawal | Run away; truancy; suicide | Fear; alarm | Indifference; some sympathy | Passive response; no improvement | Avoid hysterical reaction; encourage social participation |

| | | | | | | |
|---|---|---|---|---|---|---|
| When I prove and enjoy myself sexually | Sexual promiscuity | High level of intimate sexual activity with others | Disgust; shock; disapproval | Rejection by most; subgroup acceptance | Defiant rejection | Avoid shock and disgust; encourage desire for self-respect and respect of others |
| When I am completely supported and consoled in my shortcomings | Inadequacy | Gives up easily | Pity; hopelessness | Pity; indifference | Meager effort, then gives up again | Avoid discouraged reaction or pity; provide opportunities for small success and encouragement |
| When others find me completely charming and pleasing | Charm | Fascinating and pleasing with smooth talk and behavior | Charmed and flattered; sometimes with annoyance | Charmed; flattered; pleased; envious | Steps up charm; pouting; withdrawal | Be unimpressed but friendly; remain courteous and insist on effort |
| If I am physically beautiful or strong | Beauty; strength | Excessive attention to and dependence on physical appearance | Admiration sometimes mixed with envy or irritation | Admiration sometimes mixed with envy or irritation | Ignoring | Avoid praise; encourage nonphysical pursuits (e.g., reading, art, music) |
| When I am "super" man or "super" lady | Sexism | Boys: macho behavior; Girls: clinging-vine behavior | General approval; some annoyance | General approval; some annoyance | Rejection | Avoid blanket approval; encourage contrasting "feminine" or "masculine" attitudes and behaviors |
| When I am completely involved in learning or discussing | Intellectualizing | Very bookish | Approval | Indifference; subgroup acceptance | Argues | Avoid blanket approval; encourage social leisure activities |
| When I am fully involved in religious ideas and activities | Religiosity | Deep involvement in religious ideas and activities; regular attendance at church | Approval sometimes mixed with annoyance or concern | Ignored by most; subgroup acceptance | Pity; defensiveness | Avoid blanket approval or arguments; encourage exploratory thinking and talking |

Some examples of how each of these questions can result in natural and logical consequences for the resolution of specific problems are summarized below. These examples are taken from the experiences of teachers, counselors, and parents participating in their first workshop or discussion group on consequences. Comments after each example will highlight the significance of the actions involved.

**Example:** *"Others can reciprocate."* Each evening at 6 p.m. the parents liked to watch the news, but it was often interrupted by the children. The daughter, 12, and son, 8, each of former marriages of the parents, managed to have a fight at that time each night, which frequently resulted in bad feelings between the parents as well as with the children.

In exasperation, the husband talked with a member of discussion group, who offered some suggestions including a copy of *Children the Challenge* (Dreikurs & Soltz, 1964). The problem was solved in two nights. At dinner the evening of the first day, the parents indicated that they would no longer enter into the fights of the children and that if the parents could not watch their programs, then the children should not be able to watch theirs either. The children offered no comments or objections.

That evening there was bedlam at six! The children got into a loud argument in the bedroom and brought it into the kitchen. They finally ended up in the family room. The parents ignored it all and did not reprimand them. When the news program ended, the mother turned the television off and went to the bedroom. The father went to the bathroom to take a shower. The children howled, demanded to see their program, and even threatened to turn the television back on themselves. They did not, although both parents thought that they might. The hassle quickly subsided and the rest of the evening was quiet with everyone in his or her room.

*"No one intervenes."* The next evening as the fight progressed, they came to tattle on each other to the respective parent. Each parent responded, "We don't feel like fighting tonight. If you do, go back to Sarah's bedroom." (This room is farthest from the fam-

ily room.) Each child gaped for a few seconds, turned, and went into the bedroom. They did not fight, but the parents could hear them talking. The third night, no hassle at six!

The parents in this case are excellent candidates for a parent discussion group. Evidently they caught on quickly to the elements necessary for successful use of these methods. First, they stayed out of the fights (did not intervene) thus allowing the natural consequence to occur—no parent attention, no interest in fighting; and second, they established that if there was no television for the parents, there would be no television for the children (reciprocated with a logical consequence). Much to their surprise, the children saw the logic of this, too, and did not challenge the parents on either issue.

**Example:** *"Someone must intervene."* Each evening, Ann, a 14-year-old, would deliver her newspapers after school. She developed a habit of preparing her papers in the foyer next to the front door. Paper, wire, wire cutters, and similar debris were consistently left behind for someone else to pick up.

After being reminded, coaxed, and reprimanded numerous times, the parents decided to intervene. Without any further comments, one or the other of the parents would simply pick up the wire cutters or the carrier's bag and place them in some out-of-the-way place. After several evenings of Ann making do without these needed tools, they reappeared but without comment. No longer were reminders necessary! Occasionally, she would "forget," with a similar inconvenience the outcome.

Parents in this case were not removing the tools out of anger. They simply needed Ann's cooperation and she required theirs as well. Most workers cannot afford to leave their tools unnecessarily in others' way or in public places. Ann was learning an important lesson in social living through the use of a logical consequence.

**Encouragement.**    Encouragement in its most basic form affirms, supports, and enhances the positive attributes of another. The goal of encouragement is to nurture that quality of courage which results in individuals fundamentally believing that whatever circumstances face them and whatever the outcome, they will be able to cope. Even in the face of apparent defeat or failure, they do not feel despair nor like a failure.

Discouragement is so common that parents and teachers alike often do not realize that many of their smallest behaviors communicate a lack of faith in the child or adolescent. As a consequence, there is a need for guiding principles in the process of encouragement. Among them are the following:

1. Accept and have faith in the individual as he or she is (not his or her potential).

2. Expect him or her to handle tasks and show this expectation by your actions.

3. When confronted with misbehavior, separate the deed from the doer.

4. Confirm the fact that mistakes, defeat, or failure are common to life and not catastrophic.

5. Emphasize the joy of doing and the satisfaction in accomplishment rather than evaluations of how one is doing.

6. Recognize progress and provide ample encouragement for genuine effort.

7. Show confidence in the child's ability to be competent and avoid comparisons with others.

8. Allow for differences such as rate of learning, patience, neatness, or interest.

9. Never give up on the child, no matter how persistently he or she tries to defeat the encouragement process.

The last point is particularly critical. Very discouraged persons also have a "private logic" (i.e., assumptions and convictions about life, themselves, and others that guide their general movement through life). As useless as these notions and behaviors may seem to an outside observer, they constitute their unique notions about how to make a place in life. They will not give these up readily, for as unsatisfactory as circumstances may seem, children (and adults, too) are convinced that everything could be worse if they gave up their protective behaviors. They may think, for example, "Others know that I'm not trying and I fail. They want me to try but then everyone would know how really stupid I am—how terrible that would be!"

A strategy of successive, small approximations of the behaviors desired by the pupil are often more realistic than requiring promises beyond the probability of being kept. Until there is a repertoire of even small successes, failure is to be precluded whenever possible. One can begin reinforcing success experiences, for example, by what one says and does.

Statements that tend to be encouraging include

You seem to enjoy . . .

I enjoyed your company.

The others seem to appreciate your help.

Getting started is difficult.

What do you think . . . ?

If I can help, let me know.

Mistakes can be helpful.

Acts of encouragement are at least as important as words of encouragement. One can help others have confidence in themselves, be self-reliant, and have the courage to be imperfect. The following are some examples of acts of encouragement:

1. When children are trying to accomplish something on their own for the first time, allow them to learn by their mis-

takes as well as their successes without comment, evaluation, or intervention unless they request it. Give assistance
willingly when requested but without taking over. If verbal encouragement is appropriate afterward, try to capture
and reflect their feelings toward this endeavor without
evaluation of how they did.

2. When children are slower, less neat, doing or being different from adults, be patient, be kind—keep busy with other
matters until they catch up or finish what they are doing.

3. When others err or cause an accident, allow them to correct the mistake, clean up the mess, and try again without
reprisal. For very discouraged children, volunteer in a
friendly manner to help them if they would like assistance
but refrain from taking over or doing it all. Show them
friendliness and cooperation by example.

4. When discouragement is revealed, help the individuals
know that they have a place in the class, the family, or the
group by giving them helpful jobs that they can do or by
actions others do for them (e.g., asking them to help with
a task, saving special stamps for the stamp collector, buy-
ing a charm for another's bracelet, taking time to watch or
join them in something they enjoy).

5. When an adult enjoys a child's company or appreciates
his or her assistance, the adult can show this with a smile,
a pat, or other nonverbal behavior that the child can understand.

6. When playing a competitive game, adults can check their
motives (i.e., to win at all costs or to do the best they can
and enjoy the event, win or lose). The latter motives model
an encouraging attitude and behavior. The former reinforces a discouraged attitude in which only winning counts.

Physicians, school nurses, and teachers often hear parent concerns that relate, for example, to eating, sleeping, and toilet habits
of children. When no medical reason for these behaviors is evi-

dent, the physicians' guide found in Table 6.4 can be useful. In certain instances medical and dietary factors can precipitate bed-wetting, grouchiness, or withdrawal behaviors. When no such reason seems plausible, understanding the social value of the behavior takes on special meaning. You will note that in each case, encouragement is an essential element in restoring more appropriate behavior.

Another important dimension to encouragement was noted in chapter 5 concerning the value system underlying Adlerian methods and techniques. Adlerians attempt to help others move on a horizontal plane toward behaviors and attitudes that free them to think, feel, and act as equals to others, capable of meeting any circumstance, any consequence, in a manner suited to the situation. This value orientation causes Adlerians to question the effect of corrective recommendations that might be construed as rewards or punishment (i.e., not a logical outcome of their behavior) by the children involved. In some cases, the child's prerogative to misinterpret the intention of others is unavoidable. On the other hand, when groups of children view adult "corrective" methods as punishment or praise and reward, then the methods will be less effective. Adults in those cases may wish to reexamine whether or not their attitudes and actions are consistent with those described in this chapter.

---

Behave so as to think, feel, and act
as an equal to others.

---

Studies have shown that the use of extrinsic rewards and controls can undermine the intrinsic interest of children in the activities for which they received a reward. Even efforts to provide encouragement can be misconstrued as rewards by those for whom it is intended. Because of this possibility, efforts to empathize with the child's feelings and attitudes are important.

For example, a teacher had been attempting to encourage a low achieving girl whose records indicated above average ability. One afternoon, the pupils were doing independent projects and the teacher noted that this girl had been unusually busy working

# TABLE 6.4
## Physicians' Guide to Some Typical Nonmedical Behavior Problems

| Parents' Common Concerns | Child's Goals | Typical Adult Responses | Corrective Action[1] | Preventative Action[2] |
|---|---|---|---|---|
| Won't eat what is prepared | Attention | Become annoyed, coax, or bribe | No special preparation of food; to eat or not is his/her choice | Enjoy food yourself, make meal time pleasant—talking, sharing, etc. |
| Won't dress | Attention | Become annoyed, coax, or bribe | Take as is to sitter or dress, but no other service, e.g., breakfast | Look for opportunity to reflect satisfaction in caring for self, feeling more comfortable when warm, etc. |
| Fighting | Attention | Referee, become annoyed | Stay out—go to the bathroom or send them to their room to settle it | Give attention at times when cooperation is evident—read play games, or share a snack |
| Toilet training | Attention | Become annoyed, commotion | Relax, remain friendly friendly | Emphasize intrinsic satisfaction (e.g., reflect relief and satisfaction in elimination with attention to caring for self—personal mastery) |
| Can't sleep; "needs" water, needs lights on; has "fears" | Attention | Become annoyed; coax or bribe | Be pleasant at bedtime; ignore any calls including out-of-bed behavior | In morning or after naps, ask about good rest feelings; when bedtime approaches (child is tired), reflect how good it will feel to lie down, relax, have pleasant thoughts, etc. |

| Masturbation | Attention | Become angry; reprimand; punish | Be unimpressed; relax | Avoid moralizing; allow open, candid discussions about sexual development; encourage questions by simple, honest answers |
|---|---|---|---|---|
| Temper tantrum | Power | Become angry; reprimand | Remain calm; if in public place, remove and indicate that he or she is welcome to accompany you only if cooperation is given; if at home, go to bathroom until behavior stops; avoid talking | Give youngster a job or activity in which he or she can help or participate |
| Disobedience | Power | Become angry | Indicate a desire to be cooperative, but the choice is his/hers too; use natural or logical consequences as an alternative to punishment (e.g., doesn't wash dishes, you don't cook supper) | Hold family or classroom meeting to discuss member's strong points and how these strengths can help others; plan entertainment, picnics, etc., and establish ground rules to live by for cooperation of the group |
| Stealing | Revenge | Become hurt; punish | Be unimpressed; expect some restitution; ask youngsters to make suggestions—use consequences not punishment. | Don't give up; know youngster doesn't expect to be liked; give him/her a place by being helpful; expect cooperation; show faith |

[1]General Principles for Corrective Action: Do the unexpected; don't talk; don't act impulsively; give up the idea of controlling; use natural and logical consequences.

[2]General Principles for Preventive Action: Remain friendly; be firm, consistent, and positive; encourage responsible behavior with attention to the youngster and intrinsic satisfaction with helping, sharing, and enjoying new competence and independence; help him or her know that he or she has a place in the family or class by actions, not just words.

on her project for more than an hour without seeking help or bothering others. She watched the girl a few moments and then commented that the girl was doing a good job. The girl looked up, began to cry, and ran out of the room. At first bewildered, the teacher later approached the girl:

Teacher: Mary, what I said upset you. Do you want to talk about it?

Mary: I don't know what to say. You didn't say anything wrong.

Teacher: Hmm, I think maybe I did. I think, Mary, that no matter how hard you try, it doesn't seem good enough . . . and that really makes you feel bad.

Mary: Well . . . it doesn't seem to matter how hard I try (starts to cry) . . .

Teacher: You were really intent on what you were doing . . . really into it. Could you show me what you have planned?

Mary: Uh-huh, it really isn't finished but . . .

In this case, the teacher had overlooked the guideline that she not comment on *how* the pupil was doing but on *what* she was doing. The teacher, however, used her knowledge of the girl to empathize with her discouragement and to reorient her to what she planned to do.

The girl seemed intrinsically motivated, so that the comment by the teacher was not necessary. The comment could have been more helpful, however, if it had simply reflected the youngster's satisfaction, brought it to consciousness, and was shared by the teacher.

Not all children are discouraged in the same way. Some seek adult assurance of their place by doing everything as perfectly as possible. Teacher comments on how they are doing are solicited regularly. In some cases, not to get 100% on a test is almost catastrophic. Parents often feel great pride in such children. Gold stars, dollars for an A, ad infinitum, only add to the discouragement.

---

Through encouragement, help others
appreciate their intrinsic worth, their
equality, their place in the world.

---

The world of these persons, as children and adults, is a constant climb for success, a constant need for assurances, an unrelenting demand on energy. They can be helped, however, to appreciate their intrinsic worth, their equality, their place in the world with the appropriate use of encouragement.

### Execute with Consistency, Friendliness, and Respect

In my experience, adults have a tendency to seek relief only from the immediate problems that they are having with children and adolescents. When a reasonable amount of success is attained and the crisis of the moment has passed, further counseling or consultation ends.

A new agreement is sometimes reached between adults and children that is premature and falls far short of what is required to prevent future crises of the same type. For this reason, an understanding with adults and children to follow through on the preventative aspects of the counselor's recommendations (chapter 11) should be stressed. For purposes of execution in implementing corrective procedures, a few observations can help increase the probability of their effectiveness.

First, consistency is very important in taking corrective action. Each time adults make exceptions to the agreed upon rules, they invite further hassles on modifying other rules on other occasions. This is a testing game that every parent or teacher has experienced. Friendliness will take the harsh edge off the firmness that is necessary to maintain order.

Second, be aware that some children will cry "foul" when they finally realize the new rules have a force of their own. They will claim that something is unfair about their implementation. If the rules apply to everyone, then they will see the logic in their application. They still may try to avoid the consequences by argument. In such cases, silence is golden. Respect is reinforced by the equality inherent in these methods.

---

I'm imperfect and I'll accept you as
being imperfect.

---

Third, do not be afraid to make a mistake—have the courage to be imperfect. Occasionally an adult will feel overwhelmed by the possibilities of doing the "wrong" thing. Such notions are counterproductive to the kinds of strategies Adlerians use to help others learn. People learn by doing, by their mistakes as well as successes. If they dwell on negative thoughts, they tend to revert to the old methods and feel defeated in the process as well.

Fourth, implement only one or two recommendations at a time. Work on correcting one type of behavior at a time. Success experiences for the adults are important as well. When adults are new to these methods, they can become confused or disappointed by attempting too many adjustment too quickly.

## SUMMARY

This chapter has outlined major principles, methods, and techniques of Adlerian child guidance. Reason, respect, and responsibility are among the key components. The goals of child and adolescent misbehavior are identified. Corrective methods begin with encouragement and are supplemented by life's realities, natural and logical consequences. One final note concerns the applicability of these methods to all people regardless of age or station in life. As will be seen in subsequent chapters, Adler's observations about the "ironclad logic of social living" impinge on everyone. It is further evidence of the equality of all people. As you discover the order and harmony that can be found in living with young people, other aspects of your social life improve as well. Marriage discussion groups often are the next activity after a parent study group because participants have experienced its value and want to enrich their lives further.

Finally, chapter 12 includes group methods found useful in helping to ameliorating problems related to youth disobedience and violence in the schools. As was noted earlier, the problems of drugs- and weapons-related violence require a community effort that transcends the home and schools alone. Likewise, the serious mental health problems, teen pregnancies, and unemployment and underemployment of youth, particularly minorities, are symptoms of a society in need of a major overhaul of its philosophy, priorities, and commitments. Within Dreikurs' and Adler's approaches to human affairs, there are reasonable alternatives and some of the answers to the questions before us.

## STUDY QUESTIONS

**Directions:** Respond to the following in the spaces provided.

1. Give one illustration of each of the four goals of misbehavior and the child's "private logic" in each situation. What are the adult feelings and traditional responses in each illustration?

2. List four faulty goals of adolescents discussed within the chapter that adults tend to reinforce. Do you agree that these are faulty goals? Why or why not?

3. Isolate one child–adult incident that you observed or in which you were involved, and apply the four steps represented by CARE. How might the results have been different had these steps been applied at the time?

4. Why is talking too much a shortcoming in the corrective dimension of discipline?

## ACTIVITIES

I. You have had an opportunity to study the principles and methods of Individual Psychology in relation to guiding young people. The concept of goal-directed behavior is an exciting one when first fully understood. Initially, persons new to this approach want to apply their knowledge immediately. Naturally, successful application of this approach takes practice, creativity, and flexibility. The following exercises are designed to give you practice in recognizing the goals of misbehavior and to encourage you to begin to create alternative responses that can be applied to counseling and consultation.

A. The following paragraphs are vignettes from everyday living. On Form 6.1, identify the goal of misbehavior illustrated, the adult's usual reflexive response, and the result of this intervention. Also, propose an alternative response to the child's misbehavior. Please provide a specific response or action (e.g., mother leaves the room where the children are fighting). Hint: Try doing the unexpected. After you have completed the form, compare your responses to those in the Key to Form 6.1.

Then share your responses to the vignettes presented in the first activity and your personal experiences as a group, with your study partner, or with an interested friend. Feel free to express any concerns or doubts you have about specific interventions described. Which suggestions would you be the most uncomfortable in attempting? Each person needs to be aware of his or her own feelings in working with this approach.

**Vignette 1:** Mary is a cute little 2-year-old who has just dropped her plate of spaghetti on the floor for the second time, gleefully laughing and saying, "All gone!"

**Vignette 2:** Jim and Joe are twins who seem to fight all the time. Father has just told Jim to share his construction set with his brother. Jim screams, "You can't make me!" to which Joe replies, "I don't want to play with that old thing anyway!"

**Vignette 3:** Four-year-old Jessica brings her mother's church group meeting to a screeching halt when she loudly and clearly curses at the dog in the next room.

**Vignette 4:** Angered by her 12-year-old brother's refusal to take her along to the movies, Judy (8 years old) methodically tears up his baseball cards and sprinkles the pieces around his room.

**Vignette 5:** Although his achievement tests indicate he is able to complete the assignments, Steven rarely attempts the more difficult mathematics problems. He even refuses help from his brother.

The main purpose of this activity is to help the student see the purposiveness of behavior. Your attention is drawn to the goals of misbehavior, the adult's feelings and thoughts, and the normal responses. You will see in later lessons that new behaviors and attitudes by adults can change the relationships from fighting to friendliness.

## FORM 6.1
## Feelings and Behaviors

| Situation | Child's Goal of Misbehavior* | Adult Goal Typical Response | Outcome | Alternative Action |
|---|---|---|---|---|
| Vignette 1: Mary drops her plate of food on the floor. | | | | |
| Vignette 2: Twins, Jim and Joe, fight all the time. | | | | |
| Vignette 3: Jessica curses at the dog. | | | | |
| Vignette 4: Judy tears up her brother's base-ball cards. | | | | |
| Vignette 5: Steven rarely attempts more difficult mathematics problems. | | | | |

*The predominate goal is most easily identified by the feelings evoked in the adult or others involved. If the adult feels annoyed, the child probably wants attention; if angry—power; if hurt/disappointed—revenge; if the adult gives up, the child's goal is inadequacy.

## Key to FORM 6.1
## Feelings and Behaviors

| Situation | Child's Goal of Misbehavior* | Adult Typical Response | Outcome | Alternative Action |
|---|---|---|---|---|
| Vignette 1: Mary drops her plate of food on the floor. | attention | annoyed, and cleans up | child watches | say nothing, get clean up material, and let the child help clean up |
| Vignette 2: Twins, Jim and Joe, fight all the time. | revenge | angered, reprimands, referees | kids continue fights; Jim continues to challenge adults | sidestep power struggle, stay out of fights, send boys to their rooms to fight or at least leave immediate area (preferably with no talk from adults) |
| Vignette 3: Jessica curses at the dog. | revenge | hurt, embarrassed, scolds, paddles | calls names, fights back | remove firmly but without comment, let it be known later that she cannot go to church and disrupt others, you enjoy her company and would like her to go, but can she attend without disrupting others? If yes, no more is said; if no, she cannot go until she is |

| | | | | ready. No lectures or "what a good girl" pep talks later for cooperation—be pleasant, etc., and help make going fun, etc. |
|---|---|---|---|---|
| Vignette 4: Judy tears up her brother's baseball cards. | revenge | hurt/angry | enjoys commotion | needs encouragement (future lessons) |
| Vignette 5: Steven rarely attempts more difficult mathematics problems. | inadequacy | give up | Steven withdraws further | needs encouragement (future lessons) |

B. Describe at least two situations from your own experience in which you were dealing with a misbehaving child. Include your response and how the child reacted.

What were your feelings during and after the episode?

With your current understanding of the purposiveness of behavior, indicate what you believe was the child's goal.

How might you have responded differently?

*Personal Experience 1:*_____

_____

_____

_____

• Your Response_____

_____

• Child's Reaction_____

_____

• Your Feelings (during and after)_____

_____

• Child's Goal_____

_____

• How could you have responded differently?

_____

_____

*Personal Experience 2:* _____

_____

_____

_____

- Your Response_____

_____

- Child's Reaction_____

_____

- Your Feelings (during and after)_____

_____

- Child's Goal_____

_____

- How could you have responded differently?

_____

_____

II. In previous lessons, you have had opportunities to study the principles and methods of Individual Psychology. In this lesson you have read about some of the mistaken or faulty goals of adolescents. The following exercise provides an opportunity for you to apply the Adlerian methods to the problems associated with teenagers' disruptive behavior.

A. 1. Based on your experience and study, list three or more specific disruptive behaviors of adolescents in the spaces provided in Form 6.2.

   2. Share your examples with other members of the class or your study partner. (You may list the examples on a chalkboard if your are in a classroom. Don't worry about spelling; have the courage to be imperfect!)

   3. Think about the examples listed:

      a. Are all the behaviors generally considered "bad" behavior (e.g., talking back, being irresponsible, etc.)?

      b. If so, think about some behaviors that are more acceptable to adults but are nonetheless faulty goals, as identified in Table 6.3. List others on your form as necessary.

B. Divide into groups of three or four persons and each person in the group select one or two disruptive behaviors from his or her list to discuss. Use the form provided to determine as a group the appropriate response for each category. As nearly so as possible, the members should select behaviors that relate to different goals in order to benefit from greater variety within the group discussion.

C. 1. Following the group discussion of the selected teen problem behaviors, each member should complete the other items in Form 6.2, relating the items to the specific behavior of most interest to him or her (i.e., adult reactions, goals, thoughts, corrective responses). You may wish to refer to Table 6.3 again.

   2. When all members are finished, discussion in the small groups can begin with what each person has

**FORM 6.2**
**Typical Teenage Disruptive Behavior**

| Disruptive Behavior | Adult Reactions | Goals | Thoughts | Potential Encouraging Corrective Responses |
|---|---|---|---|---|
|  |  |  |  |  |
|  |  |  |  |  |
|  |  |  |  |  |
|  |  |  |  |  |

listed and why. Maybe others know of a youngster like that, too, and can make suggestions for successful interventions. The group members also can help ensure that goals and thoughts are consistent with the behavior and corrective methods.

III. In previous activities and lessons, I have presented and discussed the principles and methods of guiding young people. At this point in your studies, you realize that a persistently misbehaving person is pursuing a mistaken private logic, that such behavior is necessary for them to be "somebody," to be recognized. Occasionally one will experience an almost spontaneous change in attitude and behavior of a very discouraged person. More often, however, time, patience, and consistency in the reasoned use of these methods is necessary to effect significant change.

In an earlier lesson, you gave thought to identifying a misbehaving young person to determine his or her goal and what consequences and encouragement might help. In most instances, people tend to think of children pursuing the first two goals, attention and power. This is natural because they are commonly pursued goals and they annoy or anger people.

The behavior and goals of revenge and inadequacy, however, discourage people. Other individuals tend to avoid or ignore such people. Your task in this activity is to identify a youngster(s) who persistently pursues the third or fourth goals. Then using the resources of other members in a small group (four to six) or with a study partner, develop a specific plan of intervention designed to reorient the mistaken goals and behavior of the child. (Although it may go without saying at this point, the discouraged adolescent or adult also can benefit from such a plan.)

A. Identify a child whom you think pursues the goals of revenge or inadequacy. Using Form 6.3, develop a positive intervention plan. For an example, see Sample

Form 6.3. When you have a general outline, discuss your plan as a group or with your study partner. Each member should help the others

1. establish what specific behaviors are bothersome and might be changed;

2. identify the goal and likely faulty private logic the individual is using;

3. pinpoint a time or times when a discussion of natural and logical consequences might be used to establish nonpunitive rules for everyone in relation to disruptive behavior (remember that logical consequences are more easily misconstrued as punishment by the person pursuing the third goal);

4. suggest specific methods and techniques of verbal and nonverbal encouragement;

5. establish times and situations for implementation of the plan; and

6. establish guidelines for assessing progress (small steps in the desired direction are often more useful than overly ambitious outcomes).

B. At this point, you may wish to share some of your experiences in applying the methods of Individual Psychology in situations at home, school, or work. The experiences of friends and so forth also can be shared; names or other identifying information should be limited.

# FORM 6.3
## Positive Intervention Plan[1]

### Case Information

A. Description of youngster

• Age _____ Sex _____
• Physical bearing (posture, neatness, mannerisms)

• Siblings: Brothers/age ___ ___ ___
  Sisters/ages ___ ___ ___

• Ordinal Position _____

• Other Information _____

B. Disruptive Behavior(s)

•

•

•

D. Predominate Goal of Misbehavior
(based on producing feelings evoked in adult or others involved)

•

E. Private Logic (what the child's thinking)

•

F. If no change

• What misbehavior would you expect?

• What would the youngster expect from you?

## FORM 6.2
## Typical Teenage Disruptive Behavior

| Disruptive Behavior | Adult Reactions | Goals | Thoughts | Potential Encouraging Corrective Responses |
|---|---|---|---|---|
|  |  |  |  |  |
|  |  |  |  |  |
|  |  |  |  |  |
|  |  |  |  |  |

listed and why. Maybe others know of a youngster like that, too, and can make suggestions for successful interventions. The group members also can help ensure that goals and thoughts are consistent with the behavior and corrective methods.

III. In previous activities and lessons, I have presented and discussed the principles and methods of guiding young people. At this point in your studies, you realize that a persistently misbehaving person is pursuing a mistaken private logic, that such behavior is necessary for them to be "somebody," to be recognized. Occasionally one will experience an almost spontaneous change in attitude and behavior of a very discouraged person. More often, however, time, patience, and consistency in the reasoned use of these methods is necessary to effect significant change.

In an earlier lesson, you gave thought to identifying a misbehaving young person to determine his or her goal and what consequences and encouragement might help. In most instances, people tend to think of children pursuing the first two goals, attention and power. This is natural because they are commonly pursued goals and they annoy or anger people.

The behavior and goals of revenge and inadequacy, however, discourage people. Other individuals tend to avoid or ignore such people. Your task in this activity is to identify a youngster(s) who persistently pursues the third or fourth goals. Then using the resources of other members in a small group (four to six) or with a study partner, develop a specific plan of intervention designed to reorient the mistaken goals and behavior of the child. (Although it may go without saying at this point, the discouraged adolescent or adult also can benefit from such a plan.)

A. Identify a child whom you think pursues the goals of revenge or inadequacy. Using Form 6.3, develop a positive intervention plan. For an example, see Sample

Form 6.3. When you have a general outline, discuss your plan as a group or with your study partner. Each member should help the others

1. establish what specific behaviors are bothersome and might be changed;

2. identify the goal and likely faulty private logic the individual is using;

3. pinpoint a time or times when a discussion of natural and logical consequences might be used to establish nonpunitive rules for everyone in relation to disruptive behavior (remember that logical consequences are more easily misconstrued as punishment by the person pursuing the third goal);

4. suggest specific methods and techniques of verbal and nonverbal encouragement;

5. establish times and situations for implementation of the plan; and

6. establish guidelines for assessing progress (small steps in the desired direction are often more useful than overly ambitious outcomes).

B. At this point, you may wish to share some of your experiences in applying the methods of Individual Psychology in situations at home, school, or work. The experiences of friends and so forth also can be shared; names or other identifying information should be limited.

# FORM 6.3
## Positive Intervention Plan[1]

### Case Information

A. Description of youngster
- Age _____  • Sex _____
- Physical Bearing (posture, cleanliness, mannerisms)

- Siblings:   Brothers/ages _____  _____
             Sisters/ages  _____  _____

- Ordinal Position _____

- Other Information

B. Disruptive Behavior(s)
- 
- 
- 
- 
- 

C. Adults'/Others' Reactions
- Behavior

- Feelings

D. Predominate Goal of Misbehavior
   (based on predominate feeling evoked in adult or others involved)
- 

E. Private Logic (what the child is thinking)
- 

F. If no change,
- What misbehavior would you expect?

- What would the youngster expect from you?

_____

[1]Non-evaluative, focus on satisfaction in activity and relationships.

# Form 6.3 (Continued)

## Preventive Intervention Action[1]

A. Verbal Encouragement

- I Can

- When Given

B. Nonverbal Encouragement

- I Can

- When Given

[1]Nonevaluative, focus on satisfaction in activity and relationships.

# Form 6.3 (Continued)

## Corrective Intervention Action[2]

A. Natural Consequences

B. Logical Consequences

[2]Remember, "Do the unexpected; don't talk; don't act impulsively; give up the idea of controlling." The consequences should be rules on which you have agreed after the discussion. Unlike punishment, they are logical, promote order, respect individual and group rights, and are nonpunitive in nature. Note that they involve alternative choices, not ultimatums. Remain friendly, firm, consistent, and positive.

# SAMPLE FORM 6.3.  Positive Intervention Plan[1]

## Case Information

A. Description of youngster
- Age  11      • Sex  M
- Physical Bearing (posture, cleanliness, mannerisms)
  Avoids direct eye contact, slouches, bites fingernails
- Siblings:   Brothers/ages   10      ____
              (younger brother is a charmer)
              Sisters/ages    13      ____
              ("model" oldest sister)
- Ordinal Position   2nd child
- Other Information   Tom recently was transferred into my class because he was doing progressively poorer in his schoolwork, and the kids in the other class did not like him. His mother doesn't know what to do with him.

B. Disruptive Behavior(s)
- Known to lie, steal
- Fights, hits others
- Easily discouraged
- Easily off task in class—not completing work

C. Adults'/Others' Reactions
- Behavior
  —Reprimand him; send him to office
  —Make him apologize to others
  —Nag about work; tell him he can do better
  —Classmates avoid him
- Feelings
  —Hurt, resentful

D. Predominate Goal of Misbehavior
  (based on predominate feeling evoked in adult or others involved)
- Revenge, because his behavior hurts others

E. Private Logic (what the child is thinking)
- Others don't like me. Life really isn't fair, but I'll show them. I can hurt them back!

F. If no change,
- What misbehavior would you expect?
  Continued behavior problems described in "B" but would look for the behavior to intensify—ways of hurting others more—seeking ways to get even and be more disliked.

- What would the youngster expect from you?
  —Increased nagging about work habits
  —Not trusting him; accusing him first
  —Calling his parents
  —Many trips to the principal's office

[1]Non-evaluative, focus on satisfaction in activity and relationships.

# Sample Form 6.3 (Continued)

## Preventive Intervention Action[1]

### A. Verbal Encouragement

| • I Can | • When Given |
|---|---|
| Let him know that I'm glad he's in my class. | 1st day and periodically |
| Express appreciation for his help. | Each time he helps |
| In an individual conference, let him know that it must seem hard to him to have a sister who seems so good to others, but that doesn't matter in my class because I think he's showing us how really helpful and able he is. | As needed, if discouragement shows up consistently |
| Greet him with a smile and cheery hello and inquire about what's happened since yesterday. | Each day |

### B. Nonverbal Encouragement

| • I Can | • When Given |
|---|---|
| Introduce him through our classroom meeting and let him tell about his interests, etc. | 1st day of class |
| Have him help collect papers | 1st day of class and periodically |
| Smile at him | Each morning and periodically |
| Send home a note expressing positive observations about his help in my class and soliciting parents' encouragement | 1st day and periodically |
| Give him extra or individualized lesson task if skills are not up to rest of class | As needed |
| Invite him to help someone else with a job or task for which he as competence | Periodically, but especially when he seems emotionally down |

[1]Nonevaluative, focus on satisfaction in activity and relationships.

## Sample Form 6.3 (Continued)

### Corrective Intervention Action[2]

A. Natural Consequences

In Tom's case, logical consequences may be the only alternative.

B. Logical Consequences

In our class, we do not "hear" requests not prefaced with "please" or that are otherwise disrespectful. We ignore these without comment.

- Persistently disruptive behavior results in removing oneself to the "time out" table and returning when ready to rejoin the group.

- Must complete work before recess or while others play but can join in recess when finished.

- Cannot play with others when in a fighting mood but can rejoin us when ready to have fun.

- Must compensate for broken or stolen items or not have access to them in the future.

[2]Remember, "Do the unexpected; don't talk; don't act impulsively; give up the idea of controlling." The consequences should be rules on which you have agreed after the discussion. Unlike punishment, they are logical, promote order, respect individual and group rights, and are nonpunitive in nature. Note that they involve alternative choices, not ultimatums. Remain friendly, firm, consistent, and positive.

Chapter 7

# LIFESTYLE ASSESSMENT: UNCOVERING THE UNCONSCIOUS

Adler characterized lifestyle as the ". . . unity in each individual—in his thinking, feeling, acting; in his so called conscious and unconscious, in every expression of his personality. This (self-consistent) unity we call the style of life of the individual" (Ansbacher & Ansbacher, 1967, p. 175). Lifestyle analysis or assessment is an effort to make explicit the attitudes, beliefs, and convictions one uses in approaching or avoiding one's life tasks. Although the scope of this work does not provide a comprehensive introduction to methods and techniques of lifestyle assessment, an overview is appropriate and is sufficient for the purposes of beginning the process of understanding its validity and usefulness.

The best way to validate the usefulness and reliability of lifestyle assessment is through personal experience as a subject of an assessment. You may become more aware of your own perceptions with the aid of a counselor. Even more revealing is to be confronted with a genuine incongruity in one's experience or expectations, for example, with a coworker, significant other, or similar relationship. Properly done, lifestyle assessment will uncover the source of discomfort in the relationships that challenge a person. They are a part of one's private convictions, values, and expectations. The following sections of this chapter provide an introduction to the rationale and methods used in a lifestyle assessment, and subsequent chapters contain illustrations for its uses in counseling.

## DATA GATHERING

Experienced counselors learn to observe behavior as a means of understanding the motivation that makes such behavior useful to an individual. Often beginners will ask if it is necessary to conduct a formal lifestyle assessment such as outlined in this chapter. In point of fact, the experienced clinician will use a variety of sources from which to extrapolate hunches or expert guesses about the counselee. Certainly case histories, assessment instruments, family constellation, and early recollections as well as overt behavior noted by the counselor and others are all useful tools. In the latter case, symptomatic behavior such as with the goals of children's misbehavior permit intelligent guessing based on knowledge attained from work with other children. Likewise, adolescents and adults in various substance abuse programs, for example, exhibit denial behaviors that have similar purposes in their usefulness. Working with such populations is itself a source of normative data and impressions.

Adler, in *Problems of Neurosis* (1929/1964), wrote that there are many ways to detect indications of another's lifestyle. Among his early observations were those revealed through organic problems. Suggested in recent stress research is that individuals tend to respond to similar stressful circumstances with particular physiological reactions unique to their coping skills. When some individuals say that they cannot "stomach" a situation, they literally mean it! Stomach ulcers, gall bladder attacks, nausea, and other symptoms are a result.

Extensive lifestyle information generally would not be necessary in cases such as the following:

1. Individual is seeking assistance with a situational problem within his or her capability of solving without such data.

2. Child's behavior clearly reflects classical discouragement and corrective action can be taken in the home and/or classroom.

3. A major theme or movement through life is apparent and recognizable when presented by the counselor as a result of observing and attentive listening.

4. Testing information, symptomatic behavior, family constellation, early recollections, or similar data already are available to the counselor in written form or as reported by the individual.

## SOURCES OF DATA

When it is deemed appropriate to proceed with a lifestyle assessment, at least the following three sources of data should be considered: (a) family constellation questionnaire, (b) early recollections, and (c) observations. In each instance, the trained interviewer is prepared to formulate hypotheses, test them, and discard, modify, or confirm them as the case may be. Questioning techniques vary, as do styles in conducting psychological investigations. Experienced practitioners are able to integrate the sources of data into free-flowing dialogue with a client while systematically eliciting responses from which formulations are derived.

---

Lifestyle assessment underscores the holistic nature of one's being.

---

The usefulness of lifestyle assessment further underscores the holistic nature of one's being. Virtually every behavior is a small but significant piece of a larger plan or gestalt of interrelated parts.

One's choice of clothes, body posture, and movement all reveal underlying attitudes and convictions.

Essentially, lifestyle assessment allows the practitioner to reveal the private logic that the individual follows. On the one hand, most people acquire and accept certain notions of what is appropriate or inappropriate in socially living with others. Agreement on such matters may be called common sense. When individuals ignore or violate what the situation may demand as perceived by others, then these individuals are following their private logic.

Your private logic contributes to a belief that what you do is the appropriate course of action for you. Because it is a result of your earliest experiences in life and basically reinforced by selective perceptions of what you expect from life, others, and yourself, this private logic goes fairly unchallenged. Much like an invisible road map, you chart your goals, plans, and actions without an awareness of the rationale that you follow.

Your unconscious assumptions are on "automatic" so long as you are content with them, and you make choices without asking whether there is another way. Each person acts "as if" his or her perceptions are the only ones possible or correct.

Adler noted that although one's lifestyle is established by age 6 years or so, it can be changed whenever an individual considers it useful to do so. Actually most people do not require a significant change in their basic goals and learn to use their creative self-direction to accommodate others' expectations in the many social contexts that they experience.

Understanding what Dreikurs called one's hidden reason in pursuing specific behavior contributes to the kind of understanding that counselees report as useful and comforting. The author has heard Dreikurs say, "Tell a person what he is (e.g., lazy, manic depressive), so what? Tell a person how he feels, so what? But tell a person what he intends, what is his goal? Now that, the person can change!" Equally important, the counselees feel encouraged by the knowledge that someone else understands their logic and can truly empathize with some of their predicaments.

## Family Constellation

The counselor attempts, then, to understand the individual's private logic on how to be somebody, how to have a place, how to be important. Counselors look first at siblings and family for evidence of how life seems to be, how others are, and how the client makes his or her place. Dreikurs noted that the sibling closest in age and most different from the counselee has the greatest influence on the counselee's personality.

Research and clinical experience seem to corroborate this simple rule, that whatever one child likes or excels at, the other will not. If one is artistic, the other will likely be athletic. An exception is when family values help to moderate the overt differences, such as an expectation that everyone must do well in school. Differences between youngsters in the areas in which they choose to excel, nevertheless, can be discerned. Early recollections are another rich source of material. For the beginner or infrequent user of lifestyle assessment, some structure for data collection is useful. Fortunately, tools are available to assist you.

The family constellation questionnaire requires that the individual think about his or her perceptions and feelings as a child of 6 to 8 years old or younger. Some individuals can respond to this task readily, whereas others require some assistance in recapturing their childhood neighborhood, favorite places in their homes, friends, or favorite toys, pets, or things to do that are the touchstones of experiences for them as a child. Most persons become quite interested in self-disclosure and recalling earlier times without hesitation. Many persons find this is a very enjoyable experience.

The counselor is guided by a series of questions that help discover such information as the individual's ordinal position in the family, comparative characteristics with other members of the family, interaction patterns within the family, family values, and adjustment to physical and socioeconomic conditions. The following are some questions often asked in these interviews (Dreikurs, 1967):

A. *Ordinal Position.* List all the children in the family in their birth order and list their ages plus or minus years compared to the counselee's age, including siblings who are now dead and/or miscarriages that were known to the person as a child. For example:

Bob, +2
Tom, 28 (counselee)
Mary, −2
girl baby, −3 (stillborn)
Susan, −10

In this example, Tom is a middle child in a two-family constellation; that is, Susan is more likely to have the characteristics of the only child because she is more than 6 to 8 years younger than her closest sibling.

B. *Description of Siblings.* Be specific in description.

1. Who is most different from you? In what respect? (likely competitor)

2. Who is most like you? In what respect? (possible ally)

3. What kind of kid were you?

4. Describe the other siblings.

C. *Comparative Attributes.* Rate self and siblings on each of the attributes by indicating who you believed was highest or most, who was lowest or least, and if you were neither one, indicate to which sibling you were most similar.

1. Intelligence
2. Hardest worker
3. Best grades in school
4. Helped at home
5. Conforming
6. Rebellious
7. Tried to please
8. Got own way
9. Sense of humor
10. High standards
11. Most spoiled
12. Most punished

D. *Sibling Relationship*

1. Who took care of whom?

2. Who played with whom?

3. Who was favorite of mother? father?

4. Who got along best and who fought most?

E. *Parent*

1. Parent ages

2. What kind of person was each?

3. Which child liked father most? mother most? In what ways?

4. What kind of relationship existed between father and mother?

5. Who was more ambitious for the children? In what ways?

6. Did any other persons live with or significantly influence you?

Dreikurs (1967) and Shulman and Mosak (1988b) discussed the significance of questions like these and others in much greater detail. The influence of early social experiences on one's biased apperceptions is the focus of attention. From the counselee's review of these early perceptions, the counselor can begin to develop a word portrait of the individual.

**Early Recollections**

Typically, early recollections are recorded as a part of the interview process following the family constellation. Individuals frequently will begin sharing early recollections before the counselor even suggests that they do so. Adlerians note that what is remembered is done so selectively because it has significance to the individual in understanding, managing, and controlling life experiences. Specific early recollections are those recalled to approximately age 8 or 9 years.

---
Early recollections are cues for
understanding present behavior.

---

The difference between a significant early recollection and a report must be noted. Many people recall family routines, frequent interactions, or general descriptions of early experiences. For example, one individual reported that every Sunday afternoon in the summer her family made ice cream as a pastime. Even with more detail, it is not to be confused with a recollection. A useful recollection is more specific and brings attention to a particular incident. Often the early recollection will be so vivid that it takes on a "here and now" quality with an overt affective reaction as well. For example, this individual went on to say:

> I remember one Sunday afternoon it was very pleasant out-
> side and the older kids were running around ignoring the ice
> cream churn. I decided that I would make the ice cream and
> began to crank the handle. No one particularly noticed that I
> had seen the job to the end. They enjoyed the ice cream and
> so did I. I really felt pleased with myself and have liked ice
> cream especially well ever since (laugh).

In the previous example, no one in the family may have remembered her helping with the ice cream. In fact, *it may never have happened.* What is significant is that she remembers it as though it did happen. The counselor might hypothesize from this recollection that the individual believes the following:

> Among life's greatest satisfactions is seeing a job to the end,
> regardless of whether others realize who is the source of giv-
> ing. When others shirk their responsibility, I can be depended
> on to see that the job gets done. I can and do enjoy contribut-
> ing to others' pleasure.

Likewise, specific childhood dreams can be treated as early recollections. However, although recurring dreams often stand out, they are considered reports rather than early recollections.

The question that is asked to begin the process can have particular significance (i.e., What is your earliest recollection?). In my experience, when the earliest recollection is recalled easily, there is a tendency for it to contain major themes or patterns of belief fundamental to the individual's movement through life. This can be confirmed or refuted, however, by noting the content and affect in subsequent recollections.

Recording the approximate age of a recollection can be helpful, especially if the counselor observes, for example, that the individual had no recollections until a significant event occurred in the family (e.g., a birth or death, a family move, another person joined the family).

Whether the earliest recollection is remembered first or not, themes or patterns reveal themselves in a series of recollections. Some persons may remember only a few whereas most persons can recall 6 to 10 or more recollections without difficulty.

Some Adlerians have the individual respond to a family constellation and recollection questionnaire in writing. The questionnaire is then supplemented by an interview to elaborate on or clarify written responses.

To make use of the recollections requires an understanding of Adlerian psychology and further explanation beyond the scope of this chapter. Some of the activities and questions the counselor considers as he or she seeks to understand the individual are given below. This part of the process is completed after the interview, during which the counselor listened, clarified, and recorded as accurately as possible the exact descriptions shared by the individual.

In these recollections:

Is the individual active or passive?

Is he or she an observer or participant?

Is he or she giving or taking?

Does he or she go forth or withdraw?

What is his or her physical posture or position in relation to the surroundings?

Is he or she alone or with others?

Is his or her concern with people, things, or ideas?

What relationship does the counselee place himself or herself into with others? Inferior? Superior?

What emotion does he or she use?

What feeling tone is attached to the event or outcome?

Are detail and color mentioned?

Do stereotypes of authorities, subordinates, men, women, old, young, and so forth reveal themselves?

Prepare a "headline" that captures the essence of the event (e.g., in relation to the woman's recollection of the ice cream: Girl Gets Job Done!).

Look for themes and an overall pattern

Look for corroboration in the family constellation information.

To my knowledge, no single, universally established set of questions or procedures exists that standardizes the lifestyle process. Most practitioners modify or otherwise use their experience as a means of deriving information needed to assist the individual. The following is an outline of topical headings that I use to organize counselee information and tentative interpretative statements:

I.   Individual Characteristics: Family Constellation and Attributes

II.  Adult and Gender Models

III. Family/Cultural Values

IV.  Early Recollections

V. Life Convictions

VI. Approach to Life Tasks: Work; Friendship; Love; Self; Spirituality

VII. Comfort Zone—When Expectation Are Met vs. Not Met

It is not necessary to prepare an elaborate report in many instances but rather an outline of observations and tentative statements of self-talk convictions that follow from the lifestyle data. The process of summary generally results in statements such as the following (Shulman & Mosak, 1988a, 1988b):

A. I am . . .

    1. Self-concept: Who I think *I am*, what I do, like, etc.

        a. For example, I am gentle in nature

        I am short

        I am honest

        b. These may not be objectively true (i.e., a very short person may not feel short, whereas a tall person may feel short); it is the subjective evaluation of the person that must be understood.

        c. Listen for unspoken modifiers, particularly when evident in the ratings and recollections (e.g., I am *only* a woman; I *must be* honest; I am *very* short).

    2. Self-ideal: What I want, *should be*, or should do in order to have my place.

        a. For example: I want to be rich

        I should be generous

        I should work hard

        I should be a real man (woman)

      b. Family and cultural values and home atmosphere can be seen to have an influence on the self-ideal (e.g., you must get a good education to get ahead, always work to win, love cures all, men are more important than women, black is beautiful).

B. Others are . . .

    1. General: People generally are kind, dependable, and trustworthy.

    2. Specific: Women are good servants; men are strong; children should be seen but not heard.

C. Life:

    1. General: Life is full of dangers, "a great big circus," a challenge to be met.

    2. Specific: Things are exactly as they seem; nature is very unforgiving of weak persons like me; each day is a new opportunity for me.

    From the combinations of I am, others are, and life is, inferences can be made (i.e., "therefore, I . . . "):

    I am a child, but I can do what I want to do.

    Adults (i.e., those in authority) have advantages over children that are unfair.

    Life is a daily struggle in which only the strong survive.

    *Therefore, I* must show adults that they cannot defeat me.

The method of operation is revealed by the "therefore, I" statement of conviction. This does not allow the observer to predict the specific behavior of the individual (e.g., will talk back or openly rebel). With each lifestyle an infinite number of possible behaviors exist. An individual may "defeat" the authorities in his or her life by being superior to them in some positive quality or ability he or she judges significant. Someone else may choose to challenge authorities on the basis of their inconsistency, to help demonstrate to the world how they are unfair. Some of the latter individuals may become human rights activists whereas others may become members of extremist political factions. The choice rests with the individual.

To modify one's behavior does not require that the life convictions change. In fact, as individuals experience natural and logical consequences as well as punishment and reward, they modify their behavior. Adlerians simply believe that when in a new, strange, or stressful situation without the benefit of known clues, individuals resort to their earliest convictions.

## Observations

J. E. Myers (1989) discussed personality change in older persons from the perspective of their adult children. She noted with optimism that the universal tendency in older persons to share their life review (i.e., recall of early childhood, challenges, aspirations, and disappointments of life) is an opportunity to engage and encourage them. Gerontological counselors also note that as individuals get older, they tend to be more like themselves (i.e., they are even more different from others in certain specific ways). Adlerians believe such observations serve further to confirm the belief that although one's behavior does change, the orientation (i.e., characteristic way of moving through life) does not change except under unusual circumstances.

As individuals face later years and/or death, they are confronted with a new, potentially stressful task. A review of their basic life experiences and convictions seems to be a likely course to follow in attempting to cope with later years and/or death from the Adlerian point of view (Sweeney & Myers, 1986; Sweeney, in press).

This reviewing is not to suggest that one is "determined" by his or her lifestyle in an absolute way. Adlerians have observed that although people fashion their own convictions, they also tend to hold to them in the face of new data, and actually establish expectancies to prove or affirm that they were accurate all along.

Adlerians, therefore, are referred to as "soft determinants" because they have noted changes in persons as a result of psychotherapy only when it would serve individuals better, or because of an unusually significant event and/or organic trauma. Generally, Adlerians do not expect lifestyle changes, per se.

In the cases where lifestyles are reported to have changed, persons are observed to have different perceptions of their early years, and even their early recollections have changed or were forgotten (i.e., they have new interpretations of similar events or they recall "new" incidents).

---

One's lifestyle remains consistent unless . . .

---

Lifestyle analysis can involve a rather extensive review of an individual's life perceptions, including family relationships and recollections, or less extensive exploration to simply help uncover an individual's characteristic movement though life. The emphasis is on movement and motivation. Discovering how and toward what goal an individual is moving is the counselor's objective. Whether or not the individual chooses to change his or her behavior or motivation is clearly the counselee's responsibility.

The Interviewer's Lifestyle Inventory will be found in this chapter following the Summary. Also, a variety of other applications of lifestyle data will be found in chapters 8, 9, and 10 as further illustrations of this method in counseling. To assist the reader further in understanding the basics of lifestyle assessment and its application, chapter 8 contains lifestyle counseling session excerpts from an interview with a woman who is attempting to deal with her son's decision to live with his father, her ex-husband.

## SUMMARY

This chapter provides an overview of lifestyle assessment as used in Adlerian counseling and psychotherapy. Although much more can be addressed regarding this method, the reader should have an understanding of how this method is an outgrowth of the principle that all behavior is useful to individuals as they strive for a place of significance among others. With a knowledge that behavior is purposive and interrelated through one's lifestyle, discovering another's private logic becomes a matter of guessing or hypothesizing about the significance of specific behavior in relation to the whole. Through this process, you can help others in both small and large ways to understand and modify their behavior and/or motivation to the mutual advantage of themselves and others. Persons inexperienced in projective techniques and their use will need supervised experience and practice in these techniques. For although a well-developed intuitive ability is necessary, such ability is founded on knowledge of human behavior, experience, and practice in these methods.

## INTERVIEWER'S LIFESTYLE INVENTORY*

### Family Constellation

Start with your oldest sibling and list his or her name, age, and how many years older (+) or younger (−) he or she is than you; then the next oldest, and so forth. Include deceased children and note miscarriages if you know about of them. List all siblings in descending order, including yourself.

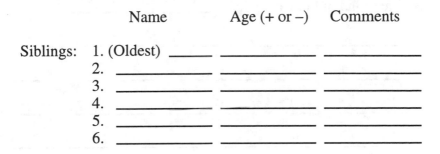

|  | Name | Age (+ or −) | Comments |
|---|---|---|---|
| Siblings: 1. (Oldest) | _____ | _____ | _____ |
| 2. | _____ | _____ | _____ |
| 3. | _____ | _____ | _____ |
| 4. | _____ | _____ | _____ |
| 5. | _____ | _____ | _____ |
| 6. | _____ | _____ | _____ |

*The questions are in large measure those in Dreikurs' 1967 work and found in various formats in both published and unpublished literature. With experience and an understanding of the potential significance of these questions, an interviewer will learn to innovate somewhat on these subject areas.

The following questions are to be answered *as you would have responded when you were a child* of 3 to 8 years of age. This is quite important and may require a little relaxed reflecting on where you lived, with whom you played as a child, and so forth. Close your eyes for a moment if it helps you to recall things more vividly or easily.

## A. Description of Siblings

1. Who is most different from you?_____ In what respect?

_____

_____

_____

2. Who is most like you?_____ In what respect?

_____

_____

_____

3. What kind of kid were you?_____

_____

_____

_____

_____

4. Describe other siblings:

Sibling 1 (oldest)_____

Sibling 2_____

Sibling 3 _____

Sibling 4 _____

Sibling 5 _____

Sibling 6 _____

## B. Ratings of Attributes

White in the space provided the name of the sibling (include consideration of yourself) whom you rate as being highest on each attribute. Then write the name of the sibling lowest on each attribute. If you are at neither extreme on an attribute, then draw an arrow ( ◀ or ▶ ) in the middle column toward the sibling most like you. If you are an only child, how would you rate yourself on each attribute in relation to other children?

|  | Sibling Highest | Self ◀ or ▶ | Sibling Lowest |
|---|---|---|---|
| 1. Intelligence | _____ | _____ | _____ |
| 2. Hardest worker | _____ | _____ | _____ |
| 3. Best grades in school | _____ | _____ | _____ |
| 4. Helping around the house | _____ | _____ | _____ |
| 5. Conforming | _____ | _____ | _____ |
| 6. Rebellious | _____ | _____ | _____ |
| 7. Trying to please | _____ | _____ | _____ |
| 8. Critical of others | _____ | _____ | _____ |
| 9. Consideration | _____ | _____ | _____ |
| 10. Selfishness | _____ | _____ | _____ |

|  | Sibling Highest | ◄ Self or ► | Sibling Lowest |
|---|---|---|---|
| 11. Having own way | _____ | _____ | _____ |
| 12. Sensitive—easily hurt | _____ | _____ | _____ |
| 13. Temper tantrum | _____ | _____ | _____ |
| 14. Sense of humor | _____ | _____ | _____ |
| 15. Idealistic | _____ | _____ | _____ |
| 16. Materialistic | _____ | _____ | _____ |
| 17. High standards of | _____ | _____ | _____ |
| a. achievement | _____ | _____ | _____ |
| b. behavior | _____ | _____ | _____ |
| c. morals | _____ | _____ | _____ |
| 18. Most athletic | _____ | _____ | _____ |
| 19. Strongest | _____ | _____ | _____ |
| 20. Tallest | _____ | _____ | _____ |
| 21. Prettiest | _____ | _____ | _____ |
| 22. Most masculine | _____ | _____ | _____ |
| 23. Most feminine | _____ | _____ | _____ |

24. In the case of females, determine when menarche began; for males, their first ejaculation or "wet dream." Who explained these phenomena to them, how they did they feel about them, and so forth? Acceptance of one's sexuality, attitudes toward men, toward women, and so forth can be understood better in

relation to attitudes associated with these events._____

_____

_____

25. Who was the most spoiled, by whom, how, and for what?___

_____

_____

26. Who was the most punished, by whom, how, and for what?__

_____

_____

27. Who had the most friends?_____ What kind of rela-
    tionship—leader, exclusive, gregarious?_____

_____

## C. Siblings' Interrelationships

1. Who took care of whom?_____

_____

2. Who played with whom?_____

_____

3. Who got along best with whom?

_____

4. Which two fought and argued the most?_____

_____

5. Who was father's favorite?_____

6. Who was mother's favorite?_____

## D. Description of Parents

1. How old was father at your birth? _____   Mother? _____

2. What kind of person is father?_____

_____

_____

_____

   Kind of job?_____

3. What kind of person is mother?_____

_____

_____

_____

   Kind of job?_____

4. Which of the children is most like father?_____

   In what way?_____

_____

5. Which of the children is most like mother?_____

   In what way?_____

_____

6. What kind of relationship existed between father and mother?

_____

_____

a. Who was dominant, made decisions, and so forth?_____

_____

b. Did they agree or disagree on methods of raising children?

_____

c. Did they quarrel openly?_____ About what?_____

_____

d. How did you feel about these quarrels? Whose side did you take?_____

_____

7. Who was more ambitious for the children? In which way?\_\_\_\_

_____

8. Did any other person (grandparent, uncle, aunt, roomer, etc.) live with the family? Were there any other significant figures in your childhood?

Describe them and your relationship to them._____

_____

_____

_____

_____

## Early Recollections

How far back can you remember? Report recollections of specific incidents with as many details as possible, including your behavior and feelings at the time, up to age 8 or 9 years. Be sure to list only true recollections, not reports told to you by your parents or others. Specific childhood dreams are early recollections. Recurring dreams are not considered early recollections.

**Age    Incident (verbatim) with Behavior and Feeling Reactions**

1. _____  _____

     _____

     _____

2. _____  _____

     _____

     _____

3. _____  _____

     _____

     _____

4. _____  _____

     _____

     _____

5. _____  _____

     _____

     _____

6. _____ _____

      _____

      _____

## STUDY QUESTIONS

**Directions:** Respond to the following in space provided.

1. What is meant by family constellation?

2. How do you distinguish between an early recollection and a report?

3. When you are completing the attributes portion of the Interviewer's Lifestyle Inventory, how might an oldest child respond compared to a middle or youngest child in the same constellation?

4. Ask a friend or acquaintance who has siblings within 5 years of his or her age to tell you about himself or herself and each sibling. Pay particular attention to their age differences and who was most alike or different, played or fought, achieved or did not, and so forth. Do you observe patterns to the responses such as were described in chapter 7? Can you see where rivals excel or have interests in different areas?

## ACTIVITIES

In chapter 6, several concepts and assumptions about Adler's Individual Psychology for understanding behavior are put into practice. Some of the major concepts include the following:

1. Humans are socially oriented toward other people.

2. Behavior is goal directed (i.e., purposive and useful to the individual) even if the behavior is not acceptable to others).

3. Individuals are self-determining (i.e., develop their own unique, private logic about life, themselves, and other people).

4. Emotions are tools that one uses to achieve goals.

5. Individuals can change their behavior whenever they perceive it as useful to them.

6. Whenever people "misbehave," they do so out of discouragement (i.e., lacking confidence first in themselves and second in others to be positive toward them).

Using these assumptions, one can recognize that understanding behavior means understanding motivation, understanding goals, and understanding one's intentions. Motivation, goals, and intentions can be changed. Therefore, this is a very optimistic, encouraging outlook to understanding how one can help people of all ages. Young people tend to be more flexible, open, and amenable to change. Using this knowledge can help you anticipate discouragement and actually avoid the misbehavior that often follows.

Another aspect to this approach concerns how one develops a private logic that guides one through life. Family, including extended family members, influence individuals' notions about life, others, and themselves. Adler noted that the person who influences another most generally is the sibling who is closest in age but most different. You have been learning about the five ordinal positions in the family (oldest, second, middle, youngest, and only child). This exercise is designed to help you explore these concepts in relation to yourself and your siblings (brothers and sisters). Parents, family values, and conflict resolution also influence one's development. One's earliest recollections also help reveal how one perceives life. Data used here will be limited but not so much so that you cannot test the general concept of sibling influence and one's desire to be unique in some respect within the family group.

I.  A.  Listing Siblings

List all siblings in descending order (including yourself). place your age next to your name and then indicate the years difference in age with a + or - for each of your brothers or sisters.

Name   Age (+ or –)   Comments

Siblings:   1. (Oldest)_____
            2. _____
            3. _____
            4. _____
            5. _____
            6. _____

B.  Description of Siblings

Record your descriptions as you remember your siblings when you were a child of 6 to 8 years of age or younger.

1. Who was most different from you?_____

In what respects? (If you are an only child, then compare yourself to others in general.)_____

_____

_____

2. Who was most like you? _____

   In what respect? _____

   _____

   _____

   _____

3. What kind of kid were you? _____

   _____

   _____

   _____

4. Describe other siblings: _____

   _____

   _____

   _____

C. Ratings of Attributes

For each of the following attributes, place in the column the name or initial for yourself or a sibling you believe was the "highest" and who was the "lowest" for the respective attribute. If you were neither "highest" nor "lowest," place your name or initial in the center column and draw an arrow to indicate whom you were most like.

|  | **Highest** | **Most Like** | **Lowest** |
|---|---|---|---|
| **Example: sad** | Bob | Me → | Jane |
| 1. Intelligence | _____ | _____ | _____ |
| 2. Hardest worker | _____ | _____ | _____ |

|  | **Highest** | **Most Like** | **Lowest** |
|---|---|---|---|
| 3. Best grades in school | _____ | _____ | _____ |
| 4. Helping around the house | _____ | _____ | _____ |
| 5. Conforming | _____ | _____ | _____ |
| 6. Rebellious | _____ | _____ | _____ |
| 7. Trying to please | _____ | _____ | _____ |
| 8. Critical of others | _____ | _____ | _____ |
| 9. Considerate | _____ | _____ | _____ |
| 10. Selfish | _____ | _____ | _____ |
| 11. Having own way | _____ | _____ | _____ |
| 12. Sensitive—easily hurt | _____ | _____ | _____ |
| 13. Bossy | _____ | _____ | _____ |
| 14. Temper tantrum | _____ | _____ | _____ |
| 15. Sense of humor | _____ | _____ | _____ |
| 16. Idealistic | _____ | _____ | _____ |
| 17. Materialistic | _____ | _____ | _____ |
| 18. High moral standards | _____ | _____ | _____ |
| 19. Most athletic | _____ | _____ | _____ |
| 20. Most artistic | _____ | _____ | _____ |
| 21. Strongest | _____ | _____ | _____ |
| 22. Tallest | _____ | _____ | _____ |
| 23. Prettiest | _____ | _____ | _____ |
| 24. Feminine | _____ | _____ | _____ |
| 25. Masculine | _____ | _____ | _____ |

D. Relationships of Siblings

    1. Who took care of whom?_____

    _____

    2. Who played with whom?_____

    _____

    3. Who got along best with whom?_____

    _____

4. Who fought most with whom?_____

_____

E.  Grouping

Using the previous data plus anything else you can recall from your childhood, compile characteristics for you and your siblings.

*Note:* In large families or in families that have children 6 or more years apart, you may have more than one oldest or youngest child or two or more only children (e.g., Bob, 18, and Mary, 8, equals two only children). Therefore, consider only siblings who are 6 years or closer in age to you to decide positions.

| **Siblings** | **Characteristics Compiled** |
|---|---|
| Oldest | _____ |
|  | _____ |
| Second | _____ |
|  | _____ |
| Middle | _____ |
|  | _____ |
| Youngest | _____ |
|  | _____ |
| Only (me) | _____ |
|  | _____ |

Others
(close
cousin, _____
friend, or _____
children in
general at _____
that time)

_____

_____

F.  Discussion

Discuss as a group or with an interested friend the following:

- The extent to which you see a pattern of similarities and differences among children.

- To what extent is the oldest, youngest, and so forth similar to the descriptions that you found in the readings, even though you and your siblings have matured?

- Can you remember incidents in your childhood that reveal influences each had on the other?

- Can you remember when you decided to stop being the "boss," the "responsible one," the "baby," the "judge," or whatever, within your family?

G.  Final Notes

The significance of this exercise is that it can reveal that all people want to have a place in every social situation important to them. Belonging, being secure, and feeling cared about are all signs of this inclination.

People bring notions to school and work about what they have to do to belong. Some expect to cooperate, others do not. Through encouragement and use of other specific methods and techniques, counselors can help all people learn to like themselves better and enjoy being cooperative and responsible members of their community.

## Chapter 8

# STAGES AND ORDER OF THE COUNSELING PROCESS

For the purposes of this chapter, a distinction between Adlerian counseling and psychotherapy will be made on the basis of lifestyle and behavior change. Adlerians note that the lifestyle of the individual is a unique, unconscious, cognitive "map" that facilitates his or her movement through life. Lifestyle is a unifying set of convictions that permit the individual to evaluate, manage, and predict events within his or her experience. Within one's lifestyle is a combination of beliefs about self, others, and the world on which his or her expectations are based. These self-determined notions become the source of direction and movement from which the individual establishes his or her place in the world.

Within each individual's lifestyle is latitude for behavioral choice (i.e., one's convictions may result in a variety of behaviors). For example, the belief that "only a real man can cope with life's challenges" may result in a vocational choice as military officer, mountain climber, astronaut, or, particularly if combined with

"I am only an ordinary man," defeated dropout, submissive husband, or philandering gigolo. The potential for pursuing socially useful or useless life activities exists within the same lifestyle.

The distinction between counseling and psychotherapy processes can be made in relation to the goals of each (Dreikurs, 1967). *In the case of counseling, behavior change within the existing lifestyle is the goal. In psychotherapy, a change in lifestyle is the desired outcome.* Although these goals can be construed as a moot point for distinguishing between two processes, considering the differences is valid. Granted that changes in attitude can result in changes in behavior and vice versa, usually counselors, teachers, social workers, or related community specialists will not have the training, experience, or time required to use lifestyle analysis successfully for significant changes in the lifestyle, per se.

---

Attitude changes result in behavioral
changes.

---

As will be illustrated later in this chapter and in chapters 11 and 12, successful use of basic educative Adlerian methods and techniques to help influence behavior change does not require graduate training in education or psychology. The counseling and consultation methods and techniques have been tested many times with much success by practitioners who, in addition to their professional training, know and use Adlerian psychology.

Success in psychotherapy by Adlerians, however, requires motivation modification. Dreikurs (1963) stated that:

> We do not attempt primarily to change behavior patterns or remove symptoms. If a patient improves his behavior because he finds it profitable at the time, without changing his basic premises, then we do not consider that as a therapeutic success. We are trying to change goals, concepts, and notions. (p. 1046)

I have experienced instances in which this distinction with behavior modification was clearly justified. An illustration of this may be found in the lifestyles of some individuals in the counseling-related professions. The motivation for some individuals' being a "helper" is intimately intertwined with their concept of self-worth and justification for a place in the social world. When unsuccessful as helper or when they receive no signs of appreciation for being helpful, persistent discouragement and disappointment develop. A change in behavior is not necessary, but an examination of why they wished to help is undertaken to determine how such notions were self-defeating.

Individuals who seek counseling, for example, often have hidden goals, such as to prove that they are beyond help, that their situations are hopeless. To defeat the counselor is unconsciously a sign of success. The counselor who believes that he or she must be successful to maintain his or her self-esteem is already at a disadvantage when the interview begins. Counselors aware of their own motivation, then, can help themselves anticipate potential pitfalls as helpers. A change in lifestyle per se is not necessary in these cases but the confrontation with clients' own mistaken notions facilitates a freeing of counselors from feeling defeated or inadequate as persons.

Many youngsters strive daily to please their parents, teachers, and others. They are rewarded for being "good" children. Although a change in behavior may not be necessary, the motivation for doing well deserves serious examination. The child striving for perfection is a discouraged person whose goal can never be attained. Encouragement for simply participating in life, including acceptance of their mistakes, could be one objective for helping such youngsters.

On the other hand, changes in behavior can open new alternatives to behavior and attitude change. For example, the counselor's knowledge of the goals of disruptive behavior can help to suggest alternative behaviors to the youngsters without conducting a lifestyle analysis. Similarly, Dreikurs' (1971) four steps for problem solving can be implemented in establishing a new agreement between marriage partners without changing basic life goals. Therefore, for the purposes of this chapter, Adlerian counseling will be defined to include those methods and techniques used within the helping relationship that encourage situational, attitude, and/or behavior changes that free the individual to function more fully as a self-determining, creative, and responsible equal within his or her environment. The methods used in counseling are essentially the same as those used in psychotherapy; the distinction between the use of the terms, therefore, relates to the outcomes.

## STAGES OF ADLERIAN COUNSELING

The assumption is made that counseling will be with individuals who are seeking assistance with concerns of an immediate social nature. Assistance will be more preventative and educative in orientation than psychotherapeutic, therapy being more corrective and remedial in the sense that discouragement is noticeably pervasive and persistent, suggesting a need for reorientation of the individual's characteristic goals in movement through life (lifestyle). The stages of intervention for both processes are alike, however.

The stages are as follows: (a) relationship, (b) psychological investigation, (c) interpretation, and (d) reorientation. Each of these stages is alluded to or illuminated in other chapters as they relate to other methods and aspects of this approach. What follows is a brief exposition of these stages as they relate specifically to the counseling process with individuals or groups. Incorporated into this process is the work of Ivey's developmental counseling and therapy (DCT) process as it relates to the investigation and interpretation stages in particular (Ivey, 1990).

### Relationship

A hallmark of the Adlerian relationship is its equalitarian quality. Adlerian counselors, while actively using their knowledge and experience to help others, also maintain respect for the individual's capabilities and power to make independent choices. They tend to assume that their counselees are capable of finding satisfactory alternatives to old predicaments if they are freed of some faulty notions. The counselor, therefore, is likely to dispel any notions of superiority by showing a genuine, nonpossessive caring for the individual, not unlike that of a friend.

Early in the conference the counselor will invite the individual to discuss his or her reasons for seeking assistance. A question that will be asked at some point during this period is, "How would life be different for you if this problem did not persist?" Other variations on this question include, "What would you be doing now?" or "What could you do that you cannot do now if there were not a problem?" The significance of these questions has to do with whether or not the counselee is avoiding some basic life tasks by having a "problem."

Dreikurs (1967) noted, for example, that there are occasions when an individual may have a medically related problem unknown to the counselee or even his or her physician. Nonmedical personnel are obviously not qualified to practice medicine. When asked, "What would be different in your life or what could you do that you can't do now if your problem was removed or resolved?" some individuals simply say, "Nothing, except I wouldn't have these headaches," or "I'd be rid of these backaches!" Adlerians have asked such people to pursue medical evaluation before pursuing counseling in depth. On more than one occasion, the physicians inquired as to how the counselor knew that there was a physical problem when initial tests or a routine physical had not revealed it. Simply stated, when basic life tasks are being met adequately, then counseling or therapy probably are not necessary.

I once saw a man who was seeking assistance related to his desire for food. He reported an almost insatiable appetite. When I observed that his weight seemed quite satisfactory, he indicated that this was true because of great restraint and careful selection of food. He had been quite overweight at one time but overcame this condition after he became convinced it was unhealthy and unsightly. He had been examined by a physician but the advice he received was to seek professional counseling.

When he enumerated that he had consumed four steaks, a whole chicken, two fish filets, salad, potato, and bread without feeling satisfied, I, too, was impressed! Exploring his work and personal relationships revealed no apparent problems. He was a willing and open counselee who showed a sense of humor even in the face of his predicament.

Further discussion of bothersome behavior revealed a tendency to nap at inappropriate times including while driving! My subsequent consultation with two physicians revealed no known condition that would contribute to these behaviors. Convinced that more medical evaluation was needed, I strongly recommended attention by specialists at a clinic or hospital with the resources required to evaluate his condition thoroughly. After three days of hospitalization and clinical evaluation, the counselee was diagnosed with a relatively rare condition known as narcolepsy. The counselee's relief and acceptance of the physician's recommendations were gratifying.

In another instance, a mother reported concern for her child who seemed to inflict injury upon himself through carelessness. Both parents reported great concern to the child's pediatrician. Accustomed to overindulgent parents, he chided them and recommended that they seek counseling. After talking with them and their children, I observed some of the unnecessary parental overindulgence but met two generally happy, cooperative preschoolers.

On following the family to their car, I noted that the child had difficulty negotiating the steps to the parking area. At first I wondered if there might be a vision problem. I suggested that the parents seek further medical consultation. Through follow-up, it was later determined that the youngster had a neurological disease, rare but insidious in its damage to the child's coordination. The parents, indeed, had good reason to be concerned.

Teachers and parents also should be alert to problems that may be responses to undiscovered difficulties with eyesight, hearing, teeth, diet, insufficient rest, and such. Physical growth during early adolescence also can be especially stressful for youngsters. Adlerians are watchful of similar circumstances that might be helped more effectively by means other than counseling.

Chapter 1 presented a discussion and a graphic illustration of the difference between low and high social interest (i.e., characteristic differences of movement through life). Adlerians believe low social interest is evidence of a lack of self-confidence and esteem. Behavioral evidences of low social interest can be detected in persistent blaming, complaining, excuses, fears, and disability reports.

If the counselor perceives the counselee as using one or more of these as a means of avoiding responsibility for his or her role in life situations, encouragement will be all the more important to the total process. Dreikurs indicated that whenever a person uses these tactics to cope with life, that person is preparing not to cooperate. Dreikurs' observation can be equally true for the counseling process unless the counselor is aware of the here-and-now aspects of the counseling relationship.

Counseling requires cooperation to work toward common goals. Adlerians establish agreements concerning the goals of counseling. An understanding of what the individual hopes to attain is established, including some indication of his or her expectations for the counselor's role. While Adlerians tend to be active participants in the counseling process, they are careful to ensure that realistic expectations are established. They will assure the individual of their interest and commitment to use their knowledge and skill for the individual's benefit. Success, however, requires an equal willingness by the counselee. Rapport, therefore, is established and nurtured throughout the counseling relationship on the basis of mutual respect, cooperation, and desire to achieve agreed upon goals. Throughout the counseling process, encouragement is a central ingredient to building and sustaining the relationship.

## Psychological Investigation

The second stage, psychological investigation of the process, will vary according to the nature of the presenting problem, the counselor's knowledge of the counselee prior to seeking counseling, and availability of data from such sources as tests, case histories, family, and so forth.

What the counselor attempts to do during this stage is understand the streams of conscious and not-so-conscious thoughts that guide individuals in understanding, predicting, and attempting to manage their environment. This action is a nonjudgmental activity. You are formulating a type of word picture of the individuals' movement through life. They are active participants in this process. It is somewhat analogous to painting an individual's portrait, with one important distinction: the portrait is not static. This aspect of movement can elude the counselor new to this method.

Individuals' respond behaviorally somewhat differently to the same convictions in their private logic when confronted with different environmental conditions. For example, concern with appearing foolish before others may evoke shy, retiring behavior in one situation and appearance of sophistication in another from the same individual. The ability to laugh at one's predicaments and not be impressed with situations that cannot be controlled could be a desirable goal in counseling. For the counselor to understand the movement toward a goal (e.g., to be in control or to avoid participation) is to begin addressing the underlying issues rather than symptoms of them.

Lifestyle assessment is one means of achieving a gestalt or holistic view of the individual's movement. Private logic is uncovered by self-disclosure and personal validation of the construct by the counselee. By this time, rapport is based solidly on respect, understanding, and caring.

My personal innovation on the traditional Adlerian process is the incorporation of Ivey's DCT assessment techniques into this and other stages of counseling where appropriate. Ivey (1986) has created a systematic approach to involving counselees in a discovery of what he calls their cognitive-developmental functioning. He has drawn on the work of Piaget (1963, 1965), the Swiss epistemologist, psychologist, and biologist, and others who have extended study beyond childhood to adolescence and adulthood.

Ivey (1986) summarizes his basic position in the following:

DCT's central assumption is that whether child, adolescent, or adult, we *metaphorically* repeat the well-known developmental stages of sensorimotor, concrete, formal, and postformal operations again and again. Piaget's strategies can be used throughout the life span. However, Piaget stressed the importance of moving to higher, more complex forms of thinking. DCT, on the other hand, values multiperspective thought, holding that there can be as much value in experiencing the world directly at the sensorimotor level as at the most complex, abstract levels. The basic tent of DCT is: *Higher is not better; each perspective is different and clarifies the whole.* (p. 126)

Like the Adlerian approach, DCT is very compatible from a multicultural perspective. Each affirms the cultural and gender values of the counselee including their identity within their primary sociological groups. Each also emphasizes the importance of the counselees' meaning attributed to prior experience as a source of understanding present and, if unexamined, likely future behavior. What DCT offers in addition to the traditional Adlerian assessment is enhancing the matching of the counselee's functional level in such a way as to be more attuned to the individual.

As will be seen in the illustrations below, we as counselors can enhance our effectiveness by systematically assessing their level of functioning and taking this into account as we dialogue with them. In short, rather than the counselee having to acquire the language and developmental level of the counselor, the counselor deliberately attempts to match the counselee's. If this is done, Ivey believes that the there is a greater likelihood that the counselee will benefit from the counseling. I agree with Ivey and believe that when lifestyle assessment is done properly this will occur. However, the use of Ivey's strategy has the potential to increase that likelihood to a greater extent, especially among clinicians less experienced with Adlerian methods. Another contribution of Ivey's approach is that the counselor may then assist the counselee to learn new levels of functioning by deliberately mismatching with a level that would benefit the counselee to experience additional coping skills.

What follows is a brief outline of concepts and steps in a DCT assessment. They include representative kinds of questions that one can use to conduct such an assessment.

**DCT Assessment Strategy.**   The process is one of co-construction, much like the process of collecting lifestyle information. The counselor is to listen to the language of the counselee in terms of content and process. Likewise, the counselor is attempting to hear, see, and feel the descriptions of the counselee as though experiencing them himself or herself. The following statements represent some of the concepts descriptive of each of the levels. As the counselee describes his or her concerns, the counselor is listening for the predominant themes in their level of development.

Cognitive-Developmental Level

| | |
|---|---|
| I. Sensorimotor | Experiences life directly in the immediate here and now; may be enmeshed in what they directly hear, see, and feel. |
| II. Concrete Operational | Describes events in great detail; "this happened . . . then this . . . "; concern is with action and objective, observable events; may be able to establish cause and effect—if/then—thought patterns. |
| III. Formal Operational | Likes to think about themselves and their personal patterns of thinking and feeling; able to look at problems at a distance but may not feel in here and now. |
| IV. Dialectic/Systemic | Capable of multiple perspectives; able to identify how family and cultural pressures affect them and their thinking processes; may be absence of emotional content. (Ivey, Ivey, & Simek-Morgan, 1993, pp. 134–135) |

**Identifying the Cognitive/Emotional Developmental Level.**
The first step in the questioning sequence is to ask: What occurs
for you when you focus on . . . (whatever issue is a difficulty at that
time). Although it is desirable for counselees to learn to function
at all levels, most will not and rapport is more easily established
and sustained, according to Ivey, when the counselor successfully
matches the counselee's predominate level. In addition, in times
of crisis or stress, individuals experience blocks in their capacity
to relate at one or more levels. Indeed, it is these very blocks to
function that contribute to the nature of a crisis. As a consequence,
by helping the counselee explore questions on the other levels
blocks can be overcome.

DCT Questioning Sequence

**Sensorimotor Questions**

Get a single image in your mind involving (issue). What are
you seeing? Hearing? Feeling? Is there a place in your body
where you particularly feel it is located?

**Concrete Questions**

Could you give me another example of when you felt this
way? Describe what happened.

**Formal Questions**

Does this happen in other situations (or ) is this a pattern for
you? Do you feel that way in other situations? Have you felt
that way before?

**Dialectic/Systemic/Integrative Questions**

How do you put together or organize all that we've been talking about? How might your thoughts and feelings about the
concern have taken form in your family of origin? How do
you see sex stereotyping and/or multicultural issues influencing your thoughts or feelings about the concern? How
could we describe this from the point of view of some other
person or using another frame of reference? (Ivey et al., 1993,
p. 140)

Illustrations of the DCT techniques will be found in the next section as well as in the Lifestyle Counseling Session Excerpts at the end of this chapter. Ivey (1986; Ivey et al., 1993) provides greater elaboration and illustration of the DCT concepts and process, including implications from a cross-cultural perspective. A broader, more in-depth study of these topics will facilitate their use in practice.

## Interpretation

The third stage, interpretation of the Adlerian counseling process, involves the use of tentative inferences and observations made by the counselor. Having listened to the individual discuss concerns, possibly exploring family constellation and/or early recollections, and having observed behavior in counseling and/or elsewhere, the counselor tentatively will offer observations that are descriptive of the individual and may have implications for meeting the individual's life tasks. A narrative outline may be prepared by the counselor using the format suggested in chapter 7.

**Intuitive Guessing and the Recognition Reflex.**   An Adlerian contribution to the process of psychological disclosure is the emphasis on what Dreikurs called deliberately "guessing" the purpose of an individual's behavior (i.e., sharing with the individual what seems to be its value and outcome or consequence). Contrary to what one might expect in the way of counselee resistance and denial, when such discussion is introduced properly, individuals feel relief and appreciation at being understood at a deeper level than is customary. Rather than a diagnosis, there is an effort to understand, explain, and interpret the motivation behind behaviors (i.e., the purpose and goals associated with behaviors). The *recognition reflex*—a knowing smile or laugh, facial acknowledgment, or verbal elaboration—is used to affirm the accuracy of psychological hunches based on the counselee's lifestyle information, one's knowledge of human motivation, and one's intuitive sense of the internal dialogue used by the individual (private logic) to make his or her place among others and cope with life's tasks. As will be illustrated in the following examples, this process helps to reach deeper levels of empathy with individuals while also helping to minimize inaccurate assumptions by the helper or categorizing individuals by symptoms.

**Interpretive Precautions.** Before proceeding to the next aspect of the counseling process, therefore, a few guidelines for the interpretive stage are needed. Interpretation is an intuitive process based upon clinical observation and judgment. For the Adlerian practitioner, it involves a caring disclosure of insights which individually may seem innocuous to the counselee until their pattern and relationship to the presenting problem become clear. It is the dissonance in beliefs and reality that creates indecision, poor judgment, and dysfunctional behavior. For the counselor's insights to be heard and understood is only a part of the process.

The ultimate goal for the counselee is to embrace and act on the new insights. Often individuals will experience the "ah, hah!" experience only to "forget" its meaning and continue with old, self-defeating behaviors. It is the skilled clinician who builds on these insights to successfully move the counselee to higher levels of readiness for change.

The following are some precautions for the interpretive stage:

1. Labeling is to be avoided; goals (purposes) of behavior are sought.

2. Encouraging the counselee to elaborate on or modify the counselor's observation is essential. Sometimes the correct wording or phrasing cannot be captured accurately without assistance from the counselee. In other cases, they can document an observation with innumerable examples of how accurately it applies.

3. Be prepared to be incorrect. Respecting the counselee's right to disagree is essential. Be particularly watchful of projecting personal biases into an observation (i.e., identifying counselor motives with counselee behavior).

4. Be aware of here-and-now behavior and feelings in the counseling relationship. Behavior and feelings expressed

in the interview also reveal lifestyle data (i.e., methods of coping and goal orientation). Not infrequently, for example, the counselor can anticipate seductiveness, anger, or withdrawal by a counselee on the basis of lifestyle information taken before the interpretation.

    5. Setting a tone of encouragement, including emphasis on the assets of the person, is an important part of the process.

Dispelling any mystical "analyst" aura that an individual may wish to ascribe to this process is essential. The counselor simply helps the individual bring to consciousness the fictive (as if) notions that are used to guide the individual and his or her feelings in life situations. Cultural and gender differences in processing this stage are worth noting as well.

**Cultural and Gender Considerations.** Men from dominant European cultures tend to be linear in their thinking processes. They tend to be outcome and achievement oriented. Personal value is found through producing and productivity. Time is like a commodity to be used wisely. Rugged individualism and personal accomplishment are prized. Religion as opposed to spirituality is the focus of personal value. These are not the values or orientation of many other cultures nor many women.

Family, friends, and community are highly regarded by Native Americans, African Americans, Asian Americans, and many other cultures around the world. To defer to the good of the family or community in lieu of personal satisfaction or gain is often the first priority of such individuals and they are personally happier and healthier for doing so. Likewise, women will process the quality of their relationships based on interpersonal satisfactions, not productivity and linear logic per se, as Caucasian men are inclined to do in this society.

Stereotypes of genders and cultures are to be avoided, but knowledge of general differences allows one to be sensitive to the possibility of assuming that others should meet one's unexamined expectations. One must be cautions about judging the value orientation of persons of the opposite gender or those who are racially or culturally different than oneself. This is especially important when the counselor is of a majority gender or culture. In an earlier illustration in chapter 1, Adler asked a social worker who sought his help in changing a person whose values were opposite to hers, "And is he happy would you say?" And when she answered affirmatively, he said, "Well, why don't we leave him alone, eh?"

**Adults.** When family constellation information and recollections are used such as is described in chapter 7, this may take the form of an interview in which the counselor sketches a verbal portrait of the individual. This summary is based on the information the individual has shared. It would reveal the characteristic ways in which the individual views himself or herself, life, and others.

The counselor may outline what he or she observes as the individual's beliefs and behaviors that are assets in coping with life tasks including, for example, work, friendship, love, self, and spirituality. The Adlerian also would present mistaken and self-defeating perceptions which, if accurate, could contribute to problems for the individual.

Without the more detailed lifestyle information, the counselor would observe and listen to the counselee to derive some means of understanding his or her goals and reflecting these to him or her. Whatever the source of data, the counselor usually would present it tentatively with a phrase such as, "Could it be . . . ?"

In addition to using lifestyle interpretation with individuals, the use of lifestyle in both premarital and marriage counseling can be very effective. The very characteristics that attract individuals often lead to some of their later major conflicts. An example may help to illustrate.

*The Case of Maria and Steve.* Early in the counseling session, each partner observed while the other partner had his or her lifestyle developed. Each was asked what qualities or attributes particularly attracted them to the other. In the case of Maria and

Steve, they reported that they were having a conflict over the husband's work and where they would live. Maria indicated that her husband left all of the decisions and responsibility for the home to her even though she had a career as well. She was an only child who grew up in a family that she described as fun-loving and affectionate. Steve worked long hours and seemed more concerned about advancement than family welfare. He was the second of two boys from a family with a strong work ethic. His older brother by 2 years, now a high school teacher, was described as able to get good grades, recognition, and social acceptance without great effort.

Maria was attracted to Steve because he was reliable, serious-minded, industrious, and ambitious. He was attracted to her because he thought of her as more intelligent (i.e., a good decision maker, a good partner, and a good, fun-loving companion). Unlike some marriages, their love had not faltered, but their confidence was shaken by the strain of recent events relative to Steve's job and moving from a house and neighborhood that Maria liked.

This case can help to illustrate both the Adlerian use of lifestyle data and DCT as a part of the interpretative stage. In this case, the counselor has determined that the wife, Maria, functions primarily on the sensorimotor cognitive-developmental level and pursues exploration of an early recollection with her:

Counselor: Maria, you described an early recollection in which you were alone and unsure of what to do about giving up your favorite game to a charity at the church. Do you remember that one? [Maria: Oh, yes!] Think back on that moment now. Try to be there now. What are you seeing?

Maria: Well, it's a pretty blue and white box. It has a bit of texture to it and it feels nice to touch. I really don't play it much because it takes two players and I rarely have anyone visit.

Counselor: Do you hear any sounds? [Maria: Not really.] And how do you feel?

Maria:    I feel torn about keeping it 'cause it's so pretty and when I do play, I enjoy it. But then again, mother wants me to contribute to the church charity. [Counselor: Anything else?] Only that I feel at a loss about what to do.

Counselor:    Where in your body are these feelings?

Maria:    Mmmm, well, I think, and this is going to sound funny, they are *in my hands*. I am holding the game in my hands and I don't want to let go but my conscience seems to be saying that I should. Does that sound funny? I mean, it's like I am sitting there alone . . . oh, no . . . Jiminy Cricket is here, too, on my shoulder. [Counselor: Oh, yes, you mentioned him in one of your other recollections. Are you feeling anything else?] Not that stands out.

*Note:* The counselor proceeds with questions on the concrete level. This level of DCT addresses the counselee's ability to relate what happened and when in a situation. It should be noted that Ivey's protocol at this point would involve asking if the counselee could think of another time when he or she felt this way.

Counselor:    Okay. Now let me ask you if you can think of another time when you felt that way? [Maria: Anytime or recently?] Well, anytime and recently would be okay, too.

Maria:    This is really weird! I was at the computer some time ago. Steve was still at work and I was typing a letter and *my hands seemed to tighten up*. [Counselor: Please continue speaking in the present tense, just like you were a moment ago.] Okay, well, I have to stop for a little while and rub them. [Counselor: Tell us more about that.] Well, I don't know. I am trying to catch up on correspondence with a friend. She has written to see how I am doing. I suddenly wish Steve was here. I mean, I feel bad but I don't know why.

Counselor:   And what are you doing now?

Maria:   I'm sitting here crying for no reason. I mean, this is crazy. I'm crying but I don't know why or what to do about it.

Counselor:   Is this still like the feelings you had a few minutes ago?

Maria:   Yes . . . yes, but now I feel sad, too. [Counselor: Uh, huh, and?] And I wish someone was here with me; I mean, it's silly, but I feel so alone, like I'm losing something.

Counselor:   Losing something like?

Maria:   [Maria looks down and continues to cry softly.] I don't know.

Counselor:   Maria, is Jiminy Cricket here? [Maria: Yes.] And what is he saying?

Maria:   He says that I know what's bothering me. [Counselor: And?] If I'm unhappy, it's up to me to do something about it. [Counselor: And what would that be?] What's right. I mean, what will do the greatest good for me and Steve.

*Note:* At this point the counselor decides to see if Maria can conceptually relate at the formal-operational level with this issue and to discern patterns to her experiencing that may help her gain insights for the future.

Counselor:   Is there any similarity between these two events? I mean any patterns within them for you?

Maria:      Well, I guess that I'm undecided about something in both situations. I feel a lot of responsibility for doing the "right" thing. [Counselor: Anything else?] Hmmm, yes, I feel alone. I wish someone would help me.

*Note:* At this point the counselor decides to see if Maria can conceptually relate at the DCT level of dialectic/systemic.

Counselor:  Could it be, too, that you feel really bad, even guilty, when you are wanting to do what might make you feel good and Jiminy Cricket says, that's not right? [Maria looks up and gives a small smile and nod, yes.] Where do you think that feeling comes from?

Maria:      I guess mother. She always said that a woman's job was to do what was right for the family. She always made sacrifices for Papa and me. [Counselor: And what does that have to do with you today?] Well, I guess that I feel I should be the same way.

Counselor:  And you if you aren't? [Maria starts to cry again.]

Maria:      It means that I'm selfish . . . that I'm not a good wife and mother.

Counselor:  So whenever there's a decision to be made, it's your job, *even obligation* to do what's best for others, even if it makes you unhappy, and you feel so alone at those times. [Maria nods and smiles even as she wipes a tear.]

*Note:* The counselor invites Steve to respond.

Counselor:  Steve, I think Maria may be wondering what you are feeling right now, too.

Steve:    I had no idea how she felt. I mean I knew that she got upset but I never understood why she'd cry over some of the things that she did. I didn't mean to hurt you, Maria, I just didn't know what to do.

The process of counseling continued, with both Maria and Steve gaining insights and a feeling for needs being expressed by Maria for more than simple reassurances so often given by him in the past. Maria was afraid to express her needs for fear of rejection and her unique (although not uncommon) set of convictions that she would be a bad partner and mother if she did. Steve's drive to be successful was discerned to be a compensation for the competition he had felt with his older brother. Maria and Steve each had sought a person as a companion who seemed to complement their needs. Maria had compensated for her hesitancy in new situations by developing a confident appearance that others assumed was based on genuinely felt, positive self-esteem.

Maria wanted a co-partner much as she had experienced between her parents, but more important, a friend in whom to confide and share decisions. Steve, on the other hand, thought he had a partner who did not need his help. Through a process of dialogue and exploration, each had an opportunity to help the other. This, of course, increases intimacy and trust as well.

Although both the early recollections and DCT questions uncovered similar patterns, each offers complementary strategies for assisting the counselee. The "rules of life" that all people create early in life are easily uncovered with lifestyle analysis. Likewise, DCT helps to bring the here and now into sharp focus and adds the dimension of using the various operational levels as a means of both more effective communication and potential intervention.

**Older Adults.**   Butler's (1963) research on the role of the life review among older individuals was the starting point and remains the focal point of much research and clinical practice using reminiscence. Research on the effectiveness of this technique has yielded equivocal results. Based on Adlerian theory, the technique of using early recollections provides an opportunity for structured reminiscence and offers several advantages over the traditional life review therapy referred to in the gerontological literature (Sweeney, 1989; Sweeney & Myers, 1986).

A variety of researchers have obtained positive outcomes in investigations of structured reminiscing in relationship to life satisfaction and ego integrity among older persons. It has proven to be effective for stimulating cognitive functioning and for improving relationships between staff and residents of long-term care facilities. Life review also has been found to be an effective therapy with depressed individuals for whom meaninglessness in life was a central problem. Some researchers, however, reported negative and/or conflicting results using life review therapy approaches, especially with depressed persons.

Perhaps even more significant is the finding that marked negative affect can occur during the course of the life review process. This may be accompanied by heightened levels of anxiety that do not diminish until near completion of the review process, if at all. As described in the literature, this process may be lengthy, leaving the older person in a depressed state for a varying amount of time, and perhaps permanently in the absence of professional intervention. This should not be the case from an Adlerian perspective.

Encouragement is used by Adlerians as the central concept to bring about change. Courage to be imperfect, courage to forgive oneself and others, courage to act even when one is very afraid, courage to do that which is no longer easy, courage to make the very best of whatever situation develops, are the basis for counseling. Adler believed that feelings of inferiority were a part of the human condition. How individuals cope with these feelings of inadequacy is reflected in their approach to life.

As noted earlier, the expert counselor can diagnose the degree of discouragement by the prevalence and persistence of reports of fears, excuses, complaining, blaming, criticizing, and disability. Some persons would contend that such behaviors are "normal" for "old" people. Although aging does indeed bring many challenges, and any person who loses a loved one, for example, will experience grief and all of its ramifications, it is still a matter of degree as to how well different individuals handle similar situations.

These differences can be uncovered, for example, through the use of early recollections. Adler noted, "Thus his memories represent his (Story of My Life); a story he repeats to himself to warn him or to comfort him, to keep him concentrated on his goal, to prepare him, by means of past experiences, to meet the future with an already tested style of action" (Ansbacher & Ansbacher, 1967, p. 351).

***The Case of Ms. Sullivan.***   One case comes to mind of a widow, Ms. Sullivan (age 67), who was having adjustment problems in a seniors living community. This particular woman had lost her husband the year before due to an unexpected heart attack. She had appeared to have coped quite satisfactorily but was urged by her daughter who lived in an adjacent state to sell her home and move into a senior citizens' apartment complex. She agreed to this arrangement at the time but never seemed entirely accepting of it. The woman who was administrator of the apartment complex made friendly overtures to Ms. Sullivan but without much success; Ms. Sullivan was cordial but distant toward the administrator.

As time went on, other residents who came to know Ms. Sullivan expressed concern about the strong angry feelings she had toward her daughter. Her son lived in California and was seen only at the time of the funeral for his father. The daughter had made more than a few efforts to visit her mother but seemed to have stopped trying of late. Those closest to her found it difficult to confront her because she would say things like, "Don't be silly, I can take care of myself just fine!" Nevertheless, these folks did not believe that she was adapting well to her new circumstances.

Because of persistent headaches, Ms. Sullivan sought a prescription from her physician. Fortunately, he had known her for several years and recognized signs of depression during his time with her. At his insistence, she agreed to talk with someone to help her sort out her feelings and priorities now that she's a widow.

On meeting with Ms. Sullivan, the counselor found a pleasant, articulate lady who seemed quite self-sufficient in outlook and manner. When asked how life would be different if she did not get headaches, she stated that maybe she could be a bit more sociable with other residents. She later expressed disappointment with her relationship with her daughter as well. After a period of general discussion about her husband's death, adjustments since then, relationships with other family members, and similar matters, the idea of lifestyle was introduced to Ms. Sullivan. She agreed quite readily to using this as a means of helping the counselor to know her better.

The lifestyle assessment, involving all the data about early relationships including siblings, parents, and so forth, and five or six early recollections, was developed into a kind of verbal narrative, focusing on Ms. Sullivan's way of coping with work, friendship, and love relationships. Because the process of collecting lifestyle information lends itself to rapport-building and further information about current life coping, this is a positive empathic experience for the counselee. This is also an opportunity for reflection and corroborating or refuting impressions that the counselor has begun to formulate.

Ms. Sullivan recounted the following experience from when she was 5 years old. It helps to illustrate the richness of information that even one recollection holds.

> I recall my mother getting ready to set out on our front porch, some of my dresses that were old and no longer fit. One of the dresses was my very favorite. I can remember my grandmother at the top of the stairs, my mother walking halfway down the stairs, and I was at the bottom of the stairs. I was begging my mother not to give away my favorite dress. She was telling me to stop making a fuss and being so silly and my grandmother saying soothing things to me.
>
> I hated both my grandmother and mother at the same time; my mother for giving away the dress and saying I was silly, and my grandmother for trying to make me feel better about the situation.

This recollection provides the counselor with an opportunity to hypothesize about Ms. Sullivan's outlook on life, herself, and other women. As a matter of practice, the counselee should also be asked to report the feelings associated with such an experience. Ms. Sullivan noted:

> I was angry at mother and grandmother. I felt I was a baby and kept telling myself as I cried to stop and be intelligent about all this. If I act like a baby my mother will really not take me serious. I also was angry at my grandmother because I felt I did not need to be taken care of.

One might hypothesize the following:

> I should be able to have my own way.

> When I don't get my way, I have a right to throw a fit!

> I don't like other women trying to talk down to me.

> When I'm mad, don't try to patronize me!

> I expect to be taken seriously and not be treated as "silly."

> I don't like feeling that I'm not in control.

All such statements are treated as tentative. They may be discarded, modified, or accepted in part or whole depending on Ms. Sullivan's responses and affirmations. The counselor begins to guess the private logic that discloses the goals of the person; in this case, to be taken seriously, to have her way with life, and to be in control. One might guess further that her relationships with women, especially with women in authority, are somewhat contentious at times of crises or stress. The transitions to widowhood and from independent living to community living certainly constitute times of stress.

Ms. Sullivan acknowledged that, for her, not feeling "on top" and in control of herself was very disquieting. Further, she recognized her pattern of being put off by anyone (but particularly women) who tried to "coddle" her. She was confronted by the counselor with the observation that "it could be" she was behaving toward her daughter exactly the way she had perceived her mother behaving toward her. This had never occurred to her before now. She reflected on this for some time and concluded that, indeed, she was probably more faithfully following that pattern than her mother had! On a subsequent visit her daughter joined her. They were both desirous of improving their relationship while there was still time.

For someone not trained in Adlerian methods or aware of the implications of early recollections, such a report may seem interesting but inconsequential. In point of fact, when Ms. Sullivan was given the opportunity to discuss its meaning for her, she reported that it helped her rethink her position on some matters of much importance to her. Certain of the insights also would be important to anyone attempting to help her cope with loss, grief, and relationships with other women in her later years. What caused her stress and how she coped with it was discussed. This was a give-and-take, interactive process. It involved a positive confrontation of life issues.

A few observations about the case of Ms. Sullivan can help to illustrate the practical usefulness of early recollections in counseling with older persons. First, even without using other lifestyle or early recollection data, one could guess that Ms. Sullivan may have difficulty with a woman counselor, unless the counselor was trained in lifestyle methods. This is based on her reaction to her mother and grandmother in the early recollection and the perception of her mother being above her. This was corroborated at least in part by the female administrator's experience (potentially an authority figure) in attempting to befriend Ms. Sullivan. Also interesting to note is that she accepted her male physician's advice, rebuffed the women acquaintances who offered similar advice based on their experience, and seemed unusually hard on her daughter who tried to make at least some visits. On the other hand, her son was not known to even make an effort to come for a visit, yet her attitude toward him remained essentially positive.

No life review need end with an older person feeling depressed, defeated, or fearful without making an informed effort to confront the negative self-talk behind these feelings. The use of early recollections and lifestyle assessment is not a panacea for all unhappy older persons. However, they can be viable alternatives or supplements to present methods (Sweeney, 1989; Sweeney & Myers, 1986).

If only a single early recollection has such potential to reveal significant insight to an individual's outlook on life, self, and others, how much more will be realized with further data, counselee behavior in the interview, and an opportunity to interact. The affect expressed in conjunction with the early recollections is always important. The feelings reveal the meaning attributed to the events. It is in these comments that courage is revealed as present or not. Life is seen as fair or unfair, safe or unsafe. Life tasks are accepted as a challenge to be met or avoided. Others are seen as helpful or threatening. Counselees perceive themselves as able or not able.

Two individuals from the same family having experienced the same event will assign different meaning to its significance. These perceptions of what happened and how they felt about it are a basis for understanding their "private logic." When counselors find discouraged attitudes and feelings in counselees' early recollections, it is not surprising to find evidence of it popping up in their day-to-day lives. Normally this reveals itself when the individual's typical way of perceiving and coping is ineffective or otherwise inappropriate for the present circumstances. Certainly, loss of one's spouse, friends, family, or home, or slowing down or loss of physical faculties will bring on a test of one's ability to cope and grow in the light of new circumstances.

Using the other precepts of Adlerian psychology also will increase the worth of these methods. They certainly have promise for work with older persons.

**Children.**   In the case of children, parent and teacher reports of behavior can be sufficient data on which to make some guesses.

In chapter 6, the goals of disruptive behavior were identified. Although observation of the child's behavior before counseling can be helpful, in many cases it is not necessary for effective counseling.

While talking with the teachers or parents, the counselor attempts to determine the child's mistaken goals and to obtain specific behavioral instances from which these goals are derived. The counselor may use these mistaken goals to confirm or refute his or her hunches while talking with the child. The counselor begins guessing, therefore, what the child expects to achieve by his or her disruptive behavior in order to help him or her assess these goals and behaviors. To have one's mistaken goals revealed can be very encouraging because what one intends to do can be voluntarily changed toward more mutually satisfying goals.

A major Adlerian technique can be described as facilitative confrontation; that is, the counselor, in a friendly, nonpossessive way, shares what he or she observes to be beliefs that the individual pursues. In working with children, the counselor may make a guess and facilitatively confront as illustrated in the following:

Counselor:   Do you know why you are here today?

Bobby:   Because I talked back to my teacher.

Counselor:   That does seem to have been a problem. Have you talked back to her before?

Bobby:   Sometimes.

Counselor:   Do you know why you talk back to her?

Bobby:   [Head nods, no.]

Counselor:   You even feel mad right now. Would you like to know why I think you talk back?

Bobby:   [Head nods, yes.]

Counselor:     I think you want her to know that she can't make you do anything, that you'll do what you want, when you want. Fellow, you have a lot on the ball and nobody's going to tell you what to do without clearing it with you first. Could it be?

Bobby:     [Smiles and shakes head, no.]

Counselor:     Even now you're going to show me, you won't agree until you're ready! [Bobby smiles.] Right? [Counselor smiles.]

Bobby:     Yep!

In instances such as this the counselor may wish to cite one or two more specific instances in which the boy has demonstrated this same goal. The recognition reflex, in this case a smile, is a fairly reliable behavioral clue that the boy's goal is power. If the counselor is mistaken, a lack of cues will be evident. In some cases, a more fundamental goal may be missed and the counselor must be prepared to revise his or her assessment accordingly. Only a few types of children resist sharing the recognition signs (e.g., those who practice being nonexpressive and those who laugh or giggle throughout a conference).

In cases such as this one, the counselor is not revealing so much about why the boy is being disruptive (what caused it) as he is revealing what the boy hopes to gain (his goal). The next question becomes one of how the boy can find his place in class without being disruptive. As was seen in chapter 6, corrective and preventative action by the teacher and parents can facilitate the decision by the boy to try out new behaviors. Adlerians believe that discouragement (i.e., lack of self-confidence) moves individuals against others. Therefore, punishment is not appropriate nor is coercion.

Although the process described in words may seem to result in authoritarian manipulation, quite the opposite is true in practice. Respect for the individual and recognition that he or she cannot be required to cooperate are uppermost in the counselor's mind. In fact, one of the most effective strategies in conflict resolution is offering appropriate alternative choices, freely made, and implemented out of the sense of respect conveyed through the relationship and process.

## Reorientation

The final stage of Adlerian counseling is dependent on the counselee's desire to institute a change. Understanding the meaning of their behaviors and the goals that they pursue frees individuals to decide what other behaviors they might wish to try. It is at this point the counselor will say, "Would you like to change?" Even when the counselees say they do, the counselor is not too quick to proceed. With the best of intentions, not everyone is prepared for the commitment. As a consequence, the counselor may "spit in the soup" of the individual by disclosing the ease with which it would be possible to fall back on old thoughts, attitudes, and behaviors. It is equally important to underscore the feelings that fortify them when an incident ensues. To maintain a friendly, accepting attitude and manner is critical at this juncture. Literally, the decision to proceed is with the counselee.

In the marriage case mentioned previously (Maria and Steve), each partner agreed to help the other in those areas that required encouragement. The husband began participating in home-related decision making. Both agreed to take more interest in the responsibility that the other carried outside of the home. One behavioral agreement they had established early in counseling was to have an uninterrupted partnership meeting for 1 hour each week. One partner would speak for 30 minutes and then the other would speak for a similar period while the partner listened. They agreed not to speak about the topics between these meeting times but would alternate who had the first session each week.

Modifications of the partnership meeting develop according to the need and desire of couples. In the beginning, however, a specific time, place, and procedure are agreed to in advance. The counselor may have the couples practice this meeting technique and similar techniques in the counseling interviews, including role-playing, problem solving, modeling, and goal setting.

In the case of the boy talking back to the teacher, the counselor suggested alternatives with the boy that he could employ to his teacher. In every case, the fact that the boy had alternatives and choices was clear. The counselor then asked the boy if he wished to change and if he would like to use a written plan or agreement of what his intentions were (e.g., not to talk back but to find other ways of expressing his feelings to the teacher). Whatever the arrangement, the counselor was working toward realistic objectives that would greatly increase the probability of success by the boy.

In some cases, the time span for success may be short intervals, or only small changes in behavior may be attempted to constitute successful progress. Failure, per se, is minimized or eliminated by careful planning and patience with mistakes or lapses.

On occasion, individuals will pursue self-defeating behaviors that seem resistant to change. Using "common sense," one would conclude that such behavior is illogical, useless, and clearly in need of remediation. Drawing on the private logic of the individual, however, reveals a rationale and purpose, to which the individual adheres without serious question.

In the case of the child who becomes characterized as a bully, fighting with other youngsters and adults becomes a source of many incidents. Punishment, lectures, and pleas for behavior change generally make little or no difference. Knowing that the child who fights is most often pursuing a goal of revenge and a private logic that "I may not be likable but I can hurt you back," one can anticipate a rationale that makes fighting, for example, a necessary behavior in his or her repertoire.

By simply listening and actively reflecting what is said, you will discover, for example, that fighting is a noble thing to do. Not unlike Robin Hood or the knights of the Round Table, they are "correcting" or "evening the score" of others' transgressions. The following is a case in point from an interview with a fourth-grade boy:

Counselor:     Do you like to fight, Daryl?

Daryl:         [He nods, no.]

Counselor:     I think maybe sometimes you do. Could it be? [Daryl shrugs his shoulders] I think sometimes you like to show others that you can hurt them, too; that you can beat them up.

Daryl:         [Smiles broadly and shakes his head, yes.]

Counselor:     So you like to fight, Daryl. And does that solve your problems?

Daryl:         [He covers a smile with his hand over his mouth.] Well, I hit them for teasing my sister, then they started picking on me!

Counselor:     Oh, I see; so it really isn't your fault 'cause they were teasing your sister.

Daryl:         [Nods, yes.]

You see a desire by Daryl to maintain self-respect. After all, who could fault the nobility of his intentions? The fact that his fights rarely involve his sister's honor is of no consequence in his private logic.

To move immediately into the next stage (i.e., reorientation) is a common error. At this point, the counselor may understand Daryl's motivation better, but asking or expecting him to change on this basis alone probably is insufficient. What I believe does help is (a) to pair the negative feelings with the misbehavior in the situation and (b) to introduce a new alternative with which only positive feelings can be associated. Using the previous illustration, the counselor may continue as follows:

Counselor:     . . . and does this make you feel happy or sad?

Daryl:         Happy and sad

Counselor: Happy that you got back at them but sad that they don't like you [Daryl nods, yes.] I wonder, do you really want other kids to like you and for you to like them? [He nods, yes.] I'm not so sure, Daryl. You see, I don't think you expect others to like you, and that's a bad feeling, so you want them to pay for your bad feelings.

Daryl: Well, I wouldn't hit them if they'd just treat me nice.

Counselor: You really feel bad when you're not included in games and stuff like everyone else. [Daryl looks down at the floor and fumbles with his fingers.] And after a fight everyone talks about how bad you are and just makes you feel worse. [Daryl looks up with a sad look on his face.] I wonder if you'd be willing to start over today on making and keeping friends.

In this case, Daryl was willing to start working on new behaviors, but helping him to focus on his new goal and the satisfaction in making progress toward it was very important to the success. So long as he gained intrinsic satisfaction from his fighting, as he chose to see it, and did not believe others would like him anyway, winning him over to changing his behavior would be difficult. Adults are just as prone to continue using ineffective, socially useless behavior unless they are helped to associate the dysfunctional behaviors with the experience of negative feelings that are evoked by the consequences.

## SPECIFIC TECHNIQUES

Convinced that individuals have the power to change if they choose to do so, Adlerians make suggestions and use techniques intended to illustrate this belief to counselees. Whether child or adult, individuals are encouraged to develop self-esteem and confidence in their ability to cope with life. The Adlerian is not impressed by fears, excuses, disabilities, blaming, or complaining.

Emotions that are used to distract others from the fact that the person wants freedom from his or her responsibilities are seen as tools that contribute to continued discouragement. Kindly but purposefully, the Adlerian will work toward avoiding the pitfalls of these expressions and instead emphasize the genuine assets of the individual's sense of belonging, security, and adequacy. Encouragement is the process the counselor uses to build the individual's confidence to cope with life.

In my experience, empathy, per se, has not been stressed by other Adlerians in their demonstrations or lectures. Persons of other theoretical persuasions sometimes are critical of this tendency. Because the Adlerian model is rationally based (i.e., mistaken evaluations or thoughts are the originating source of difficulties), feelings are not treated as an entity unto themselves. Feelings of the person are important, however, and serve as signposts for both counselor and counselee concerning the latter's intentions.

---

### Listen for three levels of feelings.

---

I have found that listening for three levels of feelings is useful in counseling and consultation. For example, in what was essentially a vocationally oriented counseling case, a high school senior expressed dissatisfaction with her part-time job. She had hoped to continue the position full time after graduation but was not happy under her present supervisor. As the interview progressed, although carefully worded, it became apparent that she wanted more independence from her parents. Later in counseling, unexpressed doubt in her ability to be independent was revealed through avoidance of serious consideration of other alternatives to her present work and home situation. This was confirmed in subsequent interviews. The feelings heard at three levels were

1. Present, obvious: dissatisfaction with work situation

2. Veiled: desire for independence

3. Preconscious: self-doubt in ability to be independent

Reasons and excuses for not considering alternatives to the presenting problem would defeat the most sincere counselor if the self-doubt was not confronted. Adlerians tend to deal with the doubts by helping to provide success experiences to overcome the doubts. Although aware of the present and veiled feelings, counselors choose to discredit the mistaken notions that contribute to the more pervasive feelings.

The reorientation stage, then, requires an awareness of the individual's thoughts and associated feelings that will affect his or her cooperation. Having cognitively decided to change does not make change happen. Therefore, a part of the counselor's function is to help distract the counselee from the advantages of his or her previous self-defeating notions and behavior.

Adlerians use a variety of specific techniques to help counselees (a) catch themselves at self-defeating behaviors, (b) become conscious of their control over their attitudes and feelings, (c) get distracted from the advantages of a hidden agenda in self-defeating behaviors, and (d) develop confidence in their ability to cope successfully with life tasks. Among the many techniques, only a few will be mentioned to illustrate.

## Spitting in the Soup

This is a vivid phrase for describing what happens when the counselor exposes the hidden agenda or goal for the counselee's self-defeating behavior. When the counselor is accurate with his or her observation ("Could it be that . . . ?") and can illustrate this clearly to the counselee, the counselee may continue this behavior, but "it won't taste so sweet" any longer! The counselee is no longer innocent of its hidden meaning.

This technique is used very effectively as a means of disengaging the individual from previous behaviors. Children can understand the goals of misbehaviors quickly and will not repeat the same behaviors unless adults or other children make them useful. It also is quite effective with adults, as in the case of the "good servant mother," the "super teacher," or "real man" images.

## Antisuggestion

This technique, used by other than Adlerians as well, is used selectively to help illustrate that individuals have control of functions not otherwise accepted by them. For example, when a counselee says he or she cannot help getting tense when talking to members of the opposite sex, the counselor may suggest that at the next such opportunity the counselee should get as tense as he or she can (i.e., try to get tense).

Occasionally this suggestion is used in the context of the interview (e.g., counselees rehearse the action as a variation of role-playing). The irony, of course, is that when invited to do their "thing'" they find themselves incapable of doing it. It has lost its value. Most counselees openly smile at their new predicament.

## "If Only I Could . . ."

This phrase often follows the important question, "How would life be different for you if this problem did not exist?" An Adlerian counselor would suggest that the person behave "as if" he or she could (i.e., act as though you can).

This suggestion can be quite effective once the individual has some insight into the mistaken assessment he or she made before counseling. Not to succeed becomes less important, thereby minimizing disappointment.

## Push-Button Technique

In response to "I can't change how I feel" or "It isn't my fault; I can't help what I do," the counselor uses the counselee's imagination to demonstrate his or her capacity to experience both positive and negative emotions by imaging situations that evoke these feelings. The counselee can experience the changes in body tension, heart rate, and so forth and the corresponding change in movement to action. Naturally, follow-up is an important aspect of the total process. Generally, the counselor can determine in advance how cooperative an individual or couple will be on follow-up.

### Adding Significant Modifiers

In addition to listening for excuses and other preludes to lack of cooperation mentioned previously, Adlerians practice reading between the lines and adding significant modifiers or conjunctions to counselee statements. For example, experience has shown that often when an individual says, "I will try," what they are thinking is, "*but* I don't think it will work."

### Assessing Probabilities

The counselor uses this information as a means of assessing the probabilities of certain suggestions being implemented. When encountering signs of discouragement, he or she tries other alternatives, smaller steps, or fewer expectations for the individual.

### Task Setting

Task setting is an important aspect of the process. "Homework" assignments to try new behaviors, participate in a study group, or simply observe others in their daily living are employed often.

Generally, limited objectives are chosen and agreed on by the counselee. The probabilities for success are high if goals are properly selected. The method of successive approximation (i.e., to move the person toward an outcome in reasonable stages for him or her) is very important. Asking a young person who uses fist fighting in his or her pursuit of the goal of revenge to "never" fight again is doomed to failure. Getting the child to agree not to fight for a defined period of time (e.g., this morning, until you get home, etc.) increases the likelihood of cooperation and success, especially if there is follow-up and encouragement for managing self-control.

**Examples of Task Setting.**   For another fellow who found a closeness lacking in his interpersonal relationships, particularly with a girl whom he liked, a variety of suggestions were explored including some developed by himself. A list was made and ordered according to his estimate of their value to him and his readiness to use them as tryout behaviors.

Among those listed first was smiling more often. He characterized himself as "Solemn Sam." More specifically, each day he entered the office, he agreed to smile quite purposefully and again at some other point in the day. The result was so dramatic that it was not necessary to list it for the second week. A number of people approached him the first morning to simply chat. Luncheon invitations followed and he soon found reasons to smile.

Another item on his list was to impulsively buy something for himself that he would not purchase normally. This action was a little more difficult because he was usually "thrifty" and very deliberate in his purchases. He had carried a notion that self-indulgence would categorically result in terrible consequences. He gave himself permission to buy a "gift" one afternoon that week and was delighted with the satisfaction he felt in being free to do what he had perceived as beyond his capability.

A more difficult item was to anticipate getting, doing, or saying something that would surprise and please his girlfriend. This item was not attempted in the first two weeks because he felt at a loss on how to proceed. The discovery of how to accomplish this task was the real challenge. He reported after successfully completing this item at least once, that he really had not been listening to her interests, aspirations, and desires. When he stopped worrying about how he was doing with her, he was freed to discover what they enjoyed together. Obviously, once is not enough, but all journeys begin with one successful step.

## SUMMARY

In my professional counseling, I have observed that the greatest prejudice discouraged persons hold against anyone is the one that they hold against themselves. The punch line in one cartoon said it well: "I know a lot of people who aren't as smart as they think they are, I just don't want to be as dumb as I think I am!" Not to believe in oneself, although not uncommon, is disabling.

The challenge for the counselor is to confront in a caring way the mistaken meaning assigned by individuals to early life events as they present themselves in the here-and-now living of today. In so doing, the counselor can help them reassess their assets and to appreciate their "shortcomings" as an expression of their membership in the whole of humanity. For it is coming to the realization that one is no more and no less than others that true social equality has meaning and purpose.

## LIFESTYLE COUNSELING SESSION EXCERPTS

### Lifestyle Assessment Information

The original purpose of this session was to conduct a demonstration of a lifestyle assessment. I also wished to incorporate some DCT techniques into the process. There was no stated reason for counseling on the part of the woman who agreed to participate in the process. As is true in many such situations, unfinished business or current events in the lives of persons not in counseling emerge as relevant because these methods uncover the unconscious thoughts, emotions, and predicaments important to the participants. As a consequence, I always provide opportunity for appropriate follow-up and inform the persons in advance that such topics may emerge for which they will desire follow-up. Naturally, volunteers are always free to decline participation at any time.

What follows is basic information gathered in an initial 1½-hour interview, including excerpts demonstrating the use of lifestyle, early recollection, and DCT methods. It may be notable only because it is typical of the kind of data, process, and usefulness that can follow from using these techniques together. The interview for gathering basic lifestyle data, as noted elsewhere, can be eliminated by having counselees complete the forms in advance. This can save time for more directed interaction in the interview within the more common 50-minute session if desired.

The data and excerpts that follow come from a typescript of the first session. Whether or not one is accustomed to Adlerian lifestyle methods, even a casual review of the data will suggest that each individual expresses expectations, intentions, and preferences in many ways by choices made each day. This woman shares a great deal about her outlook on herself, others, and life that could be relevant for topics related to her work, friendship, love, self, and spiritual dimensions as described in chapter 2. We begin to focus on one topic because it is the one most important to her at this time.

I.  Individual Characteristics: Family Constellation and Attributes

**Counselee:** Jan, female, 40s, divorced, mother of two boys, Robert, 14 years, and Norman, 13 years of age, professional person in education (bachelor's and master's degrees), brought up in a Roman Catholic family, attended Catholic schools. Attractively dressed, poised, and open to self-exploration. She was the middle child in a family of five girls. Both parents are still living (retired).

| | |
|---|---|
| Victoria | Oldest sister (+4 years) |
| Jan | I was the kid without distinction |
| Lois | (–4 years: twin; tomboy; father's favorite) |
| Loretta | (–4 years: twin; mother's favorite) most different from Jan: very determined, very outspoken, real strong personality; most like father (determined, stubborn, controlling) |
| Miscarriage | (–8 years) |
| Jackie | (–11 years: Jan's "baby doll"—she enjoyed caring for her youngest sister) |

**Attributes compared to siblings:** Jan described herself as

- the *next most* intelligent, hard working, able in school, helping around the house, conforming, trying to please, considerate of others, sensitive—easily hurt, sense of humor, idealistic (expect things to be the way that they should be), standards of achievement high, athletic, strongest, tallest, feminine.

- the *most* rebellious, wanting her own way, having a temper tantrum, materialistic, prettiest. She reported liking to be female. Her nickname was "Fancy Jan" or "Prissy Missy."

- the *least* likely to be moralistic (i.e., to go by the "book" and see the faults of others).

- the *most* punished child for "talking back" to mom and dad. (However, the family was described as loud [six women and dad] and talking back was tolerated to a certain extent among all the children.)

**Self-description:**

Counselor:  O.K. What kind of a kid were you?

Jan:  Hmm . . . the role that I played in the family is probably . . . I think and I don't know . . . but it's the *dingy* person. I mean there are a lot of things I did. I guess I probably found ways of being in the spotlight because you know *I was the kid without the distinction*. There was an oldest, there were twins, and there was a baby, but I was the second oldest; but there were things that I guess I did that drew attention. I don't know. [She goes on to say that later in life she learned to use the "dumb blonde" stereotype to get away with some things she did not want to do—she made being "without distinction" useful to her!)

II. Adult and Gender Models: Parents and Grandparents

**Father:** Insurance salesman; worked many nights; German descent; strict, very controlling, wanted children to follow rules, wanted order, not particularly patient, but he was there for them. He would play golf on Saturday morning early in order to be home in the afternoon. She thought she was father's next most favorite child (she felt he showed her off). Her sister Lois (the first of twins, a tomboy) was his favorite because they did things together. Father is an absent but important part of one recollection.

**Mother:** Homemaker; real special; she was always there for them; silly, very kind, caring, nurturing, always fun; sang songs. Mother plays prominently in two early recollections.

Parents agreed on child rearing and she had no recollections of quarreling between them. She felt no fear or anxiety about their differences. Father made the major decisions. The parents seemed to be happy together, socialized with friends, and generally provided a stable family nucleus.

**Grandmother (maternal):** Very special because she would go in the water with them (Nanny the Seal); she never knew a stranger; she'd sing silly songs; she was fun! She plays prominently in one recollection.

**Grandmother (paternal):** Strict but great cook.

**Grandfather (paternal):** Short, sweet, funny, little man; smelled of cigar smoke (the best smell in the world); fun, fun! (*Note:* Jan probably associates different fragrances with good times whether cooking or otherwise.)

III. Family/Cultural Values

There are certain values that tend to influence each child regardless of their position in the family constellation. Jan reported being brought up Roman Catholic. The fact that she notes "brought up" may suggest that she no longer practices this faith. However, the counselor would guess that spiritual beliefs are still important to her as well. Both parents practiced this faith and, as a child and adult, she admired them both as a couple and individually. Among the values in Jan's family are likely to be the following: respect and caring for one another;

respect for God as creator; hard work but balanced with fun; music and dance as a source of pleasure; order; cooperation; and attributes important to work, friendship, and love relationships.

Mother and father were reported to have openly and actively discussed their differences but they were not contentious or threatening in any way. They modeled for the children a kind of give and take that resulted in consensus or agreeing not to agree on some issues. This could be an asset to Jan when negotiating about issues with others whom she respects and who respect her. On the other hand, she may be disadvantaged in knowing how to reconcile such differences when they occur in relationships where mutual respect is not present (i.e., when the other person is not forthright and committed to a mutually acceptable solution). Her desire to be there for others could result in her taking more responsibility or giving in too much as a way to maximize the opportunity for agreement.

## IV. Early Recollections

The following are verbatim excerpts of Jan's early recollections taken from the interview. As noted earlier, Adlerians attempt to use the self-talk of the counselee in the process of interpretation and counseling in order to maximize the accuracy and relevance to the counselee. Some comments have been highlighted to assist the reader in noting some aspects of the early recollections that will be especially useful later in the counseling process regarding themes within the self-talk of this woman.

1. *I see that living room sort of, the living room window and this lamp. I think it was green glass or something and I must of been running, playing, something, but I tripped on the cord and the lamp fell and I thought, Oh, no! You know, I'm not going to stick around here for daddy to come home and get mad at me. I'm gonna run away and so my mother said, "Honey why don't you wait and daddy will take you to the bus station." I got my little doll suitcase and I put*

all my underwear in it because I was running away. She kept saying, "O.K. honey, daddy's not going to be that mad, but if you want to run away why don't you wait until he comes and he'll take you." I mean, I must of been really afraid of what he would do and I don't remember him doing anything. I remember it being funny. I think my mother must of told him what I was going to do and that I got my little doll suitcase and you know so I don't even remember him doing anything. Hmm, or saying anything, but *I do remember how afraid I was that something really awful was going to happen.* And I remember folding diapers for the twins. You know there are just mounds of diapers for these two babies and we got to help fold. I had no idea where I was going to go. I just remember packing this little red doll suitcase and just . . . and all I put in it was my underwear. (laugh) I had undershirts and I put them in there. I put socks and panties and undershirts. . . . I know that *I was scared that daddy would get mad at me and I didn't want to incur his wrath and you know I . . . My dad is a real strong domineering.*

2. You know . . . I can remember, this was in Chicago again and *I was in kindergarten and the teacher was always letting me lead the lunch line and I got to carry the milk money and this went on for half the year or so and one day I was no longer the lunch line leader and I didn't know what I'd done to fall out of this teacher's graces, but I remember feeling horrible, but I was the leader and all of a sudden I wasn't the leader.*

You know I just remember knowing . . . it felt good to lead the whole class and to carry the money and I had been chosen and probably I was taller than a lot of the kids. Hmm, but . . . you do this and I just, *that was just my role and I was very responsible about doing it and felt good about doing it and all of a sudden one day I think she put somebody else at the front of the line or something and I don't know what she said to me or how I knew that I wasn't . . . it was never explained to me. She never told me why, she never really said anything,* but that this other kid . . . it really hurt and I didn't know what I had done and I doubt that I ever went to her and said anything. I probably talked to my mother about it. I don't remember, but I'm sure I talked to my mother about it, but I don't remember what she said. *It just really hurt my feelings and I had no idea what I had done to fall out of that teacher's graces.*

3. Hmm, as a little child? Oh, okay I have a scenario. What this is about I haven't got a clue, but I was angry and we lived in Kentucky for a year after the twins were born and daddy got transferred back to Chicago so we lived in Elm Hurt in this house that was a split level and, hmm, the twins were probably three so I would have been seven and I don't know what this was about but it was summertime, but *I was mad and my mother was trying to get me to do something and I wasn't going to do it so she was coming after me and I laid on the bed with my hands and my feet just curled and I scratched my mother's eyeball.* You know, talk about . . . you know . . . she was coming after me to get me to do something I was supposed to do, to help or something and I wasn't going to do it and but . . . sometimes Victoria and I would fight and that was my defense. I would get someplace and with my hands and my feet (laugh) so nobody could get me.

Counselor: So you scratched mom's eye.

Jan: I scratched the cornea or something. She had a patch on her eye. *Talk about guilt.*

Counselor: When you say talk about guilt . . .

Jan: *I felt horrible.* I just felt you know . . . what a horrible thing to do to your mother and I don't ever remember her really saying much about it or really being mad at me or you know, but *I felt horrible that I had hurt her.*

4. I can remember being down in Texas with Nannie (maternal grandmother), hmm, at the beach, and I had to go to the bathroom and there were no bathrooms and I think that's how she got to be Nannie the Seal because she took me on the sandbar and we sat there so I could go potty.

Counselor: How did you feel?

Jan: Like somebody was taking care of me. *Like somebody was there for me.*

## V. Adlerian Interpretative Hypotheses

The following tentative hypotheses based on the lifestyle assessment including early recollections will illustrate how these data can be useful in working with a counselee. In this case, the hypotheses are designed to help her understand herself more fully and to use such understanding to cope more effectively with a problem currently causing her considerable distress.

As a middle child, Jan compared herself to the other children in the family and decided that she was the child "without distinction." She liked being female and made the most she could of gaining attention as feminine, cute, "Fancy Jan" or "Prissy Missy." In spite of these efforts, she evaluated everyone else as *very* in some positive attribute and herself as next most very or *not* very, which is a distinction in its own right.

Her parents were both strict and loving. They modeled a consistency in their parenting and gender roles where father was controlling but "there for us, too" and women provided comfort, fun, and nurturing. Women, especially mother and maternal grandmother, play prominently in her convictions about gender and personal relationships. Being "responsible and there for your loved ones" is an imperative. To hurt those whom you love even by accident is a terrible thing.

For some reason that she does not understand, her place in life can be taken away by others (early recollection: when teacher replaced her as leader of the line; more recently, ex-husband and son) and it is both confusing and hurtful. She does not know how to exercise her freedom to make choices about how she feels and responds to such incidents.

Her greatest strengths include speaking up against the norm (against parents' wishes as a child—most rebellious; Catholic orthodoxy—not going by the rules) and being attractive (i.e., outwardly looking good). Not infrequently, looking good or behaving as "dingy or the dumb blonde type" may be used to disguise feelings of *not very* in other areas of life. These often hurt more than others realize. Although she wanted more than anyone to get her own way and would show her anger to get it, she was just as likely to be disappointed and feel hurt (perceived herself as most punished and most sensitive). Besides, being too forceful in asserting yourself can result in very bad consequences (as was the case when mother's eye was scratched).

Another asset is her openness to advice from those whom she respects as well as having the courage to take steps to resolve a predicament. Her mother encouraged her to wait for her father to come home in one early recollection and, although it was father's wrath she feared, she proceeded to pack her bag and wait for him to come home to give her a ride to the bus station. As humorous as this seems, one sees that as an adult, she still listens to advice (father's advice that she return home to confront her husband) and she finds peace and calm in the midst of personal chaos when she "attends to business" and takes action of some kind (early recollection: packing her little red suitcase; more recently, doing special reading while awaiting her husband's return home). She is likely to be an excellent counselee who takes responsibility for her own actions.

## VI. Approach to Life Tasks

She has been a homemaker most of her adult life. She still enjoys the thought of doing it well, just like her mother and grandmother. She is aware of color in her environment and most likely uses color in her dress, home, and work setting to express herself to others. Appearance is important, but even more important are relationships. All of her early recollections are socially interactive, compared, for example, to someone being alone or simply observing others.

Whether in friendship or a work environment, she can be depended on to be there for others. She will do her share of work, and then some, in a most satisfactory way. Unfortunately, in moments of self-disclosure, she likely will reveal that she thinks she still is not doing her part as well as others could do it. This mistaken idea keeps her constantly striving to learn to do better.

Her family's values are consistent in their support for her faith life. In the interview, Jan reveals a deep spiritual sense of having someone there for her (God) that contributes to her transcending the chaos in her life as an adult. This personal conviction of spiritual support will be another asset throughout her life.

## VII. Comfort Zone

All persons feel most comfortable when their most basic beliefs are serving them well (i.e., they are getting along well with coworkers, friends, and family and their basic physical and spiritual life is in good order). In short, their expectations are being met. It is when their expectations for what is necessary for them to be physically, psychologically, and spiritually secure are uncertain or threatened that they become distressed. In this case, Jan has life convictions that have guided her to this point in life but are now being thwarted by her son and ex-husband. These convictions have been central to her sense of well-being.

Since her divorce, she has earned a masters degree and now applies her caring, nurturing, and intelligence through a career in education. Despite her success, she still holds a prejudice of being "not very." Her 14-year-old son who had been living with her has decided to live with his father and his father's current live-in female companion. This is a source of great hurt and frustration to her. The following segments illustrate the use of the lifestyle assessment and DCT in beginning to help her to address this issue as it unfolded during the interview.

### Early Recollection/DCT Assessment

The process progressed smoothly from data collection and assessment into interpretation and counseling. The reader will find notations throughout the interview excerpts to help explain the processes and purposes for the counselor's questions or comments. The following counselee recollection is used to help her uncover attitudes, beliefs, and feelings that are inhibiting her in coping with a current crisis in her life. Her oldest son has moved in with his father and the father's current female companion. Jan has been in the process of building a career for herself but still feels very deeply about her need "to be there for my children." The Adlerian lifestyle information gathered during the interview comes into use after successfully exploring the recollection using DCT techniques as well. The woman is first asked questions on the sensorimotor level of DCT.

Counselor:   What I would like you to do now is to choose any of the recollections and get yourself really back into it. *Imagine yourself there in the moment, what you are feeling and what you are experiencing at that moment.* We'll develop that as we go along, but just kind of get into that moment again, reliving that recollection again.

Jan:   Hmm. The one that probably, the rest of them just seem to be things that happened, but it really disturbed me that I hurt my mother. You know, when I was crying.

Counselor:   Let's go back to that. When you were laying on the bed. Can you even close your eyes, see yourself, experience yourself being on that bed? [pause] Okay.

Jan:         I can see it vividly. I was in the bedroom. The blinds were drawn or something. It wasn't real bright in there. Hmm, but I could just remember her coming after me and it was like on the edge of the bed. If Victoria was coming after me or anyone was coming after me this is what I would do. But my hands would go like this . . . and my feet. You can imagine little kids when they do that and that's what I was doing as fast as I could go.

Counselor:  *So your hands were tight and your fists were tight?*

Jan:         Well, no. My fists were like this; I was clawing. Stay away from me, like a cat.

Counselor:  *And did you hear anything?* Can you hear anything in that? You're laying on the bed. Can you hear anything? [pause] You're laying there and mom's coming at you. *Do you remember what mom looked like? The expression on her face or anything?* Do you have an image of that?

Jan:         I can sort of see her face. I can't really see an expression on her face.

Counselor:  *Anything about her body language stand out? The way she looked as she was coming towards you? As you think . . .*

Jan:         All I can visualize actually is me doing that and she's not even in the room yet. I started doing that before she even got in the room.

Counselor:  You're ready and she's coming in. *Are there any sounds? Is she saying things? Were you making sounds? Any smells?*

Jan:         No and I'm sure the other kids are around. They weren't in the room.

Counselor: *As this kept going on, it didn't happen right away, but at some point you scratched her eye. Can you talk about what happened right then?* (DCT concrete operational level questioning)

Jan: Well, then, maybe I do picture her stopping 'cause she was coming. I don't know what she was coming to do. Get me? I don't remember what this was about, but hmm, you know, then I stopped.

Counselor: You stopped.

Jan: Yeah. Then she probably left to go take care of that or whatever and Victoria may have come in and said something to me.

Counselor: Before Victoria came in, as mom's holding her eye and leaving and you're stopping, *can you get in touch with the feeling you had?* (DCT sensorimotor level)

Jan: I don't know. I just, you know, I hurt my mother.

Counselor: Were your shoulders pulled up and . . .

Jan: Probably because here I am.

Counselor: And your face tightened up. Your shoulders are tight and your arms are tight and it seems to be centered.

Jan: I hurt my mother.

Counselor: Is there anything else physically that you could describe about that feeling; sensations in your body? Where is that feeling? "Oh I hurt my mother." Where is it in your body?

Jan: All I can see is just . . .

Counselor: When you do that where do you feel it most if you do it right now? Where is the feeling?

Jan:        In my shoulders.

Counselor:  What does it feel like?

Jan:        It's probably a pain, you know, I can't really feel it.
            I was thinking that *it would probably hurt my heart
            that I'd hurt my mother.* You know, to . . .

Counselor:  *Experience that feeling. Is there another time in
            your life when you had that same feeling?* (DCT
            concrete operational questioning)

Jan:        *A hurt heart?* [laugh]

            *The only [crying] . . . the time that I can remember
            feeling a knife in my heart is when . . . I knew he
            was having an affair and wanted the divorce and*
            all that. *That was a physical heart pain. That was a
            knife in my heart. Probably, recently when my son,
            Robert, went to live with Charles. That was another
            one and that . . . now I don't know where to go with
            this but that in talking about all of these and my
            mother, she was a wonderful role model.*

            Everybody is kind and loving and caring and we
            all take good care of our children. We are all hard
            workers. They say this all the time that they have
            been so blessed and they don't know how it hap-
            pened. How they could have five daughters and all
            of us be doing very well. Not that anybody is real
            rich or any of those material things, but everybody
            has really good strong values and is very kind and
            caring and nurturing. And because I was raised that
            way I know. I mean I know what my mother [cry-
            ing] . . . and *I was growing up a teenager and col-
            lege thinking about getting married and that's all I
            ever wanted to do was to be a mother and a house-
            wife.* I mean I really enjoyed and I still do enjoy
            taking care of the house and cooking and doing all

those things and when Charles left, it was like that was all I ever wanted to do and I don't think I'm going to be anybody. I can't do this and I found that I could not be the mother that I want to be to my children. Charles blocks me from Robert and it's just a real struggle to figure out how to plan . . . because he's not doing very well right now and I'm being blocked from helping him and I don't know. It's real hard not to be able to help my son and I just keep working and searching for a different way to do something and maybe what I've got to do is nothing. That's the hardest of all.

Counselor: When asked if the feeling was similar, you said that there's two times, one is the breakup with Charles and the other one is dealing with your son. Would you be willing to talk about one of those two in more detail?

Jan: Either one of them?

Counselor: You choose.

Jan: I can look at the breakup with Charles now as that's what needed to happen. I couldn't do what I needed to do and be the mother and be anything that I needed to be in that relationship so I needed to be out of it and that's okay. I just feel tremendous disappointment about him because I always saw his potential that he's just . . . he couldn't do it and at this point, he's not going to do it, but I always knew that I could . . . that even though Robert's personality is like Charles', Robert is wonderful, Charles has a high IQ. Robert has a wonderfully high IQ. He's a wonderful child. He's creative, he's lots of things, but he's annoying as heck sometimes, which is the attention deficit disorder stuff. You know, but hmm, it's so hard to be a good mother, to be able to help him learn how to be responsible. Learn how to

. . . Robert a lot of times shifts responsibility. You know, if he gets a bad grade, well the teacher did it. Well, you know . . . that's what his father does. You know, and I don't say . . .

Counselor: Could you share a specific incident when you talked about finding out about Charles' affair. *Do you remember when you found out? Do you remember exactly what happened?* (DCT concrete operational)

Jan: Yeah. Yeah. [laugh] I was, you know, we'd just moved into this new house. We had two babies that were two and three. We were having a big July 4th party; his birthday is on the 4th and I always had huge parties. I mean the last one we had was 250 people. For some of them, I did all the cooking, hors d'oeuvres and everything, but his one was catered. Decorations, you name it. I remember him going off in a truck with one of his female coworkers to get fireworks. That was very strange. I saw them going off so there were clues that I had, but I was going out of town to my parent's wedding anniversary that the girls and I had all planned. It was a surprise. My parents had always been wonderful to Charles, but he didn't want to come. He said no. He made up all these excuses and I was really confused about that. The day after we got there Daddy sat me down in the living room and said, "Jan, Charles is either physically ill or he's having an affair" and I said "Daddy, how can you . . . Charles having an affair." If things were that bad in our marriage, I know that he would tell me. Hmm, he called that night. He never called. Charles never called me. He would go out of town. He just was very irresponsible. Hmm, but he called that night and he sounded funny. He wanted to talk to the kids. I had forgotten to ask him how his stomach was. So I called him the next day at his office and asked the receptionist and she said he's not here. I said where is he; she said, he's on vacation. I said, on vacation? I asked who else is on vacation? They said Lillian and I just knew. Daddy said you have to get on a plane and go back and take care of business. So they put me on a plane and they kept my kids and I sat on that plane . . . to this day I would love to know how I looked. I was numb. I must of looked like a zombie, but I sat on that plane and I went back and had to take care of business so I put a message on his recorder and I went to his office and talked to others. They liked me and they felt bad so the next day they didn't come to work. . . . I did my detective work and found his car and I figured out that he was on a tropical vacation because the scuba equipment was gone and I put all these little pieces together. I came home and put a note in his car saying I know where you are and who you're with, please just come home so we can figure out where to go from here and I went home and I, hmm, I had this tremendous peace. *It was the most amazing time of my life, really, because everything just turned upside down, but I was very peaceful and I spent 3 days reading all these things he had wanted me to read. . . . I was just very much at peace* and read and when he walked in that day, I didn't have any idea of when he was coming home, but he walked in the door and I said . . . hmm, and I'd always said that if my husband had an affair I'd . . . I said I'm so sorry that you are hurting so badly that you had to go to such extremes. He didn't know what to say so he set down and we started talking and we really had much better communication than we'd had in years . . . he's never been strong enough to or disciplined enough and, hmm, so we stayed together another year and a year later I found him with her again and said I'm sorry you have to leave and he cried at that point, but I was very calm again. Even then I thought we would get back together, but we never did and a 3-year horrible divorce battle ensued.

Counselor: *One of the questions that I might ask is, if given two really different scenarios, in terms of, we started with your early recollection about being on the bed with your mom and accidentally scratching her in the eye and then the circumstance with Charles and the divorce and lots of different feelings associated with that. One of them might be the sudden sense of being stabbed in the heart. I'm wondering what you see as the similarity between those two?* (DCT formal operational questioning)

Jan: I'm not sure really. I know that it hurt me to hurt my mother. I mean it just hurt tremendously to . . . you know when I think of the way Charles hurt me, hmm, there were times, there are two that I took a lot of responsibility while if I had just been a better wife or if I had just been a better mother or if I had just been a better this or that or whatever so that year that we spent together, that's what I tried to do; to get better and better and better and hmm . . .

Counselor: *So part of the pain was not meeting your own expectations.*

Jan: Yeah. Yeah.

Counselor: Something more like mom.

*Note:* The counselor uses this opportunity to ask a DCT dialectic/systemic question to explore the origin of Jan's rules about life in order to help her to see multiple perspectives (i.e., how others might see them). Jan is unclear about the question. Had the lifestyle data not been available or had the counselor had chosen otherwise, he could have clarified the question and sought to determine if Jan could establish their origin as a part of the DCT process. In this case, a more Adlerian approach was taken. It is stated by the counselor as "self-talk" in the first person. The counselor is watchful for the recognition reflex by the counselee (i.e., usually a spontaneous affirmation that the reflections are correct or not). In this case, both verbal and nonverbal affirmations are noted.

Counselor: *These messages that you give to yourself, where have they come from?* (DCT dialectic/systemic)

Jan: Which message is that?

Counselor: *In these two instances, there are some pretty strong messages.* In fact, *in the whole lifestyle,* I hear some kinds of themes that are coming through . . . *You don't want to hurt anybody. You want to be there for people* and in the situation with mom, she was coming to you and you hurt her and you felt terrible about that. *You still feel terrible about that.* Huh, when it came to your situation with Charles, you thought you were always going to be able to be there for your kids and you would be there for him and he didn't seem to appreciate that and we think about the situation with the teacher (early recollection about losing her place at the head of the line) . . . you were confused. *You couldn't understand how the rules could change. How could the rules of life have changed? The rules of life that moms and dads are there for their kids, they're there for each other, like your mom and dad were there for each other.* Hmm, *I've always believed that I was going to be that kind of a person. I was going to be that kind of a wife, that kind of a mother, that kind of a friend. To me relationships are really important and, you don't hurt people that are important to you. People who love other people are hurt and it doesn't make any sense. There's no reason for this to end.*

Jan: There's something that you . . . How can I be

> blocked from helping my son? [crying] That's the,
> . . . you know, that's what's happening.

*Note:* At this point, Jan chooses to change the focus from the lost relationship with the ex-husband to her present pain associated with her son. We can speculate that not only is the son's situation hurtful but that the pain associated with her former husband is still very present to her. The counselor follows her lead in this case, mindful that at another time she will likely revisit her feelings associated with her ex-husband to resolve them as unfinished business. In the meantime, she is unaware at a DCT dialectic level how her son has learned to think and feel as he does. The counselor guides her in a process of uncovering their origin.

Counselor: Let me see . . . you understand the relationship between mom and dad, the kids, and how you have come to think and feel . . . the rules you have for yourself and the way you've tried to live your life. Now your situation, we're saying here . . . I'm trying to live those rules and I've got a son who says that I'm not going to let you do that and an ex-husband who's contributing to that and he's acting as a support for your son and so forth. I'm also thinking of Jan who says, "Well, I don't want to do something and you're not going to make me!" Okay. Who is your son like?

Jan: Oh, he's got some of my traits . . .

Counselor: Right. Your son at this point in his life, you said when I was a teenager, my mother and I were acting like this, okay, but what was it you were doing when you were behaving like that? What were you doing?

Jan: Not doing much . . . whatever that was.

Counselor: What was your rationale? What was behind your motivation? (*Note:* guiding her toward understanding what might be her son's perspective)

Jan:          I wasn't going to be controlled.

Counselor:   And what were you going to do?

Jan:          Me?

Counselor:   You were going to be your own person.

Jan:          You're right. The only thing that Robert is doing
             this is, I mean he's got all As, two Fs. I mean there's
             . . . There's a tremendous struggle. Do I totally back
             out of this. Can parents totally back out? Can I just
             give it over to Charles? I mean I just . . . It's very
             appropriate that . . .

Counselor:   Let me ask you this Jan. *Do you even have a choice?*
             (The Adlerian counselor will encourage by making
             counselees aware of their alternatives. When the
             choice is not hers to make, it is liberating to estab-
             lish that which is within her control and take action
             there instead.)

Jan:          I don't know. I'm not sure. I keep going at it from
             every direction trying to find . . .

Counselor:   You want to be there for him and he's saying, I'm
             going to do it myself. Now you know enough from
             your own experience to say that if he wants to do it
             himself, there's nothing that you're going to do
             that's going to make any difference. Now let me
             ask you another question. What happened to you
             and your mom, I mean you described her in glow-
             ing terms, but you didn't feel that way when you
             were a teenager. So what made the difference?

Jan:          That's who she was.

Counselor:   And, what happened?

Jan:          *I don't know if I'm as good as she is.*

Counselor: You know Jan, when we were going through the list of what were you like, what were the kids like and so forth, everybody else was *very* something. Did you know that? Everybody was *very* something. There were either very good or very not good and you were always in between. *You have a prejudice against yourself that you're not* very. *How about that. Could it be?*

Jan: Oh, yeah. [laugh] (This is a typical recognition reflex.)

Counselor: Okay. Now you're a teacher, what would you say to a student who had that kind of prejudice?

Jan: You've heard me say that I'm a child without distinction, but I've never thought of myself as not very but . . . *that is how I think of myself* . . . I don't think people perceive me as feeling that I'm not very. Even my mother didn't know it, but . . . and I said something the other day, I forget what it was and she said honey, *no*, she was flabbergasted that I felt this way. You are right, though; now she and I talk every week and I can tell her anything. I guess that's true.

Counselor: When you went from that zombie state to being totally relaxed, totally at peace, totally centered when you were describing your situation, what went on in between then?

Jan: I did the things I needed to do. I went to my dear friend Sally and told her and she was there for me. I went to Charles' office and took care of business and, hmm, and to the airport and found his car and did a lot of detective work and then just came home and read and was at peace. I mean I, as I said, we grew up Catholic and when I was in college I decided that all these rules had to be ridiculous that "I

can, maybe can't"... you know, it was like there
were too many rules and I knew that there was something different that I would believe but it gave all of
us a tremendously strong sense of faith and trust
and just belief in God. That there was someone always there to turn to and to trust and that was the
beginning of that becoming really more of my core,
of finding the peace in total chaos and turmoil. Of
knowing it was there. That I could turn to that. I
practice coming back to that and I can do that sometimes . . . but that was a real turning point in my
spiritual life when that happened.

Counselor: And this is another time. So what is the business
that you think you need to get on with in terms of
Robert?

## Conclusion

At this point, the counseling evolved into an exploration of
alternative possibilities for how to think and feel about the circumstances with her son; those circumstances over which she had
control and those over which she did not. The fact that everyone
creates their own rules about life and that they can modify, delete,
or create new ones fit well with this woman's perception of herself. After all, she had practiced not following the rules of others
(those of her parents when she was a child; the Catholic Church;
her mother's when she was a teenager) and had experienced tremendous peace in the midst of chaos with her husband by reframing
her capacity to cope with what she feared (as she had in the early
recollection as a child when anticipating the wrath of her father).
The parallel between her teenage son's current behavior and her
own with her mother during her teenage years was encouraging
because it offered new hope that with time, patience, and persistence, the mature relationship that she desires with him was possible.

From a DCT perspective, this woman was developmentally
able with guidance to begin discovering her perceptual blocks and

use this knowledge to begin trying out new behaviors. She was able to relate her story at least in part on three levels: sensorimotor, concrete operational, and formal operational. The dialectic understanding of their origin and implications for her relationship with her son were blocked. Likewise, her unresolved feelings about her ex-husband and how these related to her expectations for herself as wife, mother, and friend were unknown to her.

Finally, because I believe that wellness includes the spiritual dimensions of a healthy person as discussed in chapter 2, I encouraged her to learn to call on her capacity for calm and peace through her spiritual convictions by whatever regular practices and means she chose. The belief that God will always be there for her spiritually can be a powerful asset in learning to appropriately cope with life's challenges.

The blending of Adlerian lifestyle assessment and DCT is promising. Although either of the methods alone may have been sufficient for helping the counselee over time, used together within the Adlerian approach they helped move the process of change forward more quickly and potentially with greater benefit to the counselee. Naturally, this represents only an illustration of the potential usefulness of these methods together.

## STUDY QUESTIONS

**Directions:** Respond to the following in the space provided.

1. What is the significance of motivation modification versus behavior modification from an Adlerian point of view?

2. What is the diagnostic value of the following question: How would life be different if this problem or situation were solved or corrected?

3. What do persistent blaming, complaining, excuses, fear, and "disabling conditions" have in common from an Adlerian perspective?

4. "Spitting in the soup" is a form of confrontation. Give an illustration of how you could use this technique. What conditions would be necessary for it to be effective?

## Chapter 9

# CAREER STYLE ASSESSMENT AND COUNSELING

*Mark L. Savickas*

Adler's Individual Psychology offers a perspective on vocational development that enriches the classic career counseling model (Watkins, 1984). The present chapter contains an elaboration of this assertion and a presentation of methods and materials that career counselors can use to bring the Adlerian perspective to their work. I begin with a review of the strengths and weaknesses of the most widely used approach to career counseling: matching persons to occupations. What follows is a discussion of four ways in which Adler's Individual Psychology elaborates this matching model to be more useful to counselors. The chapter proceeds with a brief section describing how Adlerian counselors apply Individual Psychology materials and methods to implement the matching model when they do career counseling as an adjunct to lifestyle counseling. The remaining two thirds of the chapter contains a presentation of Individual Psychology materials and methods specifically designed for Adlerian career counseling or, more precisely, career style counseling. The presentation of career style counseling is divided into three sections. The first section consists of a description of a structured interview that counselors use to collect data about a client's career style; the second section presents ideas on how counselors think about this data to assess the client's career style; and the third section contains a description of a five-stage model of career style counseling.

## THE MATCHING MODEL

The classic model for career counseling (Parsons, 1909) is based on the psychology of individual differences. Counselors use individual differences to match people with suitable and viable occupations. The fundamental proposition of the matching model follows the wisdom of the familiar maxim, "birds of a feather flock together." Counselors measure clients' interests and then identify corresponding occupations in which their interests may be enacted and rewarded. These congruent occupations offer clients opportunities to integrate personal needs with job demands and thereby experience job success, satisfaction, and stability.

Career counseling that follows the matching model can be likened to a translation service. A linguist translates Spanish into English; a career counselor translates a client's identity into occupational titles. For example, if clients identify themselves as nurturing and dominant, then the counselor may translate their self-concepts into occupational titles such as teacher, counselor, minister, nurse, or other occupations in which the worker helps people. The counselor then encourages clients to explore these occupations.

The matching model is embedded in the major career counseling instrument, interest inventories. These inventories automate the translation task. In responding to interest inventory items, clients describe themselves in terms of the constructs provided by the inventory's author. The scoring keys for the inventory comprise theoretically or empirically derived descriptions of successful workers in a variety of occupations or work environments. The results profile a client's similarity to workers in the different occupations. In effect, the results plotted on the profile sheet translate the client's self-concept into occupational titles. Test interpretation is the prime counseling method that counselors use with the matching model and materials (Crites, 1981). Counselors interpret interest inventory results to clients in ways designed to encourage vocational planning, guide occupational exploration, and structure career decision making.

The matching model, with its inventory materials and interpretation methods, is very popular with both clients and counselors. In fact, many clients begin their initial interview by requesting an interest inventory because they have heard from peers or teachers that inventories are useful. Counselors like interest inventories because they provide occupational titles to discuss with clients. Few counselors deny that interest inventories can be used effectively with clients who are ready to translate their self-concepts into occupational titles.

Readiness, however, is the rub. A great many clients have not crystallized their self-concepts and so they are not ready to respond meaningfully to interest inventories, especially those that present occupational titles as items. When asked to respond, they do their best, yet their indecision and confusion in dealing with inventory items produces inconsistent, undifferentiated, and unstable profiles. Every career counselor has experienced frustration while interpreting flat or inconsistent profiles to disappointed clients. Most counselors soon learn that interest inventory interpretation does not help clients who lack a clear and stable picture of who they are and what they want from life. These clients benefit from help that develops their self-concepts and clarifies their career goals. The matching model comprehends these clients but its inventory materials and interpretation methods do not work with them because they are not ready to translate their self-concepts into occupations. Career counselors need materials and methods that ease clients' identity development and goal selection. Such techniques make clients consider their own experiences and opinions instead of just reacting to interest inventory items.

Adler's Individual Psychology (IP) can broaden the classic matching model as well as its methods and materials to accommodate the needs of these clients. IP elaborates the core constructs of the matching model. It also offers methods and materials that widen the range of clients that the model addresses. IP's attention to life goals and styles can help clients develop their identities. This self-knowledge prepares them to make occupational translations that capture their spirit, not just their stereotypes of the world of work.

## THE ADLERIAN MATCHING MODEL

IP counselors appreciate matching for fit yet view it as static. Therefore, they expand the classic matching model, beyond predicting occupational fit based on individual differences in traits such as interests and abilities, to include how people use the traits they possess. IP counselors agree with Uncle Remus from the movie "Song of the South": "it ain't what you got, it's how you use it." Like trait-and-factor counselors who apply the classic matching model, IP counselors inventory clients' abilities, interests, and values. However, they concentrate on how their clients use these traits to fit in, that is, belong, contribute, and cooperate. Adler's psychology of use can elaborate the classic matching model in at least four ways because it (a) expands the core construct of fit, (b) focuses on uniqueness, (c) explains how interests develop along a career path, and (d) explicates the career decision-making process.

### From Fit to Belongingness

Individual Psychology elaborates counselors' conception of occupational fit and enhances their ability to communicate it to clients. In describing the classic matching model, vocational theorists present occupational fit as the core construct for psychological and pragmatic reasons (Dawis & Lofquist, 1984; Holland, 1985a). Empirical evidence shows that goodness of fit between a person and occupational position relates to job satisfaction and success (Spokane, 1985). IP theorists agree and add social and philosophical reasons to support person–position fit as the criterion for career choice.

The IP elaboration of the fit construct rests on ideas about belongingness and social interest. Each individual is born into the stream of history. When a baby arrives, the community already exists. The toddler's experience can be likened to someone being pushed onto center stage as the curtain rises for Act II. Without knowing what occurred in Act I, the actor must try to fit into the ongoing story and relate to the characters who share the stage. The successful actor moves toward the other characters, learns to co-operate with them, and thus carves out a role for him- or herself. In life, the child should move toward the family and community. They in turn must welcome the child in order for the child to feel belongingness. When the child feels belongingness, the child can form attachments and develop social interest. The child then responds to social expectations (also called developmental tasks) to become somebody in relation to other people. To thrive, children must make a place for themselves in the community through work, friends, and love. Thus, fit leads not just to earning personal pay-offs like success and satisfaction but also to making social contributions. People must ask both selfish and selfless questions in trying to fit in: Where can I make my place? and How can I contribute? To answer these questions, people should consider their unique goals and talents.

## From Similarity to Uniqueness

In the classic matching model, interest inventories deal with how the client is similar to workers in different occupations. The Adlerian perspective addresses these similarities yet also deals with individuality. IP emphasizes the uniqueness of a life in progress because Adlerian counselors believe that people design their own personalities. A person is both the artist and the painting. People shape and channel their movement through an ever widening social context by structuring personal goals and means. To understand clients, IP advises that a counselor learn what clients intend and how they propose to do it. Clients' goals and means reveal their uniqueness more than do interest inventory profiles. Inventories measure how clients feel about occupations not how they intend to use them to achieve their goals and become more effective and complete.

## From Interests to Career Paths

Once a counselor understands a client's life goal, the counselor knows the client's orientation to life and the general direction in which the client is heading (Csikszentmihalyi & Beattie, 1979). Adlerians call the client's way of moving to a goal "guiding lines" (Griffith & Powers, 1984). Knowing a client's goal and guiding lines allows the counselor to envision the client's career path. Think of a real path that you can walk along in your own neighborhood. What you meet along the path can attract or repel you. You have to react to what you encounter even if the reaction is disinterest or boredom. Objects on a different path require no reaction, assuming that you even know they exist. By analogy, only occupations along one's guiding lines can become interesting to the individual. Individuals recognize these occupations and, if they evaluate them as potentially useful, may become interested in them.

Life goals preoccupy the individual. They shape one's outlook, that is, how one approaches a subject. From this subjective starting point, one looks out for environmental opportunities to objectify one's life goals. When the opportunities are presented, one subjectively links oneself to these objects by forming an interest. To paraphrase Angyl (1941, p. 55), it is not an interest that defines the direction, but on the contrary, it is the direction that defines what can become an interest.

This view of the origin and development of interests fits best for careers in the professions. Blue collar workers often do not have an opportunity to select work based on their interests. They may have to select from job alternatives narrowed by the opportunity structure in their community. Often they must settle for the job they can get or choose the job that pays the most. These workers express their interests through leisure activities and family roles rather than through work.

## From Choice to Decision Making

The classic matching model and its interest inventories focus on occupational choice, not the career decision-making process. Adlerian counselors distinguish between the occupations that clients choose and how they make their choices. This expands the focus of vocational counseling to include the career decision-making process. From the perspective of IP, the career decision-making process denotes clients' search for a synthesis between their dreams and reality, that is, an integrative solution to the problems of growing up. Counselors evaluate the success of clients' attempts at synthesis by comparing their private sense (dreams) to common sense (reality). Adlerians refer to private sense as the "private logic" that clients use to orient themselves to life and answer questions such as (a) Who am I? (b) What is this world like?, and (c) How and where do I fit in? In contrast, Adlerians refer to common sense as answers to these questions that make a contribution to the community. The degree of congruence between a client's private logic and the community's common sense indicates the probability that the client will adapt successfully to the challenges of occupational choice and work adjustment.

Clients' private logic includes their "guiding fictions," that is, their conclusions about what they need to feel less incomplete and more secure. Guiding fictions are also called fictional goals because they define a client's ideal self-concept and conception of success. In the process of career decision making, clients use their private logic to evaluate occupations and to select ones along their guiding lines that move them closer to their fictional goals. An occupation that evokes interest initially attracts a person because in some way it deals with that person's guiding fiction. Thus, the occupations that interest clients have a personal meaning for them. Typically people have unexamined ideas about how certain occupations will help them reach their fictional goals and become more complete. Knowing clients' guiding fictions enables counselors to understand the "hidden reasons" (Dreikurs, 1973) or meanings behind their career goals and occupational interests.

In discussing their occupational interests with other people, clients talk in common-sense terms about the public meaning of their occupational interests. Rarely do clients spontaneously articulate the guiding fictions that direct their careers or the hidden meaning behind their occupational interests. For example, several of my clients have wanted to become physicians. They all gave the same common sense explanation of their interest in medicine: they liked people and science. Yet each client invested medicine with a different fictional goal such as being in control, overcoming clumsiness, playing with winners, being right, or pleasing father. Their hidden reasons for choosing medicine expressed guiding fictions about their needs and what it would take for them to actively master what they passively suffered.

Common sense understands this idea of occupational choice as a means of turning problems into opportunities. Probably everyone has heard stories about a person overcoming stuttering to become an orator, a girl overcoming polio to become an Olympic track star, a boy overcoming shyness to become a famous actor, or a woman overcoming her lisp to become an accomplished newscaster. Although these are dramatic examples, they are not rare. IP contends that everyone forms guiding fictions as they grow up and that everyone's private logic distorts reality to some degree. Thus, in facilitating a client's career decision making, Adlerian counselors always attend to private logic and uncover guiding fictions in general and hidden reasons for occupational interests in particular.

For example, a girl grew up with the guiding fiction that she could belong only if she could please other people. In most instances, she was able to get along well. However, with regard to career choice, her father and grandfather were displeased when she considered anything other than law. Although she wanted to become a teacher, she felt completely lost and worthless when her father was displeased. She sought career counseling for the first time during her final year in-law school. She asked the counselor to help her understand why she hated law school and to predict how she would fare as a lawyer. Her counselor helped her to examine her fictional goal of pleasing other people and her hidden reason for choosing law. She became a law professor to integratively resolve her problem in growing up.

## ADLERIAN CAREER COUNSELING

Because of their concern with belongingness, uniqueness, usefulness, and private logic, Adlerian career counselors typically do not use interest inventory materials or test interpretation methods. They implement an IP matching model through prototypal Adlerian materials such as the family constellation interview guide (Dreikurs, 1954, 1973; Shulman, 1962, 1973), early recollection report forms (Dreikurs, 1954; Mosak, 1958), and the lifestyle inventory (Eckstein, Baruth, & Mahrer, 1982; Mosak & Shulman, 1971). IP counselors use these materials to elicit clients' unique experiences and opinions so that they may assess clients' life goals and styles. Characteristic IP methods for interpreting the assessment to clients and facilitating their decision making (lifestyle management) or reorientation (lifestyle modification) are presented in chapter 7. Examples of how IP counselors use these generic Adlerian counseling materials and methods with career clients can be found in McKelvie and Friedland (1978, 1981), McKelvie (1979), Manaster and Perryman (1974), and Savickas (1989).

Counselors who try them usually report that IP materials such as the lifestyle inventory are extremely useful because they work with clients to foster identity development, enhance self-awareness, and translate identities into occupations. However, they also report three disadvantages in using the lifestyle inventory and similar materials with career choice clients. First, the questions lack face validity for career clients. When clients begin career counseling they do not expect to be asked about their childhood experiences, family relationships, or early recollections. Although communication and rapport engage them, career clients hesitate before discussing these topics. Second, the materials are extensive, taking two and sometimes three sessions to complete. Third, much of the data gathered with the lifestyle inventory pertain to career adjustment counseling, that is, helping clients cope with problems at work. Although enlightening, data about family constellation and early recollections are not needed for career choice counseling. To eliminate these disadvantages, some counselors do more than adapt lifestyle counseling materials and methods to address career choice. They have developed IP materials and methods specifically for career choice counseling. Collectively, I refer to these materials and methods for implementing an Adlerian approach to person–position matching as "career style counseling." The rest of the present chapter contains a description of career style counseling materials and methods, starting with interview materials designed to elicit career style data from clients, continuing with assessment methods to interpret career style data, and concluding with career style counseling methods.

## CAREER STYLE INTERVIEW

The career style interview consists of stimulus questions that seem valid to career counseling clients and elicit from them opinions and experiences relevant to their career choices. The questions elicit fictional goals as well as lifestyle information that reveal how clients think an interest can solve a problem or make them more complete. The stimulus questions are sequenced into a structured career style interview. The topics flow smoothly and keep clients actively engaged in self-exploration while they describe themselves to the counselor. The stimulus questions deal with (a) role models, (b) books, (c) magazines, (d) leisure activities, (e) school subjects, (f) mottos, (g) ambitions, and (h) decisions.

### Role Models

Counselors begin the career style interview by investigating a client's predicament in life as portrayed by role models. To identify a client's role models, the counselor might ask, "Whom did you admire when you were growing up?" If clients do not understand, then the counselor can ask them whom they respected a lot, maybe even enough to imitate. With clients who cannot think of anyone, the counselor may suggest that it does not have to be a famous person or fictional character. This often leads a client to name a relative or family member. After the client has named one model, the counselor asks for two other models. When the client has named three models, the counselor asks in turn for each model, "What did you admire about this person?" It sometimes takes prodding, so the counselor may ask the client to "just tell me about the person. What were they like?" The counselor closes this first topic by asking for each model, "How are you like this person and how are you different from this person?"

It is not unusual for a client to name a famous animal as a model. In fact, many clients have said that they admired Lassie. Lassie was always able to help out and save the day. A crisis counselor said he admired Mighty Mouse for much the same reasons. A gentle and kind social worker reported that his hero was Ferdinand the Bull. He went on to explain what that meant to him in relation to his angry, alcoholic father. Two different clients admired Peter Pan. Both clients had trouble accepting adult responsibilities and eventually chose occupations in which their childlike lifestyles were assets.

As clients discuss their models, counselors should concentrate on what clients admire about their models more than whom they admire. In attending to who, counselors often rely on stereotypes and what the model means to them. I recall a clear example of this mistake. I was doing a public demonstration of counseling with a disadvantaged student who said that he admired a football player. Several counselors in the audience jumped to the conclusion that the young man viewed professional athletics as his way out of the ghetto. In explaining why he admired the athlete, the young man told several stories demonstrating how the athlete was independent, artistic, and manly. This athlete modeled for him the self-confidence, independence, and vision that corresponded to his secret dream of being an architect. The young man chose this model because the athlete showed him that a person can be artistic without being effeminate. The athlete modeled a way for the young man to accept his mother's encouragement to be artistic and reject his father's admonition that, if he did, he would become homosexual.

As the client discusses role models, the counselor should think of what the model implies to form follow-up questions. Effective follow-up questions express inferences, not interpretations, so clients find them thought provoking and occasionally humorous. For example, someone who admires the Lone Ranger could be asked, "Are you a loner?" "Do you have a Tonto?" or "Do you like secrets?" and so on. The client's answers to follow-up questions increases the counselor's understanding of the client's career style.

In talking about their role models, clients describe themselves. A model shares the client's plight yet has found a way out of the predicament. In responding to questions about models, clients tell counselors about the problems that they wish to solve above all else. Thus counselors may identify the problems that structure clients' goals as well as the means that they use to move toward these goals. In other words, a client's model identifies a central life goal, articulates and labels the client's central concern, and reveals what the client thinks it will take to overcome that problem.

The value of role models to individuals who are searching for solutions to problems in growing up was succinctly explained in a thought for the day printed on a calendar. I can find no better reference than Wayne Cobb from North Carolina; I do not know the context in which he was speaking but I do recognize the beauty and truth in Mr. Cobb's statement: "My idea of a hero is someone who is to be cherished not so much for what they have accomplished in their own lives, but for what they have accomplished in mine, for how they have inspired me to grow and change and to become more of what I was created to be."

Do not confuse role models with "gender guiding lines" examined by lifestyle inventory questions about parents (Griffith & Powers, 1984, p. 47). Parents guide clients' lines of movement because they are familiar with the course of life and offer their children continuous presence or direction about the way to proceed. In a lifestyle interview, counselors ask clients to describe what kind of man was father and what kind of woman was mother. Clients respond by telling what impressed them about their parents' example. From their answers, the counselor learns about the parents as the client's standard for what it means to be a man or a woman and how to live. These archetypes are usually an unexamined part of a client's private logic. In contrast to the unexamined guiding lines that parents provide, people purposefully chose role models to show them how to work out a role and how to reduce their feelings of incompleteness or inferiority.

Experienced career counselors often ask their clients to compare a role model to a guiding line. The differences between the guide and model reveal the link between that client's problems and goals and thus map the client's line of movement from passive suffering to active mastery. For example, one client described his father as tough and his mother as tender. He loved them both and felt torn between their contradictory styles of relating to other people and situations. His way of integrating these contradictory poses was to imitate Robin Hood, whom he described as tough yet tender in defeating villains and helping people in need. The client eventually directed a social work agency, a role he enacted in a tough yet tender manner.

## Books

Counselors ask clients to describe their favorite books because a book usually includes another model or, more precisely, a life predicament and its solution. Typically, clients' favorite books portray clearly their central life problem and how someone else dealt with it. People are attracted to books in which a major character experiences a problem similar to their own problem. It comforts them to learn that other people have faced the same problem. They often find encouragement in how a character dealt with the problem and sometimes even imitate that character's coping strategy.

Some clients clearly demonstrate this idea. For example, a female premedical student frequently read *Gone With the Wind* because Scarlett O'Hara fascinated her. At an unexamined level, she was dealing with how to be a physician without deviating from her female gender guiding line. She found that this book addressed the fear that her needs for achievement and for intimacy conflicted. Another client read Hemingway's *Old Man and the Sea* as a parable that addressed his creativity and hypersensitivity. Sometimes discussing a favorite book draws the client and the counselor to the core issue. A college freshman who noted *Winesburg, Ohio* as his favorite book planned to major in chemistry. This story about a student writer corresponded to his dream—but, because of parental attitudes, he sought a "real" career. He could not envision a person like himself becoming a writer, because everyone in his family worked in a blue collar occupation. If a client cannot readily name a favorite book, then counselors should move to the next topic without probing.

## Magazines

The third topic in the career style interview is magazines. Counselors start by asking clients which magazines they enjoy reading. As prods they ask clients if they subscribe to any magazine or read one regularly. Typically, counselors try to elicit two or three magazine choices before asking clients to describe what they enjoy reading in each magazine. It is useful to get some detail about the sections that clients like most, a favorite story from the last issue, or what attracts them to the magazine.

Counselors ask about magazines during a career style interview because magazines vicariously immerse readers in an environment. Favorite magazines tell the counselor about the environments that fit the client's style. As they listen to a client's responses, counselors link them to the client's responses about role models and consider if the magazines represent environmental outlets for interests that the client finds useful. For example, the student who admired the athlete liked *Jazz Musician* and *Architectural Digest.* A client who emulated Lassie's helpfulness, enjoyed *People, National Enquirer,* and *Psychology Today.*

Occasionally, a client does not read magazines. In these instances, the counselor may ask the client about favorite television programs. It usually turns out that they watch some television programs regularly. Favorite programs reveal some information about preferred environment, but rarely as much as magazines. Magazines immerse readers into an environment more completely than television programs immerse viewers.

## Leisure Activities

The fourth topic in the career style interview deals with self-expression. Role models and books reveal a central problem and suggest which interests may be useful. Magazines indicate which environments attract a client because useful interests can be enacted and reinforced. At leisure, clients manifest their interests.

Counselors begin to examine clients' leisure activities by asking them what they like to do in their free time and, if they need a prod, what hobbies they enjoy. If they still need prodding, counselors can ask clients what they did last weekend. After identifying their leisure activities, counselors discern the role clients play in these activities. Sample roles are partner, listener, performer, host, tourist, and member. Then, within the role, counselors determine the key functions and rewards. For example, bridge partners may cooperate to win. Listeners may experience feelings in response to music. Hosts may help guests relax in order to attract friends. Sometimes clients say unexpected things. For example, one client loved bowling. I thought that physical competence or competition made the interest useful to her. Surprisingly, she said her favorite part of bowling was keeping score. Because leisure motives are intrinsic, counselors can form a clear picture of how clients prefer to interact with their environments.

In addition to self-expression, leisure presents opportunities for personal development. Through leisure activities clients can work on feelings of incompleteness or inferiority. Leisure can be autotherapeutic because in structured play, people can symbolically cope with activities or objects that they are unable to master in real life. Through leisure activities people develop skills and strategies that eventually enhance their competence and confidence and enable them to cope with the problems in real life. In this sense, play is rehearsal. So in examining a client's leisure activities, counselors consider both the self being expressed and the problem being addressed.

An example may explicate the autotherapeutic function of leisure. A homemaker who was housebound and felt unproductive decided to learn to play tennis. She played every day during one summer. At the beginning she was pale, overweight, and clumsy. By the end of the summer she was tan, slim, and a tournament winner; that was what her playmates saw. They did not recognize her increased achievement motivation, competitiveness, and confidence. She had learned that not only could she play with men, she could beat them at their own game. That fall, she started her own small business and succeeded. Through tennis she actively mastered what she had passively suffered by transforming her feeling of incompleteness and inferiority into feelings of competence and competitiveness.

## School Subjects

The fifth topic addressed in the career style interview deals with clients' preferred work environments. Counselors investigate clients' school experience to sample this aspect of their career styles. Schools present fairly uniform work experiences that shape students' work habits and attitudes. Schools expose students to a variety of work environments. For example, English classes present different job demands than do shop or chemistry classes. Counselors ask clients about their success (grades) and satisfaction (happiness) in these different work environments.

Counselors inquire about school subjects during a career style interview to find out which work environments clients liked best in high school or college. Counselors ask clients to separate teachers from subjects to avoid confusion. Sometimes clients report a particular subject as their favorite, yet this subject does not fit with their life story. On inquiry, it turns out that the client enjoyed the teacher. For example, one artistic and creative client loved ninth-grade Latin. It turned out that he disliked the subject but admired the teacher. His favorite part of the course occurred when the teacher digressed from Latin instruction to relate life experiences and personal opinions. After clients describe their favorite subjects, counselors ask them about disliked subjects. Then, they review each subject in detail by asking what clients liked about it, what grades they earned, and what effect it had on their career thinking. From these answers, counselors can picture work environments that clients prefer as well as their work habits and attitudes.

## Mottos

The sixth topic in the career style interview deals with clients' favorite sayings or mottos. In a motto, counselors listen for how clients title their life story. Some titles that clients have used are "that which flows from the heart alone brings others to your own";

"you got a mouth, use it"; "better safe than sorry"; and "shit happens." If clients do not have a motto, counselors can ask them to repeat a saying they remember hearing or create a saying. With encouragement, even reluctant clients can formulate something.

## Ambitions

As counselors approach the end of the career style interview, they ask clients to tell them about ambitions their parents had for them as children. This gives counselors some idea of the occupations to which clients have reacted. Occasionally indecisive clients say that their parents wanted them to avoid trouble or a nervous breakdown. These clients have not reacted to positive images of themselves or occupations and usually they are extremely discouraged. When asked for a positive goal, they are silent because they have not developed a dream for their life. In conjunction with the parental ambition question, some counselors ask clients about the ambitions they had for their life when they were in elementary school. It is also useful to ask which occupations they daydream about now. Planful daydreaming and fantasizing to conceptualize oneself in different occupations seems to be an essential component of effective career decision making (Crites, 1969). Moreover, the content of occupational daydreams is about as valid in predicting career choice as are interest inventories (Touchton & Magoon, 1977).

## Decisions

At the end of the career style interview, counselors ask clients to describe an important choice they have made and how they made it, in order to discern their decision-making strategies. For example, a client described how he chose a college by saying,

> I think I chose it just by the fact that it was convenient. I really couldn't decide. I applied to a lot of schools and we couldn't really get financial aid from any of them. That was how I first decided it's not practical. You know if anybody gave me any money, I'd go there. I didn't get any money, so I decided to come here because it was close to home and it

wasn't that expensive. I didn't want to go downtown. I wanted to go to a good place. You know, like I didn't want to go to a state college. I wanted to go to a good place, but I didn't want to go to an Ivy League college either. I wanted to stay in between. I don't know how I made the decision. I just kinda ended up here. I'm not sure how. I booted my girlfriend the same way. I just, one night I realized I didn't want to go out with her anymore, so I just stopped taking her out. It was like a very sudden thing. I didn't really sit down and rationally think about it. I just suddenly realized I didn't want to take her out anymore. It was more like intuition, a gut feeling. That's about how I chose this college. It's more like an intuition, rather than a rational decision.

Counselors close the career style interview by asking clients to think in between sessions about how they will eventually choose an occupation and by orienting them to the next session.

## CAREER STYLE ASSESSMENT

Before the first counseling session, counselors analyze their clients' interview responses to assess their career styles. They begin by reviewing a client's responses to the role model questions. In considering the responses, counselors attend to the central problem portrayed and the interests that seem useful in resolving this problem. Second, counselors may consider the leisure question responses to discern manifest interests and identify the roles, functions, and rewards that intrinsically attract the client. Third, counselors may review responses to the magazine questions to determine the prominence of data, people, things, and ideas in the client's preferred environments (Prediger, 1982). Fourth, counselors may consider the client's schoolwork responses to compare the client's reactions to different work environments and analyze successful and satisfying experiences as well as failures and dissatisfying experiences.

Note that the first two areas that counselors review (models and leisure) deal with the self whereas the next two (magazines and schoolwork) deal with the environment. The fifth area that counselors review deals with occupational fantasies and decisional strategies: parental ambitions, childhood ambitions, occupational daydreams, and an important choice. Consideration of these topics allows counselors to envision clients' images of themselves at work and how they might choose an occupation. It also may yield better understanding of how private logic affects their decision making.

After reviewing these five areas, experienced counselors usually can articulate a client's career style. Next, counselors relate the career style to the career choice predicament that the client presented and then identify occupations that can continue the client's life story and lead to more completeness. Usually, counselors should start informally by thinking about the occupations that the client mentioned during the career style interview. These occupations are reference points in the client's thinking and must be discussed with the client. After considering the occupations explicitly mentioned by the client, some counselors use intuition and imagination to generate a list of occupational titles. Remember that by knowing the client's career path, counselors can identify some occupations that may be useful and interesting to the client.

After using these informal procedures to generate occupational titles for a client to consider, counselors may turn to a more formal procedure. At this point, person–occupation translation materials devised to implement the classic matching model of career counseling are very useful, particularly those based on personality systematics (Dahlstrom, 1972) such as Holland's (1985a) typology of vocational personalities and work environments or Jung's theory of psychological types (I. B. Myers & McCaulley, 1985, chapter 4). For example, with Holland's typology, a counselor can assign a type code to each hobby, magazine, school subject, and self-descriptive adjective that the client mentioned during the career style interview. Using clinical judgment, the counselor can sum the results to determine an occupational type code and then use the *Dictionary of Holland Occupational Codes* (Gottfredson, Holland, & Ogawa, 1982) to identify occupations that correspond to the client's occupational type code. When they have a list of occupational prospects in hand and the client's career style and fictional goal in mind, counselors have completed the career style assessment.

**Practice Case.** The following case material may be used to exercise your skill at career style assessment. Read the following career style interview data and, before reading further, perform your own assessment of the client's career style, career path, interests, and occupational prospects. The client is a male, 19-year-old, college sophomore who dislikes the science courses in his pre-medical curriculum.

| | |
|---|---|
| Role models: | Lincoln, because he (a) lost political campaigns yet never gave up, (b) got up and gave speeches, and (c) wrote speeches. |
| | Edison, because he was (a) imaginative, (b) practical, and (c) told other people what to do. |
| | Walt Disney, because he came up with and built imaginative things. |
| Books: | *Winesburg, Ohio*, about a boy who works for a paper and wants to write. |
| Magazines: | *Time* and *Newsweek,* for movie reviews and politics; *Jazziz,* for articles about jazz music and musicians. |
| Leisure activities: | Play trumpet, build models, watch "Star Trek." |
| School subjects: | Liked history of how foreign policy was shaped and English, especially the drama in plays. Disliked science and mathematics. |
| Motto: | "The unexamined life is not worth living." |
| Parental ambitions: | Father said be an actor or use your mind; mother said be a doctor. |

Childhood ambition: Musician or teacher.

Important choice: Talked with parents about which college to attend; deferred to them and chose the one they preferred.

The counselor's goal in performing a career style assessment is not "to be right." Adlerian counselors try to be *useful* to their clients. In comparing your assessment of the above data to the assessment that follows, do not get stuck in the dichotomy of right versus wrong. Instead, look at both assessments and ask yourself, How useful would these assessments be to the client in easing self-exploration and prompting occupational exploration and career decision making?

| | |
|---|---|
| Career style: | He moves through life as a communicator who uses oral and verbal skills to entertain, report, persuade, supervise, and critique other people. His style includes the use of imagination, persuasiveness, and perseverance to identify and deal with practical problems or challenges. |
| Career path: | His future success and satisfaction may follow the line of writing or speaking about how to make decisions and solve practical problems. |
| Interests: | He appreciates the usefulness of writing, politics, performing, teaching, human relations, managing, and consulting. |
| Occupational prospects along career path: | He may want to investigate occupations such as journalist, author, lawyer, politician, actor, technical writer, human relations manager, performing arts manager, advisor/consultant. |
| Guiding fiction: | "If other people like me, then I will belong and feel secure." |

This client eventually completed a bachelor of arts degree in journalism and entered law school.

## CAREER STYLE COUNSELING

Having completed an assessment, the counselor is ready to begin career style counseling with the client. Career style counseling has a structured agenda that deals with five topics: (a) career style, (b) decision-making difficulties, (c) interests, (d) occupational prospects, and (e) choice barriers. Usually, counselors can address career style, decision making, and interests during the first session. In a second session, about a week later, they discuss occupational prospects and how clients can explore them. About a month later, counselors use a final session to confirm a client's choice or deal with barriers that block a choice. The pace of counseling varies. Occasionally, counselors deal with the first four topics during one session or deal with only the first topic during one session.

In career style counseling, Adlerian counselors use the Individual Psychology counseling methods described in chapter 7. Their methods differ for the two dimensions of counseling. Along the relationship dimension, they use empathy, encouragement, and humor to maintain collaboration and keep the client's attention on what needs to be done. Along the communication dimension, they use interpretation, confrontation, suggestion, teaching, and clarification to increase self-knowledge and vocational development and to facilitate career choice and commitment to that choice.

### Career Style and Path

The first counseling session begins with a direct presentation of a summary of the client's career style. In presenting this summation of understanding, Adlerian counselors follow principles taught by Dreikurs (Powers & Griffith, 1987). Counselors thoroughly address the strengths and limitations in clients' career styles and relate their ways of doing things to their work habits and attitudes in general and their educational–vocational successes and failures in particular. Two techniques make the discussion concrete. One technique is to identify examples of clients' career styles as expressed in their present behavior, preferably during the last 5 minutes or, if not, some things they said or did during the career style interview. The other technique is to ask clients to cite an example of something they have done during the last week that also expresses their career styles. Clients are so embedded in their own style, that they do not realize they have a style. Counselors must be sure that clients recognize their career styles before discussing where they are heading.

Counselors may move the discussion from career styles to career paths by explaining to clients that the more clearly they envision where they are heading, the more evident will be their choices. They may begin by telling clients that path is the basic meaning of career. In fact, the term career path is somewhat redundant because the word career denotes course or passage, having evolved from the medieval Latin word *carraria*, meaning road for vehicles, and the middle French word *carriere*, meaning street. Counselors may continue by describing clients' current career decision-making task as choosing a direction at a crossroads or turning point. Then counselors may relate this metaphor to clients' vocational experiences by describing the career paths that they have already traveled and project the paths over the horizon. Of course, it is most useful to use simple words and specific examples to describe clients' career paths and crossroads so that they can recognize and understand them.

To make a client's career path concrete and memorable, some counselors use success formula materials to describe a career path. I use the contents of Table 9.1 to help clients state their success formula. Together we select the three roles that best characterize the client's career style and fictional goal. Then I ask the client to complete the following sentence with one phrase from each of the three role clusters: "I feel successful and satisfied when I . . . " The client picks the phrases and together we arrange them into a success sentence that the client can use to identify and evaluate prospective occupations. For example, one client selected the following: solve problems (from the thinker role cluster), help others (from the helper role cluster), and share feelings (from the creator role cluster). She combined them into her success formula: "I feel

# TABLE 9.1
## Success Formula Elements
## Grouped by Organizational Roles*

### DOER

Work with Tools
Think with My Hands
Make or Repair Things
Use Mechanical Ability
Apply Physical Skill
Work Outdoors
Work with Animals
Work with Nature

### HELPER

Help Others
Work with People
Provide a Service
Be Outgoing and Pleasant
Help Children
Help the Elderly
Teach
Counsel
Advice

### THINKER

Solve Problems
Work with Science
Work with Math
Use Logic
Research Ideas
Figure Out How Things Work
Read
Analyze People

### INFLUENCER

Make Decisions
Convince Others
Lead a Group
Use Power
Act with Enthusiasm
Sell Things
Be the Center of Attention
Be Dynamic
Have a Lot of Variety

### CREATOR

Be Independent
Share Feelings
Be Sensitive
Paint
Play an Instrument
Write
Apply Artistic Flair
Decorate
Design

### ORGANIZER

Be Precise
Be a Part of a Team
Record Data
Type
Organize File Material
Have a Set Routine
Know What Is Expected
Carry Out Orders

*For more information about the six roles, consult Holland (1985a).

successful and satisfied when I help others solve their problems and feel better."

## Decision-Making Difficulties

After clients recognize their career styles and envision their career paths, counselors direct their attention to how clients use private logic to process career decision-making tasks. On the one hand, if common sense can comprehend and validate their private logic, then counselors may reinforce clients' private logic and apply it to their career decision-making tasks. On the other hand, if common sense cannot comprehend or validate their private logic, then counselors reveal this to clients and explain how the guiding fictions in their private logic cause their career indecision or unrealism. Invalid ideas in a guiding fiction usually take the form of preemptive distinctions, oversimplifications, or overgeneralizations (for examples, see Shulman, 1973) in a client's fictional goal (e.g., If I were . . . then I would be safe, secure, and significant). The more exaggerated these invalid ideas become, the more they delay or distort career decision making.

An example of how a client's private logic can delay or distort career decision making may be useful here. I recall one client whose ambition was to be respected. However, in his fictional goal he oversimplified respect to mean control: "If people obey me, I will be safe, secure, and significant." He succinctly expressed this mistaken idea in his motto, "My way or the highway." This exaggerated distinction distorted his career decision-making process in that he considered only occupations that offered him respect in the form of power, possessions, and prestige. Because it was irrelevant to his goal, he had not considered how he would contribute to society or how his need to control other people would impair his relations with coworkers and family members.

A client's private logic enters common sense when two people talk about it during a counseling session. By representing common sense, counselors help clients reevaluate mistaken ideas. They may begin by explaining that the mistaken idea is understandable but not necessary. This may take the form of explicating where the idea came from and why it is no longer needed. With clients who mistake respect for control, a counselor might explain how the need to control people served an adaptive purpose earlier in life, but is now maladaptive. The need to control people is understandable in light of past circumstances but not necessary in present situations. In confronting the client's mistaken idea (i.e., respect = control), the counselor should use a phrase that captures the client's imagination and compels him to reconsider the idea. For example, the counselor might impress upon the client that "our way is the highway" leads people to respect him whereas "my way or the highway" leads people to fear him. Adlerian counselors might also consider "spitting in the soup" by telling the client that his equating respect with control causes something he dislikes; maybe his hypertension, insomnia, or free-floating anger (Mosak, 1977). Another Adlerian method that a counselor might use is to confront him with a negative picture of his future if he continues to dominate other people (Shulman, 1971). Other counseling methods for correcting mistaken ideas have been presented by Adlerians in writing about mistaken assumptions (Shulman, 1968), basic mistakes (Dreikurs, 1967), or interfering ideas (Powers & Griffith, 1987), and by other counselors in writing about neurotic convictions (Horney, 1945), irrational ideas (Ellis & Greiger, 1977), private rules (Krumboltz, 1983), or irrational expectations (Nevo, 1987).

## Interests

The third career style counseling topic deals with interests as criteria in making occupational choices. After helping clients recognize their career styles and examine their private logic as it affects decision making, counselors discuss interests clients can use to move toward goals. Counselors may start by explaining that interests are not simply feelings, they have meanings, both public and private. Then they may discuss how an interest connects a career style to the environment. This lays the groundwork for naming the clients' interests, discussing the hidden meaning their interests hold, and explaining how these can be useful to them. In discussing how well various interests serve fictional goals and express career styles, counselors should be as specific as possible and cite examples from the client's life experience.

Next, counselors explain how clients can use their interests to identify occupations to explore. No one has time to explore every occupation, so each client must identify a set of plausible possibilities. Some counselors help clients do this by systematically describing their preferred work roles, activities, and settings. This discussion develops implicit interests into explicit criteria for screening occupational prospects. For example, following a discussion of this type, one client came to say that he was interested in a job that would allow him to play a leader role, use intellectual and persuasive abilities, and work in an entrepreneurial setting.

To keep clients actively involved in the career decision-making process between counseling sessions, counselors close this first counseling session by assigning two tasks as homework. The first homework task is for clients to think about what they discussed during the counseling session because the next session will begin with a discussion of their reflections on their career styles, career paths, and interests so as to reinforce, refine, or clarify the client's self-knowledge as it relates to career choice. The second homework task is for clients to learn an occupational classification system and prepare a list of occupations to discuss during the next counseling session. Counselors select one of the following for this homework assignment: (a) *The Self-Directed Search* (Holland, 1985b), (b) *Career Decision-Making System* (Harrington & O'Shea, 1982), (c) *The Career Key* (Jones, 1987), or (d) *Individual Career Exploration Student Inventory Booklet* (Miller-Tiedeman, 1976). Counselors may augment this assignment by asking clients to examine the *Encyclopedia of Careers and Vocational Guidance* (Hopke, 1987) or the *Occupational Outlook Handbook* (U.S. Department of Labor, 1996). An alternative to this assignment is to ask clients to work through computer-assisted career exploration programs such as SIGI or DISCOVER (Harris-Bowlsbey, 1984).

## Occupational Prospects

The second session in career style counseling is devoted to selecting a short list of occupations to investigate and devising an exploration plan. Counselors start the session by discussing clients' reactions to the previous session. This discussion usually leads to the occupations that appeal to clients. At this point counselors inquire about the second homework assignment, asking clients to relate the occupations they considered and to share their thoughts about how each one implements their success formula. Then counselors may ask clients to think aloud about each occupation that they mentioned during the career style interview that they have not commented on during this counseling session. Next, counselors may add to the discussion occupations identified in the career style assessment. This first half of the second counseling session usually will produce a list of about six occupations for clients to explore in depth and another six occupations to hold in reserve.

Having a short list of occupations to investigate allows the counselor and client to collaborate on constructing an exploration plan during the second half of the session. A plan consists of activities that help clients see choices clearly so their ability to decide is enhanced. Most clients do not know how to explore and clarify their alternatives. Therefore, counselors must teach them about exploratory behavior and suggest specific activities that will increase the clarity of their choices. Stewart (1969, pp. 218–221) prepared materials that are particularly useful to counselors who want to teach clients the principles of exploration as they collaborate on an exploration plan. The materials consist of four pages counselors may give to clients. One page presents examples of information sources, two explain how to get helpful information, and the fourth structures a process for using information in career decision making. To end the second counseling session, counselors use Adlerian encouragement methods (Dinkmeyer & Dreikurs, 1963) to move clients to enact their exploration plans. Counselors schedule a third career style counseling session for about a month later to allow clients time to enact their exploration plans.

## Choice Barriers

When the client and counselor reach the fifth topic (usually during the third session), career style counseling concludes, one way or another. For most clients this final session is almost casual. They tell how exploration clarified their alternatives and led them to a choice. Counselors reinforce that choice and discuss practical matters that will increase clients' commitment to their choices and help them implement their choices. For other clients, this final session is far from casual; in fact, it may be the most moving of all sessions. They begin this session by announcing that they still cannot make a choice. In these instances, distinguishing between a preference and a choice helps counselors recognize the decision-making difficulty. A preference expresses what a client would like to do whereas a choice expresses what a client probably will do (Crites, 1969). For example, a person may prefer vanilla ice cream yet choose chocolate to make it easier for the server.

The fact that some people make choices that they do not prefer makes the distinction between preference and choice critical in career counseling. If a barrier blocks turning a preference into a choice, then career style counseling is complete because clients can state viable and suitable occupational preferences. The client and counselor spend the session problem-solving how to deal with the barrier. The most frequent barrier encountered is family opposition. This occurs when family members press clients not to choose the occupations that clients prefer. Other common choice barriers include financial strain, training or entry requirements, prejudice, and dilemmas involving consorts or children. Common solutions include talking to the family in the counselor's office, moving out of the parent's home, getting a part-time job, or letting some time pass. If the client cannot state a preference during the third session, then counselors try to determine whether the inability to decide on a preference is situational undecidedness or trait indecisiveness (Cooper, Fuqua, & Hartman, 1984). In the case of situational indecision, many counselors recommend to clients that they engage in specified maturational or self-development experiences. In the case of trait indecisiveness, Adlerian counselors recommend lifestyle counseling and, if the client agrees, begin by collecting family constellation information and early recollections.

## SUMMARY

The present chapter asserted that Adler's Individual Psychology enriches the classic matching model for career counseling by elaborating its constructs and extending its applicability to a wider range of clients. Furthermore, I explained how an approach called career style counseling resolves problems that arise in adapting Adlerian lifestyle methods and materials for clients who want to make a career choice. In describing career style counseling, I dealt with the assessment of career styles, the identification of career paths, and the recognition of private logic in career decision making. The chapter presented counseling methods for interpreting clients' career styles to them and correcting mistaken ideas that delay or distort their career decision making. It also presented materials that counselors may use to perform and assess career style interviews with clients and articulate their success formulas. Hopefully, as more counselors do career style counseling, they will increase its effectiveness by developing its methods and devising additional materials.

## STUDY QUESTIONS

**Directions:** Respond to the following in the space provided.

1. Explain how the rationale for the Adlerian matching model of career counseling expands the classic Parsonian matching model.

2. Why is Adler's "psychology of use" an improvement over the "psychology of possession" that is manifest in interest inventories?

3. Use Adler's Individual Psychology to explain the origin of interests.

4. The essence of Adlerian career counseling is to clarify choices so that a client's ability to decide is enhanced. How does career style counseling clarify choices?

## ACTIVITIES

I. Perform a career style assessment with a client and administer your favorite interest inventory to that client. Before looking at the results of the interest inventory, predict the results, in as much detail as possible, based on the career style assessment.

II. Write your own "success formula" using the procedures and materials discussed in the Career Style and Path part of the Career Style Counseling section in this chapter.

III. Read the following articles that further elaborate the model and methods described in the present chapter:

Savickas, M. L. (1991). The meaning of work and love: Career issues and interventions. *Career Development Quarterly, 39,* 315–324.

Savickas, M. L. (1993). Career counseling in the postmodern era. *Journal of Cognitive Psychotherapy: An International Quarterly, 7,* 205–215.

Savickas, M. L. (1995a). Examining the personal meaning of inventoried interests during career counseling. *Journal of Career Assessment, 3,* 188–201.

Savickas, M. L. (1995b). Constructivist counseling for career indecision. *Career Development Quarterly, 43,* 363–373.

## Chapter 10

# WORKING WITH COUPLES

Love is the third and most difficult of the life tasks for individuals to master. This tends to be so because of the courage and cooperation it requires of both parties involved in the relationship. In Dreikurs' (1946) classic book on marriage, he noted that "tradition" had not prepared us for the democratic revolution that brought greater equalization into the marriage relationship. Contrary to others of that day, he was not discouraged by signs of the family's, and hence marital relationship's, demise. People's shortcomings, however, were most notable in their most intimate relationships.

> We suggest that the family is not disintegrating, but is rather faced with a serious dilemma. . . . We do not know how to resolve conflicts and clashes of interests in the spirit of mutual respect, a requisite for living in a democratic atmosphere. Our cultural inability to live with each other as equals, which we have become in fact, is most painfully felt in our closest relationship, in marriage. (p. v)

In Adler's (1936) article, "Love is a Recent Invention," he observed that, "There is no doubt that we know more about sex than our fathers did." He goes on to ask, "But do we know more about love?" These same observations could be made today. He even used a now familiar story of the father asking his son if he knew the "facts of life," to which the boy replied, "Yes, Papa, what is it you would like to know?" Humorous, yet telling, is the fact that people's attention 60 years later is still more oriented to the physical relationship than to the spiritual, intellectual, and social dimensions of their most intimate of relationships.

This by no means is intended to distract from genuine sexual problems found in some couples relationships and the need for their remediation or the substantial value to be found through planned sex education of the nation's youth. Rather, like Adler and Dreikurs, this chapter is intended to provide an introduction to the concepts and methods central to achieving a healthy relationship between couples. There are, of course, entire books written on couples counseling and therapy. The information provided in this chapter should prove useful as a basic position on which to build the theory and methods of other approaches. Unlike many other references on methods and techniques, the Adlerian model provides a value system as a basis for assessing progress in counseling or therapy as well as goals considered desirable in any such intimate relationship.

## LOVE: THE ANTECEDENT AND BYPRODUCT OF AN INTIMATE RELATIONSHIP

The reader may be distracted by the subtitle of this section. Contrary to popular belief, however, the emotion of love is not the "cause" for a satisfactory "love" relationship. This in no way minimizes its power or significance. Dreikurs (1946) noted that,

> The realization of being loved is a moment of high importance psychologically. It is characterized by a desire to give oneself and to accept the other one by a sustained and exclusive interest in the other one, by a longing to be together. . . . The existence of love [however] is threatened whenever our attitude toward the other one changes. (pp. 15–16)

Individuals, depending on their personal goals and desires, direct their affection according to how well they perceive their needs are being met by the subject of their attention. Although this process is generally an unconscious one, it operates just as deliberately as if it were by conscious intent. After considerable elaboration on the subject, Dreikurs (1946) characterized love as being highly subjective:

> Love is what one calls love . . . be it created for devotion or domination, for heaven or hell, for happiness or misery. (p. 18)

Therefore, love depends on the intentions of the lover. Left with only this assessment, one might conclude that there is little practical value in defining love for other than poetic purposes. However, Dreikurs and Adler offer further elaboration in the context of social interest.

Adler (1936) defined love in marriage as " . . . the equal partnership between a man and a woman—where two are merged into one, a human dyad, reconciling the sex urge of the individual with the biological needs of the race and the demands of society" (pp. 36 & 128). To achieve the "the perfect dyad of love," Adler went on to offer the following "rules" for consideration by all couples:

1. Don't look up to your mate and don't look down: approach love as an equal.

2. Don't expect an impossible perfection in others, of which you yourself are incapable: love a woman, not an angel; a man, not an eidolon (phantom, ideal).

3. Don't think of yourselves as one or two, but as a twosome.

4. Don't take without giving, nor give without taking, in love.

5. Don't pick out a partner who does not entice you physically, but do not entangle your fate with one who appeals to you only on a physiological basis.

6. Don't fail to cooperate with your mate on every plane, socially, economically, intellectually, spiritually, emotionally and biologically.

7. Don't lose yourself in by-paths and blind alleys: there is always a way out of emotional labyrinths—potentially all humans are fundamentally normal.

8. Be a slave neither to convention, nor to your own idiosyncrasies: remember you are not merely an individual, but a unit of your social group and the human race. (p. 128)

From these recommendations, the reader may conclude that Adler was not much of a romantic! From anecdotes of those who knew him well, we know that he was fun-loving, personable, and probably quite romantic as well. However, one must remember that emotions are tools and love is no exception! One can surmise, therefore, that Adler's admonitions would be practical and free of the entanglements into which poets would lead us.

Love, therefore, is both an antecedent and byproduct of a successful partnership. Two people decide to contribute to the other's comfort, convenience, preferences, and so forth, even when it requires discomfort, inconvenience, and overlooking one's own preferences at any given moment. Within this process of giving, there are intrinsic rewards of joy, satisfaction, and peace. Under such conditions, happiness with the relationship no doubt follows. How do people establish relationships? Dreikurs offers a psychological explanation.

## CHOOSING A MATE

Dreikurs believed that the secret personal anticipation of individuals guided them in the selection of their perspective mates. These are translated into impressions of physical, social, and psychological characteristics. They are unconscious in most respects but predictable in satisfying unspoken wants, desires, and expectations.

From the first impression until the outward expression of commitment, each individual weighs minute behaviors into a pattern of anticipation that either fits or does not fit a prototype of the "desired characteristics for me." An important Adlerian concept is imbedded within this perspective. Dreikurs (1946) believed:

> There are deep personal demands which influence the final decision; and unbelievable as it may sound, everyone gets from his mate just the treatment that he unconsciously expected in the beginning. The demands which are gratified when we suddenly or gradually accept one person as our right mate are not conventional—not those of common sense. We feel attracted when we have met somebody who offers through his personality an opportunity to realize our personal pattern . . . to continue or revive plans which we have carried since childhood. (p. 68)

Therefore, as Dreikurs described it, mating serves secret personal anticipations. These are often unspoken, even unconscious, expectations and wants of the individual. When people "feel" someone is right for them, they tend to say that they are in "love." Conversely, when they no longer perceive that the person meets their "needs," they tend to say that they have "fallen out of love." Thriftiness prior to a committed relationship becomes characterized as miserliness; generosity as extravagance; or interest in family as dull domesticity.

As strange as it may seem, in abusive relationships, when an abused partner refuses to leave at the urging of friends, family, and counselors, often what is missed is the pattern of anticipation that is being met by the abusive partner. This is not intended to minimize the real physical danger that such partners often experience as a threat to leaving. Often, however, the abused partner would benefit from lifestyle therapy (as would the abusive spouse) as a means of changing unhealthy attitudes, goals, and behaviors that sustain them in the abusive relationship. With such changes, the courage and conviction needed to accept the help and support of others to leave the abusive partner become the foundation for more and better changes.

Dreikurs (1946) characterized such a tendency as an "appeal to deficiencies." Unwittingly, some individuals are attracted to a person who offers the least possibility of a harmonious union.

> Two secret tendencies are chiefly responsible for this: the de-
> sire to maintain one's superiority, and hope of suffering. The
> one induces the selection of an inferior mate; the other the
> choice of someone who, despite certain qualities, brings dis-
> satisfaction or even torture, granting only the solace of mar-
> tyrdom. (p. 80)

The purpose associated with this inclination is to choose a partner for his or her faults. A partner who is inclined to be irresponsible, unproductive, asocial, or otherwise "socially inferior" offers
no challenge to the individual caught in a private logic requiring
continual affirmation of his or her superiority. In point of fact, more
than no challenge, the erring partner provides a readily available
stark contrast for all to see how notable, competent, or long suffering the "victim" or "martyr" is in their relationship. Again, however, one must avoid stereotypes of why categories of individuals
seek specific types of relationships. It is more important that the
counselor come to understand the private logic of the individual.

Less obvious but just as destructive are signs of discouragement revealed through marriage counseling, for example, where
one partner makes small disrespectful comments, withholds intimate disclosures of love, or exhibits nonverbal evidence of conde-
scending behaviors. These become the grounds for divorce.

Another basic concept useful in counseling relates to the observation that whatever characteristics attracted individuals in courting also will contribute to their conflicts in intimate relationships.
In fact, the very qualities that bring people together also tend to
contribute to their conflict. For example, a man marries a woman
because she is intelligent, charming, home-loving, independent,
and fun-loving. She marries him because he is intelligent, ambitious, hard-working, dependable, and gregarious.

Although oversimplified, the scenario becomes one of she feeling trapped at home or, more recently, limited career wise by a
hard-working, hardly-at-home, successful-but-too-busy husband
who may or may not show much appreciation for the sacrifices
she makes to have his career take precedence over other aspects of
their relationship.

---
One seeks companionship to
complement private logic.

---

Each partner feels justified in this discontent. They may accept some responsibility for their tension but neither may understand how fundamentally each got exactly what they sought in the other person! For couples counseling to be effective both partners need an understanding not only of their goals, convictions, and attitudes but also of how their present relationship tends to reinforce mistaken notions that bring conflict.

## COUPLES COUNSELING

Counselors must ask themselves at some point when one or more partners approaches counseling, What is the status of the relationship? Are both partners committed to the relationship? Are both prepared to enter counseling with a desire for success in achieving a "twosome" or dyad? There are, of course, assessment instruments available to pinpoint trouble spots and areas of discouragement. The measure of commitment to continue the relationship, however, is not so easy to determine.

As Vaughan (1986) found from interviews with 103 individuals of various types, ages, and descriptions who went through what she called the "uncoupling" process, there are discernible stages and patterns that can be useful for the counselor to recognize. She characterized the unhappy member as the initiator and the other as simply the partner. She notes that often counselors are confronted by a situation in which the initiator has unsuccessfully tried to communicate unhappiness, and, only after he or she decides the relationship is "unsavable," does the partner realize the depths of their predicament. At this juncture, the initiator already has begun the process of leaving, psychologically if not physically. She notes that when a counselor is sought:

> Partners will push for a professional whom they believe will
> be committed to saving the relationship. . . . Initiators on the
> other hand, will lobby for a counselor with no apparent bias
> toward keeping relationships together. . . . Both compete for

> support of this third person who has now entered the fray. . .
> . All things are possible. . . . Nonetheless, counselors note
> that in most cases by the time a couple seeks counseling, it is
> too late. (pp. 176–177)

"Too late" is not an Adlerian viewpoint, however, from which to approach counseling. First, many couples join parent study groups and discover that they could learn much to improve their relationships. Many discover through structured programs such as those sponsored by community agencies and churches that there can be much benefit from outside assistance with improving their relationship. Second, if in doubt, an Adlerian counselor would inquire about the probabilities each partner would predict that they would still be together in five years. So long as each offers any prospect that they will be committed in the future, no matter how small, then there is hope worth pursuing. If no hope is present, then the assistance expected by one or both partners may be divorce or separation counseling. This most certainly needs to be as clear as possible from the outset.

## Establishing the Relationship

Getting started will be more difficult for some couples and partners than others. "Initiators" are likely to be more anxious than their partner because their own motivation is in question (i.e., they harbor thoughts that the relationship probably is not savable). Conversely, the partner still hopeful of saving the relationship is emotionally distraught over the prospect of it ending. Worth noting is the fact that Vaughan found instances where partners had been initiators on other occasions or in other relationships. One can imagine over the life of a relationship how each member may have become discouraged enough to think of terminating it.

The uncoupling process is a natural evolution when one or more partners becomes so discouraged, so fatigued by fighting, thinking, arguing, trying, and so forth, that, at some times, they feel too physically and emotionally drained to imagine going on for 5 more minutes, let alone five more years. As a consequence, they begin to explore other alternatives, if not in fact, at least in their mind. They tend to begin disengaging themselves from the frustration, guilt, hurt, anger, and related feelings associated with this relationship by pulling away from their partner.

In effect, the initiators have begun the opposite process to how they originally became engaged with their partner. As one might guess, they can think more quickly of the partner's faults than they can of what is attractive, encouraging, and desirable. Empathizing with these feelings, reassuring them that these are normal, understandable feelings under the circumstances, and offering support to both partners can do much to diffuse the discouragement.

The counselor, then, strives to put both parties at ease by establishing rapport with each in a genuine way. This is not as difficult as it may seem if you can imagine that both parties are most likely emotionally in pain and yearn for empathic understanding. Without taking sides, simply asking each person to describe what has brought them to this point and what they have been doing to resolve their differences gives the counselor sufficient basis for empathizing with each partner's predicament.

Establishing rapport includes reaching some agreement on goals and process. One goal with which both partners can usually agree is that the outcome should result in the promise of a happier life for each of them. At this juncture, the assumption can be expressed that they are there because the relationship needs improvement and that this could move each of them toward this goal.

Even though it may be apparent that one partner is resistant, some agreement is desirable for short-term goals. For example, you can explain the value of lifestyle assessment. This is true for both partners, whether or not they continue counseling or the relationship beyond the sessions needed to complete it. Assuming that they are agreeable to participating in this process, then they should be agreeable to scheduling another four or five sessions with an opportunity to renegotiate after that point.

### Assessment

The assessment process can be done formally or informally. As noted above, the counselor is alert to unspoken words as well as nonverbal cues between the couple that are important to the counseling relationship.

The process includes determining what they hope to achieve through counseling. When the relationship seems in serious question, ask the partners to individually write what they consider to be the likelihood of it surviving five more years. Each writes the percentage (e.g., 20% chance) on a piece of paper and gives it to the counselor. How closely their opinions match may give an indication of how much discussion has preceded seeking counseling. It also can indicate who the initiator is (i.e., who is unhappy and has begun the process of leaving) and which partner believes the relationship is savable.

The individual with the lowest percentage often poses the greatest challenge to cooperation. Their discouragement is likely to have begun before their partner's and they have exhausted much of their hope for a happy resolution. As a consequence, they may unwittingly, if not deliberately, attempt to prove that there really is no hope after all. If you suspect that this is the case, then kindly but deliberately raise the issue. This can be done in such a way as to explain how the process of "uncoupling" works, as noted above.

In the initial interview, issues related to finances, in-laws, parenting, shared responsibilities, and expressions of love (sexual as well as otherwise) are common. These are an expression of the issues related to cooperation. Most often, these reveal the areas where the partners have focused their unsuccessful efforts at cooperation. Decision making, problem solving, and conflict resolution strategies are teachable. In the homework and reorientation phase of the counseling process, these can be developed. The real issues, however, concern clashes of the lifestyles. For this to be uncovered, lifestyle assessment is helpful.

The counselor also must listen for what is not said. Serious symptoms of lack of success will be found in alcohol abuse, other substance abuse, partner or child abuse, and triangulating by one or both partners. Triangulating may seem relatively innocuous as when a parent is overinvolved with a child or one is overly ambitious at work. But both are at the expense of the relationship and both erode its foundation.

Obviously, when alcoholism and other more serious conditions are involved, the challenge to successful counseling is that much greater. These are frequently "secrets" that the couple keep to themselves. The counselor must be alert to uncovering them when they are not presented by the couple. In some cases, it is as easy as asking how much and how often they consume alcohol. Depending on the family background, values, and so forth, they may see their abusive drinking behavior, for example, as perfectly normal. In other cases, they will attempt to minimize or deny it.

Another serious impediment to a successful counseling relationship is triangulation by the partners with others outside of the relationship. These can be well-intended friends or relatives or a lover of one of the partners. If the precipitating crisis for counseling came from an affair of one of the partners, the type and length of the relationship and availability of the third person should be determined. These can be indices for the likelihood that one partner will be tempted to seek refuge there when counseling is difficult or seemingly unsuccessful. The affair itself, however, is usually an expression of the discouragement in the relationship. Statistically, few of the "third party" persons ever enter into the lives of the partner even after a divorce. They definitely can be a factor, however, during this fragile time in the life of a struggling marriage or partnership.

The relative or friend who supports the partner against the other is also a problem. What both partners need are friends who support their efforts to be a couple and who are willing to do so in a genuine, loving way. As a consequence, the counselor may need to spend some time helping the couple identify such people and consider how to involve them in their social lives at this point in time. Some of these people may be old mutual friends who were dropped as the relationship deteriorated; coworkers with common interests; church members looking for couples of like age, family life, and so forth; or acquaintances newly met through a recreational activity such as dancing, card playing, or bowling. Such persons and couples can constitute a social support network for normalizing their relationship.

## Lifestyle Assessment for Couples

Lifestyle assessment and the interpretation of what this means in relation to their conflicts provides a nonthreatening pairing of beliefs, behaviors, and feelings. These pairings become the basis for new understandings, trying on new behaviors, and dissipating negative feelings. As noted in chapter 7, it provides a method for uncovering, for example, the views one hold about men, women, and the way that they relate to one another in resolving conflicts, meeting life tasks, and so forth. This method provides a useful way of constructing the individual's unique patterns that can be made immediate, relevant, and concrete to a counselee.

The process includes the childhood family constellation and early recollections. In each case, the partner is present during the collection of data and interpretative observations of the counselor. This activity itself tends to diffuse some of the anxiousness of both parties and generally evokes some greater hopefulness. It may be one of the few truly cooperative, nonthreatening activities for them together in some time.

Prior to collecting the lifestyle information, you may wish to ask each of the partners to write on a piece of paper how their relationship would be made better if their partner were different in certain ways. These should be shared with the counselor but not the partner until later in the interpretative phase of counseling. At the point when the counselor has enough insight to see the connection between the individual's life convictions and the "offending" behavior, then they, counselor and client, can disclose this to the observing partner.

Another technique allows a quick assessment of trouble spots early in the counseling process. Partners are asked first to rate themselves on seven areas of life tasks (i.e., occupation/work, love and marriage/partnership, friendship, getting along with oneself, finding meaning in life, leisure and recreation, and parenting). They do this using a scale of 1 to 5 with 1 as high. Next, partners are asked to indicate where they believe their partner would rate them in each of the areas. These are plotted on a paper or board for all to see.

The discrepancies as well as agreements become the focus of attention. Depending on the couple and circumstances, this technique can be used for partners to rate other areas such as coping with finances, in-laws, or spiritual issues.

## THE CASE OF NEL AND MARK

Mark and Nel came in for counseling after referral by their pastor. He had talked with them and concluded that they would benefit from a trained counselor's assistance. Mark was wary and not altogether communicative. Nel was obviously distraught and very tense. Early in the first session it was disclosed that Mark had had an affair with a woman where he worked. The woman did not work near him and had changed shifts since Nel had confronted Mark with her suspicions. Nevertheless, Nel was not sure that it was really over or simply waiting to start again.

When asked how their relationship would be better if their partner were different, Mark wrote that Nel would be more fun to be with, less bossy, and less task oriented. Nel said that Mark would be more responsible and more sensitive to her feelings and desires. On the basis of what had been said, I was inclined to think that Mark was the initiator and Nel was only now realizing the potential loss of their relationship. Obviously, trust was going to be a large factor in the success of the relationship as well.

The need for structure and encouragement to help them get unstuck from the emotionally draining dialogues that had been going on for the last several days seemed evident. Prior to beginning lifestyle assessment, it can be revealing to have the couple describe a typical day. Listening for cues as to how roles are structured, unspoken rules and ways of relating to one another, children, coworkers, in-laws, and so forth, helps the counselor develop

notions about the unconscious goals and movement of each partner in this relationship as well as how external influences may be
important. This can be the counselor's first opportunity to assess
the possibility of later family counseling, including in-laws when
their influence impinges on the success of the relationship.

This was a tension-relieving activity for the couple; both of
them got involved and showed some evidence of cooperation. As
will be revealed a little later, my hunches about the priorities of
this couple were corroborated by the lifestyle assessment.

As the lifestyle assessments progressed, both Mark and Nel
became engrossed in the process itself and let down their defenses.
Occasional laughter came into the telling of childhood stories, recalling friends, family situations, and similar information.

Mark was a youngest child. He had been doted on by his mother
and taken care of by his sometimes reluctant sisters. Two of his
recollections:

> I remember Beth [+4 years], my oldest sister, telling me that
> I'd have to wait until Mom got home to get my dessert. When
> she wasn't looking, I got it anyway. I thought, I'm old enough
> to get my own dessert. I felt good. I don't think she ever knew
> that I got it.

* * * *

> I remember Beth and Nancy [+2 years] holding my hands
> between them. We were going somewhere and I didn't want
> to go. They held on tight and dragged me along. I didn't like
> it and they knew it, too!

Mark is telling us a lot about his approach to life and about his
priorities. Adler characterized four types of number one priorities:
ruling, getting, avoiding, and socially useful. Not to be confused
with labeling or categorizing, these offer one way of attempting to
understand the dominant themes in an individual's life. One sees
in Mark's case a young man who has decided that, "I should get
what I want when I want it and not a minute later!" or words to

that effect. When confronted with this assessment, Mark smiled his agreement.

Building on the prior theme, I continued, "and no woman can stand in my way of getting what I want." Nel could not resist saying that this had certainly been true in their relationship. Surprising to some people, Mark was not defensive about this; indeed, he was proud of it! For him, it was true, so what's wrong with that?

You might guess that Nel was an oldest child. She had a younger brother, Bill, by 4 years. Each had a special position within the family. Although she helped with her brother, she had not considered it a problem. He was "a pretty nice little kid" and, aside from getting into her stuff sometimes, he was kind of fun to have around.

Now for a couple of her recollections:

> One evening, Billy was supposed to be helping me do something in the kitchen. As it turned out, I think I did all the work but I remember he was so funny clowning around that I didn't mind.

\* \* \* \*

> One Sunday we were at church and I remember the minister talking to my mother and father out on the front steps. It was a lovely day. The grass was green, the trees were in bloom (it must have been Spring), the sun was shining, everything was just great. And I remember overhearing the minister say what a delightful little girl I was, how fortunate my parents were to have a child so responsible that she could go to the adult church and never be noticed. My parents agreed and I know that it made them feel really good. Me, too.

## Interpretation

Without getting into a great deal of detail, I was already able to do some guessing about this relationship. Unless, for example, it was a family value to go to church in Mark's family, guess where he would resist "being dragged" by Nel? This guess was on target and both were fascinated by this small insight. It had been a bone of contention between them since the early days of their marriage. One also can guess who has taken on the responsible and "pleasing" role within this family; Nel, of course.

Mark, on the other hand, is supposed to at least come home, lighten up the environment, and provide some entertainment. Nel readily acknowledged, if there was to be any fun or social activity, it was up to Mark to be the "social director." He, however, tired of this expectation. At this point, they were invited to share what was on their "how our relationship would be different" list. With a little prompting, both could see how Nel's preoccupation with being "responsible," "seen but not heard," and in charge of "pleasing" was a heavy burden and impediment to their relationship.

Although Mark had married Nel because she was pleasing, responsible, and so forth, he did not like her bossiness. She countered that a little help around the house and with the kids could make it possible for her to be less bossy. At this point, I intervened to ask if they would like to do something about it. This redirected the energy and we moved to the next phase of the process.

This is not a lock-step process, however. There were many more insights gained from the family constellation, images each developed about how men and women behave toward one another, how they had learned either to cooperate and collaborate or merely cohabitate, how they handled disagreement, conflict, and so forth. Likewise, these and other early recollections provided additional useful insights. And throughout the process of counseling, we would occasionally refer to the lifestyle material.

**Reorientation**

Reorientation is the process of reframing old outlooks and attitudes such that they produce new and better feelings and behavior. The case of Mark and Nel is used to illustrate reorientation.

For Mark, we had to confront the mistaken, adversarial role he assigned to women in general, and Nel in particular. An interesting aside to Mark's insight was the realization that a recurring difficulty that he had with a female coworker was rooted in his private logic about women. In relation to Nel, helping him to gain intrinsic satisfaction in a role as helpmate and willing companion was going to take time. On the other hand, the trust that Nel had lost in him was to be regained only after some emotional, soul-searching experience. Time and deliberate effort were necessary for these and more to be accomplished.

Adlerians have observed that couples tend to be attracted by patterns, for example, in which one partner is concerned with power and the other control or one in pleasing and the other in comfort and being served. In this case, Nel and Mark could see that each of them had contributed to the growing discontent within their marriage. Nel was clearly tired of the domestic role alone, and yet it was comfortable to her and a lot safer than stepping outside of the home. She had felt satisfied in pleasing Mark and her children.

Now Nel was needed less by the children and Mark was not happy with her efforts to please him. Mark could be a source of support and encouragement. This was to be a new role for him, as Nel had always been the one to listen to his concerns at work, plans for promotion, and so forth. For the first time in a long time, and maybe ever, Mark and Nel were going to collaborate on working toward mutual goals. Until now, each contributed to the household by performing different tasks in conjunction with different people, using different resources, and on different time schedules. Each succeeded in their own endeavors with the cooperation but not necessarily collaboration of their partner.

Mark meets people easily. One of his contributions was to help Nel learn to do the same for herself. Nel agreed that she would like to "lighten up" and be able to enjoy more recreational time with friends as a couple. She also expressed a desire to take an adult continuing education course to see how that would do for finding new activities outside of the home. Mark acknowledged that he would work alongside Nel to get evening chores done so that they could have more quality time together.

In the process of counseling, Nel had willingly characterized herself as "Super Mom." Although that image had served her purposes previously, she was ready to take off the proverbial cape (and apron, too!) to see herself as a person, not as one in a perfectionistic stereotypic role.

One assignment that they, like many couples, found difficult but necessary to their relationship was dialogue and communication time. There are many variations on this as a method but the goals are the same: to establish or reopen authentic communications between the partners.

One recommendation to a couple is to establish a mutually agreed upon time to share feelings about anything that they care to share. One way to do this is by one person talking first for a fixed time such as 15 to 30 minutes without response from the partner. The partner then has an equal amount of time. They alternate who starts first each time. A variation on this is to have partners write a letter to each other, to share the letters, and then to dialogue on the messages in each letter for a specified period of time. The topics of the letters can be suggested by the counselor until the couple catches on and can create their own.

Because the purposes of these activities are to increase intimacy and to cultivate better communication skills, the counselor will need to teach or review some basics of such communication. For example, when attempting to communicate feelings, the person should learn to use feeling vocabulary such as is found in chapter 5. A quick technique for discriminating between "feeling" and "thinking" communication is by substitution of the word "think" for the word "feel" in the sentence. If the sentence makes good sense, then it is not a "feeling" communication. For example:

| | |
|---|---|
| *Not* a feeling communication: | I *feel* that we should stop pointing out each other's faults! |
| | I *think* that we should stop pointing out each other's faults! |
| A feeling communication: | I *feel* so hurt every time you say something ugly in front of our |

friends! (makes sense as a feeling)

I *think* so hurt every time you say
something ugly in front of our
friends! (does not make sense!)

The use of "I messages" as described in chapter 5 is also an
important addition to many couples' communications skills. These
can be reinforced by participation of such couples in group counseling or, as they have a stable foundation, in couples enrichment
groups.

There are many other topical areas with which the counselor
can be a resource and/or direct assistance. These include child-
rearing attitudes and practices, financial management strategies,
coping with in-laws or former spouses, blending families, or encouraging career and other life planning, because the foundation
for all of these is basic life coping strategies. Conflict resolution,
democratic decision making, and encouragement techniques such
as found in other chapters of this book are fundamental to the repertoire of successful couples.

On the other hand, the counselor must be prepared to let go of
the relationship as the goal of counseling when and if it becomes
clear that the goals of one or both of the partners is separation or
divorce. In these cases, the process of coping with all that moving
apart entails will be important. Both parties will have emotional,
social, physical, and financial challenges before them. In cases
where there are children to consider, they, too, will have need of
support, encouragement, and ideas of how to cope.

There are, of course, many issues to deal with related to legal
separation and divorce that are beyond the scope of this chapter.
Kranitz's (1987) book, *Getting Apart Together*, is an excellent example of an Adlerian type approach to dissolution by couples who
agree to cooperate at least in separation. Dreikurs said that it takes
an agreement to have a fight. If a couple can see that turning the
agreement to cooperation, at least for the purpose of minimizing

hurt to themselves, their children, their careers, and so forth, then they may learn from this experience what they never could learn when they were together.

Even in separation and divorce, there is hope for some good to come from the experience that can follow them into another relationship. This is an important point for the partners intent on ending the relationship to understand. The relationship most often has a life of its own beyond the legal termination. Emotionally, financially, and family-wise, when children are involved, partners continue to experience the presence of the old relationship. The longer the marriage or relationship, the deeper, more long lasting the impressions and memories. As a consequence, the more "unfinished" business of an emotional nature that is sorted out and directly confronted, the better off both partners will be in the future.

## SUMMARY

Adlerian counseling has an essential ingredient within it that all marriages and partnerships require: hopefulness. Without hope, there can be no successful couples counseling. Hope can be cultivated with genuine, uncompromising encouragement. The business of counseling persons in troubled relationships is challenging and fraught with pitfalls. In spite of one's very best effort, the ultimate responsibility for the hope of success rests with the individual partners. Adlerian counselors strive to use all of their knowledge, skill, and caring to nurture whatever hope exists within the partnership. If the relationship changes from that of marriage or living together, there is still positive work that can be done to help all of the parties involved cope with the inevitable changes and adjustments.

## STUDY QUESTIONS

**Directions:** Respond to the following in the space provided.

1. Why does the author believe that Adlerian philosophy and methods related to coupled relationships are even more relevant today than in generations past?

2. What is meant by, "Love is an antecedent and byproduct of a happy marriage"?

3. How can the fact that one got exactly what he or she wanted in a partner result in discord?

4. Why do you think Adlerians maintain an optimistic outlook when a couples relationship may seem almost hopelessly lost?

Chapter 11

# WORKING WITH FAMILIES

Adlerians work in a variety of settings and deal with many kinds of problems, persons, and situations. Dreikurs noted on different occasions that there would be no significant or unresolvable social problems if persons had confidence in their own equality. Without the courage to be imperfect, small problems become large ones. He also taught that the issues disagreeing parties bring to a counselor or consultant are most often not the real source of their difficulty. The major source of difficulty is most often who wins and who loses. Whatever the social conflict, who gets the upper hand or who loses respect is the hidden agenda in negotiations.

To solve conflicts requires an awareness of the hidden agenda and a strategy for establishing a new agreement in which no one wins or loses. For this reason, Dreikurs recommended four steps in problem solving and conflict resolution:

1. Establish mutual respect (i.e., grant each the legitimacy of his or her feelings and perceptions).

2. Pinpoint the real issue(s) (i.e., personal concerns about one's relative status or loss of it).

3. Change the agreement from one of fighting to a genuine concern for what the situation or task requires (i.e., the facts of the situation, what I am doing, and how I can change my behavior to help provide for the welfare of others in the resolution of the problem situation).

4. Allow all parties to participate in making the decision (i.e., listen to each other, help each other, decide together how to solve the problems, and each assume responsibility for a part in the new agreement).

Adlerians, therefore, approach different social relationships (e.g., teacher–student, employer–employee, husband–wife, parent–child) with essentially the same problem-solving, conflict-resolution strategy. In addition, Adlerians tend not to make a distinction between counseling and consultation, per se. Whether a counselee or consultee, the individual involved will be conscious of the fact that how he or she thinks, feels, and acts are subject to influence and change as a part of the resolution of a situation. A definition of consultation, however, may be useful as a means of distinguishing between it and other methods of helping relationships.

---

Consultation involves three or more persons.

---

Adlerian consultation involves:

1. At least three persons, directly or indirectly: the consultant, the consultee, and the consultee's clients, students, children, and so forth.

2. A problem or situation among persons that could benefit from a third party's view and expertise.

3. An equalitarian, collaborative relationship in which the consultee is free to accept, reject, or alter consultant suggestions.

4. The same conditions necessary in any helping relationship (e.g., genuineness, caring, empathy, facilitative confrontation, specificity).

The consultant, then, is a third party who provides assistance on an ad hoc basis. The consultant's goal is to effectively share his or her knowledge and skills in such a way that empowers the consultee and further referral for similar concerns is no longer necessary.

Unlike counseling, which tends to focus on the private logic, emotions, and behavior of an individual, the focus of attention in consultation tends to be directed more toward solving problems and resolving conflicts with a person and a group (e.g., supervisor–supervisees) or between groups (e.g., races, union–management). In chapter 10, marriage counseling, while dealing with conflict resolution as well, is shown to be approached from the phenomenological perspective of each partner. Later in this chapter I provide an example of a case in which a counselor works as a consultant to parents to help them cope more effectively with their children.

## ADLERIAN AND SYSTEMS THEORY

In their book *Family Therapy*, Nichols and Schwartz (1994) correctly noted that Adler and Dreikurs were among the earliest community group practitioners. Particularly noteworthy are their observations about Dreikurs' contributions to family therapy:

> Dreikurs' technique with families combined emotional support and encouragement with interpretations and suggestions about modifying unhappy interactions. He encouraged families to discuss their mutual problems in an open, democratic spirit, and he urged them to institute regular "family council," in order to carry the model of family group therapy into the family's daily life.
>
> Despite the fact that his approach anticipated many later developments in family therapy, Dreikurs' work did not gain wide attention, nor did it have much influence on the field. . . . He is one of those people who possess foresight and imagination, but whose ideas do not take hold because they are not developed in a receptive professional context. (p. 232)

Systems theory essentially builds on the idea that individuals influence and are influenced by the human "systems" within which they live and work. The systems proponents believe that the identified patient is simply an expression of a dysfunctional family of which the identified patient is a part. Depending on which approach to systems theory one follows, the practitioners variously use communications methods, strategies to restructure family interaction, or techniques to help their counselees reframe their perceptions of the family dynamic.

These variations on systems offer a different and potentially complementary way of conceptualizing and intervening with families from an Adlerian perspective. Although not developed as a systems approach, as noted by Nichols and Schwartz, Dreikurs preceded most of the current theorist-practitioners by several years. On the other hand, systems proponents such as Minuchin (1974; Minuchin & Fishman, 1981) have made contributions to family therapy from which Adlerians can benefit.

In Minuchin's approach, research has demonstrated particular effectiveness with family situations involving anorexia nervosa, adult drug addiction, and similarly difficult-to-treat cases. Because structural theory and methods are well suited to comparison with Adlerian concepts and methods, a brief discussion follows.

Minuchin, like Dreikurs, worked in inner-city, low-income (slum) areas. He found that establishing rapport involved what came to be known as *joining* with the family. Although not becoming a part of the family system (as some other theorists propose), Minuchin makes a quick assessment of whether the family is dysfunctional or simply transitional in the life cycle of the family (e.g., when children are born or leave home).

Like Adlerians, Minuchin prefers to have the entire family present in order to assess their here-and-now functioning. He keeps young children and the parents together during assessment. Rather than a distraction to the process, the child–adult interactions are seen as an essential part in the early assessment of the family's functioning. If he concludes that the family is dysfunctional, he moves quickly to intervene as his assessment dictates. Like Adlerians, he is very conscious of normal developmental family concerns. He cautions others to be slow to categorize a family's functioning as dysfunctional. He accepts a broad range of coping behaviors and interactions as "normal." He is quick to remind others that most, if not all, families deviate from the mythical norm to a greater or lesser extent especially in times of crisis or transition.

One important tenet is related to what he terms *subsystems* within the family. If the mother–child subsystem is treated without consideration for its purpose in relation to the other subsystems (e.g., father–mother), then the intervention is not likely to result in a lasting change. Subsystems are elements of the family based on function. Therefore, if the mother's goal is to maintain distance from the father or if the father is aligned against the mother with another child, techniques such as going to the bathroom to side-step excessive attention or power struggles (as Adlerians often suggest) will only address a part of the problem.

Minuchin believes that subsystems are circumscribed and regulated by emotional boundaries. Normal families have clear enough boundaries to protect individuals and the subsystems, but all receive freedom for autonomy and mutual support as well. Interpersonal boundaries regulate the amount of contact with others. With not enough boundaries, individuation is hampered. With too much, individuals experience little or no emotional support.

With what he terms *enmeshed families*, the boundaries are diffused. Such families "smother" the individuality of its less powerful members. The enmeshed subsystem offers a heightened sense of mutual support but at the expense of autonomy. The challenge to the counselor is to help members of the family to think, feel, and behave independently. This is certainly consistent with Adlerian goals as well.

*Disengaged families* have rigid boundaries. These families have members who literally go their own way and "do their own thing." These members feel no loyalty, support, or commitment to the members of the family. Adlerians would move quickly to encourage family members toward greater emotional and related support. These are difficult families to help and Minuchins have been lacking with them as well.

Having diagnosed a subsystem that works against a healthier environment for the family members, Minuchin attempts to restructure the family by activating dormant structures. For example, if he finds the mother and child in a subsystem distancing mother from the father, he may deliberately have the parents sit together and place the child at some distance away from them, possibly next to another family member or himself. He may ask the parents and children how this feels. He then reinforces the benefits of this arrangement and asks them to continue practicing it until the feelings are comfortable.

Techniques like these are creatively developed to fit the situation. Then family members are encouraged to replicate these activities outside of the counseling office. An Adlerian counselor often recommends a discussion or counseling group for parents or couples to help deal with some of these issues.

Minuchin notes that family structure involves a set of *covert rules*. Like Adlerians, he brings these to the awareness of the family members to be examined. When necessary, these rules are exposed as counterproductive to the best interests of the family. Because they are covert, when left unexamined, they tend to be self-perpetuating.

Although this is only speculative, I believe that Adler would have enjoyed exchanging points of view with Minuchin. Likewise, Adler would have been interested in the work of others as well.

Adlerians will continue to follow the basic tenets of Adler. However, the value of extending the family history to include generational issues (e.g., history of alcoholism, person abuse, health conditions, etc.), assessing the subsystems within the family beyond mother–father–child (which Dreikurs did as well), studying ethnicity as an influence on values, feelings, and behaviors within both the nuclear and the new families, and, potentially, adopting specific techniques that further the work of assessment and intervention merit consideration.

## UNDERLYING ASSUMPTIONS OF ADLERIAN CONSULTATION

Among the assumptions underlying the Adlerian consultation process are the following:

1. We are all in the same boat (i.e., we share common human frailties and assets and can benefit from this fact as we work together to overcome common problems). No one needs to act on feelings of inadequacy or compensatory superiority if he or she understands and accepts the reality of the human condition.

2. What is shared by the consultant is basically educative in nature (i.e., he or she is teaching a philosophy and process of social democracy in which the logic of social living is predicated upon the equality of persons). Techniques and methods help to establish this approach as a useful way of living together for all people. Pathology or abnormality is not assumed to be the source of difficulty nor is therapy the modus operandi.

3. The consultee is willing to consider changing his or her behavior and attitudes first (i.e., an acceptance of responsibility for helping to establish a new agreement).

4. Although many of the recommendations generally are effective with certain types of problems, the consultant is prepared for the unexpected (e.g., most children respond to specific recommendations in a particular way, but you can be equally sure that some will not, and this, too, should be expected).

5. Encouragement is a keystone to the entire process. Attentiveness, friendliness, and general supportiveness are fun-

damental to the relationship. When recommendations are made, they are offered in a clear, concise manner without harsh evaluative implications that everything done before was wrong. In fact, the consultee is encouraged to build on his or her strengths to help prescribe new alternatives to behaviors that he or she considers potentially more useful than others.

6. With proper consultation and desire by the consultees, they will make innovations on the consultant's suggestions and, eventually, will function independently of the consultant quite successfully.

## CHARACTERISTICS OF STRONG FAMILIES

In chapter 2, a model for wellness based on the Adlerian constructs for life tasks provides a review of the characteristics of healthy persons. This model and the assessment instrument developed from it represent an extension of Adlerian theory based on empirical studies across the disciplines. Naturally, family as a social unit constitutes an essential component in the development of individuals. Likewise, individuals are essential to the health and development of the family. Research has been conducted with thousands of families that reveal common characteristics of those considered to be healthy. There are parallels between the characteristics of healthy individuals, healthy marriages, and what some researchers call family strengths. They have gathered data on a diverse group throughout the United States and abroad, from all economic levels, single-parent and two-parent families, all educational levels, many religious persuasions, across generations, and cultures and races. Among the characteristics of strong marriages and families are the following (Curran, 1983; Fenell, 1993; Guarendi, 1990; Johnson, 1992; Olson et al., 1983; Stinnett & DeFrain, 1985; Wallerstein & Blakeslee, 1995):

1. *Commitment.* Members are dedicated to promoting each other's welfare and happiness. They value the unity of the family.

2. *Appreciation.* Members show appreciation for each other daily.

3. *Communication.* Members have good communication skills and spend a lot of time talking with each other.

4. *Time.* Members spend large quantities of quality time with each other.

5. *Spirituality.* Whether they go to formal religious services or not, members have a strong sense of a greater good or power in life, and that belief gives them strength or purpose.

6. *Coping ability.* Members are able to view stress or crises as an opportunity to grow.

These characteristics are consistent with those found in Dreikurs' works as well as the underlying foundation of those found throughout this book. In my experience as a counselor, they are consistent with the goals that counselors typically attempt to achieve. Having such a list, however, can make one's efforts more focused, more positive, and, hopefully, more effective. They represent areas for assessment and strengthening in all families who seek assistance.

## INTERVIEW

The one area in which Adlerians have had the most experience is adult and child relationships. Dreikurs (1971) does refer to other situations, including labor relations, in which he used Adlerian methods successfully as a consultant. Likewise, I have used Dreikurs' methods successfully as a consultant and workshop leader in business and organizational settings. The remainder of this chapter, however, will be devoted to illustrating Adlerian intervention primarily with parents and children.

From my experience and observations of demonstrations by other Adlerians, the following section outlines the major sequential stages of the interview. In this case, the illustration is based on the parent–child relationship. The family and marriage relationship are fundamentally healthy. As a consequence, rather than counseling the family per se, the counselor functions as a consultant to the parents in helping them learn more effective attitudes and methods of working with the children.

With minor modifications, teacher–pupil examples could be used as well. Because demonstrations or large group participation are common with Adlerian methods, reference is made as to how this is taken into consideration by the counselor-consultant. A full, only partially edited, two-parent-family interview appears in Appendix A.

### Establishing Rapport

Whether in the counselor's office or in a group setting such as a family education center, the counselor-consultant will be concerned first with helping to put parents at ease. Friendliness and sensitivity to the newness of a group situation for parents can reduce their apprehension early in the conference.

Generally, Adlerians work with parents in a group setting only after parents have had one or more opportunities to observe a similar demonstration. In any case, structuring statements often are used to help establish ground rules for the group conference and to clarify the parents' expectations for the conference as well.

Because experience has shown that families have much in common concerning parent–child relationships, the counselor uses his or her knowledge and experience to dispel the notion that this family and these parents are more troubled or less competent than others. While being aware of and empathizing with the parents' concerns, the counselor attempts to provide a new perspective on family living for them. If necessary, he or she helps to unite them with the larger body of parents who experience similar problems but also have begun to learn new methods for coping with them.

Among the types of ground rules for a group setting consultation are the following:

1. Parents and children are invited to ask questions of the group as well as the counselor whenever they desire.

2. The group may ask questions or comment but the parents may choose not to respond and/or the counselor may intervene if he or she believes that is necessary.

3. Labeling, evaluating, or otherwise categorizing the family or its members into static terms is definitely avoided.

4. Support and encouragement from the group members is used whenever appropriate (i.e., to show solidarity or common concerns, validate usefulness of methods from others' experience, or help reduce distance among participants).

5. What is discussed with the family remains within the group, although most of what is discussed will be behavior relatively public to others as well (i.e., neighbors, friends, and even strangers often know about the problems of a given family). On the other hand, respect and even admiration can be shown best by limiting discussion or comments about the family to the group of which they are a part.

6. Questions or comments relating to other families are not discussed.

7. The method of teaching by demonstration is explained and the fact that therapy, per se, is not the orientation for helping is clarified if necessary.

## Parent Interview

Once the preliminary aspects of the relationship are established, the counselor will begin by requesting information about the family constellation. This information requires a listing of the children by name, age, and sex, including any children who are deceased, were stillborn, or were miscarried. The latter information can be significant with respect to special or unusual treatment of living children.

Other children living in the same household or significant other adults with whom the children interact regularly may be noted. Grandparents, for example, who keep the children while the mother and father work have a substantial influence on the children. They, too, may be invited to participate in the sessions with the parents on occasion.

Frequently, in the case of a two-parent family, the mother will be seated nearest the counselor and will tend to answer the questions as they are asked. This may suggest that the mother is considered to be more responsible for the children. This is one reason why an effort should be made to include both parents in all phases of the process as much as possible. Fathers, obviously, are a very important part of any success with the children's development. In dual-career marriages, more fathers are getting involved with responsibilities formerly thought to be those of a mother. On the other hand, surveys of working mothers suggest that, as a group, mothers still handle more of the load than their spouses.

Some Adlerians take notes as they talk with the parents. If this is the case, a mention of the fact and how it is helpful in recalling important information may allay concerns the parents feel about this process. A short-hand system allows maximum eye contact when used properly. However, notetaking is discontinued if it is a distraction.

---

Family constellation information is
essential in consultation.

---

Generally the parents are quite prepared to report their reasons for seeking assistance. One or more of the children are a source of difficulty and they feel unable to cope successfully with it any longer. On the basis of the initial family constellation information including birth order, the counselor may make a guess about the characteristics of one or more of the children after hearing the parents' description of the presenting problem. On the basis of simple probabilities, the counselor often can determine who among the children fits the following descriptions:

1. Tries to please

2. Gets best grades

3. Helps out at home

4. Tries to be considerate

5. Is happy-go-lucky

6. Is cute

7. Gets own way easily

8. Demands own way

9. Is rebellious

10. Is critical of others

11. Is easily hurt, sensitive

12. Is bossy

13. Fights with whom

14. Takes care of whom

As noted in chapter 6, such guesses are based on the experiences of many families. The value of guessing is twofold: (1) It tests a working hypothesis against that of the family being interviewed. If it is incorrect, better that it be discarded as early as possible. (2) It can be a source of interest and encouragement to the parents that a relative stranger already understands their family in just a short time.

Although some general descriptions of the problem that they confront can be helpful, Adlerians find reports of specific incidents necessary to an adequate understanding of the parent–child interaction. For example, parents give general reports:

1. The two oldest are fighting constantly.

2. Someone is doing poorly in school.

3. They won't help out around the house without a big hassle.

4. They won't obey even simple requests to get up in the morning, do their homework, or get ready for bed at night.

On the other hand, the Adlerian will request a description of specific situations, representative of the types most troublesome to the parents. Frequently these come from events of the last 24 hours. The following excerpt from a group session will help to illustrate this technique. The parent is a working mother of three boys: Jose, 6; Juan, 4½; and Jesus, 2½ years. The father was unavailable for this session.

Mother: I've been trying everything I know to get them to help out around the house, but nothing seems to really work—even bribes of things I know they really want. Now they even talk back to me when I try to straighten out their fights.

Counselor: It's really discouraging to be trying your best and see things getting worse. Could you give me specific examples of some incidents that have happened recently.

Mother: Well, yes, uh, just this afternoon they started fighting over who could wear what coat as we were getting ready to come over here.

Counselor: Okay, what exactly did they do. Just tell us how you remember the situation at the time.

Mother: Well, I was working in the kitchen when I heard the boys beginning to get into a fight. Evidently Jose was trying to help Jesus with his coat and Juan felt that something was not being done properly. The next thing I knew, Juan was shouting at Jose and they were getting into a fist fight. I went into the hallway to see what was happening and proceeded to scold the boys for the noise and their fighting. At this point, Juan turned to me and said that it was not fair for me to stick up for them. He ran upstairs and began crying.

Counselor: So when the fight started, you found yourself going to find out what was happening. Juan felt that you were interfering on behalf of the other boys. How were you feeling at that point?

Mother: Well, I was angry at first, but then I was shocked by his turning on me like that. I found myself feeling a little bad, like maybe I had jumped in too soon and made the assumption that he was the trouble maker.

Counselor: How did the other two boys react when Juan ran upstairs crying?

Mother: Well, they just went on getting themselves dressed and didn't seem to bother too much about it.

Counselor: Do you have any other situations that are troublesome to you that we might be able to help you with?

Mother: Well, every morning I find myself going through a routine of trying to get the boys up before their father and I get off to work and I have to get down to the kindergarten with Jose. Generally, Jose's not too bad to get up in the morning, but he can be awfully slow about getting dressed. In fact, all three of them are quite a problem to get organized in the morning. I find that Jose will often try to help with his brother but it only becomes a fight because Juan doesn't want to be helped and . . . well, that's only part of the problem because the boys don't like to have the same kind of breakfasts. Some mornings I can make something, and Jose and Juan will be quite satisfied but the baby will want something besides what I fixed, but, the next morning, one of the other two won't like what's been made . . . and I just find that if it's not one thing it's another.

Counselor: So, from the time you get up in the morning, the boys begin a routine that manages to keep you pretty busy.

Parent: They sure do.

Counselor: Well, I think maybe we can help to get you out of that situation. We find that many families like yours start out with disagreements in the morning, some of which are small in nature, but nevertheless an aggravation. Sometimes these aggravations are more intense and, as a result, some of the bumps in daily living. I wonder how many parents here in the group have had similar problems to that described by our mother this morning. [At this point, the counselor turns to the members of the group who are observing.] I see we have several people here who evidently share some of the same problems that you have experienced with your boys.

Opportunities to bring the parents and group participants closer together are always important. It reduces the distance in such a way that the parents no longer feel self-conscious or concerned about the fact that they are the center of attention.

After the parents have had an opportunity to explain the concerns for which they have come to this conference, the counselor generally will invite them to describe the happenings of a typical day in their family. This description begins with a report of getting up in the morning and how the day is typically started. This is also an opportunity to assess the family with regard to family strengths noted earlier.

In most families, one finds that the "good" mother is a servant par excellence. She is the first or one of the first persons to rise in the morning. It falls to her to begin waking the younger members of the family, to prepare breakfast for the morning and lunches as well. In families such as the one just described, it is not uncommon for the mother to lay out the children's clothes, see that they have brushed their teeth, and make sure they have their lunches, books, and other paraphernalia ready (when of school age). For the youngster who is staying home with mother, it is a matter of getting the child ready for the day, including possibly an outing where he or she is entertained by the mother.

The typical day may be different to some degree for each family, but it usually involves the children coming home from school, leaving their materials, clothing, and so forth wherever they find themselves as they enter the house, proceeding outside to play with friends, and potentially coming in late for supper. This might be followed with some discussion and reminders about getting their homework done, preparing for bed, and, finally, for the last hour of the day, hassling over going to sleep and being quiet. Most families experience these circumstances to a greater or lesser degree at any given time. It is when these become persistent and augmented by frequent fights, evidence of lying or stealing, or similar behaviors that parents seek consultation.

After the major aspects of a typical day have been covered, the counselor should have a fairly clear idea of (a) which parent feels responsible for the children, (b) what goals of misbehavior the children pursue, (c) what behavior the parents might be willing to change initially, and (d) which procedures to offer as alternatives to the children. If it is not already clear, the counselor might ask if there is some behavior that the parents would like to work on with the children. The use of encouragement and humor, if appropriate, can be very helpful in expressing confidence in the parents' ability and judgment. The counselor should not press for goals beyond the willingness of the parents to be consistent.

If resistance is encountered, often it helps to identify one recommendation that they would be willing to implement for a week.

This can be facilitated by asking, "Has what you've been trying worked? Have you anything to lose by doing this for one week?" Although the parents may have some doubts about the new recommendations, they are just as ready to admit that what they have been doing has not worked. This being the case, the parents realize that not trying something new will in all probability not change the situation, so why not give it a try?

The counselor might ask the parents if they know how the children are likely to respond in the interview situation. They also might speculate on whether the children know why they are coming in for the interview and how they are likely to respond to the recommendations that have been discussed. In those instances when older children or adolescents are involved, the counselor may wish to indicate to the parents that suggestions by the youngsters may modify to some degree the goals and methods that have been discussed already. Unless there are further questions or comments from the parents, this portion of the conference ends and the parents are excused in order to allow the youngsters their opportunity to meet with the counselor.

## Children Interview

As in the case of the parents, the counselor will note who among the children comes first, who leads and/or speaks first, and who supports whom among the children as they begin their discussion with the counselor. It is important for the counselor to realize that children deserve the same respect shown for their parents. As a consequence, the counselor will talk *with* the youngsters, not at or down to them. The counselor will encourage the audience not to be overly impressed with the small size of the little children or to any overt signs of fear and discomfort.

Persons not familiar with Adlerian psychology occasionally are critical of the seemingly adult-like expectations the counselor holds for the children. Normally this direct, adult-like approach is accepted by even very young children. Baby talk or talking down to children is definitely not Adlerian. On the other hand, the same empathy and attentiveness shown to the parents is exhibited with the children. Being distant or otherwise stern with the children would be a misuse of this approach.

Putting the youngsters at ease, then, is the first order of business. With very young children, even getting names and ages may be a bit of a problem if a group of adults surround them. However, they usually forget their concerns quite readily and join in the discussion at the first opportunity.

An early question asked of the youngsters is, "Do you know why you are here?" then "Do you want to guess?" (or "Do you want to say more about that?") Generally the youngsters do know why they have come for this conference but may be reluctant to admit it. The counselor may volunteer why the parents have chosen to come in for the conference. Then the counselor may say, "Do you know what your parents say about the problems this causes?" (the counselor may tell them) and "Do you feel that way too?" The counselor then may inquire about their feelings and attitudes concerning their parents' behavior toward them.

---

Youngsters can identify what behaviors
bother their parents.

---

Much to the surprise of many parents, the children understand the ground rules of family living quite well. For example, it is not unusual for the youngsters to know exactly how many times their mother must call before they are to get up in the morning. In other cases, they realize that it is the inflection in her voice or choice of words that determines when she is at her wit's end. Equally important, the youngsters can discern when their fights are aggravating the parents even though they may not be in the same room. When asked what behaviors bother the parents most, the youngsters identify them without hesitation. This is not to suggest that the youngsters have consciously planned and plotted every one of their activities. Quite the contrary, they, too, operate very much on a day-to-day, moment-by-moment basis. On the other hand, when given the opportunity to examine their behaviors in relation to their parents, they have little difficulty identifying the key factors in their relationships.

After the youngsters and the counselor have had an opportunity to become acquainted, the counselor may ask, "Do you know why you do what you do?" "Would you like to know what I think?" and "Could it be . . . ?" The counselor has established some hypothesis about the goals of misbehavior for the children. He or she will have identified some specific behaviors that help to illustrate this point. On occasion, youngsters will not immediately recognize the significance of their behavior by a simple statement related to its goal. On the other hand, when given two or three instances that help to illustrate this point, the youngsters cannot resist a recognition reflex (smile) or other evidence that validates the counselor's observation.

The following excerpt from an interview with Jose (6), Juan (4½), and Jesus (2½) (discussed earlier by the mother) can help to illustrate how this process takes place.

| | |
|---|---|
| Counselor: | Boys, I wonder if you know why you're here today? . . . Do you know why your mother brought you down here with her today? |
| Jose: | I think she doesn't like the fact that we fight. |
| Counselor: | Well, Joe, that's very good. As a matter of fact, that is one thing she had on her mind. Can you think of anything else? |
| Jose: | [Shakes his head, no.] |
| Counselor: | What about you, Juan? Can you think of some things that your mom might want to talk to us about? |
| Juan: | [Shakes his head, no.] |
| Counselor: | And what about you, Jesus? |
| Jesus: | [Has his thumb in his mouth and is looking off at members of the group with his big, brown eyes.] |

| | |
|---|---|
| Counselor: | Do you boys feel that fighting is a problem for you? |
| Boys: | [Nod their heads.] |
| Counselor: | Are there any other things that you feel your mother and father are concerned about? |
| Juan: | Mama doesn't like to get us up in the morning. |
| Counselor: | Oh, I see. Is that a problem, too? [Juan nods his head.] Are there any other things that you feel have been a problem for your family? [Boys seem uncertain.] Do you know why you do the things that you do? [Boys shake their heads, no.] Would you like to know what I think? [The boys nod their heads, yes.] Could it be that you like to keep Mom busy, and you like Mom to know that you'll do things when you want to do them? [Both of the older boys smile a little and the younger one begins to pay attention.] Can you think of times when you managed to keep your mom pretty busy and also have your own way, too? |
| Juan: | I don't get to have my own way. In fact, I don't get to have my way at all. |
| Counselor: | I see, Juan. You feel that you're the only one in the family who doesn't get to have his own way. Hmmm . . . so life is just not fair to you. I wonder, Juan, could it be that you'd rather be right than have your own way sometimes in order to let people know how unfair they've been? |
| Juan: | [Shakes his head tentatively, no.] |
| Counselor: | I wonder. You might want to think about that, Juan. Could it be that when Jose and Jesus are getting their way, you'd rather complain about not get- |

ting your way so that you can make Mother feel bad, like she's done something wrong? Could that be? [Juan looks on.] I think, Juan, it must make you happy sometimes seeing your mother uncomfortable and feeling that she's wrong and you know that she's wrong. What do you think about that? [Juan smiles and nods his head, yes.] Tell me, Juan, what would be more important to you, having your own way more often or having the satisfaction of knowing that your mother was mistaken and that you know she was wrong?

Juan:        Having my own way more often.

Counselor:   Well, that certainly is a possibility, Juan, but it's for you to decide; and it may be hard, because sometimes in the past you've had some real fun knowing that your mother is wrong. Am I right? [Juan nods his head, yes.] Would you boys like some help in changing some of the problems in your family?

Jose/Juan:   Yes.

Counselor:   And what about you, Jesus? Would you like to see some things different in your family, too?

Jesus:       [Nods his head, yes, also.]

The counselor then explains to the boys some alternatives that had been discussed with the parents. The boys are given an opportunity to discuss how they think it will help to improve their situation at home. In some cases, working out details with the children (e.g., about getting themselves up in the morning) allows the counselor to ask them, "Do you think your parents will agree?" Such questions can help the counselor assess mutual confidence between the parents and children. It is also an indication to them of how people begin to improve their relationships. With young children, the counselor may conclude by summarizing aspects of what is to follow at home, indicating when they will return, and generally expressing friendliness and encouragement.

The counselor may express thanks to the youngsters for talking before the group if that is the circumstance. As was true with the parents, the youngsters will have been given the opportunity before the conference to volunteer that they would be willing to speak before the group.

## Consolidation

For the parents of young children, the remainder of the conference will be conducted without the presence of the youngster. When teenagers are involved, they frequently are included in the wrap-up session. This session is an opportunity to review behavioral goals and recommendations upon which agreement has been reached. It is also an opportunity to answer questions that the parents or youngsters may have. Details of how, when, and where the next conference will be held also should be covered. Comments from the group might be in order if they have had experience with the recommendations that the family is preparing to implement. Such responses often provide encouragement and general support to the family as evidence that they, like others, have it within their capability to make changes in a positive direction. Attention may be given to encouraging the family to focus on areas that would strengthen it, such as research suggests (e.g., spending more quality time together, listening to one another's stories of the day at dinner time, or expressing appreciation for one another's contributions to the family and each other on a regular basis).

## TYPICAL RECOMMENDATIONS

Because certain family situations are so common, Adlerians have found that many of the same recommendations are effective for different families. The following are among the recommendations that have been found to reduce the number of hassles in many families.

## Alarm Clock

Many families have discovered that one of the finest inventions of all time is the alarm clock. This is due in no small part to the fact that even young children can learn to set the alarm in the evening in order to get themselves up in the morning. Contrary to what many parents expect, children appreciate the fact that they are given the responsibility for taking care of themselves in the morning. This is a very basic way to demonstrate that the children can assume responsibility.

Parents often will feel that the youngster will sleep in spite of the alarm clock. This is not normally the case. In the event that it should happen, however, parents should be instructed to allow the natural consequences of the youngsters' behavior to follow. If the youngsters normally get themselves up but sleep late one morning because of a particularly late activity the night before, there certainly would be no reason for not awakening them, as one might do for a friend. The only concern would be with not establishing a pattern or expectancy that sleeping in is alright because someone else will take care of them.

## Dress Before Breakfast

Many parents are surprised to find that a very simple change in the ground rules in the morning can save them a great deal of time and hassle. An illustration of this might be helpful:

> One mother reported that her 5-year-old son, Frank, was the last one to be dressed every morning. Because the mother worked outside of the home, this presented a number of problems. The other children managed to get themselves dressed and come down for breakfast, but Frank would linger until the very last minute and then finally require that his mother get him dressed. As a consequence, the mother would be late getting to work.
>
> After two or three evenings of discussing chapters in *Children the Challenge* (Dreikurs & Soltz, 1964), members of the group suggested that she might wish to consider a new ground rule for their family. The new ground rule was simply

this: All members of the family, including Frank, would be expected to get dressed before breakfast in the morning. The logic of this was that the mother was busy making breakfast and preparing for the remainder of the day while Frank should be getting dressed. If Frank was unable to get dressed, then it would be necessary for his mother to help him, which took time from her day. The result would be that Frank would not have breakfast and would be going to the nursery without breakfast. This would be explained to the nursery teacher in the event that this should be necessary.

The following week the mother returned to the discussion group quite delighted to report that Frank had gotten himself in the habit of dressing before breakfast in the morning. This did not happen the first morning, however. The evening of the parent discussion group, the mother had tucked Frank into bed and said, "We will have a new rule in the morning. It will be necessary for everyone to be dressed for breakfast in order that I can go about my chores, too."

The next morning Frank arrived in his pajamas as he had so many mornings before. The mother said nothing to Frank and he simply sat and waited for his breakfast to be served. The other children began eating and Frank received no breakfast. Shortly after sitting for a time, he proceeded to go back upstairs and returned with his pants and shirt on but no socks and shoes. He waited again for breakfast to be served and still no breakfast was served. During this time the mother said nothing.

Frank then proceeded up the stairs again and came back down with one sock and shoe on but not the others. It was again a short period of time and Frank was back upstairs, whereupon he returned completely clothed. He had to rush, but he did get his breakfast. The mother reported that every morning since he has dressed himself before breakfast.

The success was largely to the mother's credit that she did not remind Frank or in any way make a fuss over the fact that he had done what was expected of him. Many other examples could be cited in which the same recommendation was used and worked just as effectively.

## No Reminders

It becomes increasingly obvious to the person using Adlerian methods that a lack of effectiveness of recommendations is almost directly proportional to the amount of talking the parents do with the youngsters about a behavior. Parents have a tendency to want to talk about the aggravations that come about as a result of the youngsters' behavior, both past and present. An important lesson to be learned by all adults who work with children concerns the value of silence. Allowing the reality of consequences to operate is the key.

Although most children have clocks and watches, parents are often in the position of being timekeepers. They remind the youngsters that it's time to get up, it's time for breakfast, it's time to get ready for school, it's time to put away their materials, it's time to study, it's time to stop watching TV, it's time to do the dishes, it's time to get ready for bed, it's time to go to bed, and it's time to go to sleep. In one of my parent discussion groups, it was determined that a mother of five children was spending approximately 29 hours each week telling her children what to do. Principal among the activities was reminders of when it was time for the children to accomplish the various items listed previously.

So the new rule is, no reminders. If there is an understanding of when it is time to get up, to go to school, to eat supper, and to go to bed, parents of even young children may avoid the problem of having to remind them several times. The adults in the family can provide a routine and order that is very helpful to the children. The logic of the routine and order is based in no small part on the social activities in which the family is engaged.

Generally no one needs to explain that the school bus arrives at a certain time, or that the father or mother have to be at work at a given time, once the pattern is established. Equally so, if there is a regular eating time and a regular time to go to bed, there is no need for the parents to continually remind members of the family. The logical and natural consequences that follow from one's behavior should be the source of learning.

## Bedtime

Bedtime is one of the most common problem periods for children and parents alike. Part of the problem is that parents sometimes bribe the children to be good when they have company, or in other cases, threaten them with punishment of the severest sort. Unfortunately, these work some of the time, but certainly not all the time. As a result, the parents have a tendency to resort to them periodically with the hope that they might work again. These tactics simply plays into the youngsters' expectations that if they apply themselves diligently, they can have what they want when they want it.

In most cases, the consultant can help the parents and children reach a new agreement about the time that the youngsters should go to bed. In fact, the youngsters will be responsible for getting themselves ready for and into bed. For the children who cannot tell time, the parent simply mentions the time without particular reference to going to bed. Once bedtime has passed, however, the parents are instructed to ignore completely any of the behavior of the youngsters that demands their time or attention. Another illustration from parent discussion groups might be helpful:

> The father of three youngsters was having difficulty with the youngest girl going to bed at night. She was 4 years old and, as a consequence, aware of when the other children were going to bed and when she should be going to bed also. She would slip out of bed when the lights were out and the parents were back downstairs going about whatever activities they had before the evening was completed. At these times, she would talk to the father and mother about things that they were doing or things that she had done during the day that would peak their interest in what she was saying. Usually the parents would tell her to go back upstairs and begin to ignore her behavior. However, she was quite persistent and, as a consequence, normally ended up having one or the other of the parents carry her upstairs.
>
> As is true of many families, the parents had tried many methods but had not been consistent in any of them. So it was

recommended to the father that on the next occasion of the youngster getting out of bed, he and the mother ignore the daughter when she came downstairs. He reported at the next meeting of the group that the daughter had indeed come down that very next night and proceeded to talk to him while he tried to complete some work that he had that evening. His wife was a teacher also and was grading papers. the little girl went from one to the other until she found that she was getting no satisfaction. She remained up for approximately 40 minutes, alternately making distracting noises, playing, and attempting to bring attention to herself.

The next evening, she came downstairs and tried even more persistently to distract her father. At one point, without saying a word, the father simply pointed to the room and went back to his work. The girl immediately returned to her room and that was the last evening that she got out of bed. It is noteworthy that although the father did give an indication that he was aware of her presence, he said nothing. He simply emphasized that this was not the time for play or talk.

In instances such as this one, when the parents are advised to ignore the children, they are also informed that it is very important to plan for opportunities to talk and play and generally have fun together. The parents can be important contributors to pleasantness during those times of day when the family members are all present. Very often, during breakfast in the morning, dinner in the evening, and just prior to bedtime, the parents can inject humor, pleasantness, and a general appreciation for each member of the family. Some parents read to their children, others talk of events for the day ahead, and others pray with them offering thanks, petitions, and general prayer.

## Establishing New Agreements

Although it comes in many forms, the consultant often finds himself or herself helping to negotiate new agreements between the warring parties in the family. Parents and children alike need to learn ways for resolving differences. As has been noted before, even when there is a conflict, there is agreement. In fact, without an agreement, there can be no conflict.

Therefore, many of the recommendations involve a negotiation between the parents and the children. For example, at bedtime they can establish an understanding about what is a reasonable expectation for time, each others' role, and the advantages of such a change. On the basis of this agreement, all parties know what is expected of them and generally act accordingly.

Another frequent problem of parents is establishing a satisfactory arrangement with respect to the children doing their homework. Often, parents believe they know what the best solution is for children. Time and again, however, children surprise their parents, when, in the course of discussion with the consultant, children propose alternative ways of handling the homework situation that turn out to be quite satisfactory and even more effective than what parents had imagined. Building confidence in the children's ability to understand the problem and to propose solutions is one of the greatest lessons of the consultation process.

Very often children will recommend, for example, that on certain evenings they be given the option of completing their homework after they have had a chance to play with their friends. On other evenings, because of certain television programs they like, they prefer to do their homework as soon as they arrive home and then play for as long as time will permit before the television programs begin. Experiencing success with their solution becomes a significant source of satisfaction.

Helping with chores around the house is handled in a similar way. The children want to indicate they have good sense and can determine when things need to get done. For this reason, given the opportunity to decide when the dishes should be washed, when the garbage should be taken out, or when the grass should be cut, their attitude toward getting the job done changes and they find it much more agreeable to be contributing members of the family.

## WHEN RECOMMENDATIONS FAIL

Frequently, parents will report that certain recommendations did not work for them. On such occasions the consultant should determine exactly what transpired in the situation to which the parents refer. Generally certain conditions have contributed to the recommendation's not succeeding. The following are among the most common factors for the consultant to note.

## Talking

As noted earlier, adults have a tendency to talk too much and at the wrong time. When trying to utilize the advantages of natural and logical consequences, parents must learn to not talk and to not draw attention to the fact that they are aware a youngster is experiencing the outcome of an ill-advised act. The most obvious example of this is the "I told you so" comment that many adults feel compelled to insert whenever they gain the satisfaction of having the upper hand. Such remarks only deepen the conflict and increase the probability that the youngster will learn how to get back when he or she has the opportunity.

The following example is taken from the case of a mother whose daughter, a teenager, was using her as a bus service. In this case, the mother demonstrates unusual patience and an awareness of the importance of not talking at important times. As a result, both she and the daughter learned a very important lesson.

> Karen basically got along well with her family and friends. Her mother did have concern, however, that Karen was increasingly depending on her as a source of transportation to school and other functions. The mother realized that Karen could not drive, but she was beginning to resent the fact that Karen would take advantage of her at times when it was not necessary. This contributed to words between the mother and daughter and was a source of increasing tension in other matters that were of lesser consequence. The mother did not work and felt that she was obligated to help Karen even though it was sometimes inconvenient for her.
>
> The recommendation to the mother was simply that she give consideration to Karen as she would to any friend. When the mother found it not convenient or not in the best interest for Karen to have a ready taxi driver, the mother was simply to allow the consequences of Karen's behavior to follow as it

might for a friend who had not planned sufficiently in advance.

The next week Karen was up late one night and slept late in the morning and missed her school bus. When this happened previously, the mother had rushed to get dressed and hurried to get the girl to school on time. On this particular morning, however, the mother decided to finish reading the newspaper and have a second cup of coffee. The girl stood by in disbelief until she finally went outside, slamming the door behind her, and sat in the automobile. The mother proceeded to straighten up the kitchen as she normally would before she left the house. As she approached the car, she could tell that Karen was quite upset with her.

On the way downtown, the mother mentioned that she had an appointment this morning and would be a little late unless she kept to her schedule. They conversed about one or two matters that concerned Karen and activities for the coming week. Because the traffic was heavy, the mother asked Karen to walk the last few blocks to school in order that she would not have to get out of the main flow of traffic. Karen looked surprised but agreed somewhat reluctantly.

That evening during supper, the mother found herself in a conversation with Karen about the events of the day. The mother reported that she caught herself just as she began to ask Karen if she had made it to school on time. The next morning, Karen was on time for the school bus and nothing was said about that particular incident.

The mother found that on subsequent occasions when Karen needed a ride she asked her mother well in advance. The mother found this much more agreeable and was inclined whenever she could without feeling resentment or, in other cases, guilty when she did not.

## Inconsistency

Inconsistency in following through with recommendations of the counselor is another problem found in learning to apply Adlerian methods. This is why the counselor will attempt to ensure that parents not only understand the recommendations but also are pre-pared to continue them in the event that recommendations are not effective when initially applied.

What is acceptable to one parent as a recommendation can be quite unacceptable to another. Most parents find that allowing their children to get themselves up in the morning is quite acceptable. On the other hand, bedtime can be so important in the minds of parents, that they will be unwilling to negotiate the time for going to bed during the first few interviews. Later on these same parents may find negotiating bedtime more agreeable because the meth-ods recommended previously worked for them and served the pur-pose of a more cooperative, harmonious family life.

---

Integrating respect for others and respect for self is an art worth practicing.

---

Adler emphasized the importance of order and routine in the lives of children as a means of helping them to feel more secure. The fact that children test the limits to various rules of order might lead one to believe that they generally do not desire such guide-lines. Quite the opposite is true of the rules related to the logic of living together.

Being able to make an exception to rules and still maintain the order is a fine art not always understood by parents. Kindness and firmness are needed in child guidance. Kindness might be charac-terized as respect for the child's well-being. This involves making judgments that allow occasional exceptions to rules. Firmness in-dicates a respect for oneself, which should preclude being ma-nipulated or otherwise used in ways not in the best interests of the adult or the child. As new ground rules are established for interact-ing within the family, both of these ingredients will be important as parents learn to be consistent in their guidance of children.

## Overcorrecting

Parents and teachers sometime find that once they have begun to understand some of the principles of Individual Psychology, they become embroiled in situations involving two or three misbehaviors of children. The misbehavior that adults focus on initially becomes secondary as another behavior is exhibited. Adults inadvertently take away the effectiveness of the first corrective measure by making mistakes on subsequent behaviors. The following illustration will help to clarify this error:

> Clancey was outside playing with his friends. His mother heard a disagreement ensuing. As she watched the proceedings, Clancey was attempting to boss the other members of the group and they would have no part of it. In his frustration, Clancey grabbed his friend's truck and began to hit him with it. At this point, the mother called to Clancey that he should come in. When Clancey came in, she simply indicated that until he was able to play without getting into a fight, he would have to stay in the house.

> A few minutes later, Clancey was throwing toys around the room. His mother then proceeded to scold him for making a mess. He talked back to her and said that he would do what he pleased. She became angry at this point and sent him to his bedroom and said that he would not have supper until he came out and apologized.

In this case, the mother had begun to use the principles and methods recommended by the counselor. Unfortunately, she did not understand yet that only one behavior can be dealt with successfully at a time. What Clancey did until he decided to stop fighting should be ignored. Upon her return for consultation, this principle was pointed out to her so that in subsequent instances she would not find herself frustrated by attempting to deal with too many situations at one time.

## Self-Fulfilling Prophesy

Unfortunately adults often verbally or nonverbally communicate to children that they do not expect the children to behave in a way that would be helpful to the family or class. Adults also might indicate that they have little or no confidence in the children's judgment to handle a new situation. The children respond in kind and perform in much the way the adults indicated that they had expected.

As indicated previously, it is important that adults believe that they can follow through on recommendations and be consistent. Having faith in themselves and in the youngsters is a critical factor in helping to bring about a change. The counselor needs to listen carefully to the language used by those who are agreeing to implement recommendations. Generally, "I'll try" is silently followed by the conjunction "but," as in "I don't think this is going to work"! If necessary, change the homework recommendation to something that is less difficult or of less duration. In every case, ensuring success in implementing the new methods must be a high priority, otherwise, a negative self-fulfilling prophesy may be the result.

## FOLLOW-UP

As is true with any attempt to be helpful to an individual or family, it is important that consultees be given an opportunity to evaluate their progress since the last conference and to clarify any questions they may have. At this point the counselor has an opportunity to determine the extent to which the recommendations were understood and implemented properly. On the assumption that some recommendations will have been useful, new suggestions will be made as there appears to be sufficient progress to avoid overloading consultees with new tasks.

If the adults are not already in a study group, they should be encouraged to join a group. Such groups can be very helpful in providing the kind of insight and support needed to implement the recommendations of the counselor. Children also can benefit from discussion groups in their classes or in counseling groups that might be established through the school.

Occasionally adults and children alike tacitly agree to stop having conflict over the original presenting problems. Although still not functioning in a spirit of genuine cooperation and equality, they settle for a new agreement of services and contingencies not far removed from the original problems. The counselor-consultant should attempt to help them anticipate this pitfall and overcome it by following through with study groups, class or family meetings, and follow-up consultation or counseling as necessary.

## FURTHER APPLICATIONS

As noted at the beginning of this chapter, there are as many applications of these methods as there are social conflicts. Family physicians and pastors often hear the plight of the frustrated mother. A physician's guide to some typical nonmedical behavior problems for children appears in chapter 6 (Table 6.4), and excerpts from a family interview are included in Appendix A. These are provided as a means of extending the theory into practice.

With respect to adult relationships, the same steps are followed although techniques will vary. The most commonly violated aspect of conflict resolution concerns the first step, mutual respect. When individuals believe that someone else is mistaken or has done something wrong, they tend to begin their interaction by asking accusatory questions, blaming, or pointing out the error. In short, they tend to undermine the other person's sense of belonging, security, or adequacy. Action statements follow as to what should be done to correct the situation. Even though the suggestions may address what the situation requires to correct it, the violation of step one almost precludes successful resolution. Winning and losing become the goal of such situations.

On the other hand, if respect is established through active listening, good eye contact, and empathic communication, the other steps may not be executed optimally but the situation can still be resolved satisfactorily. When others perceive openness, flexibility, and respect as elements of efforts to solve differences, there is a greater probability of success in achieving a satisfactory outcome.

## SUMMARY

Adlerians use principles and practices of Individual Psychology to help mediate differences between individuals in groups of various types. They approach each situation with a strategy for conflict resolution originally outlined by Dreikurs.

Dreikurs was active particularly in demonstrating the effectiveness of the Adlerian approach in marriage conflicts, union negotiations, multicultural conflicts, and similar circumstances. By using his strategy for conflict resolution and the logic of social living based on social equality, he taught others how to apply the approach in a wide variety of situations. He would say that people are limited only by their imagination and their will to cooperate.

As is true with any approach that is new to someone, application requires patience and a willingness to be in error in order to find out the most effective ways of using it in one's life. For this reason, the consultant is an important source of encouragement and instruction as others seek to use the new approach effectively in their lives.

## STUDY QUESTIONS

**Directions:** Respond to the following in the space provided.

1. Illustrate the four steps of social conflict resolution using a situation with which you are familiar. If the conflict was not resolved satisfactorily, explain why this was so from an Adlerian perspective.

2. What are the hallmarks of a consultative relationship?

3. Identify two or more basic assumptions of the Adlerian consultative process that you consider particularly important and explain why.

4. What are some promising insights or methods from the family systems approach to complement Adlerian methods?

## ACTIVITIES

The following activities provide an opportunity for you to apply the techniques of conflict resolution. Please note that the situations in section I are especially well-suited to group activity. Individuals working alone or with a study partner would review the first section and then, using the same principles and techniques, respond to the marital conflict vignette in section II.

I. Role-Playing Critical Incidents in Parent–Teacher Conferences

Following are several initial incidents that could occur in parent–teacher conferences. In each case, the approach used by the teacher could have a strong impact on the parent–teacher relationship and on the child's school progress. Divide into groups of four persons. Each group should role-play all three situations. Try to act realistically, identify as much as possible with your role, and attempt to reach a solution. After each activity, participants should rotate roles.

| Role-Play Activity 1 | Role-Play Activity 2 | Role-Play Activity 3 |
|---|---|---|
| Teacher | Teacher | Teacher |
| Father | Parent | Father |
| Mother | Child | Mother |
| Observer | Observer | Observer |

In preparation for your roles as the observer and the teacher, you will find the following hints helpful:

*Observer:* Note as unobtrusively as possible which teacher responses are the most helpful in establishing a constructive atmosphere and, in general, observe the interactions of the group (note behaviors, dialogue, and so forth).

*Teacher:* Consider the following as you play the teacher's role:

- At the beginning of the conference, get up and greet the person(s) using his or her name(s).

- Be pleasant and look the person(s) directly in the eye.

- Avoid physical barriers between you (e.g., a desk).

- Speak quietly and listen carefully.

- Respond empathically, accepting feelings as nondefensively as possible.

- Attempt to establish what the situation demands. Be prepared to show examples of the student's work.

- Determine the willingness of the other person to cooperate in a plan of action.

- Establish a concrete plan of action.

- Summarize and establish a follow-up contact.

**Role-Play Activity 1**

*Situation:* The parents of a bright child (select grade level and gender) have requested a conference.

*Parents:* Father and mother express concern (feeling) that the son or daughter is not receiving enough enrichment in the class. He or she seems bored, less interested in school than they think is good. They are eager for him or her to do well. They expect the teacher to do something.

*Teacher:* The teacher should reinforce the following concepts: listening skills, communicating feelings, clarifying (values)— what parents expect, encouraging child, and specific home–school cooperation tasks.

*Observer:* Note the interchange among the three. As much as possible, note how, when, and by whom Adlerian concepts were utilized and how doing so affected the meeting.

Following the role-play activity, respond to the following:

1. *All participants:* How did you feel in your role? Was it especially difficult, or did it seem to come naturally?

2. *Parents:* Did the teacher seem interested and involved? How did he or she react to your expectations? Did he or she seem to understand your concern? Were you satisfied with the outcome? Would you have liked to have done something differently?

3. *Teacher:* How did you feel about the parents expecting you to "do something"? Did you find yourself defending your position? How did you feel about the outcome? Would you have liked to have done something differently?

4. *Observer:* Share your perceptions of the parents' and teacher's roles. Which teacher responses did you note as being particularly facilitative? Can you suggest different

approaches to the teacher? In general, how did this group discussion relate to the principles presented in this and previous chapters?

### Role-Play Activity 2

*Situation:* The teacher has asked a parent to come in for a conference because the son has been a persistent problem in school. His level of achievement is below what his standardized test scores indicate he is capable of achieving.

*Parent:* Parent is at least initially defensive and will observe that the son did not have this problem with other teacher(s) previously. Feelings of anger, resentment, and being uncomfortable in the school can be shown either verbally or behaviorally, or both. This position can be modified at least somewhat if the teacher uses insight and skill.

*Teacher:* In addition to the suggestions listed previously, the teacher should enforce the following concepts: listening skills, accepting feelings, a shift from blaming to what the task requires (e.g., "How can we help you, [son's name]?"), and specific encouragement tasks for the son agreed on by the teacher and parent.

*Child:* The son is present, but he says nothing unless asked. He is well-behaved throughout and willing to respond to questions. He feels uneasy in this situation and will either quietly enjoy the teacher's predicament with parent or become genuinely encouraged by the adults working together to help.

*Observer:* Note the interchange among the three. As much as possible, note how, when, and by whom Adlerian concepts were utilized and how doing so affected the meeting.

Following the role-play activity, respond to the following:

1. *All participants:* How did you feel in your roles? Were you able, as you perceived your role-playing, to utilize Adlerian concepts?

2. *Parent:* Did the teacher seem interested and involved? Did the teacher react to your comments as you expected? Were the teacher's comments helpful to you as a parent?

3. *Teacher:* Did you feel accepted in your interaction with the parent? Did you believe you were being helpful to the parent? How did you perceive the child's reaction to the meeting?

4. *Observer:* Share your perceptions. How, when, and by whom did you see the Adlerian concepts being utilized.

## Role-Play Activity 3

*Situation:* The principal recently called the parents to ask their permission to refer their child to the school psychologist for diagnostic testing on the teacher's recommendation. The parents asked to talk with the teacher.

*Parents:* The parents are distressed by the idea that something is wrong with their child. They want an explanation of why their child is being singled out as "defective" or not altogether "right." They don't see anything wrong with him at home. They're afraid that he may get labeled for life by psychological jargon.

*Teacher:* In addition to the suggestions listed earlier, the teacher should reinforce the following concepts: listening, empathy, expressing attitudes toward "slow" students (e.g., teacher's position on mainstreaming all children), helping parent understand referral.

*Observer:* Note the interchange among the three. As much as possible, note how, when, and by whom Adlerian concepts were utilized and how doing so affected the meeting.

Following the role-play activity, respond to the following:

1. *All participants:* How did you feel about playing this role? Which, of the three, was the most difficult for you? Can you explain why?

2. *Parents:* How did you think the teacher felt about your child? Were your fears allayed or are you now more anxious than before the conference? What kinds of information did the teacher impart? Is the psychological testing justified in your eyes?

3. *Teacher:* How effective did you feel in explaining your reasons for testing? Did you find yourself defending your position? What might you have done differently to obtain more cooperation from the parents?

4. *Observer:* Share your perceptions of each member's role. Which teacher responses did you note as being facilitative? How, if at all, might the teacher have approached this situation in a more constructive manner? Share any other observations you have of the group's interaction.

II. Responding to a Marital Conflict Situation

Bob and Mary have been married a little over a year. Both are working, and they have no children. Each night Mary comes home to cook supper. She cleans the apartment and does the laundry on weekends. Bob washes the cars and generally looks after their maintenance.

Due to increased responsibility at work, Mary has asked Bob to share more responsibility for the chores. He says that he does not know how and that it isn't man's work. Mary is developing deep resentment about this situation and has begun to show it in small but significant ways (e.g., "accidentally" burning supper).

Bob brings up the subject. Mary immediately becomes defensive but looks to you for support. Respond to the following:

1. What is the real issue?

2. What can you do and say to remain a "friend" and help them understand the conflict?

3. What does the situation require to restore harmony?

4. How can that be achieved?

When you have completed this exercise, share your responses with your study partner or an interested friend. Following your discussion, compare your responses with those suggested below. They are illustrative of the kinds of answers that would reflect an Adlerian solution to Bob and Mary's conflict:

1.  The real issue is Bob's fear of losing his masculinity and privileges as the "man of the house" and Mary's resentment at Bob's perceived disrespectful attitude toward shared responsibility. Bob's priority is comfort and Mary's has been in pleasing him.

2.  You can follow the four steps of conflict resolution by (a) helping each person's position be stated and respected; (b) clarifying that each would rather not fight (i.e., prefer cooperation and harmony through mutual agreement); (c) facilitating establishment of what Mary thinks she needs in the way of assistance, what Bob knows or can learn to do, and what a new agreement can accomplish; and (d) reaching an agreement on what to do to establish a new arrangement.

3.  The situation requires a responsible, flexible, division of shared responsibility in keeping up the apartment, cooking, laundry, and related "chores" for daily living.

Chapter 12

# WORKING WITH GROUPS

Probably no other method is more compatible with Adlerian psychology than working with groups. From the assumption that people are understood best in relation to their social environment follows that in a variety of instances, group situations can be used to teach and encourage others in the logic of social living. Adlerians wish to dispel the notion that problems of social living require secrecy and one-to-one specialized treatment. For this reason, Adler and his followers established child and family education centers wherever Adlerians worked.

Frequently, audience or group observers will inquire about the effectiveness of these methods with other than middle-class families. In the absence of more empirical data, Adlerians note that in Chicago, for example, the earliest child guidance centers were established in inner-city neighborhoods. Much of the work there was necessarily volunteered and many lay leaders were found to be at least as effective in discussion groups as the trained counselor. In fact, paraprofessionals have been the backbone of the Adlerian family education movement in working with participants who do not require therapy.

My experience, like Dreikurs', also indicates that economically advantaged persons will request participation in discussion groups on child rearing and marriage at least as readily as any other persons. Marriage discussion groups at any socioeconomic level, however, have not been nearly as prominent in the activities of Adlerians as the child-rearing groups. In my judgment, there is and will continue to be a decided increase in marriage education and counseling among Adlerians.

## TYPES OF GROUPS

The group methods used most often by Adlerians can be classified as discussion, consulting, and counseling, although psychodrama and group therapy are used as well. Common elements in these methods relate to principles of Individual Psychology. Whether working with children or adults, in consulting, counseling, or discussion groups, participants are

1. Inherently equal and are expected to behave as such (i.e., have a place that no one can rightfully challenge).

2. Considered to be capable of assuming responsibility for their behavior.

3. Individually understood best in a holistic, unified way as creative, purposive beings.

4. Considered as social beings meeting the same life tasks as others.

5. Capable of changing their attitudes and/or behavior.

6. Able to help as well as be helped in the process of giving meaning to life.

The climate or conditions that exist in these groups are typically those of any helping relationship. Expectations are for sincerity, caring, trust, empathy, support, cooperation, and honesty in transactions between members. In addition, a good measure of humor and friendliness also are present. In counseling or consulting groups, confidences are kept among members out of respect for the context within which information was shared (i.e., among those with common interests or concerns who have a commitment to assisting each other). In public demonstrations, such as described in chapter 11, respect for the participants is uppermost in the leader's mind.

The amount of training and/or knowledge a leader needs in Individual Psychology as well as in group procedures varies with the types of groups and their objectives. In discussion groups, for example, leadership can be shared or rotated among the members for a session or more. This rotation is particularly possible when the group is using a common reading source to provide structure and information.

In consultation or counseling groups, portions of sessions may be influenced significantly by one or more members but the leader would likely maintain a share of the responsibility for clarifying, summarizing, or otherwise directing the group. Co-leadership is recommended whenever possible because it increases the probability that what one person might overlook, another person would not. Compatibility of co-leaders in these cases requires cooperation and a general sense of equality but not necessarily similar training or background. In some cases, a counselor and teacher or parent might co-lead a group with considerable effectiveness because of their complimentary insights and experiences.

## DISCUSSION GROUPS

### Discussion Groups for Children

Although the same observations can be made for persons in any of the Adlerian groups, one of the most important outcomes for children concerns their realization that individually and collectively they can use their intellect to solve problems that they experience in their daily living. In fact, earlier studies have found that the extent to which young students feel they have control over their own destiny is strongly related to their achievement.

To believe in their own capabilities, to mobilize and cooperate in the use of other's capabilities, and to expect that problems can be solved in constructive, rational ways are important lifelong lessons to be learned through group discussions. These discussions also can help to counteract some adults' tendency to overemphasize the importance of subject matter in school. Discipline per se can be a subject of learning instead of an adjunct, in the sense that "good" students know how to behave and others must be shown through rules, merits, demerits, lectures, and punishment. Discouraged students misbehave or do poorly in school because that appears to them to be their best solution. They need guidance in learning alternative behaviors and attitudes.

**Classroom Meetings.**   Unfortunately, school and home tend to reinforce mistaken notions of discouraged children by emphasizing their shortcomings and overlooking opportunities to offer new or different alternatives. Classroom meetings are one important way to ensure that each child has opportunities to discover his or her unique talents and strengths. This meeting is an excellent way for children to overcome whatever real or imagined limitations they perceive as roadblocks to a more satisfying life for themselves and others.

---

Responsible behavior is possible
for all children.

---

Both Dreikurs and Glasser provided valuable principles and specific procedures on classroom meetings for counselors and teachers. Although Glasser (1969) referred to his approach as reality therapy, his principles are very compatible with Individual Psychology and his methods are equally helpful. He believes that responsible behavior is possible for all children when they are given the opportunity to become involved, to learn the significance of valuing, and to make a commitment to activities that provide a sense of worth and belonging or love.

Borrowing from Glasser's (1969) three types of classroom meetings (open-ended, educational diagnostic, and social problem-solving meetings), I discuss my use of each in the following.

***Open-Ended Meetings.*** Children are invited to discuss any thought-provoking question that interests them. In these discussions the teacher aims to stimulate both the creative and rational thinking capabilities of the children.

Facts or known answers are not the major focus of an open-ended meeting. For example, I have asked the following questions of second-grade elementary school pupils:

> Have you ever wondered what would happen if we could not buy toys in stores? Do you think that would be good or bad?

> Have you ever had a toy that was made especially for you? Would you like that as well as a store-bought toy?

> Have you ever made a toy or pretended you had a toy? Did you enjoy playing with it?

> Have you ever made someone else a toy? How many of you would like to make a toy you could share with a friend? What kind of toys could we make?

In this case, the teacher could follow up with other activities and discussions on giving and receiving or what makes people happy or sad, and possibly even devote an activity time to making toys for others out of pipe cleaners, common household articles, or materials readily available in the children's neighborhoods. On the other hand, such sessions do not have to be planned, followed up, or scheduled. In fact, some of the most meaningful sessions for the children will be spontaneously suggested by them or by events in the news that cannot be programmed in advance. As the pupils learn that there are no "correct" answers, they will look forward to these opportunities.

***Educational Diagnostic Meetings.***    These sessions are related to what the class is studying. They allow the teacher to determine quickly whether what the class is studying is being understood by the pupils. In my experience, pupils often memorize what is required for classroom tests without seeing its relevance for daily living. Without relevance, motivation to learn the subject is lost or misplaced on values unrelated to the subject itself (i.e., grades to show superiority).

Challenging the pupils to examine concepts and to transfer their knowledge to current events is often the focus of these sessions. I found the following questions useful in helping a seventh-grade teacher evaluate the class's use of concepts and facts being studied in social studies:

Why do you think we have never had a woman president?

What role have women played in the history of our government? Can you name a few who have made a significant contribution to this country?

Can you name other countries who have women as the recognized head or leader of their country?

Do you know of any women who may have an opportunity in the future to run for president?

What knowledge or experiences which women traditionally have had might contribute to their being a good leader and president?

At the time of the previous meeting, the primary election campaigns were in progress. Students had been studying current events as well as history. After class, the teacher reported some disappointment in their responses to the questions. Approximately 6 weeks later, after an average of two or more class meetings a week for 25 minutes each, I observed a substantial improvement in the quality of their discussions and a noticeable increase in responses from the quieter, less academic students.

I usually co-lead with the teachers on at least two occasions and simply observe at other times. Normally a demonstration and assistance on a few other occasions is sufficient help for the teachers to carry on the activity. Learning to listen and respond empathically, to withhold evaluation, and to encourage any genuine effort to participate are the key ingredients for success of group activities. Teachers will find the educational diagnostic meeting most informative when someone else leads the discussion. Sharing time for this purpose, as in team teaching, could be a meaningful way for teachers to assist one another. Otherwise, teachers leading such a discussion will want to use caution when children do not relate what has been studied in class to what they perceive as an open-ended discussion. Reminding or reprimanding will discourage future participation.

*Social Problem-Solving Meetings.*   These meetings are held to discuss and potentially solve individual and group educational problems of the class and the school. Social problem-solving meetings are more difficult for an outsider to lead than they are for the teacher. This tends to be true because problems often cannot be solved in one meeting and follow-up with involvement by outsiders is difficult, even if students accept them as members of the group. A few rules of thumb can help identify the hallmarks of the social problem-solving meetings:

1. All problems relative to the class as a group and to any individual in the class are eligible for discussion. Home problems may be included if the pupil or parent wishes to bring them up.

2. The discussion itself should be directed toward solving the problem. Fault finding or punishment should never be a part of the discussion of the solution.

3. The teacher remains nonjudgmental but the class may be judgmental and then work toward positive solutions. The teacher helps sustain the understanding that everyone has value and a place in the group—even the misbehaving individual. The class members, however, have a right to de-

cide how they will respond to a lack of cooperation by members in the class.

4. The meetings should be conducted in a tight circle with everyone visible to everyone else. (This arrangement is also important in the other types of meetings.)

5. Meetings should be relatively short for younger children (10 to 30 minutes) and longer for older pupils (30 to 45 minutes). Meeting regularly, however, is more important than undue concern for the length of the meetings.

6. The principal can be an important partner in presenting the possible alternatives open to the class. The principal may be involved in discussing a problem situation of a class or of individuals. His or her role would include helping students to examine what they did that contributed to a problem and what they can do to solve the problem, and asking for a commitment to follow through on a plan to resolve the problem. When punishment is completely out of the question, frank discussions between students and the principal are entirely possible.

7. No one problem or individual should be allowed to dominate these meetings one session after another. Once the negative aspects of a situation are identified, future attention should be directed to progress and positive steps that can be taken. Behavioral problems per se should not be the only basis for discussion. Concerns with friendship, loneliness, vocational choice, sportsmanship, dating, and many other topics can be discussed quite profitably.

I was invited to join a teacher of high school seniors in a family living class to discuss student attitudes toward male and female roles in society. The teacher reported a problem of overt reactions directed at her by some of the boys because of her presentation of women's equality, opinions, information, and so forth. She became upset by the boys' comments, including what she considered disrespect for women, in general, and for her, in particular.

Although the class had had discussions before, they had not met in the circle nor had they met me before. There was a noticeable tenseness in the group as they entered the room and a few audible comments suggesting that, although the teacher had asked if a visitor could join them, a few of those boys were less than ecstatic about the prospects. A few of the boys resisted joining the tight circle initially but became full-fledged members as the meeting progressed.

After the teacher's opening comments concerning her perceptions of the problem, I was asked to help lead a discussion that might allow them to take a fresh look at their feelings and attitudes. Sensing that some members of the class suspected there may be a hidden agenda, I assured them that none existed other than an open attempt to have them discuss their true attitudes and feelings. To facilitate this process, I invited them to share their opinions and ideas on the following.

*What does it mean to be a human being?* The first remarks came from a few of the more academically inclined students. The reluctance to participate by a few of the boys was still obvious but they were attentive. Nonevaluative, reflective, and clarifying comments were the primary responses to the remarks of the students. They sought to distinguish human beings from animals and other living things. They identified characteristics and abilities that they considered important aspects of being a human being. They mentioned living cooperatively and responsibly among the qualities of being a human being.

*What does it mean to be a person?* The discussion was much more relaxed and counterquestions followed comments. To be a person meant different things to different people, but all agreed that to be a person was important to them. Persons are human beings and they have many qualities in common.

*What does it mean to be a man?* and *What does it mean to be a woman?* At this point in the discussion, the reluctant participants were actively sharing their views. There were no signs of hostility or disregard for others' views. Quite the contrary, there was much agreement on the general equality of men and women as persons and human beings. Three of the boys, however, stated that they still did not like to consider women as equals even though they agreed with the logic of the discussion.

The period was about to end as their attention was turned to considering prejudice. The view was offered that being aware of one's prejudice can be a significant step toward examining it. They were not being asked to change their views, only to be honest in accepting them as their own. Further discussions on the assumption that everyone holds unexamined values, attitudes, and prejudices might be helpful to everyone in the class.

The teacher reported further discussions were held and a unit on careers allowed the class to consider the issue further but from a different point of view. Of importance to the teacher, the behavior of the boys improved noticeably and she found them more cooperative in the class.

Children need specific training in group participation. Natural leadership from within the group usually will emerge in a few weeks so that the teacher can relinquish leadership to members of the group. The teacher functions as a consultant once the members have learned fundamentals of group discussion. In the beginning, he or she provides guidance by doing the following:

1. *Helping establish ground rules.* In other words, talk about what it means to have friendly discussion and how a few simple rules can help them work and play together in a cooperative, friendly way. Order is important to a democratic setting, but it evolves from the logic of the situation and respect for self and others.

2. *Ensuring total group participation.* There are topics, questions, or issues about which any pupil can safely express an opinion. By observing which children are not participating, the teacher can ask a question and invite the quiet students to share their views. Any genuine effort by these students to participate can receive recognition by the

teacher's responses to them. Normally, these students will slowly but willingly join in the class discussions.

3. *Modeling through initial leadership.* The teacher's leadership is directed toward relinquishing the responsibility for leading. The teacher models how the children can think through their own experiences, how they can question and evaluate what they have heard in order to reach a conclusion or solve a problem.

4. *Handling touchy problems.* Keeping the discussions focused on constructive thinking and devoid of meaningless or derogatory comments particularly is important when pupils discuss the misbehavior of other students. Fighting, lying, stealing, or cheating can be topics that bring about lively discussions. As students become experienced in dealing with such matters, certain ones will become the moderators in the sense that they will intervene when unnecessary or unkind comments are made. Until that time, the teacher will redirect comments or suggest alternatives in a friendly but purposeful way.

5. *Stimulating ideas.* Introducing problems, questions, or ideas that require the pupils to observe, evaluate, and reach conclusions is an important function of the teacher. In the activities of a year, pupils will have ideas or topics that they will wish to discuss. At other times, and especially when they are still learning how to participate in a discussion, the teacher can anticipate topics that will motivate them and possibly be of help in acquiring the confidence to deal with situations that face them in the future.

6. *Encouraging group decisions and avoiding premature interventions.* Learning to make group decisions and to accept the consequences of them are the necessary ingredients for democratic living. Some groups make ill-considered decisions and the teachers prematurely intervene to save the class from the consequences of their choice. If the class chose to disregard suggestions or otherwise over-

looked important considerations, better that they discover the outcome for themselves. Equally important, the teacher can increase the satisfaction gained from the many occasions when sound decisions help individuals or the class as a whole.

An example of how group decisions, whether soundly considered or not, can be valuable sources of learning to students is illustrated in the following situation:

A sixth-grade class had had enough experience with classroom meetings that they were feeling some expansiveness in their ability. They had decided that if they could get all their week's work accomplished by Friday noon of that week, they would like to have a "free" afternoon for a class picnic at a nearby park.

The teacher injected that permission notes from their parents and approval for a picnic by the principal would be needed. She also suggested that they check with the principal as early as possible to avoid any problems. The teacher observed that they seemed confident of their ability to get along quite well without her suggestions.

The following week plans moved along enthusiastically and they worked diligently in all of their studies. They requested permission slips for their parents' signatures from the teacher and proceeded to collect them.

On Thursday afternoon, they sent a committee to the principal for permission. The committee returned in a short time with their faces revealing a dilemma. The principal willingly gave them permission and hoped that they enjoyed the picnic as much as the other children enjoyed the surprise circus visit planned for Friday afternoon!

Needless to say, a reassessment of their alternative was made and they decided to see the circus and work diligently for a second week in order to have the picnic. This time they agreed to gain permission and check on conflicts ahead of time. The teacher was asked if she had any suggestions or thoughts on how to plan more effectively. To the teacher's credit, she never said "I told you so" or mentioned her earlier admonitions.

7. *Summarizing and evaluating progress made.* Groups should make an assessment periodically of their performance and consider plans for the future as well. They might ask, "What have we done?" "In what ways has it been of value?" and "What other things might we do that could be helpful or needed?"

**Peer Mediation and Conflict Resolution.**   In chapter 11, steps to conflict resolution are outlined and illustrated. As with problem-solving meetings, the use of the peer group to help resolve conflicts in schools can be very powerful with minimal intervention by adults. Many schools are now using mediation training of students as a means to alleviate some of the problems among students. An Adlerian approach to such training and intervention naturally evolves through group work. Training involves basic listening and responding skills plus practice under supervision in the process of mediation. The conditions for an effective intervention are trained mediators and the support of the school administration. Basic principles for a successful intervention include the following:

1. *Commit time.* Essentially, all parties must make time for training, supervising, and conducting the interventions. Students, including those in conflict, must be agreeable to meeting for the purpose of resolution of differences.

2. *Accept mediator.* The students in the conflict must agree to accept the mediator and the process of mediation.

3. *No interruptions.* Students must agree to listen to one another without interrupting.

4. *No labeling.* Students must agree to no name calling, labeling, or such.

5. *Keep cool.* Students must agree to remain calm and in control of their behaviors.

6. *Win/win goal.* No one leaves a loser; therefore, the process continues until all are agreeable to a mutually acceptable solution.

7. *Brainstorm solutions.* Solutions require openness, creativity, and full participation of all parties.

8. *Commit to solution.* One's word is an honor-bound bond.

School personnel are often surprised to learn that some of the most effective mediators were their greatest trouble makers in prior years. By giving students a responsible part in the classroom and school, they are able to channel the students' need to belong into positive roles and responsibilities. In my experience, teaching young people the principles of basic human relations is not difficult. They are quick to understand the practical implications of the guidelines and the methods that follow.

Once students are trained in mediation, other students as well as administrators can call on them for reconciling differences with or between other students. This helps to de-escalate problems and keep many of them out of the administrators' offices. Equally important, there is a transfer of learning that can permeate the school environment. Empowerment of the students for the good of the entire school is an important byproduct of this process.

One illustration of how mediation was helpful relates to a school where difficulties with an eighth-grade Hispanic boy were growing progressively worse. His family was Spanish speaking and had limited contact with the school since they had moved into the community. Among the school administrators' concerns were reports that he had been reading questionable Spanish magazines in the school library. He was told that they would be returned if after review they were found to be acceptable. In addition, local police reported that he was "running around" with a "gang" of other Hispanic kids whose dress and manner suggested that they might be trouble makers. When confronted about his apparent disrespect for the school and community, Juan seemed defiant and continually referred to his "familia." He claimed that he is the victim of racism and resented the harassment from school officials, teachers, and the police.

Fortunately, another Spanish-speaking bilingual student was a member of the student mediation team. After explaining the mediation process, this student asked Juan if he would be willing to meet with him to explain his position further. After this session, the mediator came to the school counselor with the following insights. First, the "gang" that the police described were Juan's cousins. They all wear "dickies," which are an inexpensive pair of casual pants of the same type traditionally worn by his grandfather and uncles. Second, the magazines that were confiscated from him were of cultural interest to him and included articles about cars, foods, and similar topics suited to his age. Indeed, no one had had any difficulties with Juan prior to these recent reports. In short, he was being victimized and the result was a growing distrust and anger directed toward the school and community.

Under the circumstances, the counselor realized that there was an immediate need to develop and implement a cultural awareness among the staff and administrators. Juan, among others, was invited to participate in planning a program for this purpose. In this case, the school administrators were the second party in the dispute and wisely agreed to the resolution of differences through a collaborative project. The difficulties with Juan and his cousins subsided and Juan eventually became a trained mediator. Although many disputes are between students and must be resolved by them through mediation, the preceding illustration makes clear that it is a process worthy of adult consideration and use as well.

**Guidelines for Cooperative Classrooms.** The following are guidelines for teachers of the democratic classroom:

1. A group cannot run democratically without order and ground rules.

2. Limits are necessary.

3. Children should participate in establishing and maintaining rules necessary for functioning in an orderly group.

4. The group needs leadership and the teacher needs to know how to exert democratic leadership.

5. Mutual trust and faith in each other in a class is essential to function democratically.

6. The teacher must learn how to win the cooperation of the students through creative solutions, decision making, consequences, and encouragement.

7. A spirit of cooperation must replace competitiveness in the classroom.

8. The teacher needs group dynamic skills to integrate the class for a common purpose; each child has to have a sense of belonging to the whole class.

Dreikurs believed that the problem of more effective education lay in teaching adults as well as children the methods of democratic living. Whenever children have the opportunity to move from autocratic to democratic settings, they do not know how to behave in responsible ways. Equally important, adults do not know how to guide children in the methods of democratic living.

Laissez-faire leadership as an alternative to autocratic leadership is a poor idea. And yet, in the search for more human, child-oriented methods, many teachers and parents mistakenly subscribe to these methods and create even more havoc in their lives. When autocratic methods are set aside, adults and children alike require guidance and a period of training. In addition, Dreikurs was quite critical of teachers whose methods did not encourage curiosity and intrinsic satisfaction in the process of self-discovery and learning. As a consequence, he devoted much of his personal efforts to writing about classroom methods and teaching teachers his methods through demonstrations and lectures.

**Study Groups.**    Teachers need opportunities to study and observe others leading democratically based classroom meetings. Similarly, parents are not likely to lead family meetings successfully without some instructions and encouragement. For this reason, Adlerians have experienced some of their most enthusiastic support from participants in parent discussion groups.

Parent study groups using Dreikurs and Soltz's (1969) book, *Children the Challenge*, and teachers using Dreikurs' classroom behavior books, meet under the following conditions:

1. Participants customarily gather together in groups under the leadership of a counselor or someone with similar interests to themselves (who may or may not have previous acquaintance with the material).

2. They mutually discuss the philosophy, principles, values, and methods found in the book.

3. They share their views and understanding of this approach in guiding young people.

4. They learn new basic principles and their application in the art of democratic family living.

The leader of a study group is simply to facilitate the discussion, help avoid pitfalls of digressions from the topic, and leave responsibility to members for accepting or rejecting what is presented through the readings. There are leaders' guides available for *Children the Challenge* through most bookstores.

In my experience, groups usually meet for 10 sessions of approximately 1½ hours each. Group size varies from 8 to 12 persons. In the parent groups, evening sessions allow those who work outside the home to attend, although daytime sessions have also been well attended by parents. A male co-leader seems to help increase the probability that men who come to the first session continue to attend. Having both parents participate is very helpful but not necessary if one or the other desires to benefit from the sessions. Having parents and teachers in groups together can be very helpful to both groups, although dual relationships should be avoided among parents with children in their classes.

Leadership for the individual sessions can be rotated among those willing to do so by sharing the leader's manual. This procedure seems to contribute to the confidence of participants and increases their interest in the discussion. Frequently, persons who participate in their first group can be encouraged to lead or co-lead groups for others who desire this opportunity. Because every group is somewhat unique, new ideas are discovered or learned ones reinforced. Therefore, an individual can reread and discuss principles and examples many times and continue learning from the group discussion.

### Family Meeting or Council

The family meeting or council is a logical extension of the democratic process into the home. As was noted in chapter 11, strong families have characteristics that contribute to their cohesiveness. Among them are (a) members are dedicated to the welfare of each other; (b) members spend time together on an ongoing, regular basis; (c) members have good communications skills and use them to talk with each other about all manner of topics; (d) there are strong spiritual values that fortify the family in meeting life's demands; and (e) members cultivate coping strategies that sustain them in times of crisis.

In the mobile, dual-career or single-parent families of today, the challenge to establish and sustain the characteristics of the strong family requires extraordinary effort. The average child spends 900 hours in school each year, whereas more than 1,500 hours is devoted to watching television. In fact, 66% of U.S. families report watching television while they eat dinner. These statistics are the tip of the proverbial iceberg, because it is not only the time devoted to watching that is unhealthy for the average family.

More than half of the news time on television is focused on crime, disaster, and war. The average child in the United States sees more than 8,000 murders on television before they finish elementary school. The average family has the television on approximately 7 hours per day. With so much time devoted to television viewing and the lessons about life that it offers, only the most spiritually strong and deliberately family-oriented families would seem to have hope of eluding the seduction of a contrary value system. Now, more than ever, the need for the family meeting as a preparation for family living is evident. Like the classroom meeting, this is a time when all members learn to express their points of view, concerns, and questions in a safe, respected atmosphere. It is also a time to seek support, celebrate, and plan events together.

**Guidelines for the Family Meeting.** Each family establishes its own rules for meeting. Sometimes these rules are elaborate; in other cases, they are minimal. Recommended considerations include the following:

1. Establish a mutually agreeable time and place to meet.

2. Establish a procedure for keeping minutes and chairing the meeting. A rotation of chairing is often effective.

3. No one is urged or required to attend.

4. Anyone can enter or leave at any time.

5. Decisions can be made that affect absent members.

6. Decisions can be changed at other meetings.

7. Decisions are made by consensus. When consensus cannot be reached on an issue, the decision should be made by voting, and all agree to abide by the majority vote or the issue is tabled until another time.

Parents and teachers alike who are new to these methods sometimes worry that the children will be irresponsible and uncooperative in these meetings. With patience and a willingness to learn together, such concerns will pass away. A foundation in principles is important, however, if adults are to help the children in this process.

**Excerpts from a Family Meeting.** In the following excerpt from a family meeting, an important principle is introduced by the oldest daughter (9 years old) at the first meeting. She has a rule for father, but the family discovers, rules are for everyone!

| | |
|---|---|
| Father: | Is there anything else to discuss today? |
| Mother: | No. |
| Son: | No. |
| Oldest daughter: | Yes, you should tell us the days that you're going to come home late so that we can have things fixed for you and dinner and such. |
| Father: | Well, what do you think I ought to do; I'm not sure what you are saying. Are you saying I should tell you when I'm coming home? |
| Oldest daughter: | Uh huh, so we'll know. And sometimes Mother cooks food and she doesn't expect you home and you come home. And she has to cook more supper after she's all done. |
| Father: | Well, I see. that's a good point. Would that . . . is that a rule for everybody then? In other words, when Mother's out and she's coming home late, she should let us know? And when you're out, you should let us know when you're coming home so we know? Is that what you're saying, too? |
| Oldest daughter: | Not exactly. |
| Father: | I mean is it just a rule for me, or is it for everybody? |
| Oldest daughter: | It should be sort of like a rule for you. |
| Second daughter: | I think it should be a rule for everybody. 'Cause everybody doesn't know when everybody else is coming home. |

Mother: Yes, that's right because it sometimes gets dark before you children decide to come in. I've called and called. Right?

Second daughter: Yeah.

Father: How about that? Is it a good rule for everyone? [All nod their heads, yes.] Does anyone want to say more about it before we go on? [no] We'll want to put that in our minutes and I'll make a point of calling if I'm not coming home on time. Will everyone try it? [nods]

In this case, important lessons have been learned by parents and children alike. First, the children now know that they can safely confront the parents with behavior that they believe needs improvement; second, they also have learned that rules are for everyone and they are not to be applied in a discriminatory manner; and third, the parents have learned that not only are the children capable of observing and reporting behavior that the parents need to improve but also they are very rational about how to resolve it successfully. Equality is well illustrated in this situation, and from it, more open dialogue can be expected. Appendix B contains a full transcript of the family council from which the previous excerpt was taken. Because such an example is not available elsewhere, parent study group leaders should find it a useful reference for parents interested in starting their family council.

**Why Family Meetings Fail.** As was true of the classroom meetings, the ages of children and the agenda items that evolve generally determine the length of meetings. When members consistently leave early or begin complaining about the meetings, the meeting may be too long. Other common contributors to unsuccessful family meetings are

1. Not starting on time

2. Not holding meetings regularly

3. Meeting at mealtime or while the television is on

4. Parental domination instead of modeling good listening and responding skills

5. Giving up because agreements are not working

6. Not following through on agreements

Parents, like teachers, must realize that learning to participate in a democratic meeting with children requires experience and an inclination to be patient. There will be some excellent meetings with outstanding progress and there will be some relatively poor meetings with regression to old ways. The meetings can improve the quality of living significantly, however, when the spirit behind them becomes an integral part of the family's way of relating to one another.

## Marriage Discussion Groups

Because the principles of Individual Psychology apply to all interpersonal relationships, participants in parent groups often see its implications for their marriage relationships as well. As a result, marriage discussion groups, organized and conducted much in the same manner as the child-rearing groups, are formed to satisfy the interest of those individuals wishing to pursue study further.

Marriage discussion groups are not counseling or therapy groups, although some individuals may be in counseling outside of the group. When questions are asked in the meetings, no attempt is made to relate them to problems or concerns of members in the group. Members may volunteer examples of behaviors that illustrate certain principles when they fit into the flow of the discussion, however.

As was true of the parent groups, participants may be encouraged to record questions or concerns that they hope will be answered through the discussion. If at the end of 10 sessions their questions have not been answered, they may bring them up for discussion. Occasionally, a member of the group will volunteer to tell how the application of these principles has improved a specific situation that was troublesome for husband and wife. An illustration of such improvement is the following:

> A husband had a habit of calling his wife (a group member) late in the afternoon to announce that he was bringing home a visiting business associate for dinner. This habit was a source of regular anguish to her because the food might not be what she considered suitable for a guest or she simply had other things to do. Being a dutiful servant, however, she would do what she thought was expected and then feel resentment because of his insensitivity.
>
> After reading sections of *The Challenge of Marriage* (Dreikurs, 1946) with the discussion group, she decided to discuss her observations with her husband and propose an alternative. She suggested that in the future, if it was inconvenient for her to do the cooking, he should be responsible for the meal. Much to her surprise, he was very agreeable and actually enjoyed cooking for the guests he brought home. She was then able to meet the guests, enjoy the conversation before dinner, and gain a new appreciation for the work her husband had chosen as a career.

Another case involved a husband who frequently came home late for dinner. The wife would be angry because "supper was ruined " and many an evening was ruined as well. She decided that trying to keep supper warm beyond the time that was agreed upon was unnecessary. She discussed this fact with him, saying simply that if he was late, she would first put it in the refrigerator for him to warm up when he got home. After the first two occasions when she did this but made no complaint or comment, he came home much more regularly. Equally important, their evenings together were friendlier and more enjoyable.

Dreikurs' (1946) book on marriage has been a useful reference for discussion groups even though it was written in the mid-40s. Participants often are surprised at the accuracy of his predictions with respect to social change and the relevance of his suggestions for today's marriages. The organizer and/or leader of the group will need to develop a few questions for each session that will help the group to discuss the principles involved. After the first few meetings leadership can be rotated to members of the group as they show a willingness to assume it.

## CONSULTING GROUPS

Consulting groups for parents and teachers are designed to capitalize on the principles and methods of Adlerian theory while empowering the group to use them in applying them in their life situations. The purposes of these groups are threefold:

1. To help adults understand the practical application of Individual Psychology in their relationships with children.

2. To help them understand their feelings and behavior in adult–child conflicts.

3. To help them integrate their understanding into beliefs and values that will help them work more effectively with children.

Groups vary in size from four to six persons for teachers to slightly more in parent groups. They meet for approximately 1 hour each week for six or more times depending on their previous background and experience with Adlerian methods. Through the group experiences, the participants are taught four procedures for improving communication. They are particularly attuned to the fact that they communicate emotional as well as intellectual messages. The procedures involve

1. Learning to communicate caring responses

2. Stating own feelings about the impact of the child's behavior on them in a respectful way

3. Learning conflict resolution to reach mutual agreement

4. Utilizing logical consequences when children choose not to help in conflict resolution

The leader must be the one who is competent in group processes as well as Adlerian methods. Group interaction can stagnate or otherwise remain inconsequential without appropriate leadership. For this reason, the goals of the group must be clear and agreed upon before starting. Attention to the effective development of the group is essential.

Generally, after a period of getting to know one another through structured exercises, groups begin by learning how to establish alternative approaches to the disruptive behavior of children. The methods and procedures described in chapter 6 are involved in this process. For example, the group uses a specific teacher–child or parent–child conflict to identify the goals of misbehavior and alternative corrective and preventative actions for the adult.

Among the important considerations in conducting such a group, the leader must encourage collaboration among the members on common goals; model and encourage effective listening and responding skills; establish trust through understanding about confidentiality and respect by "agreeing to disagree" when necessary; maintain an open, positive yet intellectually challenging atmosphere; and obtain a commitment to follow through with specific recommendations after each session.

Studies of parent and teacher groups reported in the 1970s generally supported their effectiveness in positive changes in the classroom behavior of children in elementary schools. In addition, high school interventions with teacher groups proved even more effective than working with students alone. A difference between the study groups and consultation groups is the focus on implementing recommendations and seeking consultation from the group before and after implementation. Whether there are differences in the effectiveness of each method remains to be tested. More important to the practitioner is that each appears to be effective in helping to bring about positive changes in children's behavior.

# COUNSELING GROUPS

Although a distinction between counseling and consulting has been made for the purposes of this introduction to Adlerian methods, much of what has been presented under consultation and discussion groups also applies here. Actually, there has been very little reported in the literature on Adlerian group counseling per se. For example, classroom meetings, parent and teacher study groups, and teacher and parent consultation study groups have been referred to by others as forms of group counseling. One distinction I make with respect to the methods in the next section is their emphasis on the private logic of the individual as they relate to self, others, and life in general. The focus is on I, me, and self, not others. It is both intra- and interpsychic in nature. Such focus can result in profound, life-changing results. As was noted earlier about the difference between behavior and motivation modification, a change in one's life purpose will affect every dimension of personality. On the other hand, lifestyle exploration does not require psychotherapy in order to be meaningful.

# LIFESTYLE GROUPS

My experience with groups employing lifestyle as a means of self-exploration and potential change suggests that these groups may be different from others, primarily in the degree of emphasis on discovery of one's life plan. Purposes of the lifestyle groups include

1.  To help each member understand the application of Individual Psychology in his or her own development.

2.  To help each member discover his or her characteristic ways of approaching and perceiving his or her basic life tasks.

3.  To help each member test his or her perceptions of self, others, and life with those of others in the group while also validating the lifestyle technique.

4. To help each member resolve any specific conflicts with which he or she desires assistance.

## Starting Lifestyle Groups

Usually the first group session deals with ground rules for establishing trust, cohesiveness, and administrative details necessary in any group that expects to involve self-disclosure for promoting personal growth. Structure and task orientation are provided for early sessions by the educative function present in learning the theory and technique.

The leader of the group interviews and presents a lifestyle analysis for one of the members of the group in the first sessions. Members of the group are asked to record the information and ask for collaboration or clarification as co-participants in the process. In this manner, they are actually involved in learning how to collect and use information. This also facilitates the collection of their own lifestyle information on forms that they can complete at home. Examples of forms are the ones provided in this book and the *LSI— Life Style Inventory* (Shulman & Mosak, 1988a). For a member unfamiliar with Individual Psychology, recommended readings and instructional sessions on basic principles are conducted. Shulman and Mosak (1988b) have provided a *Manual for Life Style Assessment*, which describes the process in detail.

## Lifestyle Sessions

As members become more familiar with the process and theory, they are asked to preview the lifestyle information of one or members of the group, to interview them in teams of two, and to develop from that a lifestyle summary that includes the following:

1. Characteristic ways of making their place

2. Characteristic ways of approaching work, social relationships, and love relationships

3. Characteristic attitudes about self, others, and life

4. Possible self-defeating fictive notions as well as notions that contribute to their coping successfully with life circumstances (All members are invited to write a journal entry regarding social issues in their lives early in the group. Invariably, the private logic convictions associated with the issues are uncovered through the lifestyle assessment.)

Members of the group have access to the lifestyle information of a member one week before the session at which the individual's lifestyle is presented for reaction. All such information is treated as confidential and is in a secured location.

Individuals who interviewed the member usually present their observations first, although questions and observations from other group members are always in order. Observations are offered tentatively with a preface such as, "It seems as though . . . " or "Could it be that . . . ," rather than as dogmatic statements of fact. Generally, it is best to frame statements as though spoken in the self-talk of the individual (e.g., "For me life is full of surprises that often leave me confused" or "I am most comfortable in the company of women who appreciate my interest in nature, the arts, and the beauty all around us." Generally, interpretations can be validated by direct reference to the lifestyle information as well as by the individual's behavior within the group.

The group is watchful of the presenter projecting to other members attributes possessed by the presenter. The recognition reflex has proven to be a valuable index to accuracy of an observation. The smile or laugh comes readily in these groups because the genuine caring and empathy that develop make defensive maneuvering quite unnecessary.

---

Genuine caring and empathy that
develop make defensive maneuvering
quite unnecessary.

---

Caring confrontation becomes a natural adjunct to the relationships that develop. After two or three lifestyles summaries have been completed, the level of disclosure and trust are established to a degree that honestly offering or rejecting observations is not a threat to the warmth and supportive nature of the group.

At the beginning of the group, members are asked to write as specifically as possible any concerns or relationship problems they wish to resolve through the group. After all the lifestyle assessments have been completed, members are asked if any of the recorded concerns have been resolved by the group activities. If there is unfinished business, they may wish to bring it to the group's attention. Depending on the circumstances, the group may reexamine the person's lifestyle summary to discover how the individual may be experiencing difficulty because of mistaken notions. Behavioral homework goals, role-playing, and similar techniques may be suggested or used in the process.

Usually six to eight individuals compose a group. They meet a minimum of once a week for two hours. Everyone is expected to attend each session and to participate actively in all activities of the group, although leading a session on someone else's lifestyle assessment is voluntary. When used with trainees of one of the counseling professions, members are better prepared to judge the value of the theory and technique from full participation. For those solely interested in personal insight and development, reports indicate that the process is highly valued and considered useful in coping more effectively with basic life tasks.

When do lifestyle sessions cease? When the group perceives that there is no further business of individuals or the group, the group will cease to meet.

## SUMMARY

The significance of group work in the growth of Adlerian methods is apparent. Most illustrations of principles and methods in the literature are taken from reports of parents, teachers, and others who have shared their experiences in discussion, consultation, or counseling groups. One reason lifestyle techniques per se may have remained somewhat obscure is that they apparently had not been adapted to group work. This is likely to be less true in the future as their use in public demonstrations, marriage counseling, and groups such as described here become more common.

## STUDY QUESTIONS

**Directions:** Respond to the following in the space provided.

1. Identify three or more characteristics of all Adlerian groups whether with children or adults and whether the focus is therapy or discussion.

2. What are relative strengths and weaknesses of open-ended, educational diagnostic, and social problem-solving class-room meetings?

3. (a) If family meetings are to succeed, what rules of thumb should be followed?

   (b) What are some precautions?

4. What are some distinctions between study groups and con-sultation or counseling groups?

# APPENDICES

# FAMILY COUNSELING

The following transcript is taken from an interview by the author with a family: mother, father, and four children. The oldest child is a girl, Teryl, 11 years; John, 8; Paul, 3½; and Michael, 2½. Michael has braces on his legs because of a birth defect. In this interview, the two youngest were at home with colds.

The interview is conducted in the presence of a graduate class of approximately 40 persons. This is the first opportunity the parents have had to talk with the counselor; therefore, the preliminary remarks help serve the purpose of providing an orientation to both the parents and the class. After the discussion with the parents, the children are interviewed, and then the session concludes with the parents.

## PARENT INTERVIEW

Counselor: We're sending around pictures of Mr. and Mrs. F's youngest children because they have the flu today. Mr. and Mrs. F have four children. Of the two oldest children, Teryl is 11 and John is 8. The other two boys you'll see in pictures are Paul and Mike. Paul is 3½ and Michael is 2½. He is the fellow with the braces.

Now, we want you to be as comfortable with us as we can possibly make it. These class members are for the most part a group of teachers and counselors and a couple of school administrators. But, more important, also many parents are here. Our purpose in being here is to discover together what others have found to be some principles that relate to living together as families, and as groups in classrooms and other social places. We know from experience that there's a great deal that you experience in your family that's just as true in our family. As a matter of fact as we go along, on occasion I'm going to ask these folks how many of them have something like this going on in their families, and I think you're going to be surprised to find out you've got a lot of companions here. Most of the things that we think are hassles in our family, other people experience as well. There's nothing terribly unique about it. As a result of that, we can learn a lot from each other. We really appreciate the fact that you're willing to come in and talk to us about what's happening in your family because it allows us to learn something about our own. There may be some things that these folks might want to know, and I'm inviting them to ask questions although I may censor it and say I don't think it's going to move us in the direction that we want to go; or you may say "I'd just rather not answer that," or "I don't know," and that's perfectly fine. There's absolutely no expectation that you talk about anything you don't want to talk about. You may ask them questions if you like. You may say, "Well, what would you do about this?" and see what they say. I've found out already that they're very willing to correct me! [laugh]

Now, I see here, an oldest child—a girl—and three boys. Ron [Father], you did mention that you were having difficulty with one of the boys but that didn't surprise me. It wouldn't surprise this group either because we have been looking at other families and we know that when you have an oldest child who is a girl, she tends to get along better with the parents than the second child right behind her. Does that tend to be true in your family?

Mother: Yes.

Counselor: OK. [We got a nice smile there.] Again, I don't know Teryl, but we'll see if we're wrong and if we are it's OK to correct us. Teryl's probably a girl who would be helpful to her mother. She won't always do what you ask her to do, but she will follow through and do things more readily than the other children. In fact, she'll try to be a pleaser; she'll go along with what your expectations are, Mother and Father, in terms of how an oldest child should be, helping out with the younger children. She will probably get along pretty well in school. In fact, she might even be a model child in school. She may try very hard to do a good job, and, if she has difficulty, it will probably be with the second boy. That's where there is likely to be fights, but with the younger children she'll try to help out as much as she can. Now how does that sound to you?

Mother: Pretty good!

Counselor: O.K. Now, we know one of the children is having some difficulty with John. It may be that all of them do. In fact, I think you're going to discover that all of them work together to keep both of you pretty busy. You're smiling again. But, in all probability, John will be the most rebellious and independent. Most likely he'll look at the other side of the coin. If there's a rule for the family, he'll find an exception to the rule. He'll try to say it's not fair, that this rule applies to him only in certain situations. Does that sound like something John would say?

Father:      Absolutely!

Counselor:    This is not to say that John is what is sometimes called a bad child, in fact, we don't even think about bad kids. We're thinking about kids who experience some discouragement. By discouragement we mean that they feel that life is such that right now they're not getting their way—they think the way things "ought to be." They may feel defeated and become very discouraged. I suspect that because you're in here and interested in talking to us, there may not be serious discouragement. You're probably concerned enough to want to try and help out and see that the children are given love and attention and care. But, nonetheless, in most families you'll have one youngster like John who, because the other kids seem to be having their way by doing well and helping out, chooses to make his place by being troublesome at times.

           In the case of Mike, he's special in a couple of ways. He's the youngest and, because he has braces, he has some disability that requires that he receive special attention. Maybe even at birth, it was known that he was going to need some special help and special attention. You see, he won it right away. Paul gets his attention very likely by being cute. He smiles, he's charming, he gets along with just about everybody, and he gets his own way pretty well because others will take care of him. Is that what it's like?

Mother:     Yes. It seems like you have known them for years!

Counselor:    Well, in a manner of speaking, that's true. It's because your family is like my family, and it's like other families here, too. I guess one of the important things to realize from this is that what works in helping my children may help your children, too.

Mother:     I think the group here know that we didn't tell you about the children.

Counselor: I didn't have any foreknowledge of these kids; I hadn't met them before they came in the door. This is something which is not unusual, but it does sometimes surprise people. Some people may think that I'm simply saying this and you're being agreeable because you feel you must be. I think they can see the smiles on your faces showing that I'm not putting words in your mouth!

Now, knowing that you have a lot in common with others, let's become specific because, frankly, every family is different from every other family. Now, that may sound contradictory to what I just said, but it's true. I believe that not one of your children is like another and, that you folks aren't like any of us in some respects. We're each unique. As we talk about your kids, I want you to know that we're going to be trying to understand how the kids are unique and how your family is unique. OK?

Father: OK.

Counselor: All right. Would you tell me why you choose to come in this morning?

Father: Well, we thought it would be a different type of experience. We're having some problems with John and it has raised some questions about what we should do; should we encourage him to knock somebody's teeth out; should we encourage him to be a tattle-tale; how should we treat him? We haven't got any drastic problems, but John gets the idea he wants to run away from home once in a while. He had those ideas when he was a year and a half old!

Counselor: Are there some specific behaviors that you can think of; something that happened recently or persistently that you think you'd like to get some help in working with?

Mother:     John? He has been a problem on the bus. I think he's well controlled in class. Maybe he's worn out by the time the bus gets there. I'm not sure. Awhile ago there was a little boy whose birthday came up and John was very determined that he was going to the birthday party. He didn't have an invitation and when it got a little closer we suggested that they call to invite John to the party. Well, then it's, John, you can't go. Teryl always gets to go to parties. Then, John wasn't going to get on the bus at school until the principal assisted him. When he got off the bus, he was quite upset and wanted to run away. I said, "Well go ahead. It's rather cold out." He packed his suitcase and out the door he went. I watched and thought, "I wonder how far he's going to go before I have to get him." He's a very strong-willed child. He doesn't like to back down when he's done something. Pretty soon he came back and snuck in the door. When I looked out to see which way he went, there he was.

Counselor:  So now we know for sure that he won't go too far in his efforts to impress you. Let's see if I can help you by starting with a typical day. How do things proceed with breakfast and getting dressed and things of that sort?

Mother:     Well, just since last Christmas, I started working at the day care center in New Lexington. Ron usually wakes up first and tries to get me up. Then he usually gets Michael and Paul up. They're usually awake. It's just a matter of getting them up out of bed and taking them out to the table. Breakfast is served . . .

Counselor:  Excuse me a minute. You said you get Mike and Paul up. Are they on a high bed?

Father:     Michael can't get up by himself. He's totally paralyzed from the waist down. Usually between 5:30 and 6:30, he hollers, "Daddy, come and get me, I want my cereal." And I usually take Paul and Michael out, set them up at the table, and give them something to eat. Then Pam [Mother] gets up and gets dressed and makes her bed. I make a pot of tea and she comes out and has some breakfast. Then, about a quarter til seven Teryl and John get up before their mother leaves. They come out and although I don't insist that they eat right away, usually by five of seven they're having their breakfast when she's leaving.

Counselor:   Do they make their breakfast or do you?

Father:   We're changing that right now. This is a mistake I suppose we've been making. We have never felt that our kids ought to pour their own cereal in the bowl but this is one of the things they're teaching Michael and Paul at school. We've cut their meat up and put it on the plate and things like this. In the last 2 weeks we've started to put their meat on their plate and although they didn't know what to do with it, they're finding out.

Mother:   It was ridiculous. They were finished eating by the time we were starting. We could all be eating together. It really works.

Counselor:   Letting them learn to take care of themselves really works.

Mother:   It does! [Laughter] I've learned quite a bit in just a little while at the day care. We've had an eating problem with Paul. He just didn't want to eat anything at all. He liked snacks but not basic good food. And now that he's serving himself he's eating real well. They have a counselor at school who suggested that we don't make any kind of a fuss if he doesn't eat. We do brag when he's cleaned his plate. Now that we're not talking about it, he's eating. So serving themselves has worked.

Counselor: If you had come in two month ago before you had had this experience and I had said this to you, I think you would probably have thought I was out of my head. Right?

Mother: Well, that was my first reaction. I thought, "They just can't do it. They're too little." But they can!

Counselor: Sure. They can do a lot more than you realize. When Paul wanted his food differently, he was getting attention and a special service. The youngest children generally know how to press other people into their service. While John feels its hopeless, he can't get what he wants, Paul's convinced he can get everything. All he has to do is want it and it will be taken care of. [Mother smiles and nods agreement.] On the other hand, they can now learn the satisfaction of being able to care for themselves. But it does require that you work with them early. Now what I'd like to suggest is that when you see the youngsters doing something that is showing progress toward taking care of themselves, self-reliance, more independence, more responsibility, and so forth, think not so much about *how* they're doing as about *what* they're doing. If you can just make that distinction, not *how* they're doing but *what* they're doing, and say, for example, to Paul when he's just finished eating, "My goodness, you must have really enjoyed what you ate," rather than "Oh, I see you ate everything on your plate." There is a difference because the process of eating can give you a great deal of enjoyment and satisfaction; you like what you eat and feel some satisfaction upon eating a good meal.

The reason for this is it avoids the chance that kids will compare themselves. You know, Teryl didn't finish, John didn't finish, I finished; therefore, I did better. You don't want to encourage the competition between kids. So if you simply say, "Hey you really seem to have gotten enjoyment out of eating that meal," or when they bring a report card home, "You seem to like your reading better than you do your math," emphasizing the areas in which they have the strengths; or saying, "Maybe you would like some help with this or that." And, "What has the teacher said about these other areas?" or "Do you have any concern about it?" You'll find that by not being terribly impressed by grades, they'll do as well as they can with proper encouragement.

Mother:      Teryl is an all-A student. She does quite well without an effort. It's really disgusting! [Laughs] She doesn't work up to her capacity and she's still getting straight A's. She isn't, she isn't . . .

Counselor:   Challenged?

Mother:      Right, she can do it without an effort, and I'm afraid it's going to make her not work quite as hard as she really could. I think this is another conflict for John because he does have a harder time with his lessons. It is work for him to get the grades that he gets, and he sees she can do nothing and get good grades.

Counselor:   Just another confirmation that life is unfair. [Mother murmuring assent.] "Look how hard I have to work." I would like to say that I'm not so concerned and this may influence what I say to you about trying to get Teryl working harder.

             Let's go back to breakfast. So we've got Paul who had something of an eating problem, but now he's taking care of himself and the whole eating pattern for the family is beginning to change and get better.

Father:      Right. Then following breakfast, Pam has gone off to work, and Teryl and John are usually dressed by 7:30, and they have had their breakfast. Then Teryl usually goes and makes her bed. John is beginning to make his bed and get it done. Then he goes on to Paul and Michael's beds and usually makes them.

Mother: Teryl practices her piano usually in the morning before she goes to school.

Father: Right. She practices her piano between 8:30 and 9:00 when I'm not there to see whether it's happening or not. I think it's happening.

Counselor: Now one thing here, Ron. You're at home with the kids. Pam, you've gone off to work. Michael and Paul are still there?

Mother: No, they go with me.

Counselor: In terms of Teryl and John getting dressed, do you have to remind them about that?

Father: No, I don't think there's much of a problem there.

Mother: They've dressed themselves for quite some time. Usually we have to remind John to comb his hair. . . .

Father: He combs his hair, but not good enough. Or he comes out with a short-sleeved shirt in zero weather.

Counselor: Isn't that beautiful, he just leaves a bit of something, just one little thing so you have to be sure to remind him about it.

Mother: Thursday they went on a field trip and it was really surprising. He came out and he had every hair right where it belonged. So he can do it.

Counselor: Yes, he knows how to do it.

Father: Usually I leave for work about 8:00 and leave Teryl and John home for an hour by themselves. They've done real well. There have been no problems there.

Teryl usually packs her lunch in the morning while John makes the other two beds. She does that on her own.

Counselor: And John?

Father: Well, she fixes John's also. John has some trash to take out. There's usually a couple of diapers from Michael that he takes out and puts in the trash for me.

Counselor: Now, he does this without you telling him?

Father: No sir! [Laughter]

Counselor: I'd have been surprised if you'd have said yes.

Student: Dr. Sweeney, I have a question. [To Mother] When you decided to go to work, did you talk this over with the two older children and decide what they would do differently in order for you to work? Or, was this just a decision made between you and your husband? Were the children involved in it?

Mother: Somewhat, yes, I told them that I had an opportunity to go to work and that they were going to have to accept certain responsibilities. We didn't sit down and say, "We're going to have a discussion about going to work."

Father: I don't know that there was much discussion between Pam and me. I wasn't too sure I could agree with it in the beginning, but it hasn't been bad leaving the children by themselves.

Mother: He obviously doesn't want me to work.

Father: I wasn't against her going to work; I just wasn't sure what it would do to the family relationships. We have so many commitments with Michael. What happens if the kids get sick? It's working out though. I guess they understand at the day care because they work with children. John and Teryl watch Lassie in the morning on television. I'm so drastically against TV, but I do let them watch Lassie in the morning. When Lassie goes off they have to turn the TV off and come back upstairs. I would say that TV is John's number one love. He does enjoy it and this is what we pull away from him as his main punishment. I think this hurts him worse than anything that we could do. They turn off the TV at 8:30 and the bus comes at ten after nine . . .

Counselor:   OK, so they're off to school by now, and you're off to work. Who comes home first and what happens then?

Mother:   I do. I'm home by four before Teryl and John get home. They come home from school at about 10 after four, and come in and have a snack and watch TV in the afternoon. Then we usually have dinner around six.

Counselor:   Are there any fights between home time and dinner time?

Mother:    Not usually. It's usually pretty quiet. There are certain programs they like to watch on TV and they'll go down and watch those. Paul's beginning to watch some program. There for a while he would go down and stand in front of the TV to see if John would yell. But he's beginning to watch, too. We have a large basement and they have their riding toys. They play on their toys usually until dinner time. Teryl doesn't watch too much TV; she likes to read quite well. She has scouts one day a week. We usually have dinner about six.

Counselor:   Is it pretty quiet at dinner time?

Father:   The children want to talk.

Mother:   It's more of a . . .

Father: . . . complete runaway during dinner. They want to relate everything. John wants to tell you everything he's seen on TV.

Mother: I've had to tell him, "If I wanted to see what the program was I'd be down there sitting with you. I don't want to hear it." And so we hear it all the more.

Counselor: Excuse me. Isn't it interesting. Dad hates that TV and what's John want to talk about? [Laughter] So at supper time the TV talk is a nuisance. How do you usually handle that?

Father: Well, it's not always TV. John talks about everything.

Mother: Everything that has gone on through the day. It's like a competing thing. Paul may be talking and John interrupts because he's got something really important he has to say. And then Paul talks a little bit louder so that he can get in what he wants to say.

Father: Teryl is challenging, also, at this time.

Mother: It goes back and forth between each of them—talking about nothing important, just babbling to hear themselves.

Counselor: Is that enough of a problem that you'd like to change it?

Father: I don't know. We've been trying to listen a little bit to what they're saying but it's difficult to know what's important to an 8-year-old. We try to listen to part of it and try to stop them enough so they have time to eat their dinner.

Mother: This is the thing that has really caused most problems. They have so much to say that they don't eat.

Counselor: So what do you do?

Mother:     Just say, "Well, why don't you eat your dinner," and "We'll talk about it later."

Counselor:  What are you doing while all this is going on?

Mother:     Usually we have dinner when Ron comes home, so there's talking that we would like to do. I think they realize this, and I think maybe this is the reason why they're talking.

Counselor:  Everybody wants to talk at the same time and they know that you two want to talk. Would you like to know some things to do about that?

Mother:     Right.

Counselor:  OK. Let's move on and finish the day and we'll come back to this talking at the table. I don't want to flood you with too many things. Actually, we just want to come back to one or two. There are a few situations that you've mentioned that you said you'd like some help with. One is how to handle the fights. You've mentioned that all the kids are in the fights. Paul's bedtime. Talking at the table. Can you think of any others that stand out in your mind that you especially want to work on?

Mother:     Teryl just the last little while has been putting off bedtime with her reading. Is there a way that we can work around this, or should we just say, "This is the time that you're supposed to go to bed. Whatever you're doing has to be stopped." Or should we allow her more time? Maybe she's not requiring as much sleep.

Counselor:  I suspect that the answer that I might give you would not be acceptable, but let me suggest this. You might consider finding out what time the kids think they should go to bed. In other words, ask them what time they should be in bed at night. I mean, "What time do you feel that you should be in bed at night? Is that an agreeable time?" And, once they know the time, then you really shouldn't have to talk about it any further. Now the younger children won't know how to tell time but they'll know by the routine what time to go to bed. I think we can ask Teryl what time she thinks she should be in bed, and then she is responsible for it. One of the mistakes that we often make is that bed- time becomes a big struggle with some families. If it's an occasional problem, I don't think I would make much of it. Can she read in her own room?

Mother: Yes.

Counselor: I think if she goes to her own room and reads, she's the one who's going to be tired the next day. I just wouldn't make too much of it. Do they have their own alarm clock?

Mother: No. Well, built in. There's not an oversleeping prob- lem.

Counselor: Well, I thought if they had a clock they would know the time.

Mother: She has a clock-radio in her room but she doesn't use it for that purpose.

Counselor: You're most fortunate that they get themselves up. With many families that's where we start—with an alarm clock.

Well, let's focus then for the moment on the fighting and the table talk, because these seem to be two big items. With regard to the fighting, you need to appre- ciate, first of all, that the fighting is done for your benefit. And, because it is solely for your benefit, you've got to get yourself out of the situation. Now, one of the things that's recommended is that, for ex- ample, you go to the bathroom. If you're home alone and the kids are fighting, go to the bathroom, have a magazine, have a transistor radio and just be oblivious of what's going on. You don't want to say anything about it.

Now, that may sound like it's going to be very difficult and it may well be, until you understand they're fighting for your benefit. Now, I'm going to tell the kids this. We're going to talk about how they are all conspiring together, and how Teryl will allow certain things to happen so that she'll come out looking good; how Paul will have the satisfaction of knowing John got in trouble; and how Mike stands by enjoying the whole free-for-all. So, you want to remove yourself from that situation. Now, if this happens, for example, at a time when you're watching your favorite TV program, then everybody goes to their room and they can fight all they want to until they're ready to come back, either individually or in a group. Now, in mind of the fact that you're really not that keen about TV anyway, I could see how you could very well turn off the TV and when the kids have left, talk or read or do whatever you choose to. If it's a program that you want to watch, or if you are where you need to be, then it's for them to remove themselves physically. Now, what I'm saying is, the kids know that it bugs you. You may have to talk about this together.

From what we've heard so far, the fighting probably won't happen when you are there by yourself, Pam, so the bathroom technique may not need to be used. But it may happen when you've all had supper and both of you have sat down to watch TV, read the paper, or do whatever you do. They may start their fussing and fighting, but we've set a new rule in the family, "When you fight it takes place in your room, not in our room. The TV room is our room and we're not involved in fights, so you must leave the room. When you're ready to come back you can." Well, who wants to fight if nobody's going to pay attention?

Mother: I do the books for a company, and I've been doing this in the basement. The table's separate from the TV room but usually when I go down there, the children are right there. This is upsetting and I think they could play there when I'm not there. Yesterday, I had gone down and finished my work. They were playing and didn't upset me, but when I went upstairs to do something every one of them, Michael included, trooped up. I thought, "Gee, I'm being followed." How would you combat that?

Counselor: Which part? The part about going . . .

Mother: All of it.

Father: Ignore them again?

Counselor: Well, have you gone into an area where they usually play in order to do your work? Is that what you're saying?

Father: Well, yes, that's usually their playroom. But they don't go down there to play unless she's down there.

Counselor: OK, so they wait until you're there to hassle you. It may be that if the rule applies to everybody, maybe you need to find a space where you're not where they are. The kitchen might be a better place to do your work. Could that be?

Mother: No, I think they would be in the kitchen.

Counselor: Well, no. They can't have it both ways. See, I can ask them a question: "Where should you be when your mother has her work to do?" and let them decide where they should be.

Mother: OK, I see what you're saying.

Counselor: They can't have it both ways, so what I can do is help you find a place where they won't bother you.

Mother:     OK.

Father:     About this squabbling situation, Paul just teases John enough that John hits him on the back or pats him a little hard. I don't think he ever hurts him. You say ignore them, but Paul, you don't ignore him. He comes and climbs up or stands up on top of me or bangs into me to make sure I know that he's crying.

Counselor:  Paul comes to you?

Father:     Right.

Counselor:  So you go to the bathroom or your bedroom. Even children understand the bathroom is a place where you get privacy. It's sacred.

Father:     Not at our house.

Counselor:  Well, it is when the door is closed and locked. The same thing can be true of your bedroom. If both of you want to go, then you can go in the bedroom and lock the door, put your music on and do your work or read your books or whatever. Now many parents have images of being locked in a room for hours. It doesn't happen and it requires confidence. Now, if you don't want to do this, that's fine. Just let us know right from the beginning that you don't see yourself doing that. Then we won't work on that.

Father:     Mmm.

Mother:     We can try.

Counselor:  It will be important to be consistent, because most parents find it will take one or two times. We've had kids who stop and say, "Don't go in the bathroom." . . . [Laughter] . . . It really happens.

Mother:     Even at the dinner table, if they're squabbling, you're saying . . .

Counselor: Oh no, at table time we've got another suggestion.

Father: I think I'm not so concerned about feeling locked in my room all the time, but I feel that I ought to be accessible to those kids at any second that I'm there. It would hurt me that they couldn't get to me.

Counselor: We've got the "good father" here. "At any moment they may need me."

Father: We've never shut ourselves out from them when we're there and no matter where we are, they know they can come to us.

Counselor: You're not shutting yourselves out except to the extent that they want you to be shut out. That's the message. They decide. All we're trying to do is win their cooperation. They've decided they're going to throw a fit in order to get your attention and you've said, "You can get my attention in other ways. This way I won't let you have it." And you just withdraw. As soon as they stop the noise, and stop making the cries and so forth, you can go back out. You've seen cartoons I'm sure where kids walk blocks to get home to be able to cry and complain about what happened at the playground. They can wait that long. They can turn it on and off just as . . . we call it "water power." It's a way of managing other people. So, how do you feel about this now. If you're uncomfortable with it, it's OK.

Father: Now I am, but I'll try it and see.

Counselor: Okay, let's take a little break and then I'll talk with the children.

## CHILDREN INTERVIEW

Counselor: Now, do you know why you came down today?

Teryl:     [Murmurs] "No."

Counselor: You have no idea at all?

Teryl:     Not really.

Counselor: Do you want to guess? [Silence]

What about you, John, would you like to guess? You don't want to guess at all. Well, your parents have some situations at home that they're not real sure how to handle. They think that the situations that deal with you kids fighting, for example, they're not sure how to handle. So they don't know what to do with you kids. How about that?

[Silence]

Do you know what to do with your Mom and Dad? [Some nonverbal response] Ah, I think I know better than that, John. OK. Well, what are some things that you consider to be kind of a hassle at home? Do you have any problems that you can think of?

John:      Brothers bugging you when you don't want bugged.

Counselor: OK, brothers bug you. All the brothers? One more than the other?

John:      Mostly the middle one.

Counselor: Mostly the middle one.

John:      Yeah, Paul.

Counselor: Is that Paul? OK, Paul wants to get your attention a lot, huh?

John:        He takes things away from me.

Counselor:    OK, so Paul takes things that you want to play with and that bugs you. Any other kinds of things?

John:        He bites.

Counselor:    He bites you, too? Uh, hmm. Does he bite hard?

Teryl:       Yes.

Counselor:    Does he bite you, too? . . . Not so much I think. I think he bites John more. Right? Yeah, OK. You guys, do you have fights in the family? So you agree with your mom and dad, hmm? How many times a day do you fight?

Teryl:       At least once every day.

Counselor:    At least once a day. John doesn't think so. Is that right John? Does once a day sound right?

John:        Maybe.

Counselor:    Yeah, maybe. You're trying to think back on how many times you get bit, I think. You don't always get bit, but there are some hassles. About one a day. What happens when you have a fight? Can you describe a fight that's just gone on recently?

Teryl:       One wants to watch one TV program, and the other wants to watch another.

Counselor:    OK. So then what happens?

John:        We get to arguing, and finally one walks off and lets the other watch it. Then the other turns it to the channel the other one wants to watch.

Counselor:    Ah ha, so when one guy walks off then another guy enters the fight. He'll come in and change . . .

Teryl:          No, the guy that you were fighting with will change the channel to the one you wanted to watch.

Counselor:      Oh, I see. OK so you resolve that yourself then? Huh? OK. Do you have any fights where you don't resolve it yourself? [Nods, yes] OK, what happens? Can you think of a fight like that? Something that maybe's happened recently?

Teryl:          You can get sent to your room.

Counselor:      OK. Oh, you can get sent to your room. Who sends you to your room?

Both:           Usually our mother.

Counselor:      Oh, I see. Is Mom generally the one who comes in and helps with the fight?

Teryl:          Hmm, not al . . . No.

Counselor:      Not always.

John:           Not usually.

Counselor:      Not usually.

John:           Paul fights the most.

Teryl:          Yeah, he comes in and decides to fight.

John:           He comes in and he'll knock me down on to the floor and start wrestling me.

Counselor:      Paul comes in. Now let's see, Paul is what, he's 3½. Is that right?

Teryl & John:   Hm, hmm.

Counselor:      Paul comes in and knocks down . . . and you're about 8?

John:       Hm, hmm.

Counselor:  He knocks you down, and beats you up.

Teryl:      Really, John lets him knock him down.

Counselor:  Oh, I see. Is that right, John?

John:       No.

Teryl:      I think he really likes to fight with Paul though.

Counselor:  Uh, huh. What do you think, John? [Laughter] John's smiling again. I think you like to fight, John. Sometimes, hmm?

John:       Not really.

Counselor:  OK. All right. So sometimes when you have your fights, your mother or maybe your father more often, comes in on a white horse and like the Lone Ranger saves you? What does he do?

Teryl:      Gets mad.

Counselor:  Does he get mad?

Teryl:      Sometimes.

Counselor:  Uh, hmm. So, it really bugs Mom and Dad when you guys get into a fight then. Uh, hmm. Why do you think you get into fights?

Teryl:      Hmm? [Murmurs "I don't know."]

Counselor:  Don't know why? What purpose would be served by it?

John:       If I want to watch a different cartoon than she wants to watch, she will end up flipping the channels 'til we finally decide on one.

Counselor: Uh, hmm. But when you don't flip the channels and find one?

Teryl: We get in a fight.

Counselor: Uh, hmm. Do you want to know what I think? . . . Well, you said yes, John said no. I guess I have a choice. Do I have a choice? I think, John, that you like to get in a fight because it gets your mom and dad involved. I think it keeps them busy with you. Could that be?

[Silence]

Teryl thinks "maybe, yes." What about you John?

John: I agree with her.

Counselor: You'll agree with her; you won't agree with me though, right? So fights are very often to keep Papa and Mama busy. You know what I've suggested to your mom and dad? I've suggested that they not get involved in your fights. What do you think about that?

John: I think that's better.

Counselor: You think that's better. I don't really think you'll like that, John. If Mom and Dad don't enter into your fights, you won't have anybody to bother with you. Oh, you think Teryl will? Teryl, are you going to come in on your white horse and save the day? [Nods, no!] Teryl says she's not going to do it, John. How about that?

John: Well, she'll . . . I don't think she'll give up the minute I hit her.

Counselor: Oh, you're going to hit her, is that it? Well, Teryl . . .

John: We always get hitting each other.

Counselor: Well, let me tell you what I've suggested to your mom and dad and maybe Teryl might do this too. I've suggested to your Mom and Dad that if you guys are downstairs and you're into your own fight that they just closet themselves away somewhere, or do something that they want to that takes them completely out of the noise range, and completely out of any being bothered by it all. They won't even know you're fighting. They won't even be concerned about it.

John: They won't even hear it. I know how they'll do it. They'll run the vacuum. It makes too much noise.

Counselor: Oh? They'll run the vacuum and ignore whatever it happens to be. There will be no reason to come in and get involved in your fights. I don't think you're going to like that John. What do you think? . . .

[Silence]

Not so sure. No. You see, John, there are a lot of things that go on that are to get your folks involved, but from now on they won't. They'll let you kids take care of it yourselves.

OK, one other thing that Mom and Dad talked with us about is the fact that dinner time sometimes gets to be kind of a hassle. Everybody wants to talk at the same time. Is that true?

Teryl: Hmmm.

Counselor: Well, I suggested maybe there'd be a new rule at dinner time. The new rule is that everybody will get a chance to talk, one at a time. And if somebody wants to talk and get loud, and begin making it difficult for everyone else to be able to eat and enjoy dinner, then they leave the table until they're able to come back and join in with the rest of the family.

John:       My mom and dad already know that.

Counselor:  Do they already know that? Do they tell you to leave the table, John.

John:       Uh, hmm.

Counselor:  OK. Can you come back to the table when you want to?

John:       Hmm?

Counselor:  Kind of. OK. Well, we're just clarifying that so you know that when you leave you can come back. Now, this applies to Mike and to Paul also. There is one other thing that maybe you can help with. That could be true of any of these things by the way. If you see some things you'd like to see handled a little differently, we would like your suggestions. Mother reports that she has work to do at home, and her place to do it so far has been down in the TV room where you kids play very often. She said sometimes it's difficult to work because she wants to work when you kids are down there playing.

John:       Maybe we could go in and watch TV while she's working, and not get on the toys that make a racket.

Counselor:  OK. Now is the TV in the same room where she works?

Teryl:      No.

Counselor:  Oh, it's in another room. OK. The toys are in that room?

Teryl:      No.

John:       The toys are in the room where the TV is.

Teryl:      They end up in the other room though.

Counselor:  Oh, I see. They end up in the other room where she
            needs to work, and that becomes a part of the prob-
            lem then. I didn't understand that. Well, let's see if I
            understand now, John. I understand you're saying that
            maybe when Mother has to work you kids will watch
            the TV quietly and not play with any toys that would
            be noisy. Does that sound like it would be possible?

Teryl:      It would be a little hard.

Counselor:  And how would that be hard, Teryl?

Teryl:      Paul and Michael.

Counselor:  You don't think they would go along with this rule?

John:       Yes, but there's another problem with the TV. When
            Mom types it messes up the TV and it makes a racket.

Counselor:  Oh, I see. So when she's running the typewriter it in-
            terferes with the TV. Could it maybe be that you kids
            could go outside or go up to your bedrooms, or play
            someplace else besides down there while she's work-
            ing? Would that be a reasonable solution to suggest?

John:       Yes, but I don't think Paul and Michael would.

Counselor:  You don't think they'll go along with that?

John:       Um, nah.

Teryl:      They might.

Counselor:  They might, though. Maybe the family could sit down
            and talk to the boys and see how they feel about that?
            I guess you two would have a chance to show them
            how to do it. That way they could learn how from you

guys. Do you think so? [They nod, yes.] Well, I'll tell you what, John. I'll tell your mother what you've suggested. It seems like Teryl's agreeing. Maybe you can talk as a family with Mike and Paul when you get home and see what they think about that.

Are there any things that you would like help with? Is there something that's going on at home, or some things that Mom and Dad do that you wish they didn't do. [Silence] Nothing? John, what about you? . . . OK. Well, I get the feeling that you really have a nice family, that your Mom and Dad really care a lot about you. They pointed out some things that I was really pleased to hear; for example, that Teryl helps to make John's lunch in the morning, and that John takes out the trash. We really need to do these kinds of things for each other in a family. One of the things that I suggested to your mom and dad is that a couple of times a week you kids all plan together with your mom and dad what you can do to have a good time together as a family. Maybe you will choose someplace to go, or a game to play, or some way to have a good time together. Would you like that? Do you think Mike and Paul would? [They nod, yes.] We want to include them.

You really have folks who care a lot about you kids. They want to have you grown up being able to take care of life and take care of yourself. I have a feeling they're going to be doing everything they can to help you find ways that you can deal with your life situations and have a good time. They're going to be looking for you to give them some ideas to help them out and it's going to be important that you talk to them about it. Now, this thing about fights and talking at the table. It's simply a matter that if we're going to live together we need to find ways to do it so that we're not hassled. So, they don't bug you and you don't bug them. Do you think this conference has been helpful? [Both smile and nod, yes.]

## PARENT INTERVIEW RESUMED

Counselor: . . . About the fighting thing, Teryl and John didn't really like the idea that you wouldn't get into it. You may be surprised to know that John knows that you run the vacuum when you don't want to hear him.

Mother: Gee!

Counselor: Well, he knows that. He said, "She'll run the vacuum and then she won't know we're fighting." So he already understood. I think I've said to you before that kids sometimes know how many times they have to be called, and so forth. They know also how you're likely to respond.

Student: Is it a coincidence that you're busy and you run the vacuum cleaner or do you really turn it on to drown out the noise?

Mother: Oh, I don't think I ever have!

Counselor: Well, it's occurred to him that you have. In his mind he wanted you to come in and save him and you were busy with that darn vacuum. He was not too keen about the idea that you're not going to come in on your white horse and save him. What he said was that Teryl would do it. Well, of course Teryl's hearing everything we're saying. Being a good surrogate momma, she will probably pick up on this, and if she doesn't then you can point this out to her the next time.

About the table talk, they said that you've already done this, probably with the one difference that when they left the table maybe they could come back, but not always. Now, if someone leaves the table and doesn't come back, you clean up and put away the food. One of the outcomes is that someone misses supper so there's some motivation for wanting to come back and fit in. You want to take advantage of that by not leaving the food so that they get to eat some more later. Follow me? In other words if they act up at the table, you say, "Hey, if you're going to be that way, you know the rule." Now, on some occasions, especially with the little people if they're into a power kind of thing, you may actually have to remove them. That's unusual, and I don't think you'll have to do it with your kids. So don't do that first. First is simply, "Hey, you know the rule. Leave. When you're ready to come back you may." Now if they leave the table and dilly-dally, and you leave the food, you've made it easy for them not to experience the full consequences. It's not punishment. It's just what happens when dinner's done. We clean up. Now, I didn't say anything about the cleaning up yet. I think that if you make straightening up after dinner a fun thing to do, they'll swing right into it. They really care for each other, and they like you. It's obvious they really don't want to hassle you too much, just a little bit. So, its really a low level of hassling that you've got. That's really a good sign. It's going to be very easy to deal with these things.

Now, the question about mother working, where could she be, where could they be. I think they concluded that they couldn't be downstairs while you're working because the TV gets interference from the typewriter, and the other boys wouldn't go along. That part they really shared in most. If you talk with them a little further about it you may find other alternatives, but allow them to help decide where they can be while you're working. The point is, Mom has to have time to be able to get her work done so that she can cook the supper, so that she can have time to play with them, and so that you can have time to be together. And I did mention to them, that I had also suggested that you plan one or two times a week when you're going to play together. It may be Sunday after church, or Friday night when everybody's at home and the work is behind you. Whatever is a mutually good time for all of you. They liked that. They felt good about that, and that's very promising.

[The parents responded with comfort in the recommendations and pleasure with what they learned.]

*Note:* Subsequent interviews involved the younger children. The youngest boy's solicitation of special service was quickly identified and corrective recommendations implemented. Parents and children alike reported fewer "fights" and greater cooperation on helping mom get her work done, and the parents found playtime with the children a good time investment with fewer hassles.

# FAMILY COUNCIL

What follows are excerpts from the actual transcript of the first family council meeting of the author's family. Besides the mother and father, there are three children. The oldest daughter (Elizabeth Rose) was almost 9 years old, the second daughter (Ann) was 7, and the youngest (Tom) was 3. This session was videotaped in the home.

The oldest daughter is about to leave on her first Girl Scout camp adventure for 1 week. At one point in the meeting, she gives an indication of being uncomfortable with leaving but it is more nonverbal than verbal. The reader will note the youngest child (son) leaves the group periodically, makes faces at the camera, and finally evokes a response from the middle child (second daughter), who responds in a characteristic way. Even the transcript reveals how skillfully the youngest gained attention.

This was a first and by no means model family meeting. As relative neophytes to the Adlerian approach, the mother was reading the section on family meetings in Dreikurs' *Children the Challenge* while the father was giving the children an introduction to the purpose of the meeting. Note that the oldest daughter catches on quickly to the equalitarian concept and starts in on "new rules" just for Dad! The second daughter is a willing, if not enthusiastic, participant.

For families who regularly talk over events and problems during the course of a week, a meeting such as this one is probably rarely if ever needed. On the other hand, for the family where members tend to see each other rarely altogether, the family meeting has merit. Although the recommendation is that a time be adhered to regularly, I suggest that once everyone learns how to participate in a meeting, these skills carry over and can be called on even on an irregular meeting time basis (i.e., meeting occasionally).

Father:     Do you remember us talking about a family council before?

Children:   Yes.

Father:     Well, I wanted to do this now because I was hoping that before you got away, Elizabeth Rose, we would be able to talk about it and get out of the way whatever things we needed to so that the next time you came home, we'll be able to meet again. Your mother's still reading the book now and trying to rind out something about . . . What are you laughing about?

Mother:     I'm just laughing because I'm reading here—this is the way to do it. Read the directions as you "fly the plane"! [Laugh]

Father:     Got to find out what you're supposed to do. [Laugh]

Mother:     Yeah.

Father:     Well, you know Mom and I have attended discussion groups where we've been talking about how to rear children and also how to have a better family. A lot of the things that we've done, and still do for that matter, we feel are not good for you children or us. So we're trying to find better ways to do it and we think that the best way to do it is for you to help us. Now one of the things that is really important is for us to learn how to treat you as equals, like real people, and also how to, for us as a family, to work together cooperatively. You know I've said a lot of times, you've got to cooperate. We have always felt as though we have a good family, we've always been happy, but we do have problems at times and you have problems with us. [Children nod agreement.] So, if we get together at a fixed time when we agree say every week, then anybody who's got something they want to talk over with the whole family, knows that they'll be able to do it at that time.

One of the things we need to do is to learn how to listen to each other and for Mom and Dad not to talk so much. We should listen. The only reason I'm talking so much today is because I feel I need to tell you about the meetings to help us get started.

One of the things they say is really important is everybody has an equal vote. I thought one of the ways we could show that, just to show that we're all equals, I have these five pieces of paper and they are all the same size. Just for fun we can start by putting your name on one, Elizabeth, put your name on one, Tom, Ann's name on one, put Mother's name on one and I've got one. Now, if there's anything that we need to vote on or that would be helpful to vote on, then we all have the same vote. In other words, oldest daughter's, second daughter's and son's and Mother's and mine are all the same.

From what I can tell from people who have done this kind of thing before, it is important that we not use this as a gripe session alone. It isn't for me and Mother to tell you girls what you're doing wrong. It's just a good time for us to sit down and talk to find out how each other's doing and things that are on our minds.

Oldest
Daughter:    And what's going on.

Father:      Right. And if somebody's not cooperating in the family, we can talk about that. One of the things that we can do is talk about it and decide what might be the best solution for us as we see it. Not as I see it or as Mother sees it.

Second
Daughter:    I don't get the voting.

Father:      You don't understand the voting?

Second
Daughter:    No.

Father:      What would we vote about? Is that what you mean?

*Note:* Dreikurs in his works later concluded that voting is not conducive to the spirit of cooperation desired. There always tend to be winners and losers. The author now recommends efforts toward consensus as much as possible.

Second
Daughter:    No. I don't understand how you do it.

Father:      Well, let's pretend for a moment that we all felt that the dishes ought to be cleaned up, or that there ought to be a time when we all get together. Let's try one for real right now. I know that I keep real bad hours in terms of work and things I do. I can't always be depended upon to be at home. I'd like to be here. How would you feel about meeting on Sunday mornings?

Oldest
Daughter:    Don't we always?

Father:      Well, I mean that would be the time that we would meet for our council. This is generally when I'm home.

I go to church with the family, whether it's morning or evening, but we agree that we meet on a Sunday, probably on Sunday morning after breakfast.

Mother: Instead of just sitting around the house, we would make it a point to sit down together and talk together and we would call it our council. We would call it our family council time, even though you are right, we are always all here on Sunday morning.

Second
Daughter: Almost.

Mother: Well, yeah. Usually, we're all here, but we're all doing something else. You're watching TV, he's reading the paper, and Tom's playing so we would make . . .

Son: Will we be taping next time?

Father: Maybe, maybe we will. Now, if you don't like the taping, we can always stop. We don't have to do that.

Children: No, no I don't care . . .

Father: Well, is Sunday OK with you girls?

Both
Daughters: Uh huh, yeah.

Mother: Then we need to vote on it to make sure.

Father: Right. All right, everybody who's in favor of meeting on Sunday put your hand up. All agreed?

Mother: Four in favor and one abstaining. [Son had left the group.] You've come back. Maybe we ought to ask him.

Father: All right. Son, do you, would you like to meet on Sundays like we're meeting today? Would this be an OK day for you?

| | |
|---|---|
| Mother: | OK, that's your vote. You can put it down on the table. |
| Father: | Yours is just as good as everybody else's. Now do you understand? Sometimes we may not want to just vote, we may say that we agree, and that constitutes a vote. I guess when it would be critical would be when we didn't agree, then we would vote. When we vote, if three people say it ought to be one way and two say it ought to be another way, the three would have the say as to how it should be. |
| | And if we make mistakes, that's OK. In other words, if we decide to do something and find out in between times it is not such a good idea, at the next family meeting, the next Sunday, we can talk about it and change our decision. |
| Mother: | It doesn't have to stay. |
| Father: | Right, but during that week we decided to do something, we'll have to try the best we can, and . . . |
| Second Daughter: | But how long will we meet? We won't have time. |
| Father: | Do you think it best, that there be a time that would be better to do it than mornings? |
| Second Daughter: | What times does everybody get up? |
| Oldest Daughter: | That's a good question. |
| Second Daughter: | Because when there's some that get up at seven and some that get up at eight and then some that get up at ten and nine. |

| | |
|---|---|
| Oldest Daughter: | And eleven, too. |
| Father: | Do you have any suggestions? |
| Mother: | Some at twelve, go ahead and say it. [laughs] |
| Father: | Sometimes, huh? |
| Daughters: | Yeah. [smiles] |
| Father: | Sometimes, and you know who it is, don't you? [laugh] |
| Daughters: | Yeah. |
| Father: | The last one out of bed. |
| Oldest Daughter: | Everybody's just got this habit of getting up when they. . . |
| Mother: | How about if we make the point of getting up at ten o'clock? |
| Father: | Be up by ten? |
| Mother: | Be up by ten and that will give us a chance to get ready for 12:00 Mass. |
| Oldest Daughter: | And then we could vote on those that would make the breakfast. |
| Second Daughter: | Yeah! |
| Father: | You'd like that wouldn't you? |
| Mother: | That sounds like a winner already! |

Oldest
Daughter:     First we got to vote on me.

Second
Daughter:     If we would start off like Sunday, we'd vote first on who would do it and then, that same Sunday, we'd vote on who would do it next week and so on.

Oldest
Daughter:     Of course, you're not going to go alphabetically!

Mother:     You don't think so, huh? [laughs]

Second
Daughter:     No.

Mother:     I think I'll make that suggestion!

Second
Daughter:     No, no!

Mother:     I suggest we go alphabetically!

Oldest
Daughter:     Okay.

Mother:     I wouldn't have even thought of it 'til you opened your mouth!

Second
Daughter:     Okay, first daughter, you can go ahead and do it first!

Father:     Well, are we saying that we're going to meet at 10:00 on Sunday mornings, then?

Daughters:     Um hmm.

Father:     Is that all right with you, son?

Son:     And from 10 to 10:30. It doesn't have to be that long.

Father:        In other words, it doesn't have to be the exact time.

Son:           Yeah.

Father:        Well, we'll be meeting next week on Sunday.

Oldest
Daughter:      We'll vote next week who makes breakfast!

Father:        For whoever's here.

Second
Daughter:      Not me!

Father:        I just remembered that I'm likely to be out of town next week, so you folks make it to the meeting without Rosie [oldest] and me. Do you have any questions about the council?

Oldest
Daughter:      Not about it, but—it wouldn't make any sense anyhow.

Father:        Well you can ask. You know, in this instance, for example, Tom is making noises to get our attention and so far we've been able to ignore him. Now if he interferes with your being able to think or talk, we can ask him to . . . [no one seems bothered] Well, can we think of anything else we need to talk about?

Oldest
Daughter:      The dogs.

Father:        What about the dogs?

Oldest
Daughter:      Well, ever since you started feeding them, I remind you about the dogs and you say—um, like at night, I think, this is only what I think, I hear the car drive up, and then, I hear a click click at the door, and after that

I hear some footsteps and I think that after I hear the car come in, I should hear something go like plunk, like the garbage can being opened to get the dog food.

Father: And you listen for it and you don't hear it?

Oldest
Daughter: Um huh.

Father: You're thinking I don't feed the dogs.

Oldest
Daughter: Right, just like you did with . . .

Father: In other words, what I was getting after you about, not feeding the dogs, now you notice that I'm not feeding the dogs.

Oldest
Daughter: Yeah!

Father: Okay. I don't know. Mom and I have talked about this and this is something we didn't get real clear. In fact, I think we thought we would meet sooner than just now, but you remember that we said to you one day . . . We're the ones that bought the dogs, you didn't. In fact, at that point, you were young enough that we didn't expect you to do anything about the dogs. And along the way, we said that they were your dogs, or at least one of them was your dog, and that you should take care of them. Well, we decided as we began to learn about how to be fair about this as parents that we had really stuck you with that job and that we were making you feel bad about it when it really wasn't fair. It wasn't fair of us to expect you to do things when we were the ones who bought the dogs, so we should take care of them if anybody did.

Now, what Mom and I decided was that we had been threatening to get rid of the dogs as a way of trying to make you feel bad . . .

Oldest
Daughter:    Making me feed them . . .

Father:      Right, and so we said that that isn't right. So, we'll
             take care of the dogs because we got them and if we
             got them, then it's our responsibility. Now, if we can't
             take care of the dogs, then we have to decide what to
             do about it. In other words, if we should get rid of the
             dogs then we'll do it, but we shouldn't make you feel
             bad about us getting rid of the dogs . . .

Mother:      Right, we can't really say "We're gonna get rid of the
             dogs because you don't take care of them." That's not
             really fair. If we get rid of the dogs, it's because we
             don't take care of them.

Father:      Right. And we don't really want to get rid of the dogs.
             We'd like to keep them, too. We really love them. I
             think you have every right to say to me, "And you're
             not taking care of these dogs either!"

Second
Daughter:    You know when I got Boots, I thought it was unfair if
             I had two pets and the rest had one, and Tom didn't
             have any, so I gave Mac to him.

Father:      Yeah, now he feels better knowing he's got a dog and
             you've got a cat. And yet it's still Mom and my re-
             sponsibility to take care of the dogs. Now I'm tickled
             to death to have you help. You know, just like every-
             body else, sometimes I forget and sometimes I don't
             get around to doing it, but I have been doing this, if I
             don't feed the dogs at night, I try to be sure and do it
             in the morning before I leave for work. So it may be
             that you haven't heard me because you're asleep in
             the mornings.

Oldest
Daughter:    Except for this morning.

Father:          Yeah, well, I fed them last night.

Oldest
Daughter:        Yeah, I know. I watched you!

Father:          Right. And I'll feed them tonight again. But you're
                 right, I've missed a couple of times and Mom knows,
                 she's told me about it. Now, Mom has fed them a
                 couple of times for me and I've been keeping the dog
                 pen pretty clean, I think, and I'm trying and I see it's
                 a lot harder sometimes when you don't get credit for
                 it.

Oldest
Daughter:        Yeah.

Father:          It's kind of good to know the problem, isn't it? To
                 know where you are, too.

Oldest
Daughter:        Um huh. [Teary eyed over first time leaving for Scout
                 camp shortly.]

Father:          You know, we really do love you, don't you? Some-
                 times I don't act like that, do I?

Oldest
Daughter:        One thing, Dad.

Father:          We're going to miss you, too. [Speaking to her ex-
                 pression and tears]

Mother:          You're going to write us and tell us what you're do-
                 ing, aren't you?

Oldest
Daughter:        Um huh.

Mother:          Are you going to write us postcards?

Oldest
Daughter: Um huh, and letters.

Mother: Okay. Are you going to write to your Grandmas and
Grandpas. Now be sure to write Grandma and Grandpa
a card, though, because you know they'll be going off
on the 20th.

Oldest
Daughter: Okay.

Father: We'll have to give you some stamps before you go.

Daughter: No, I can get them at camp.

Mother: She can get them up there at the trading post. I gave
$6 credit, and a dollar and a half, I think, is for . . .

Son: Look at my name!

Mother: And 75 cents is for . . .

Son: Look at my name!!

Mother: So that leaves about $4 . . .

Son: Look at my name, Daddy!!!

Second
Daughter: I have something to complain about. He keeps interrupting people when they're talking. That bothers me.

Mother: What are we going to do?

Father: I think he feels like he's being left out. Do you feel
like you are being left out, Tom? That's not a good
feeling to be left out, is it? I think what happens, Tom,
is that when you start making noise people try to, you
know, keep on with what they're doing. But if you
want to talk to us about something that's on your mind,

|  |  |
|---|---|
|  | we'll sure give you our attention. We'll be glad to listen to you. |
| Mother: | We'd be glad to. The only reason we don't pay any attention to you is because when you're making noise we don't want to encourage you, to make you think that's the thing to do. |
| Second Daughter: | That's the way to get attention! |
| Mother: | Right. If you have something to talk about, we'll listen to you. |
| Father: | Now he feels put out. |
| Mother: | Well, don't. We just want you to know. |
| Father: | If you want to say something, Tom, you just do what Annie does. Put your hand up to let us know. |
| Mother: | Hold it up this way. And we'll listen to you. |
| Father: | Your paper is just as big as mine, did you notice that? See here. Okay, is that what you wanted to say? |
| Second Daughter: | Yes. |
| Mother: | Now, how do you end one? |
| Father: | When everybody feels like they've said everything they wanted to say. Is there anything else that you need to bring up? |
| Mother: | No. |
| Oldest Daughter: | You? |

Father:     I'm trying to think. I feel like there probably ought to be, but I don't know.

Mother:     Are you finished, Tom? You don't have something to say do you? Okay.

Father:     When you want to come back, Tom, you come on back.

Oldest
Daughter:   You should tell us the days that you're going to come home so that we can expect you and we'll have the place clean for you and we can have a good meal, besides coming in at twelve and ten and one.

Father:     Well, what do you think I ought to do. I'm not sure what you're saying. Are you saying I should tell you when I'm coming home?

Oldest
Daughter:   Uh huh, so we'll know. And sometimes Mother cooks food and she doesn't expect you home and you come home. And she has to cook supper, after she's all done.

Father:     Well, I see. Would that, is that a rule for everybody then? In other words, when Mother's out, and she's coming home she should let us know and when you're coming home you'd let us know. Is that what you're saying too?

Oldest
Daughter:   Not exactly.

Father:     I mean, is it just a rule for me, or is it for everybody?

Oldest
Daughter:   It should be sort of like a rule for you.

Second
Daughter:   I think it should be a rule for everybody. 'Cause ev-

erybody doesn't know when everybody's coming home.

Oldest
Daughter:  Yeah, like if Daddy comes home from work, nobody knows.

Mother:    Yes, that's right because it sometimes gets dark before you children decide to come in. I've called and called. Right?

Second
Daughter:  How about the time Daddy came home and the door was unlocked and he scared Lucy [cleaning woman] and you.

Mother:    Yeah.

Father:    You mean the time all the doors were locked and you were supposed to be in the house and you couldn't get in?

Second
Daughter:  No, I'm talking about the time you . . .

Mother:    No, don't you remember the time you came home, we didn't expect you and I was sitting in here and Lucy was in here and I saw this shadow going down the hall and you really scared the both of us. Lucy, too. You really scared us! We didn't know who was in the house. Nobody else was supposed to be here.

Father:    I didn't remember that one. I remember one night I called the children and nobody came home and I locked all the doors cause I figured everybody was gone. Nobody answered and, then, everything was locked up and I had the TV on and everything.

Second
Daughter:  He was back in the back room.

Father:    Yeah, that's right.

Second
Daughter:    I was banging on the windows, saying, "Daddy, let us in!"

Father:    Well, I guess the way I feel about it is this: If you're asking me to let the family know when I'm going to be home on any given day, I'll try it. I also know that there are going to be days when I'll have to change it, but if what you're asking me is to call and tell you, I'll be agreeable to doing that if everybody else is agreeable to it. In other words, if you're going out and you're going to be playing and say it's 6:30 or 7:00 and you say, "Mother, I'll be home before dark," when you're going out the door you let her know that; then, if we all do that I think that would be very good. I think your suggestion is very good.

Oldest
Daughter:    'Cause there was one time when everybody went off. So I turned on the light, walked in, and I locked all the doors and turned on the TV, and nobody was there. Somebody knocked on the door so I asked who it was, I just heard footsteps and so I didn't know what to do, so I called the neighbors.

Father:    So if you'd known when we were going to be home, it would have helped you not to be scared.

Oldest
Daughter:    Yeah.

Father:    Well, you know, Ann said something a little different there, too. Ann was saying, maybe I ought to set a time when I'm going to be home. Is that what you were saying?

Oldest
Daughter:    Uh huh.

Father:  It'd be a little hard for me, Ann. I mean, there are certain days, now, for example, in the Fall, when I know what my schedule is, I could say I will be home. Otherwise I can call and say I can't make it. But I have been very loose about this in the past. A lot of times I wouldn't even tell Mother at all when I was going to be home and I would come early sometimes and sometimes I'd come in late. You're right, she didn't know. And you didn't know either.

Oldest
Daughter:  And she didn't expect you and you knew she would have supper for all of us and you walk in the door and say, "Where's supper?"

Father:  Yeah.

Oldest
Daughter:  And there we are, eating.

Father:  Right. So, okay. Now, are we saying that we're all in favor and we're all voting for keeping the whole family informed when we're coming home and stuff?

Mother:  Why not . . . I hate to leave notes on the door in obvious places. If you want to leave notes, then leave a piece of paper like this cause it's so handy, why not—and everybody knows where the Scotch tape is—why not.

Daughters:  We don't.

Mother:  You know where the masking tape is.

Daughters:  Yeah.

Mother:  What differences does it make whether it's Scotch tape or whatever?

Daughters:  Uh huh.

Mother:          Okay. Why not leave notes on the inside of the first door, where the drawers are, on the inside of that door.

Second
Daughter:        Yeah, but what if the door's locked?

Mother:          What door?

Second
Daughter:        Any door. I mean if the whole house is locked.

Mother:          No, a note to tell you what time I'll be back.

Oldest
Daughter:        Oh! Outside the door.

Father:          And if we come home and we don't know where they are we'll look behind the door.

Mother:          Exactly.

Father:          Okay. And . . .

Mother:          On the inside of the door.

Father:          Okay. Then the other thing is that if we have left a written note and we find that we're not getting home for some reason, then we could call.

Mother:          We call. Yes.

Father:          Right. Okay. Any more suggestions?

Oldest
Daughter:        We could also keep records of our meetings. Me and Ann have these record things.

Second
Daughter:        And Mother has already used a couple of them. She typed them and she uses them.

Oldest
Daughter: We've got little folders and we can just have, you know, what we voted on and the dates, and the times that we missed the meetings. And we could go during the week and make it up for that.

Father: Who's going to ask for that . . .

Second
Daughter: And then while they are gone we would pick up things and, you know, think about what goes on and during the meeting . . .

Mother: That's right. We would be able to tell you when you're not here on a Sunday, what we decided last Sunday.

Oldest
Daughter: And then . . .

Father: That would be important wouldn't it? That's a good point.

Second
Daughter: I have a notebook . . .

Oldest
Daughter: And then, the person that's been gone, why they would know what's been going on there.

Father: All right. Maybe we ought to write down some things we decided today so that we won't forget them.

Second
Daughter: I have a notebook. It has paper in it. I'll go get it.

Father: Do you have a pencil, too?

Second
Daughter: I think so.

| | |
|---|---|
| Mother: | A little note. That would be a way of tallying them up. 'Cause I won't even remember. |
| Father: | I bet you they will! |
| Mother: | I know they will! |
| Oldest Daughter: | If we don't, we'll use the back of Mother's paper. |

[Son is away from the meeting]

| | |
|---|---|
| Father: | Tom, We're going to write down the things we decided today. If you want to join in with us, we'd be pleased to have you. |
| Mother: | You want to sit down with us? |
| Son: | Daddy, let's do it on TV. Let's bring the stuff down there. |
| Father: | You think it was a lot of fun. |
| Son: | Let's watch us up there in the air and watch me on TV. |
| Oldest Daughter: | I have a pen. |
| Second Daughter: | Okay. |
| Father: | It's a lot more fun when everybody doesn't want to be serious, huh? |
| Mother: | Did you get your notebook? |
| Father: | We should have it in color, do you think? |
| Son: | Please! |

Mother:     Okay, now what were the things we decided?

Father:     We can't open that up now, Son. We're not finished yet.

Mother:     First of all, we decided what day we were going to have our meeting. That I remember.

Oldest
Daughter:   Yeah, Sunday. Okay, second.

Mother:     What time everybody should be up by. 10:30.

Oldest
Daughter:   Okay, third. About Tommy, wasn't it?

Second
Daughter:   Umm, about calling, about writing the notes.

Mother:     Yeah, where to put the notes. If you're going to be going off and nobody's home, or if somebody's—notes to be left . . .

Oldest
Daughter:   Put where?

Mother:     Inside the first storage door. Is that what you call it?

Father:     Okay. I think I was asked—what it started with was Ann saying to me that I ought to have a time to come home and we were agreeing that we would call . . .

Oldest
Daughter:   That was me.

Father:     That's right. It was you.

Oldest
Daughter:   Yeah, I said Daddy . . .

Mother: Okay, then put down, he agreed he would call and let us know.

Father: Well, but that was for everybody.

Mother: Yeah.

Father: It wasn't just me. We agreed to let the family know when we would be home. That's worthy of note, I think.

Mother: Well, put in all.

Oldest
Daughter: Okay. There.

Mother: Was there a fifth one?

Mother: Okay. What was the fifth one?

Father: Well, was there a fifth one?

Second
Daughter: I think there was.

Mother: I don't know.

Second
Daughter: Yeah. About Tommy. Remember about interrupting?

Oldest
Daughter: Oh, not that.

Second
Daughter: You know when Tom started to . . .

Mother: That's another topic. I'd like to wait.

Father: You're saying you don't want to do more today?

Second
Daughter: We don't have to limit. Because if we did limit then we'd have to say, Okay, we can stop right now!

Mother: We might cut somebody off.

Father: It might be a good idea to set a time limit, though. In other words, we might agree to spend no more than 45 minutes or an hour. Do you girls want to continue talking a little longer or would you like to finish as soon as we can? [This was the beginning of the end!]

Daughters: Finish it.

# REFERENCES

Adler, A. (1904). The physician as educator. In *Healing and education: Medical-educational papers of the Society for Individual Psychology*. Chicago: International Publications.

Adler, A. (1907). *Study of organ inferiority and its physical compensation: A contribution to clinical medicine* (S. E. Jelliffe, Trans.). New York: Moffat-Yard.

Adler, A. (1936). Love is a recent invention. *Esquire Magazine, 4*(1), 36, 128.

Adler, A. (1938). *Social interest.* London: Faber & Faber.

Adler, A. (1954). *Understanding human nature* (W. B. Wolf, Trans.). New York: Fawcett Premier. (Original work published 1927)

Adler, A. (1964). *Problems of neurosis* (original work published 1929). New York: Harper Torchbooks.

Angyl, A. (1941). *Foundations for a science of personality.* New York: Commonwealth Fund.

Ansbacher, H. L. (Ed.). (1969). *The science of living: Alfred Adler.* Garden City, NY: Doubleday Anchor Books.

Ansbacher, H. L., & Ansbacher, R. R. (Eds.). (1967). *The individual psychology of Alfred Adler.* New York: Harper Torchbooks, Harper and Row.

Archer, J., Jr. (1991). *Managing anxiety and stress* (2nd ed.). Muncie, IN: Accelerated Development.

Arciniega, G. M., & Newlon, B. J. (1995). *Counseling and psychotherapy: Multicultural considerations.* In D. Capuzzi & D. R. Gross (Eds.), *Counseling and psychotherapy: Theories and interventions* (pp. 557–587). Englewood Cliffs, NJ: Merrill.

Are you eating right? (1992, October). *Consumer Reports, 4,* 3.

Argyle, M., & Furnham, A. (1983). Sources of satisfaction and conflict in long-term relationships. *Journal of Marriage and the Family, 45,* 481–493.

Baumeister, R. F., & Leary, M. R. (1995). The need to belong: Desire for interpersonal attachments as a fundamental human motivation. *Psychological Bulletin, 117,* 497–529.

Beall, A. E., & Sternberg, R. J. (Eds.). (1993). *The psychology of gender.* New York: Guilford Press.

Beck, A. T. (1984). Cognitive approaches to stress. In R. L. Woolfolk & P. M. Lehrer (Eds.), *Principles and practice of stress management* (pp. 255–305). New York: Guilford Press.

Beck, J. S. (1995). *Cognitive therapy: Basics and beyond.* New York: Guilford Press.

Benson, H., & Stuart, E. M. (1992). *The wellness book: The comprehensive guide to maintaining health and treating stress-related illness.* New York: Simon & Schuster.

Berkman, L., & Syme, S. L. (1979). Social network, host resistance, and mortality: A nine-year study of Alameda County residents. *American Journal of Epidemiology, 109,* 186–204.

Berne, E. (1964). *Games people play.* New York: Grove Press.

Blankenhorn, D. (1995). *Fatherless America: Confronting our most urgent social problem.* New York: Basic Books.

Bolen, J. S. (1979). *The tao of psychology.* San Francisco: Harper and Row.

Bortz, W. M. (1991). *We live too short and die too long.* New York: Bantam.

Borysenko, J., & Borysenko, M. (1994). *The power of the mind to heal.* Carson, CA: Hay House.

Bradshaw, J. (1992). *Creating love.* New York: Bantam.

Branden, N. (1994). *The six pillars of self-esteem.* New York: Bantam.

Burg, M. M., & Seeman, T. E. (1994). Families and health: The negative side of social ties. *Annals of Behavioral Medicine, 16,* 109–115.

Burnett, J. W., Anderson, W. P., & Hepner, P. P. (1995). Gender roles and self-esteem: A consideration of environmental factors. *Journal of Counseling & Development, 73*(3), 323–326.

Burnett, P. C. (1988). Evaluation of Adlerian parenting programs. *Individual Psychology, 44,* 63–76.

Butler, R. N. (1963). The life review: An interpretation of reminiscence in the aged. *Psychiatry, 26,* 65–76.

Campbell, A. (1981). *The sense of well-being in America: Recent patterns and trends.* New York: McGraw-Hill.

Capuzzi, D., & Gross, D. R. (Eds.). (1995). *Counseling and psychotherapy: Theories and interventions.* Englewood Cliffs, NJ: Merrill.

Cohen, S., & Syme, S. L. (Eds.). (1985). *Social support and health.* London: Academic Press.

Cook, E. P. (1985). Psychological androgyny. Elmsford, NY: Pergamon Press.

Cook, E. P. (1987). Psychological androgyny: A review of the research. *The Counseling Psychologist, 15,* 471–513.

Cooper, S. E., Fuqua, D. R., & Hartman, B. W. (1984). The relationship of trait indecisiveness to vocational uncertainty, career indecision, and interpersonal characteristics. *Journal of College Student Personnel, 25,* 353–356.

Coopersmith, A. (1967). *Antecedents of self-esteem.* San Francisco: Freeman.

Corey, G. (1991). Invited commentary on macrostrategies for delivery of mental health counseling services. *Journal of Mental Health Counseling, 13,* 51–57.

Cosse, J. W. (1992). Who's who and what's what? The effects of gender on development in adolescence. In B. R. Wainrib (Ed.), *Gender issues across the life cycle* (pp. 5–16). New York: Springer.

Cousins, N. (1979). *Anatomy of an illness as perceived by the patient.* New York: W. W. Norton.

Cowher, S. J. (1995). Recognizing and addressing gender issues in the classroom. *Journal of Humanistic Education and Development, 34,* 35–41.

Crandall, J. E. (1975). A scale for social interest. *Journal of Individual Psychology, 31,* 187–195.

Crites, J. O. (1969). *Vocational psychology.* New York: McGraw-Hill.

Crites, J. O. (1981). Integrative test interpretation. In D. H. Montross & C. J. Shinkman (Eds.), *Career development in the 1980s: Theory and practice* (pp. 161–168). Springfield, IL: Charles C. Thomas.

Crocker, J., & Major, B. (1989). Social stigma and self-esteem: The self-protective properties of stigma. *Psychological Review, 96,* 608–630.

Csikszentmihalyi, M. (1990). *Flow: The psychology of optimal experience.* New York: Harper Collins.

Csikszentmihalyi, M., & Beattie, O. V. (1979). Life themes: A theoretical and empirical exploration of their origins and effects. *Journal of Humanistic Psychology, 19,* 45–63.

Curran, D. (1983). *Traits of a healthy family.* New York: Ballantine.

Dacher, E. S. (1991). *Psychoneuroimmunology: The new mind/body healing program.* New York: Paragon House.

Dahlstrom, W. G. (1972). *Personality systematics and the problem of types.* Morristown, NJ: General Learning Press.

Dawis, R. V., & Lofquist, L. H. (1984). *A psychological theory of work adjustment: An individual-differences model and its application.* Minneapolis: University of Minnesota Press.

Dillon, K. M., Minchoff, B., & Baker, K. H. (1985). Positive emotional states and the enhancement of the immune system. *International Journal of Psychiatry in Medicine, 15,* 13–17.

Dinkmeyer, D., & Dreikurs, R. (1963). *Encouraging children to learn: The encouragement process.* Englewood Cliffs, NJ: Prentice-Hall.

Does exercise boost immunity? (1995, April). *Consumer Reports on Health, 7*(4), 37–39.

Dreher, H. (1995). *The immune power personality: 7 traits you can develop to stay healthy.* New York: Dutton.

Dreikurs, R. (1946). *The challenge of marriage.* New York: Hawthorn Books.

Dreikurs, R. (1953). *Fundamentals of Adlerian psychology.* Chicago: Alfred Adler Institute.

Dreikurs, R. (1954). The psychological interview in medicine. *American Journal of Individual Psychology, 10,* 99–122.

Dreikurs, R. (1963). Psychodynamic diagnosis in psychiatry. *American Journal of Psychiatry, 119,* 1045–1048.

Dreikurs, R. (1967). *Psychodynamics, psychotherapy, and counseling.* Chicago: Alfred Adler Institute.

Dreikurs, R. (1968). *Psychology in the classroom* (2nd ed.). New York: Harper and Row.

Dreikurs, R. (1971). *Social equality: The challenge of today.* Chicago: Henry Regnery.

Dreikurs, R. (1973). *Psychodynamics, psychotherapy, and counseling* (Rev. ed.). Chicago: Alfred Adler Institute.

Dreikurs, R., & Grey, L. (1968). *Logical consequences.* New York: Hawthorn Books.

Dreikurs, R., & Soltz, V. (1964). *Children the challenge.* New York: Hawthorn Books.

Eckstein, D., Baruth, L., & Mahrer, D. (1982). *Life style: What it is and how to do it* (2nd ed.). Dubuque, IA: Kendall/Hunt.

Ekman, P. (1989). The argument and evidence about universals in facial expression of emotion. In H. Wagner & A. Mansted (Eds.), *Handbook of social psychophysiology* (pp. 143–163). New York: Wiley.

Ekman, P., & Davidson, R. J. (Eds.). (1994). *The nature of emotion.* New York: Oxford University Press.

Ellenberger, H. (1970). *The discovery of the unconscious.* New York: Basic Books.

Ellis, A. (1962). *Reason and emotion in psychotherapy.* New York: Lyle Stuart.

Ellis, A., & Greiger, R. (1977). *Handbook of rational-emotive therapy.* New York: Springer.

Erikson, E. (1950). *Childhood and society.* New York: Norton.

Exercise: A prescription for health. (1992, April 11). *USA Today,* pp. D1–2.

Exercise for the ages. (1996, July). *Consumer Reports on Health, 8*(7), 73–74.

Falk, D. R., & Hill, C. E. (1992). Counselor interventions preceding client laughter in brief therapy. *Journal of Counseling Psychology, 39,* 39–45.

Fenell, D. L. (1993). Characteristics of long-term first marriages. *Journal of Mental Health Counseling, 15,* 446-460.

Freeman, A., & DeWolf, R. (1992). *The 10 dumbest mistakes smart people make and how to avoid them.* New York: Harper Perennial.

Fromm, E. (1956). *The art of loving.* New York: Bantam.

Gallup, G., Jr., & Castelli, J. (1989). *The people's religion: American faith in the 90s.* New York: Macmillan.

Gardner, H. (1983). *Frames of mind: The theory of multiple intelligences.* New York: Basic Books.

Getting in shape: It's more important than ever. (1996, January). *Consumer Reports, 8,* 2.

Girdano, D. E., Everly, G. S., Jr., & Dusek, D. E. (1993). *Controlling stress and tension* (4th ed.). Englewood Cliffs, NJ: Prentice-Hall.

Gladding, S. T. (1995). Humor in counseling: Using a natural resource. *Journal of Humanistic Education and Development, 34,* 3–12.

Gladding, S. (1996). *Counseling: A comprehensive profession.* Upper Saddle River, NJ: Merrill.

Glasser, W. (1969). *Schools without failure.* New York: Harper and Row.

Goldberg, K. (1993). *How men can live as long as women: Seven steps to a longer and better life.* Fort Worth, TX: Summit Group.

Goldberger, L., & Breznitz, S. (1993). *Handbook of stress: Theoretical and clinical aspects* (2nd ed.). New York: Free Press.

Goleman, D. (1995). *Emotional intelligence.* New York: Bantam.

Goleman, D., & Gurin, J. (1993). Mind-body medicine: How to use your mind for better health. Yonkers, NY: Consumer Reports Books, a Division of Consumers Union.

Gottfredson, G. D., Holland, J. L., & Ogawa, D. K. (1982). *Dictionary of Holland occupational codes.* Palo Alto, CA: Consulting Psychologists Press.

Gottman, J. (1995). *Why marriages succeed or fail: And how you can make yours last.* New York: Simon & Schuster.

Greever, K. B., Tseng, M. S., & Friedland, B. U. (1973). Development of the social interest index. *Journal of Consulting and Clinical Psychology, 41,* 454–458.

Griffith, J., & Powers, R. L. (1984). *An Adlerian lexicon.* Chicago: American Institute of Adlerian Studies.

Guarendi, R., with Eich, D. (1990). *Back to the family: Proven advice on building a stronger, healthier, happier family.* New York: Simon & Schuster.

Hafen, B. Q., Frandsen, K. J., Karren, K. J., & Hooker, K. R. (1992). *The health effects of attitudes, emotions, relationships.* Provo, UT: EMS Associates.

Harrington, T. F., & O'Shea, A. J. (1982). *Career decision-making system.* Circle Pines, MN: American Guidance Service.

Harris-Bowlsbey, J. (1984). The computer as a tool in career guidance programs. In N. Gysbers (Ed.), *Designing careers* (pp. 362–383). San Francisco: Jossey-Bass.

Hattie, J. (1992). *Self-concept.* Hillsdale, NJ: Erlbaum.

Herr, E. L., & Cramer, S. H. (1988). *Career guidance and counseling through the life span.* Glenview, IL: Scott, Foresman.

Hoare, C. H. (1991). Psychosocial identity development and cultural others. *Journal of Counseling & Development, 70,* 45–53.

Holland, J. L. (1985a). *Making vocational choices: A theory of vocational personalities and work environments.* Englewood Cliffs, NJ: Prentice-Hall.

Holland, J. L. (1985b). *The self-directed search.* Odessa, FL: Psychological Assessment Resources.

Hopke, W. (1987). *Encyclopedia of careers and vocational guidance* (7th ed.). Chicago: Ferguson Publishing.

Horney, K. (1945). *Our inner conflicts.* New York: Norton.

Huyck, M. H. (1990). *Gender differences in aging.* In J. E. Birren & K. W. Schaie (Eds.), *Handbook of the psychology of aging* (3rd ed.) (pp. 124–132). San Diego: Academic Press.

Ivey, A. (1986). *Developmental therapy: Theory into practice.* San Francisco: Jossey-Bass.

Ivey, A. (1990). *Developmental counseling and therapy.* Pacific Grove, CA: Brooks/Cole.

Ivey, A. E., Ivey, M. B., & Simek-Morgan, L. (1993). *Counseling and psychotherapy: A multicultural perspective* (3rd ed.). Boston: Allyn & Bacon.

Izard, C. E. (1977). *Human emotions*. New York: Plenum Press.

Johnson, C. (1992). *Lucky in love: The secrets of happy couples and how their marriages thrive*. New York: Viking.

Johnson, D. W., Maruyama, G., Johnson, R., Nelson, D., & Skon, L. (1981). Effect of cooperative, competitive, and individualizing goal structures on achievements: A meta-analysis. *Psychological Bulletin, 89,* 47–62.

Jones, L. K. (1987). *The career key*. Chicago: Ferguson Publishing.

Kabat-Zinn, J. (1990). *Full catastrophe living: Using the wisdom of your body and mind to face stress, pain, and illness*. New York: Delta.

Kabat-Zinn, J. (1994). *Wherever you go, there you are: Mindfulness meditation in everyday life*. New York: Hyperion.

Karasek, R. A., & Theorell, T. (1990). *Healthy work*. New York: Basic Books.

Kelly, E. W., Jr. (1995). *Spirituality and religion in counseling and psychotherapy: Diversity in theory and practice*. Alexandria, VA: American Counseling Association.

Kelly, E. W., & Sweeney, T. J. (1979). Typical faulty goals of adolescents. *School Counselor, 26,* 236–246.

Kennedy, J. F. (1956). *Profiles in courage*. New York: Harper and Row.

Kenrick, D. T. (1987). Gender, genes, and social environment: A biosocial interactionist perspective. In P. Shaver & C. Hendrick (Eds.), *Sex and gender* (pp. 14–43). Newbury Park, CA: Sage.

Kiecolt-Glaser, J. K., Malarkey, W. B., Chee, M. A., Newton, T., Cacioppo, J. T., Mao, H. Y., & Glaser, R. (1993). Negative behavior during marital conflict is associated with immunological down-regulation. *Psychosomatic Medicine, 55,* 395–409.

Kleinke, C. L. (1991). *Coping with life challenges*. Pacific Grove, CA: Brooks/Cole.

Knoop, R. (1994). Relieving stress through value-rich work. *Journal of Social Psychology, 134,* 829–836.

Kozora, E. J. (Ed.). (1987). *Nutritional guidelines.* Seattle, WA: American Holistic Medical Association.

Kranitz, M. A. (1987). *Getting apart together.* San Luis Obispo, CA: Impact Publishers.

Krumboltz, J. D. (1983). *Private rules in career decision making.* Columbus, OH: The National Center for Research in Vocational Education.

Lazarus, R. S. (1991). *Emotion and adaptation.* New York: Oxford University Press.

Lazarus, R. S., & Folkman, S. (1984). *Stress, appraisal, and coping.* New York: Springer.

Leak, G. K., & Williams, D. E. (1989). Relationship between social interest, alienation, and psychological hardiness. *Individual Psychology, 45,* 359–375.

Lee, C. C., & Richardson, B. L. (1991). *Multicultural issues in counseling: New approaches to diversity.* Alexandria, VA: American Association for Counseling and Development.

Lehrer, P. M., & Woolfolk, R. L. (1993). *Principles and practices of stress management* (2nd ed.). New York: Guilford Press.

Levin, J. S., & Vanderpool, H. Y. (1987). Is frequent religious attendance really conducive to better health? Toward an epidemiology of religion. *Social Science and Medicine, 24,* 589–600.

Levin, B. H. (1991). *Your body believes every word you say.* Lower Lake, CA: Aslan Publishing.

Locke, S., & Colligan, D. (1986). *The healer within: The new medicine of mind and body.* New York: New American Library.

Locke, S., Kraus, I., Leserman, J., Hurst, M. W., Heisel, J. S., & Williams, R. M. (1984). Life change stress, psychiatric symptoms, and natural killer cell activity. *Psychosomatic Medicine, 46,* 441–453.

Loehr, J. E., & McLaughlin, P. J. (1986). *Mentally tough: The principles of winning at sports applied to winning in business.* New York: M. Evans.

Lorig, K. (1992, September 28). Self-care boosts esteem, cuts medical costs. *American Medical News,* p. 1.

Losing weight: What works, what doesn't. (1993, June). *Consumer Reports on Health, 5,* 3.

Luks, A. (1992). *The healing power of doing good.* New York: Fawcett Columbine.

Lynch, J. J. (1977). *The broken heart: The medical consequences of loneliness.* New York: Basic Books.

Maccoby, E. E. (1990). Gender and relationships: A developmental account. *American Psychologist, 45,* 513–520.

Manaster, G. J., Painter, G., Deutsch, J., & Overholt, B. (1977). *Alfred Adler: As we remember him.* Chicago: North American Society of Adlerian Psychology.

Manaster, G. J., & Perryman, T. B. (1974). Early recollections and occupational choice. *Journal of Individual Psychology, 30,* 232–237.

Maslow, A. H. (1968). *Toward a psychology of being* (2nd ed.). New York: D. Van Nostrand.

Maslow, A. H. (1970). *Motivation and personality* (2nd ed.). New York: Harper and Row.

May, R. (1969). *Love and will.* New York: Norton.

McClelland, D. C., Ross, G., & Patel, V. (1985). The effect of academic examination on salivary norepinephrine and immunoglobulin levels. *Journal of Human Stress, 11,* 52–59.

McDaniels, C., & Gysbers, N. C. (1992). *Counseling for career development: Theories, resources, and practice.* San Francisco: Jossey-Bass.

McKelvie, W. (1979). Career counseling with early recollections. In H. A. Olson (Ed.), *Early recollections: Their use in diagnosis and psychotherapy* (pp. 99–118). Springfield, IL: Thomas.

McKelvie, W., & Friedland, B. U. (1978). *Career goals counseling: A holistic approach.* Baltimore: F. M. S. Associates.

McKelvie, W., & Friedland, B. U. (1981). The life style and career counseling. In L. Barut & D. Eckstein (Eds.), *Life style: Theory, practice, and research* (2nd ed.) (pp. 57–62). Dubuque, IA: Kendall/Hunt.

Michelson, L., & Ascher, L. M. (1987). *Anxiety and stress disorders: Cognitive-behavioral assessment and treatment.* New York: Guilford Press.

Miller, E. E. (1991). *Opening the inner "I": Discover healing imagery through elective awareness.* Berkeley, CA: Celestial Arts.

Miller-Tiedeman, A. (1976). *Individual career exploration student inventory booklet.* Benesville, IL: Scholastic Testing Service.

Mintz, L. B., & O'Neil, J. O. (1990). Gender roles, sex, and the process of psychotherapy: Many questions and few answers. *Journal of Counseling & Development, 68,* 381–387.

Minuchin, S. (1974). *Family therapy techniques.* Cambridge: Harvard University Press.

Minuchin, S., & Fishman, H. C. (1981). *Families and family therapy.* Cambridge: Harvard University Press.

Money, J. (1973). Gender role identity. *Journal of the Academy of Psychoanalysis, 4,* 397–403.

Montagu, A. (1981). *Growing young.* New York: McGraw-Hill.

Moody, R. A. (1978). *Laugh after laugh: The healing power of humor.* Jacksonville, FL: Headwaters Press.

Moore, T. (1994). *Soul mates: Honoring the mysteries of love and relationship.* New York: Harper Collins.

Mosak, H. H. (1958). Early recollections as a projective technique. *Journal of Projective Techniques, 22,* 301–311. (Also in Lindzey, G., & Hall, C. S. (Eds.). (1965). *Theories of personality: Primary sources and research* [pp. 105–113]. New York: Wiley.)

Mosak, H. H. (1977). *The controller: A social interpretation of the anal character. On purpose: Collected papers of Harold H. Mosak.* Chicago: Alfred Adler Institute.

Mosak, H. H. (1987). *Ha, ha and aha: The role of humor in psychotherapy.* Muncie, IN: Accelerated Development.

Mosak, H. H., & Dreikurs, R. (1967). The life tasks III, the fifth life task. *Individual Psychologist, 5,* 16–22.

Mosak, H. H., & Dreikurs, R. (1973). Adlerian psychotherapy. In R. Corsini (Ed.), *Current psychotherapies* (pp. 126–157). Itasca, IL: F. E. Peacock.

Mosak, H. H., & Shulman, B. H. (1971). *The lifestyle inventory.* Chicago: Alfred Adler Institute.

Myers, D. G. (1992). *Pursuit of happiness: What makes a person happy and why.* New York: William Morrow.

Myers, I. B., & McCaulley, M. H. (1985). *Manual: A guide to the development and use of the Myers-Briggs Type Indicator.* Palo Alto, CA: Consulting Psychologists Press.

Myers, J. E. (1989). *Adult children and aging parents.* Alexandria, VA: American Counseling Association.

Myers, J. E., Witmer, J. M., & Sweeney, T. J. (1995). *Wellness evaluation of lifestyle.* Unpublished assessment instrument, University of North Carolina, Greensboro.

Myers, J. E., Witmer, J. M., & Sweeney, T. J. (1996). *The WEL workbook: Wellness evaluation of lifestyle.* Greensboro, NC: University of North Carolina, Greensboro.

Naisbitt, J., & Aburdene, P. (1990). *Megatrends 2000: Ten new directions for the 1990s.* New York: William Morrow.

Nehru, J. (1958). *Toward freedom.* Boston: Beacon Press.

Nevo, O. (1987). Irrational expectations in career counseling and their confronting arguments. *Career Development Quarterly, 35,* 239–250.

Nichols, M. P., & Schwartz, R. C. (1994). *Family therapy: Concepts and methods* (3rd ed.). Boston: Allyn.

Notarius, C., & Markman, H. (1993). *We can work it out: Making sense of marital conflict.* New York: Putnam.

Olson, D. H., McCubbin, H., Barnes, H., Larsen, A., Muxen, M., & Wilson, M. (1983). *Families: What makes them work?* Beverly Hills, CA: Sage.

Ornish, D. (1990). *Dr. Dean Ornish's program for reversing heart disease.* New York: Ballantine.

Ornstein, R., & Sobel, D. (1989). *Healthy pleasures.* Reading, MA: Addison-Wesley.

Parsons, F. (1909). *Choosing a vocation.* Boston: Houghton-Mifflin.

Pederson, P. (1994). *A handbook for developing cultural awareness* (2nd ed.). Alexandria, VA: American Counseling Association.

Pelletier, K. R. (1981). *Longevity: Fulfilling our biological potential.* New York: Delacorte Press/Seymour Lawrence.

Pelletier, K. R. (1994). *Sound mind, sound body: A new model for lifelong health.* New York: Simon & Schuster.

Pennebaker, J. W. (1990). *Opening up: The healing power of confiding in others.* New York: William Morrow.

Peterson, C., & Bossio, L. M. (1991). *Health and optimism.* New York: Free Press.

Piaget, J. (1963). *The origin of intelligence in children.* New York: Norton.

Piaget, J. (1965). *The moral judgment of the child.* New York: Free Press.

Powers, R. L., & Griffith, J. (1987). *Understanding life-style: The psycho-clarity process.* Chicago: The American Institute of Adlerian Studies.

Prediger, D. J. (1982). Dimensions underlying Holland's hexagon: Missing link between interests and expectations? *Journal of Vocational Behavior, 21,* 259–287.

Prochaska, J. O., & DiClemente, C. C. (1984). *The transtheoretical approach: Crossing traditional boundaries of therapy.* Melbourne, FL: Krieger.

Prochaska, J. O., & Norcross, J. C. (1994). *Systems of psychotherapy: A transtheoretical analysis* (3rd ed.). Pacific Grove, CA: Brooks/Cole.

Renwick, P. A., & Lawler, E. E. (1978, May). What you really want from your job. *Psychology Today, 11*(3), 53–65, 118.

Rosenfeld, I. (1995). *Doctor, what should I eat?* New York: Warner.

Sagan, L. A. (1987). *The health of nations.* New York: Basic Books.

Santrock, J. W. (1995). *Life-span development.* Dubuque, IA: Brown and Benchmark.

Sarason, B. R., Sarason, I. G., & Pierce, G. R. (1990). *Social support: An international view.* New York: Wiley.

Savickas, M. L. (1989). Career counseling. In T. Sweeney (Ed.), *Adlerian counseling: A Practical approach for a new decade* (3rd ed.) (pp. 289–320). Muncie, IN: Accelerated Development.

Scarf, M. (1995). *Intimate worlds: Life inside the family.* New York: Random House.

Schafer, C., Coyne, J. C., & Lazarus, R. S. (1982). The health-related functions of social support. *Journal of Behavioral Medicine, 4,* 381–406.

Scheier, M. F., & Carver, C. S. (1987). Dispositional optimism and physical well-being: The influence of generalized outcome experiences on health. *Journal of Personality, 55,* 169–210.

Schwartz, M. S., & Associates. (1995). *Biofeedback: A practitioner's guide.* New York: Guilford Press.

Segall, M. H., Dasen, P. R., Berry, J. W., & Poortinga, Y. H. (1990). *Human behavior in global perspective: An introduction to cross-cultural psychology.* New York: Pergamon Press.

Seligman, M. E. P. (1990). *Learned optimism.* New York: Knopf.

Shealy, C. N., & Myss, C. M. (1993). *The creation of health: The emotional, psychological, and spiritual responses that promote health and healing.* Walpole, NH: Stillpoint Publishing.

Shulman, B. H. (1962). The family constellation in personality diagnosis. *Journal of Individual Psychology, 18,* 35–47.

Shulman, B. H. (1968). *Essays in schizophrenia.* Baltimore: Williams & Wilkins.

Shulman, B. H. (1971). Confrontation techniques in Adlerian psychotherapy. *Journal of Individual Psychology, 27,* 167–175.

Shulman, B. H. (1973). *What is the life style? Contributions to individual psychology.* Chicago: Alfred Adler Institute.

Shulman, B. H., & Mosak, H. (1988a). *LSI—Life Style Inventory.* Muncie, IN: Accelerated Development.

Shulman, B. H., & Mosak, H. (1988b). *Manual for life style assessment.* Muncie, IN: Accelerated Development.

Simon, S. B., & Simon, S. (1990). *Forgiveness.* New York: Warner Books.

Six convincing reasons to exercise. (1994, February). *Health After 50. The Johns Hopkins Medical Letter, 6,* 1.

Smith, E. M. J. (1985). Ethnic minorities: Life stress, social support, and mental health issues. *The Counseling Psychologist, 13,* 537–579.

Smith, E. J. (1991). Ethnic identity development: Toward the development of a theory within the context of majority/minority status. *Journal of Counseling & Development, 70,* 181–188.

Smith, J. C. (1993). *Creative stress management: The 1-2-3 cope system.* Englewood Cliffs, NJ: Prentice-Hall.

Sorokin, P. (1967). *The ways and powers of love.* Chicago: H. Regnery.

Spencer, H. (1885). *Education—intellectual, moral, physical.* New York: P. D. Alden.

Spokane, A. R. (1985). A review of research on person-environment congruence in Holland's theory of careers. *Journal of Vocational Behavior, 26,* 306–343.

Stewart, N. R. (1969). Exploring and processing information about educational and vocational opportunities in groups. In J. D. Krumboltz & C. E. Thoresen (Eds.), *Behavioral counseling: Cases and techniques* (pp. 213–234). New York: Holt, Reinhart, & Winston.

Stinnet, N., & Defrain, J. (1985). *Secrets of strong families.* New York: Berkley Books.

Stone, A. A., Cox, D. S., Valdimarsdottir, H., Jandorf, L., & Neale, J. M. (1987). Evidence that IgA antibody is associated with daily mood. *Journal of Personality and Social Psychology, 52,* 988–993.

Strength training for everyone. (1991, November). *University of California at Berkeley Wellness Letter, 8*(2), 4–7.

Strickland, B. R. (1978). Internal-external experiences and health-related behaviors. *Journal of Consulting and Clinical Psychology, 46,* 1192–1211.

Sue, D. W., & Sue, D. (1990). *Counseling the culturally different: Theory and practice* (2nd ed.). New York: Wiley.

Sulliman, J. R. (1973). The development of a scale for the measurement of social interest. *Dissertation Abstracts International, 34,* 2914B. (University Microfilms No. 73-31, 567)

Summary statement—workshop on physical activity and public health. (1993). *Sports Medicine Bulletin, 28*(4), 2.

Sweeney, T. J. (1989). *Adlerian counseling: A practical approach for a new decade* (3rd ed.). Muncie, IN: Accelerated Development.

Sweeney, T. J. (1995). Adlerian theory. In D. Capuzzi & D. R. Gross (Eds.), *Counseling and psychotherapy: Theories and interventions* (pp. 171–206). Englewood Cliffs, NJ: Merrill.

Sweeney, T. J. (1997). Early recollections: A source of healing and encouragement with older persons. *Therapeutic Strategies with Older Persons, 3*(5), 3-14.

Vaihinger, H. (1965). *The philosophy of "as if."* London: Routledge and Kegan Paul.

Vaillant, G. E. (1977). *Adaptation to life.* Boston: Little, Brown.

Vaughan, D. (1986). *Uncoupling: Turning points in intimate relationships.* New York: Oxford University Press.

Wainrib, B. R. (Ed.). (1992). *Gender issues across the life cycle.* New York: Springer.

Wallerstein, J., & Blakeslee, S. (1995). *The good marriage: How and why good love lasts.* Boston: Houghton-Mifflin.

Warner, R. (1993). Work in progress: Toward a new paradigm for the sociological study of religion in the United States. *American Journal of Sociology, 98,* 1044–1093.

Watkins, C. E. (1984). The individual psychology of Alfred Adler: Toward an Adlerian vocational theory. *Journal of Vocational Behavior, 24,* 28–47.

Watkins, C. E. (1992a). Adlerian-oriented early memory research: What does it tell us? *Journal of Personality Assessment, 59,* 248–263.

Watkins, C. E. (1992b). Birth-order research and Adler's theory: A critical review. *Individual Psychology, 48,* 357–368.

Watkins, C. E. (1992c). Research activity with Adler's theory. *Individual Psychology, 48,* 107–108.

Watkins, C. E. (1994). Measuring social interest. *Individual Psychology, 50,* 69–96.

Weil, A. (1995). *Spontaneous healing: How to discover and enhance your body's natural ability to maintain and heal itself.* New York: Knopf.

Wheeler, M. S., Kern, R. M., & Curlette, W. L. (1991). Life-style can be measured. *Individual Psychology, 47,* 229–240.

When mental illness strikes. (1993, July 7). *USA Today,* p. A11.

Williams, R. (1989). *The trusting heart: Great news about type A behavior.* New York: Times Books.

Witmer, J. M. (1985). *Pathways to personal growth: Developing a sense of worth and competence.* Muncie, IN: Accelerated Development.

Witmer, J. M. (1989). Reaching toward wholeness. In T. J. Sweeney (Ed.), *Adlerian counseling: A practical approach for a new decade* (3rd ed.) (pp. 31–79). Muncie, IN: Accelerated Development.

Witmer, J. M. (1996). *Reaching toward wellness.* Unpublished monograph, College of Education, Ohio University, Athens.

Witmer, J. M., & Rich, C. (1995). *Optimism as generalized outcome expectancies for coping with stress.* Unpublished manuscript, College of Education, Ohio University, Athens.

Witmer, J. M., Rich, C., Barcikowski, R., & Mague, J. C. (1983). Psychosocial characteristics mediating the stress response: An exploratory study. *The Personnel and Guidance Journal, 62,* 73–77.

Witmer, J. M., & Sweeney, T. J. (1992). A holistic model for wellness and prevention over the life span. *Journal of Counseling and Development, 71,* 140–148.

Witmer, J. M., Sweeney, T. J., & Myers, J. E. (1994). *Wellness Evaluation of Lifestyle.* Unpublished inventory, University of North Carolina, Greensboro.

Wurtman, J. (1986). *Managing your mind and mood through food.* New York: Rawson.

Yankelovich, D. (1978, May). The new psychological contracts at work. *Psychology Today, 12*(3), 46–50.

# INDEX

Sweeney, T. J. (in press). Adlerian theory. In D. Capuzzi & D. R. Gross (Eds.), *Counseling and psychotherapy: Theories and interventions* (2nd ed.). Englewood Cliffs, NJ: Merrill.

Sweeney, T. J., & Moses, M. A. (1979). Parent education topical bibliography. *School Counselor, 26,* 254–263.

Sweeney, T. J., & Myers, J. E. (1986). Early recollections: An Adlerian method for use with older persons. *Clinical Gerontologist, 4*(4), 3–12.

Sweeney, T. J., & Witmer, J. M. (1991). Beyond social interest: Striving toward optimum health and wellness. *Individual Psychology, 47,* 527–540.

Tart, C. T. (1986). *Waking up: Overcoming the obstacles to human potential.* Boston: New Science Library, Shambhala.

Temoshok, L., & Dreher, H. (1992). *The type C connection: The behavioral links to cancer and health.* New York: Random House.

Terner, J., & Pew, W. L. (1978). *The courage to be imperfect: The life and works of Rudolf Dreikurs.* New York: Hawthorn Books.

Thayer, S. (1988, May). Close encounters. *Psychology Today, 22*(3), 31–36.

Touchton, J. B., & Magoon, T. M. (1977). Occupational daydreams as predictors of vocational plans for college women. *Journal of Vocational Behavior, 10,* 156–166.

University of California at Berkeley. (1993, February). Fascinating facts. *Wellness Letter, 9*(5), 1.

U.S. Department of Labor. (1996). *Occupational outlook handbook: 1996–97 edition* (Publication No. 2470). Washington, DC: U.S. Government Printing Office.

U.S. Public Health Service. (1979). *Smoking and health: A report of the Surgeon General* (DHEW Publication No. PHS 79-50066). Washington, DC: U.S. Government Printing Office.

U.S. Public Health Service. (1990). *Healthy people 2000: National health promotion and disease prevention objectives* (DHHS Publication No. 91-50213). Washington, DC: U.S. Government Printing Office.

Matching model
    Adlerian, 332-336, 358
    classic, 330-332, 358
May, R., 3, 77, 525
McCaulley, M., 347, 527
McClelland, D., 57, 525
McCubbin, H., 528
McDaniels, C., 72, 73, 525
McKelvie, W., 337, 525, 526
McLaughlin, P., 60, 524
Media, as a life force, 83
Michelson, L., 65, 526
Miller, E., 96, 526
Miller-Tiedeman, A., 355, 526
Minchoff, B., 57, 519
MINDGARDEN, 86
Mintz, L., 66, 526
Minuchin, S., 386-388, 526
Money, J., 66, 526
Montagu, A., 57, 60, 71, 526
Moody, R., 60, 526
Moore, T., 77, 526
Mosak, H., 2, 10, 17, 30, 60. 243,
    247, 337, 354, 423, 526, 527, 530
Moses, M., 30, 532
Motivation, extrinsic, 26, 141
    intrinsic, 26, 141, 174-176
Mottos, 344-345, 348
Multiculturalism, 31-34, 39, 68-69
Multiple intelligences, 58-59
Muxen, M., 528
Myers, D., 52, 53, 69-70, 159, 527
Myers, I., 347, 527
Myers, J., 44, 45, 49, 84, 85, 86,
    249, 287, 292, 527, 532, 534
Myss, C., 96, 530

**N**

Naisbitt, J., 82, 527
*National Enquirer*, 342
National Wellness Institute, 85
Native Americans, 19, 280

Natural consequences, xi, 101-112,
    113, 174, 199-207
    example, 206-207
Neale, J., 57, 531
Nehru, J., 124, 527
Nelson, D., 176, 523
Neurosis, 21
Nevo, O., 354, 527
Newlon, B., 31, 33, 526
*Newsweek*, 348
Newton, T., 523
Nichols, M., 385, 386, 528
Norcross, J., 2, 37, 98, 529
North American Society of Adlerian
    Psychology, 7
Notarius, C., 79, 528
Nutrition, 61-62, 126

**O**

O'Neil, J., 66, 526
O'Shea, A., 355, 522
Observations, 239, 249-250
*Occupational Outlook Handbook*,
    355, 532
Occupational prospects, 355-356
Ogawa, D., 347, 523, 528
*Old Man and the Sea*, 341
Open-ended meetings, 431
Ordinal position, see Birth order
Organizational roles, 352
Ornish, D., 96, 528
Ornstein, R., 54, 528
Overholt, B., 5, 525

**P**

Painter, G., 5, 525
Parent interview, 393-400
    examples, 396-398, 459 477,
    487-489
Parsons, F., 330, 358, 528
Patel, V., 57, 525
Pederson, P., 68, 528

# ABOUT THE CONTRIBUTORS

**Mark L. Savickas**, Ph.D., is Professor and Chairman of the Behavioral Sciences Department at the Northeastern Ohio Universities College of Medicine, which is in consortium with The University of Akron, Kent State University, and Youngstown State University. He also serves as an Adjunct Professor Educational Psychology, Administration, Technology, and Foundations in the College of Education at Kent State University.

Dr. Savickas became dedicated to the discipline of career counseling during the 5 years he served as a college counselor. Each semester for the last 17 years, he has taught career counseling to graduate students in community counseling, rehabilitation counseling, counseling psychology, and college student personnel. His approach to the practice of career counseling emphasized helping clients make educational and vocational choices by integrating their subjective interpretations of their lives with objective assessments of their abilities, interests, and opportunities. He has concentrated his research activities on vocational maturation and the process of career decision making. Currently, he serves on the editorial boards of the *Career Development Quarterly* and the *Journal of Vocational Behavior*. Dr. Savickas frequently has presented his ideas to colleagues at professional meetings and has presented more than 300 in-service workshops to career counselors and educators.

**J. Melvin Witmer**, Ph.D., LPCC, is Professor Emeritus of Counselor Education at Ohio University, where he taught from 1966 to 1989 and continues to teach one quarter each year. He is a licensed professional clinical counselor, a licensed psychologist, and a national certified counselor. He has been a professor, consultant, and workshop leader in counseling and human development for more than 25 years. His experiences as a teacher in elementary, secondary, and higher education gave him a developmental perspective on how people grow and learn. Experiences in school counseling and school psychology continue to motivate him to search for barriers that inhibit growth and the beliefs and behaviors that develop human potential. Dr. Witmer has received 16 professional awards and honors from state professional organizations, colleagues, and Ohio University.

For the last 20 years, Dr. Witmer has directed research in stress management and conducted classes and workshops on stress and wellness. Through teaching and professional organizations, he has worked to improve the quality of counseling services by implementing ethical and licensure standards. Recent presentations at professional conferences and continuing education workshops include the characteristics of psychologically healthy people and assessment and planning of a wellness lifestyle for the life span. His 1985 book, *Pathways to Personal Growth*, and subsequent publications describe the process of developing one's potential, striving for wellness, understanding emotions, encouraging others, teaching values, and coping with stress. He has directed 51 dissertations, 14 of them related to stress and its intervention. He continues to research the factors that contribute to wellness.

His application of a model of wellness has been presented throughout the United States to groups in education, business and industry, community agencies, and mental health. Dr. Witmer also has presented the model to professional groups of counselors, psychologists, and psychiatrists at several international conferences held in Europe and Saudia Arabia. He continues to refine the wellness model in collaboration with colleagues Drs. Tom Sweeney and Jane Myers. Together they are developing a wellness assessment instrument, the Wellness Evaluation of Lifestyle (WEL Inventory), that has application in counseling and personal development.

Personal interests include photography, indoor and outdoor gardening, tennis, sailing, traveling, and visiting the family. He lives on his fantasy island off the South Carolina coast where a favorite pastime is walking along the beach.

# ABOUT THE AUTHOR

Thomas J. Sweeney, Ph.D., Professor Emeritus of Counselor Education at Ohio University, consultant, author, and Executive Director of Chi Sigma Iota International, became interested in Adlerian concepts and methods as the father of five children and, professionally, as a counselor and consultant. The second son in a family of two children, he perceived the validity of Adler's observations and teachings in his own development. His history of trying harder as a second child is readily discernible in his accomplishments.

Dr. Sweeney has been president of state, regional, national, and international organizations in his chosen field of counseling and counselor education. He has held both state and national certifications as a counselor in addition to being a licensed professional clinical counselor. Formerly a junior and senior high school counselor and teacher, he has been an administrator in higher education for more than 18 years as well as a professor for more than 30 years.

The author of numerous articles, chapters, monographs, and reviews, he also authored the American Counseling Association (ACA) positions on counselor licensure and accreditation. He chaired each of these respective activities during their formative years to move them forward for the profession.

The recipient of many awards and consultant/lecturer in the United States and abroad, he reports his greatest satisfaction with winning both state and national awards for the telecourse/film series, "Coping With Kids," based on Adler's and Dreikurs' teachings. He has since helped produce a national video series on counseling older persons that incorporated Adlerian methods and techniques into its programs.

Dr. Sweeney currently teaches one quarter per year at Ohio University, from which he took early retirement in 1992. As Executive Director of Chi Sigma Iota Counseling Academic and Professional Honor Society International (CSI), Dr. Sweeney continues to travel this country and abroad as well as to write, teach, and consult professionally, particularly on the applications of Individual Psychology and the practical merits of a wellness orientation to lifestyle.